Project managing ITSM from hell

(implement ITIL that works!!)

Brian Johnson
Paul Wilkinson

Van Haren
PUBLISHING

Sejanus was a liar but so fine a general of lies that he knew how to marshal them into an alert and disciplined formation which would come off best in any skirmish with suspicions or any general engagement with the truth.

Robert Graves
from 'I, Claudius'

Thanks.......

In keeping with latest publishing traditions to thank everyone connected with a book, Brian and Paul wish to thank those featured in the following short list:

Rudolf, Comet, Cupid, Vixen, Dasher, Dancer, Prancer, Donner and Blitzen, the Lone Ranger and Tonto, Silver and Scout, Happy, Dopey, Sneezy, Grumpy, Sleepy, Smelly, Fatty, Snotty, Wally, Bashful and Doc, Alex, Pippa, Sue, Jacqueline, Claudia, Kate and Naomi, Hugh Hefner, Earthworm Jim and Peter the puppy, Queen pulsating, bloated, festering, sweaty, malformed, pus-filled Slug-for-a-Butt, Psycrow, Evil the Cat, Professor Monkey for a Head, the Justice League of America, Eric and Erica, Mick McCarthy, Vic Halom, Peter Reid, Ian Porterfield, John Stewart, mam and dad, Paul's mum (they're posh in his house) and dad, Dillon, the Men from UNCLE, Eric and Ernie, Mark van Onna, Bob the Killer Goldfish, Robert van Oirschot, Paddington, Michael Foot, Tony Benn, Theresa Hyphenated-Surname, Bob Stokoe, Colin, all Scottish Goalkeepers, James Stewart, Dalglish, Basil d'Oliveira, Frasier, Daphne, Niles, Martin, the gorgeous Ros and (especially) Maris, Sandra, Liz, Annelise, Geoff Boycott, Willie Donachie, Super Dave, Ivor Cutler, Roy Harper, Priscilla Queen of the Desert, George of the Jungle, Lassie, Rin Tin Tin, Tin-Tin, Tex Avery, Tom and Jerry, Champion the Wonder Horse, Skippy the Bush Kangaroo, Dave Dee, Dozy, Beaky, Mick, Titch, Ginger, Posh, Scary, Sporty and Baby, John, Paul, George and Ringo, Johnny Ringo, the Ringo Kid, Wyatt Earp, Pans People, Legs and Co., John Carpenter, Johnny Rotten, Joe Strummer, Neil Young, Richard Thompson, Tom Waits, Ry Cooder, Mick, Keith, Charlie, Brian, Mick (the other one), Ronnie and Bill, Fred, Barney, Betty and Wilma, lots of names to make you think we are intellectuals such as Camus, Kierkegaard, Mies van der Rohe, Sartre and Eddie Murphy, Stacy and Leslie, Irene, Enid Blyton, Capt. W.E. Johns, , APM, PUG, GUP, GUPPY, PUPPY, SPAM and SMUG, SMERSH, THRUSH, BUSH and MUSH little doggies, Hush Puppies, Slush Puppies, Posh Slushies, Aspirin, Penicillin, Oxytocin, Wednesdays, Marilyn Monroe, Monica Lewinsky (no jokes, they'd just leave a bad taste in the mouth), Hans Ringnalda, Wellington, Boot, Marlon and Maisie, Wellington (the other one), Winston Churchill, Avon, Cally, Jenna, Blake (even if he was a bit wet), Gan, Vila, Zen, Orac, Servalan (phwoar) Einstein, Eisenstein, Frankenstein and Stein remover and last but not least, Kylie Minogue.

Acknowledgements

John Stewart and Frances Scarff at CCTA for their advice and assistance. Particular thanks to John who was forced to locate a second hand sense of humour for use while he reviewed this piece of work and whose smile muscles had to be surgically restructured before the review could begin.

Thanks also to the First Aiders at CCTA who helped the authors after John had finished reading the acknowledgement.

Brian Johnson
Paul Wilkinson

Concept & text: Brian Johnson and Paul Wilkinson
Illustrations: Paul Wilkinson
Making the illustrations funny: Brian Johnson
Honorary Dutch Publishing Expert: Ivo van Haren
First edition, second impression with minor amendments, May 2005
Coverdesign & prepress: DTPresto Design & Layout -Zeewolde-NL

Contents

Foreword

'We are all in the gutter, but some of us are so hammered we can see the stars.'

I wrote that (it is a work in progress, I have to say) to illustrate the wit and ready repartee that epitomises the apocalyptic approach to ITSM redolent in this work. I tried Sado-Masochism when I was a bit younger and more supple, which is of course............what?   not sado..? really?,   oh, sorry.

Start again. IT Service Management?? Of course it is. And project management?. OK.

This piece of work claims to be politically incorrect, sexist and IT-centric. And it achieves all three. I recommend this book to you unreservedly if you wish to provide the worst possible services to your customers. Which is of course NOT the reason that Brian and Paul wrote this warped vision of project management and ITSM. Be aware, that most of the items raised as comic issues make uncomfortable reading, because we can all identify someone who really believes in them!

I know them well enough to believe that they really ARE being ironic. Of course, I know Paul very well but best not to mention that before the trial.

Oscar Wilde
Reading Gaol

Token woman

Token Frenchman

Token Chinese philospher

The cast of characters

The Business executive
Aim: to find a method that helps projects to finish on time and within budget.
Hobby: trying to finish the Financial Times crossword within 5 minutes.

The Senior user
Aim: to discover a project deliverable that remotely resembles what was initially requested.
Hobby: trying to finish the FT crossword.

The Senior supplier
Aim: to be able to understand what exactly projects were promising to deliver.
Hobby: trying to understand FT crossword clues.

The project manager
Aim: Trying to create a permanent project that takes over the whole organisation.
Hobby: writing the FT crossword.

The project resource
Aim: not to be dumped upon from a great height when projects go wrong.
Hobby: trying to start The Sun crosswords.

IT Director
Aim: to build a user free IT empire and eventually outsource the whole of the business.
Hobby: talking about himself and praising his own achievements.

IT Professional
Aim: to be able to walk on water.
Hobby: sliding under doors and making customers and users feel totally inadequate.

Customer
Aim: to be able to make sense of the IT reports.
Hobby: asking the IT organisation bloody silly questions and being boring.

Help Desk operator
Aim: to retire at 25.
Hobby: biting the heads off users.

User
Aim: to be able to use IT effectively (no, stop laughing... he means it!).
Hobby: ...who cares.

You will notice that the cast of characters is miniscule in comparison to the millions of people and roles recommended by project management experts or IT organisational consultants. Our method is based on maximum involvement of the minimum number of people necessary for you to have an easy life. Of course, if you want to hedge your bets by employing boatloads of people, in order to more easily pass the buck or point the dirty digit of blame, you should consult a method such as PRINCE 2.

1

Highlights and heroes
in the history
of
project management

"I went shopping
for some
camouflage trousers,
but I couldn't find
any"

Osama Bin Laden

1.1 Project management - What is it?

Why have we included a number of chapters on project management within this IT publication?. Figures reveal that more than 70% of IT projects are over time or budget or fail to deliver anything even resembling the expected results, something we in IT are proud of and intend to maintain. This makes the business even more dependent upon us in IT for fixing the mess delivered by IT projects, which in turn keeps us in work. As I said this is an achievement we intend to maintain and the first six chapters in this book help you to achieve this major goal.

Also IT Infrastructure Library best practice recommends using a method to manage IT projects (or process implementation projects, or pretty much anything with a pulse. Or without a pulse. In fact, anything.) and recommends PRINCE2 so that even more money goes to the office of administrative affairs to be wasted by Sir Humphrey and his mob of procurement Nazi's. Or as this is more often described, used to fund the development of best practices.

To get back to the question however, philosophers as diverse as Descartes, Kierkegaard, Sartre, Cantona, Camus and, er, other people, were asked to debate the question 'What is project management?'. Needless to say this caused them to wobble a lot. To avoid having to answer such a mind bogglingly tricky question, they resorted to hiding themselves behind the cloak of Epistemology - the theory of knowledge, or what is knowable. Bishop Berkeley an English philosopher, declared 'for an object to exist (a project) it must be perceived.' If it were not perceived it would not exist...as a project cannot be perceived it cannot exist. Therefore the concept of 'project management' is meaningless.'

They all looked mighty smug after that. Berkeley asked the famous French philosopher Rene Descartes for support. He thought long and hard about it and then said 'I want a SPAM sandwich'.

As philosophers, they then invented Spam, that, until that time had not even been an existentialist concept.

They had to come up with something else however, and finally, they agreed on the following:
- An invisible organisational parasite that eats resources and money......
- An opportunity for lonely people to call meetings.
- A bureaucratic monster that vomits forth vast quantities of paper...
- An excuse for not doing something that the line

organisation should be doing... (by forging incomprehensible decision making algorithms and project organisational structures that go around in circles before finally disappearing up their own spiral staircase)...

- An excuse to appoint a project manager who can take the blame when the project fails to achieve what everybody knew was impossible in the first place...
- An opportunity for IT organisations to make themselves indispensable by first messing things up and then having the task of cleaning it up again.
- An oxymoron.

Of course, being philosophers, they were all talking out of their hindquarters. And soon they started arguing that all generalisations were false. As that statement included itself so to speak, it sent the assembled company into a series of gibbering arguments and some years elapsed before Cantona could again make a sensible philosophical point.

There are as many types of project as there are definitions. Each type has easily identifiable characteristics.

Project type	Characteristics
dinosaur:	Huge and lumbering. Impossible to control. It usually becomes obsolete before realising its purpose. Reasons for destruction are never clear.
hit & run:	A short, seemingly purposeless exercise that is over before anybody even realised it had begun (many women recognise this particular characteristic, for reasons that the authors have found difficult to identify (or admit to)) and before the project plan had been agreed.
damp squib:	A project that fizzles out after the first project board meeting because the project board is bored. Or fail to turn up.
black hole:	A project that seems to consume vast sums of money and boatloads of resource and nothing ever emerges from its clutches.
gridlock:	A project that never goes anywhere because it is always tied down in meetings (Inertia)and decision moments to decide if another decision moment needs to be created. Hence the study of 'Moments of Inertia', in itself indescribably boring no matter what the opinion of my old physics teacher.
	A decision moment should definitely not be confused with a Minute. Minutes, especially from Project Board Meetings, have been known

to take hours - come to think of it, decision moments have been known to take days, sometimes days take months, then after a while, those memories of your youth intervene and you recall talking to that special girl for the first time and the way she said 'Get lost you spotty little creep' and - er, are you sure you wouldn't prefer to study philosophy?

NB a 'gridlock' is often accompanied by detailed status reports that identify the status of all status reports.

virus	begins as a single project and develops into a full grown programme that devours the whole organisation.
barge pole	A project that smells like a dead fish.
sure thing	Perceived as being absolutely infallible, see also - black hole, gridlock, virus and hot brick
the banker	(also known as the career builder) That once only, usually minuscule, project that you bring in on time (well almost) which allows you to continue forever as a project manager. It's called the banker because it is your 'ace in the hole' whenever you're asked to name one, just one, successful project that you've managed. It also sounds similar to your nickname.
hot brick	A project that is a hot issue in the organisation and for which success is critical. Failing to secure project success is a 'career limiting move'; wise project managers throw this sort of project from one to another like a hot brick.

And yet the project plan has still been authorised.

PROJECT MANAGEMENT
'ULTIMATE PROJECT'
• unknown finish date
• unknown resources
• unknown deliverables

1.2   Why do it??

Think about being wholly responsible and accountable for:
- The management of cost,
- deployment of resources out of number,
- communications,
- knowledge creation, assimilation and distribution.

All of these and more can be yours. Or you could try project management. With project management, you get all of the benefits of being in charge, allied to the important knowledge that you can make someone else responsible for all of the problems.

So, consider the following:
- If you use the guidance in this book correctly you could create for yourself a huge, 'permanent' project structure in which you are the supreme ruler and wielder of organisational power as your project consumes the whole organisation...
- You can put people in extremely uncomfortable positions forcing them to make decisions they really don't want to make and then watch them squirm.
- You can take a hike before the finger of blame extends its dirty digit.
- You can avoid having to commit yourself to anything even vaguely resembling a deliverable.
- You can insist the business has a role in the project and when things go horribly wrong you can blame the business, because you know they won't turn up for the project meetings anyway.

The PRINCE 2 method is important to this book; we will tell you how it was developed and how to ignore all of the rubbish it spouts in favour of the one or two good ideas it houses to help you find easy street. Project management is not idiot proof. No method can achieve this target. And anyway, if project management became idiot proof, a better class of idiot would soon arise.

The central principle of project management is to do nothing whilst becoming indispensable, like politicians. Or actors. Or TV football pundits. Or the European Parliament. And to spend lots of money, and (occasionally, but this is not the reason for being a project manager, it is merely to keep up appearances), to deliver a successful project.

Using the European Parliament as an example, you can see that power, lack of responsibility and a huge budget spent on, well , just about anything, has never been held up as a reason for them actually achieving anything. Quite the opposite. It is a well-known fact that the EU spent six billion ECU educating French Farmers to speak English to imported sheep. The fact that imported sheep from the UK were then found to be Welsh speaking (well, that's what the French thought when the Farmers found that the sheep appeared to find English incomprehensible) enraged the Farmers who promptly set fire to the Bastille in protest and arranged for wheel barrows to run on the tracks of the Paris Metro to really screw up public transport and, well, be French about things.

The disruption and the rebuilding of the Bastille cost another 14 billion ECU. Damage to the reputation of the French Farmers was estimated as nearly 30 centimes. And the EU had to create numerous sub committee's of MEPs to travel the world to assess the capabilities of sheep to understand French. Which didn't half cost a packet.

What has this got to do with being a project manager? The fact that even failure can be richly rewarded with new projects to manage so long as the failure is massive, costly and embarrassing. And not your fault (or rather, that you can find a suitable scapegoat).

Convinced? Then read on.

1.3   Where it all began

Some 50 years ago, the then head of CCTA, asked his management board 'Why does nothing ever get delivered when I want it??'. The question was passed to a new recruit, Hugh Jeegoh, (family motto; if you don't know what you're doing, do it neatly) who had a brainwave. They would ask the new computer (of course this theme was used some years later by the famous Douglas Adams, without credit to the young Jeegoh). Thousands of operators prepared punch cards (this was an old computer) and some 20 years later came the reply 'I'm still thinking'. This reply was not a complete waste of time since it has been used ever since by every project manager involved in mechanisation projects. Five years later, the computer came up with *'Come back in another five years'*, also used by project managers everywhere.

How they all laughed.

Finally, twenty years ago the computer issued invitations to a gathering at CCTA where 'the answer' would be given.

The answer was 'Because projects don't finish on time'. Hugh was assigned a project, to define a method to enable projects to finish on time. This was the infamous PROMPT method (named so that projects was created would now finish promptly.) It was a dismal failure. Undeterred, the PROMPT project was transmogrified into the PRINCE project. This too was a complete fiasco. To disguise the less than glorious origins of their current method therefore, CCTA decided to start again with a completely different name, PRINCE 2; that would fool them.

Then a method was added as an afterthought. Not much of a method, but enough to confuse anyone who thought that a project could be managed by government.

The method has nothing to do with real project management, which is the subject of part of this book.

1.4 Great moments in the history of project management

Many great moments are the province of the space industry. Man and technology focused on achieving seemingly insurmountable project tasks. Enormous projects, with seemingly inexhaustible supplies of money

NASA The Apollo project.

A multi billion dollar project spanning two decades, all in an effort to capture a few pounds of rocks. However to be fair, there were spin off benefits: Alan Shepherd got to practice his golf swing in zero gravity, further advancing mankind's understanding of how to avoid a slice in weightless conditions, and my mam got to buy a non stick frying pan.

ESA Ariane 2 project.

The customers thought they were having their multi million dollar satellites launched in to orbit, whereas ESA were planning to go into direct competition with the Chinese in producing the worlds most expensive and spectacular fireworks display. The project was directly responsible for the production of the following joke, extracted from the stand-up act of the great Chinese Communist comedian, Ho Bludi Ho:

The Chinese were asked *'What do you put in your fireworks?'* they said *'Gunpowder'*; the French were asked 'What do you put in your fireworks?", they replied *'Satellites'*.

It seems to lose a little in the translation from Cantonese.

Other great moments include:

- The seven wonders of the world (the contractors were asked to create seven wonders, but the project manager knowing the limits of travel agents BC, built only the pyramids and printed some really natty brochures for the other six wonders, and of course went over budget).
- The leaning tower of Pisa. This wasn't actually due to the incompetence of the architect but was in fact the fault of the project manager. He was asked to build a Learning Tower for Pisa.

- the Channel Tunnel (it is not widely known that 37 tunnels were excavated by the French and 43 by the English contractors before they were fortunate enough to find a pair that met in the middle without too great a kink in the tracks. Why else do you think the budget was exceeded by such a large amount?

In keeping with the traditions of good project management, the superfluous tunnels will be developed as nuclear waste dumps - in fact this will be the only part of the entire project that is likely to show an immediate return on investment).

This section cannot end without further reference to the CCTA project to create PRINCE 2: it was delivered late.

1.5   Heroes of project management

Before we start, let us consider the myriad attributes needed by a project manager.

They should be male (of course), unless a scapegoat is needed when a female should be recruited. A pulse in the candidate is generally considered mandatory, as is an ego the size of Birmingham. Ideally, shiftless and lazy, the best candidates also lie as smoothly as an American President.

Briefly, we would like to mention some real heroes of project management.

Jules Rimet; the man credited with creating the world cup: old Jules did not realise his project manager was actually a football hooligan who wanted regular punch-ups with neighbouring foreign hooligans. The project team organised a tournament with the help of Jules that is so successful, that every four years people organise the opportunity to fight on their behalf and even better, countries compete to find the hooligans an exciting new location!

Wellington is an English national hero because of his project to beat the French (his slogan, "anywhere, anytime, anyplace", being later adopted by a famous drinks manufacturer).

Perhaps unsurprisingly, all Scottish goalkeepers are heroes to the English because of the SGBP (Scottish Goalkeeper Breeding Project). Managed by an Englishman who will have to remain anonymous, the most successful project in the history of the English FA is the project to ensure that all goalkeepers who play for Scotland are bred to be hopeless. Mind you their BEFWB (Breeding English Footballers With Brains) project clearly has a long way to go. The gene pool in use could use a little chlorine.

1.6   The frog that turned out to be a frog despite all the kissing

This the project that will not go away. The project that despite all efforts keeps on going, consumes money, changes direction faster than New Labour and is under the microscope because it is in the public eye, requiring media manipulation on an epic scale to focus blame on suitable scapegoats.

In other words, The Millennium dome. History, as they say, beckoned.

2

Risk Management

"No american soldier will ever set foot in Baghdad"

Saddam Hussein

2.1   Risk management - What it is

What is Risk management? It is the business of managing risks, what the hell do you think it is?

Well, now that the technical discussion is over, what are project risks? Examples include:

- a project sponsor that nit-picks and insists upon concrete, clearly defined results,
- sponsors who take an interest in the project,
- well-trained team members,
- appointing a project board,
- some idiot insisting that go/no go decisions are necessary,
- clearly defined business cases with specific objectives,
- sponsors who insist upon meaningful status reports with accurate resource and financial figures and will definitely not accept a load of very colourful graphs and pie charts.

2.2   PRAM, PRAT, CRAMM and CRIB

There are varied methods for managing risk.

PRAM	Sponsored by an organisation we have no intention of publicising and anyway it is named after a baby's carriage so it can't be any good, ask any mother, they all use push chairs nowadays.
PRAT	This is more like it, Project Risk Assessment Technology; buy this expensive software from us and you can ignore all of the rubbish about using techniques to manage risk (PRAT has now been adopted as the official term of endearment for the Project Quality Control Manager).

I can't get the PRAT to work!

Which particular PRAT are you refering to? ... I've never seen any of the users work!

CRAMM	The CCTA Risk Assessment Marmalade Method or whatever, we don't know, go and ask them. It'll be no use. And anyway its now owned by the spooks at MI5 or 6 or whatever and they probably won't tell you what it is unless you have forms E123 and E567 and

FU2 signed in triplicate and you agree that your kids can be held hostage if you even smell like you told anyone that you've seen the stuff, so its not worth it is it?

The best method is the tried and trusted method shown below.

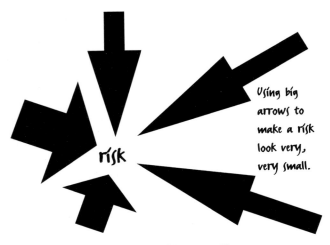

Managing risks with very big arrows diagram

As you can see, this technique involves drawing very big, angry looking arrows around the risk. It must work, otherwise it wouldn't appear in so many books.

2.3 Critical path analysis

Also known as analysis of the path that is critical. It is explained fully in the diagram below.

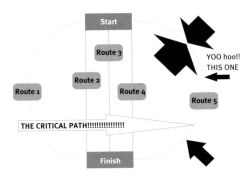

If politicians understood a little about critical path analysis, they may have chosen to provide a cheap reliable means of public transport, (rather like the one that existed before trams were axed and railway stations closed, and huge pots of money were put into out of town development and equally huge pots of money were withdrawn from subsidising rural transport services), before defining a transport policy to cut reliance on the private car. But that's the beauty of having inept management; more projects and more money to spend.

3

Getting started,
planning
and
other stuff

"1 in 5 people are
Chinese; there are 5 in
my family, and ma and pa
ar not chinese, so it has
to be my brother Ho Chin
Wa or my brother Jeb.
I think it is Jeb."

(George Bush)

A Fable

One of the greatest examples of the discrepancy between project planning and implementation may be found in the creation of the universe. God (Industries) Ltd a well known contracting firm in the universe creation business claimed that a universe could be created in seven days. That promise was made in writing in their brochure, The Bible. Naturally the promise of such an impressively short time span won them the contract. The initial project kick off known as the big bang, supervised personally by God Herself, took place some 18,000 million years ago. It then took another 17,900 million years (give or take a week or two) to get around to forming the Sun and the Earth and the other slightly less useful bits of our solar system. It took even longer to create really useless stuff like project management methods.

Some mathematicians detected a slight discrepancy in this planning/implementation scenario. Fortunately for God Industries, their brochure points out various punishments (known as Divine retribution) for mathematicians (or anyone else come to that) who questions discrepancies between what was promised by God and what She actually delivers. Many people have been trying to get in touch with God to, er, communicate with Her (politely) ever since but She seems to be permanently unavailable for comment.

3.1 Doing nothing

Getting started is actually known as doing nothing, a task that curiously can have many activities. Often you have to be very busy in order to do nothing, it is therefore suggested that you hold meetings at regular intervals in order to avoid doing anything at all. Meetings, especially QA meetings, are called by the very best project managers all over the country (outside if possible, because there is obviously less risk of anyone noticing how little you are actually doing) with as many people in attendance as can be conned into travelling (a well known ploy being to arrange the meeting at some swish hotel - on the pretext that you will be away from the interruptions of the office and able to achieve something meaningful, like getting absolutely, er, informed at company expense).

If you are lonely, or boring, or perhaps simply disliked by all sensible people, you will find meetings to be an excellent method of forcing yourself into their company.

3.2 Continuing to do nothing whilst looking like doing something

Time management is only mentioned here because some smart Alec will mention it to you. If you have time to go to the pub, finish early, arrive late and all the while produce nothing whilst appearing to be working your fingers to the bone (and at the same time being able to submit huge expenses claims) you don't need any more advice from us.

For those of you looking for advice, we suggest the technique known as timewasting. We could go on about this for hours but would be wasting our time. In brief, run around conspicuously, preferably carrying lots of files and GANTT charts (see chapter 4). When not running around, put your feet on your desk, look serious and phone everyone you know, talking to them in a low voice. Position your PC so that the screen cannot be seen while you play 'Minesweeper' (all the clicks and swearing will convince everyone that you are hard at work).

3.3 Managing the risk of being caught doing nothing

This is a brilliant opportunity to try out all of the risk management methods. This way you can find the one that wastes the greatest amount of time whilst still producing a complete rainforest of paperwork and at least three pretty graphs (or better, GANTT charts -see chapter 4- to hang on your wall).

Should you actually be caught doing nothing the best defence is to draw up a project exception report (see section 6.1 Report writing) in which you pass the buck to some objectionable line manager who you may accuse of failing to deliver the promised resources. Incidentally, if you are wondering about the role of project planning, well what do you think the first three items in this chapter were covering?

3.4 The business case

The business case is vital to methods such as PRINCE 2. It allows management to specify the objectives, resources, costs, benefits and risks for the project. The method is quite handy for us because a good (or bad, depending on your point of view) business case will enable you to identify projects without:

- a customer,
- a sponsor or owner,
- the means of knowing whether the project will, achieve its objectives (as there aren't any),
- requirements,
- justification.

The business case will also identify projects in conflict (because of multiple customers each having different goals) and projects where the sponsors tell you what they don't want (but not what they do want). The business case is vital therefore to assure you that no one has a clue about what is required. Since such information is a powerful weapon in providing you with an easy life, it is worthwhile therefore pretending to the organisation that you support the development of a business case.

About 50 people ... sometime next year ... delivering a really useful thingymajigg written on the back of a beermat isn't what I would call a detailed project plan!

A good reason for adopting a project management method is that initially the idea is greeted with great enthusiasm within the organisation. Project briefs and PIDs fly about like shrapnel. Adoption of a project management method is however, almost always accompanied by a rise in sickness as project managers fall victim to the deadly 'Post stage plan stress disorder'. It was examination of post stage plan stress disorder that led army psychologists to discover 'Post traumatic stress disorder' which strikes down soldiers following active combat duty. It has been rumoured that Saddam (a misspelling of SSADM, was secretly arming his warheads with PRINCE 2 stage plans with the intention of firing these at allied troops. The Americans sadly failed to realise that evidence of weapons of mass destruction were at their fingertips and instead searched for useless stuff like biological weapons.

3.5   Phases of a project

Much to the disappointment of Star Trek fans project phases are not those cute, trendy looking hand held blasters that can be used to transform your opponents into a cloud of cosmic dust particles. A project phase is something that must be gone through. Like the sound barrier, it is also accompanied by loud noises (the disgruntled moans and wailed objections of the project sponsors).

The best advice we can give you here is to find someone with the standard number of fingers on each hand (ie not from remote areas) and get them to remind you that phase two follows phase one, phase three follows phase two and so on. So long as you have lots of serially numbered phases and you don't forget to count them off in the right order, you will be thought of as extremely smart and talented. If you want to appear really clever you can discuss the interdependence of the phases and

even illustrate them. It's quite simple really, it just involves drawing lines that randomly link up different bits of the GANTT charts. You can also produce reports for each phase. As a guide try adding a semblance of structured thought to the phasing by adopting the examples included here.

Starting up a project

This is the difficult phase in which you often have to explain to a bunch of morons, in laborious detail, what you are going to do so that they can agree to let you do what you've already started doing.

Project brief

A project brief is rather like a summons. Once you pick it up, it is officially served and you are obliged to do something about it. Never pick up or physically handle a project brief until you know what surprises are lurking within.

Scoping

This is where you tell the project sponsor that you are going to do and deliver what they want to hear you say you are going to do and deliver, when really you know differently. To the project manager this is known as 'scoping out'. It is essential in this phase to build in ambiguity, contradictions and misleading statements.

Project planning

Project planning is one of those paradoxical situations in which the line organisation, characterised by the fact that nobody knows who is supposed to do what, where, when or why, demands that you as a project manager specify all of these things in your project plan insisting it's the only way that they can keep control of things and to ensure that there isn't a clash with the line organisations activities and planning.

The phases of a project embrace a number of natty processes and committees and other stuff that no one understands. They waste time very effectively and so we include a selection here that you may choose to employ.

Project board

Best practice insists you have to have a project board to ensure the quality of the project deliverables, make decisions, make meaningful comments on reports, ask difficult, probing bloody awkward questions that put the project manager on the spot. The trick here is to create a project 'bored'. A group of people far too 'bored' to bother reading the status reports and let you get on with it.

A project board should consist of no more than three people ... two of whom are absent.

For us IT specialists the PRINCE2 project board is an ideal way for us to find an unsuspecting scapegoat when the project does go over time or budget and fails spectacularly to deliver a solution even remotely resembling what the business requested. Meaning we have years of maintenance work and changes that we can charge to the business.

So how does it work? PRINCE2 insists that the role of 'Business executive' or 'Business sponsor' or 'Senior user' or some other such nonentity role from the business is involved in the project board. Business people are generally either too frightened, too confused or too superior to get their hands dirty by becoming involved in an IT project or to take this role seriously (lucky for us). So when things do go wrong we simply blame the business for lack of involvement.

Project Evaluation

The purpose of a project evaluation is to identify scapegoats and to allocate blame (proportionate with the degree of aggravation caused to the project manager by the various project 'issues', such as those line managers who failed to give up all claim to their manpower resources, controllers of

A famous American president had a sign on his desk that proclaimed 'the buck stops here'. As a Project manager we live by the maxim 'the buck stops there!'.

The buck stops anywhere but HERE!

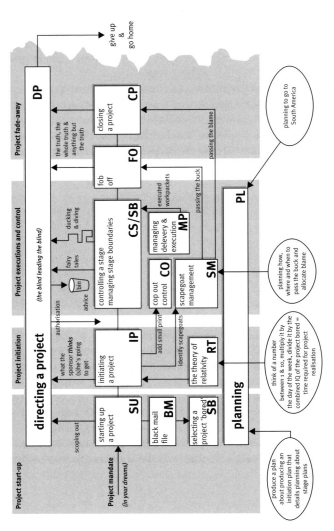

Example model

the corporate purse strings who failed to cough up the necessary readies, project board members, who questioned the validity of the projects, or started raising awkward bloody questions about status reports, demanding to be kept up to date...., self righteous, megalomaniac, meddling gits....er where was I again, yes... evaluations)..

3.6   Go/not even if I can marry Claudia Schiffer situations

Decision making is hard, eg watch the telly, or go to the pub? And an inevitable fact of life in the world of project working is the need to make decisions. The 'Go/not even if I can marry Claudia Schiffer situation' is one wherein the decision not to do something (eg commit yourself to delivery on time, under budget) is so ludicrous that you would not do so , even if..........

Now that is a decision!

3.7   Baling out

It is perfectly possible to get a track record as a successful project manager without ever doing or finishing anything. The technique is known as baling out and it can be employed at various times. The exact moment is dependent on you knowing just when the brown stuff is about to make its inexorable march towards the air conditioning (the actual moment is known as 'the balloon going up'). The more experienced project manager can bale out very close to the moment that the balloon actually goes up. Ideally, you should find an excuse for leaving (or to use a recommended phrase - to hand over the reins), between 50% and 75% of the way through your original project plan timescale. Obviously if the balloon has gone up, you will need a parachute (usually a scapegoat) so it is recommended that you learn to bale out long before anyone realises that the project is a dud.

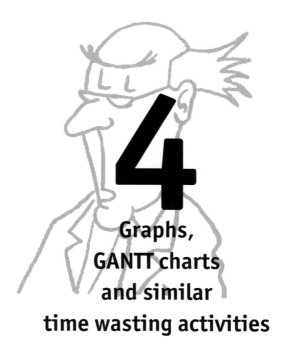

4

Graphs,
GANTT charts
and similar
time wasting activities

A committee (or project board) is a group of people
who individually can do nothing but as a group
decide that nothing can be done.
Fred Allen

"83.7 percent of statistics are made up on the spot"

Albert Einstein

4.1   Graphs and GANTT charts

Graphs are fine but easily understood. Therefore you need to avoid using them. You should consider using the much more complex GANTT (Got Another New Timewasting Toy) Chart. Prepared correctly, these also can be useful but by following detailed instructions to map everything that moves, they can be prepared in such a way that they look marvellous and mean sod-all.

The central characteristic of your GANTT chart must be that the time spent on actually looking at and trying to understand it should be entirely disproportionate to the production effort. A really useless GANTT chart is a work of art which though created in thirty seconds flat, is a thing to be treasured, and talked about, and admired long into the night, when 'resting' project managers gather for their annual conference. A GANTT chart should aim to be so aesthetically pleasing, and, well, colourful, that business managers can pin it on the wall behind their desks. It should be gargantuan, with more lines than the BT network, and with myriad highlighted milestones so that the business manager can feel suitably important and proud of displaying the thing (despite the fact that neither they or the architect of the chart has a clue what all those lines and funny shapes mean). And it should be supplied with coloured pens so that extra useless information can be added at will by its owner when it is desirable to look like they understand it.

4.2   Costs

A good, expensive, project should, like a good pair of shoes, last for years. The analogy runs deeper than you might believe. Shoes will need to go to the cobblers every so often and you will have to talk cobblers. Also, every so often you will end up stepping in something brown and smelly and you will be forced to find someone to clean up the mess (after all, you won't want to do it yourself). The best advice is to make the project so outrageously expensive, busting more budgets than the average local council, so that writing-off the cost cannot ever be countenanced.

4.3   Slush funds

You may find it useful to siphon off a pile of money into a slush fund that can be used when things go seriously out of control (eg to buy back incriminating end-stage reports), or to grease the palms of people who can help you. These people are known as slush puppies. Do not underestimate the power of bribery (or indeed the cost). One more thing. It is important to be sincere, even when employing bribery and deception. If you can fake sincerity, then you are on your way.

4.4   PRINCE 2

Right out in front in terms of timewasting is of course PRINCE 2. We have covered the usefulness of the business case and the role of the business sponsor or senior user as a scapegoat, now we turn our attention to the only other use you can make of the method and that is to 'scope out' (remember our earlier reference to this useful technique) everything that might remotely cause you to work to a formal process. You don't even have to tell lies, simply use the actual diagram reproduced from the PRINCE 2 handbooks and shown below.

As you can see from the above; Organisation, Planning, Controls, Stages, Management of Risk, Quality Control, Configuration Management and Change Control are completely outside the bounds of a project and should definitely not be attempted.

5

Activities taking place

"raise my hand
all those who believe in
telekinesis"

Stephen Wright

5.1 Estimating how bad things are

We rely on the following trusted methods:
- if you poke your head around the office door, does anyone shout or hurl abuse at you,
- does your boss strike you on a regular basis,
- is your job being advertised,
- are board meetings attended by money lenders,
- are all of the original sponsors still alive, or at least not in retirement,
- in project board meetings, mention how wonderfully well things are going and see if anyone starts frothing at the mouth, or going purple in the face or shaking uncontrollably (when they haven't been drinking),
- has anyone mentioned outsourcing.

Curiously enough, if you find that everything is coming along within budget, on time etc, then this is actually rather good and things may not be that bad really. Which is an event about as likely as a Barmitzvah in Baghdad.

5.2   Troubleshooting

Something that still takes place today in some countries, is that trouble makers and petty criminals are taken to packed football stadiums where they are shot. This is considered to be entertainment. It is an appealing method for project managers to use when dealing with troublesome individuals but it tends to be frowned upon by the unions and namby pamby human resource and personnel departments.

Another useful technique is to join a users group (the PRINCE 2 version has the unlikely name of PUG, but you can't do much with the three letters you have to play with). These users groups often involve real project managers, so you can use the meetings as an opportunity to steal their ideas.

5.3   Manipulating results

This is easy. Some examples to help you are given below.

Reality:	**The project is running late**
Your version:	*I wasn't there when that happened*
Reality:	**The project is running late**
Your version:	*It was her job*
Reality:	**The project is running late**
Your version:	*No it isn't*
Reality:	**The project is running late**
Your version:	*Are you talking in terms of real or elapsed time and have you taken into account:*
	- daylight saving
	- the use of the Julian calendar
	- the time zone
	- the Project Management Tool (PMT) only accepts dates in the American format which can be quite confusing

Reality:	**The project is running over budget**
Your version:	*I wasn't there when that happened*
Reality:	**The project is running over budget**
Your version:	*It was her job*
Reality:	**The project is running over budget**
Your version:	*No it isn't*
Reality:	**The project is running over budget**
Your version:	*Are you talking in terms of real money or ECU's and have you taken into account:*
	- the strength of the pound/lira/yen/franc/ deutschmark/euro/kroner
	- the National Debt
	- international exchange rates
	- inflation
	- VAT

Reality:	**Project management is incompetent**
Your version:	*Despite constant attention from me, it is the fault of everyone else, especially her and did you know she said that you were a brainless git who has need of under-pants bearing 'Left' and 'Right' identification symbols to enable you to put your bum in the right place?*

Reality:	**Project management is incompetent**
Your version:	*No it isn't*
Reality:	**Project management is incompetent**
Your version:	*Its all to do with PMT*
Reality:	**Project management is incompetent**
Your version:	*Define incompetent*
Reality:	**Project management is incompetent**
Your version:	*Oh I do so agree - that's bound to throw them for a while, then snarl 'No it isn't'*

You can wear anyone down through insistent gainsaying of their point of view. Therefore 'No it isn't' is a phrase that you should commit to memory.

5.4 Damage limitation

In 5.2 we described hiring trained project managers to take the blame for any mismanagement. The technique is known as scapegoating and is a recognised form of damage limitation. Other recognised methods include:

- ✔ Risk management (bit too technical though)
- ✔ reporting problems at the earliest opportunity (as if......)
- ✔ lying
- ✔ cheating
- ✔ offering to commit hara kiri (popular in Japan, but ensure that the offer will not be considered seriously before you make it)

✔ moving to another job before the brown solids and the air conditioning meet in a deathly embrace.

5.5 Lying through your teeth

Practice in front of a mirror saying 'This project will finish on time' without sniggering, giggling or bursting into laughter. There is not much more to add really. Look to any President of the USA for role models and to the avoidance techniques employed by any British politician when faced by a direct question.

A tip: borrow somebody else's dentures so that you can lie through their teeth.

No..no there is very little chance that we will overrun budget estimates.

5.6 Travelling in South America

OK. It has all gone pear shaped and your lies have been wasted and no amount of crying (see chapter six) can help. Adopt the escape kit retailed by the authors (false nose, glasses and moustache, new identity, passport and one way ticket to South America) and get the hell out before compensation is sought.

Once in South America, the authors can put you in touch with some friendly Germans who will have places for you to stay, nice new uniforms and can arrange a job. You may be asked to attend the occasional midnight rally, er, we mean picnic and some of the party games will be unfamiliar, but in general, well you should have paid more attention to the guidance in here, shouldn't you?

6

Laughing in the face
of failure
and
smacking the bottom
of criticism

"I wish I had stayed on at school to learn latin; it would have been so useful in my visits to latin america"

Dan Quayle

6.1 Report writing

Adopting an industry recognised project management method means burdening yourself with a responsibility for producing a mass of reports thereby doubling the amount of time required to complete the project.

Arguing that all this nonsense about report generation will only delay project completion, eat up valuable skilled resources and waste the valuable time of project board members in having not only read, but also to make sense of the complex sets of facts and figures (not to mention the fact that it will significantly add to the cost of the project) may help you get out of having to produce some reports. Unfortunately, there is always someone, somewhere in the organisation who says 'How much money has this fiasco...er project cost us so far?'. And who will ask for an answer in writing.

The thing to do is ensure that reports are used to underpin your objectives and that information about costs is presented in the most complex manner possible (this is where accountants earn their corn). The following table identifies some of the documents and reports you will be expected to deliver; more importantly it identifies what your objectives should be for these products.

Document	project brief
Objective	telling the project board what they want to hear
Characteristic	a confidence trickster's handbook
Document	project initiation document (PID)
Objective	convincing the project board they're going to get what they think they want.
Characteristic	the sting
Document	progress reports
Objective	jargon, acronyms, masses of meaningless facts and figures and don't forget the updated GANTT and Pie charts.
Characteristic	the fob off
Document	stage plan
Objective	convincing the project board you're going to do what they think you should be doing had the PID borne the slightest resemblance to what was really going to happen.
Characteristic	the British Rail timetable
Document	end stage report
Objective	the truth, the whole truth and anything but the truth

Characteristic	the fairy tale
Document	exception reports
Objective	passing the buck
Characteristic	the buck stops there

Document	evaluation reports
Objective	allocating blame
Characteristic	the back stab

6.2   Hard and Soft benefits

What do we mean by the terms Hard and Soft benefits? A hard benefit is , er, hard. Oh wait, now I remember, it is one that you can measure, like slush money. A soft benefit is intangible; that is to say, it is an excellent technical term to use to describe things that do not exist, have no value and fool people into believing that a complete and utter waste of time actually provided benefits. Only they can't see them, or touch them, smell them, hear them, or do anything with them. Or anything like that.

6.3   Crying in public (the benefits)

After taking on board all of this advice, what happens if you are discovered to be a con artist? Well, in many organisations you can get promotion, because they need people like you at the top, making decisions and deciding policy to rip off customers instead. And your proven track record will stand you in good stead.

If this is not the case, then bursting into tears and explaining that your family will be condemned to the poorhouse etc is bound to help. If you can cry in public (maybe even on TV), the effect is all the more striking. TV evangelists such as the magnificent Jimmy Swaggart spring to mind as a role model. He didn't just cry, he cried buckets. And he got his wife to cry, his children to weep; he even had bags of peeled onions passed around the studio audience. His bull terrier Bush was crying, his poodles Blair wept openly: his budgie Derek, his pet rabbits Marilyn, Pippa, Frances and Keith, his neighbours Hiram and Cindy-Lou, Chet and Maybelline, Walt and Mary-Beth-Bobbie-Jo, Bill and Hillary you get the picture.

Throw yourself on the mercy of your accuser. And if that doesn't work, move into programme management where your talents will be better appreciated.

"Probably the most important management fundamental that is being ignored today is staying close to the customer to satisfy his needs and anticipate his wants. In too many companies, the customer has become a bloody nuisance whose unpredictable behaviour damages carefully made strategic plans, whose activities mess up computer operations, and who stubbornly insists that purchased products should work."

Lew Young
Editor-in-Chief, Business Week

7

Not ITIL.......

**"Why did
Kamikaze pilots
wear helmets?"**

Anon

7.1 Introduction to ITIL and ITSM

"Why did Kamikaze pilots wear helmets?"

We don't know, but increasingly we in IT need to wear a helmet to protect ourselves from the flak coming from business managers, or 'customers' as they are known throughout the charted universe. It is time to declare war on business managers and business users of IT. Business managers and business users of IT do not understand IT and yet they consider themselves qualified to 'demand' to make use of IT. What is more, they insist that IT functionality is tailored to fit their individual needs. What arrogance! For nearly fifty years IT professionals have kept businesses afloat through their grasp of technically complex, intellectually demanding, er, stuff. And just because a few business 'managers' find they can 'surf the net' (sad, very sad) and cause two-dimensional images to lop-off one another's heads, to a soundtrack that would induce migraine even in the average heavy metal fan, they think that they should control the way in which IT is used!

Anway back to the introduction. ITIL, meet ITSM; ITSM, meet ITIL. There's the intro done. Only joking!. The difference between ITIL and ITSM is that they are spelled differently. Oh yes and that people working in ITSM are so important that they need their own method and certificates to show how really vital they are to pretty much everything.

The cartoon presents a rather extremist viewpoint...NOT!! Can you not tell how much this poor guy must have suffered at the hands of customers? This guy probably read and implemented the IT Infrastructure Library and then found all of

his good work thrown back in his face as users of the IT services demanded more and more for less and less. The thanks you get from some people! Well, we think these people have had it their way for too long.

ITSM will help you to regain control of the destiny of IT, putting IT back in the hands of those who know and love it. Us. We will be able to spend more. We will once again be guru's. We will make IT responsible for IT again. Use the project management guidance you read earlier to put this stuff together and you and the project team are set for life!

Customers (or 'users' as these tyrants are also sometimes known) should of course, not have a say in what IT they get. They should take what they're given. And what they are given is what they are fit for, based upon the professional, sound judgement of the IT experts that are charged with IT infrastructure management.

Has it ever occurred to you the curious, no, supernatural significance of the words *customer* and *user*?? Think about it:

c**US**tom**ER**s

Yes! A subliminal message, devilish in its simplicity. But are users and customers one and the same? Is it simply that the clever so and so's are trying to make us IT experts try to think of different ways to keep the same person happy?

7.2   Customers and Users

We've all heard frustrated IT professional say something like *'I'm just taking my brain out. I have to go and talk to some users (or customers)'*, when having to face the usually time wasting challenge of meeting business user representatives wanting to talk about IT.

But do you know how to tell the difference between 'customer' and 'user'? To identify a *'user'*?? These people, users, are far more dangerous to you than simple 'customers'. Customers live in blissful ignorance of the power of IT (and we intend to keep it that way). Users however, *know* something. It is these critters that have PCs at home. And as we all know, a little knowledge is a dangerous thing, especially in IT. Look at the Year 2000 problem, whose fault was that then? Er, maybe that's not such a great example.

The term user, within the IT social environment conjures up the image of 'abuser'. Somebody who will do anything to satisfy his individual needs regardless of impact upon, or respect for others. They have little or no respect for IT. They use it for their own selfish aims with little care for the impact they have upon the IT infrastructure management departments (or other 'abusers' of IT). For example they are responsible for a huge amount of requests for changes to IT, problems and questions about IT and make excessive and uncontrolled use of IT, causing performance and workload demands. Need we say more?? No wonder they are always complaining that IT is so expensive.

It has been suggested by industry experts (well, us actually) that users should be 'means tested'. That is made to undergo IT literacy tests - supervised by us IT experts - before being allowed use, or more accurately, abuse IT.

Sorry Dobson, you've been 'means-tested' and the best we could get from the IT department is a calculator that plays 'jingle bells'.

We would recommend making a distinction between 'customer' and 'user' in the following way. Draw up strategies and service levels agreements with customers (ie the bosses of the user communities) because you can pull the wool over their eyes. Then these 'user' types, the people that actually receive IT services at the sharp end have no one to blame but their bosses. We can then sympathise with these users, tell them we understand, etc, while all of the time taking steps to isolate them from being able to actually do anything about the lousy service. You must constantly be on guard against them, in case they start to influence their bosses (yes, the customers) into actually trying to understand IT and to obtain service levels and strategies that actually support the business.

Users also can be aggressive; for example they can be very dangerous if they are startled. Therefore always make plenty of noise when walking in their territory so that they know you are arriving. It is also a wise precaution never to feed them after midnight and never ever allow them to get wet.

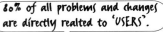

We propose that the purpose of IT infrastructure management (and therefore the premise of any method) is 'to understand and minimise the impact of users upon the IT infrastructure'. And we can do this in many ways, even if they have the bright idea of finding someone better to provide their IT.

Let's begin with a worst case. The business is looking for a new IT provider. Clearly, you have been negligent. For, as you will see in later chapters, you should have spotted the warning signs and gotten rid of the business ages ago. Still, the first thing you will need to know is how to stay in a job, so you need to know about the intelligent customer function.

7.3 The intelligent customer function

What's this then? (other than an oxymoron). Well, when businesses outsource IT, purportedly to save money or improve efficiency (as if they have any idea of the fact that the business is the cause of the problem), someone comes along and offers to buy the IT infrastructure and its people, and run the whole shebang more effectively. The business appoints a small group - often comprised of the people in IT who spotted the likelihood of being sold into slavery and who moved into non-transferable jobs - to manage the people now in charge of the IT.

Now this small group, the buffer between the no-nothing business and the know-all new supplier is known as the intelligent customer. Well, obviously the guidance on this issue can't be up to much because there's clearly more than one person in the group. And what were these self same individuals known as when they did the same job pre-take-over, for the in house IT? Thick customers, that's what. And where was the flaming guidance for us Thickies then? Left to our own devices were we not? No wonder we got sold down the river. Just because we were too thick to, erm, to, to, act intelligent.

7.4   Using consultants

If you need expert help, use these guys. They can really fool users because they're impossible to understand. And customers love them because they're clean. However, avoid the ones with 'models'. These consultants spend most of their waking hours drawing pictures on whiteboards and sadly, most of them have their own pet theories to match their boring models.

There really should be a consumer watchdog for this lot, they could be termed 'The Model Police' and given authority to bring charges against consultants relating to models, such as:

- using a model without due care and attention,
- displaying a model in a public place, with malice aforethought,
- drunk in charge of an offensive model,
- causing an affray in a public toilet through indecent exposure of a dangerous model,
- using an offensive model with intent to corrupt a minor,
- providing models with intent to cause a breach of the peace,
- using a model as an offensive weapon,
- being stupid.

Actually, you probably couldn't charge them for being stupid, but it is a hell of a good idea. Maybe we could also include being ugly, or wearing the same suit for the past ten years, or perhaps failing to buy us lunch.

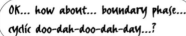

The cartoon strip illustrates a very serious problem for us IT professionals. What our hero really wants to say is 'Earth calling user, come in' or: 'I thought not, basically you don't have a clue as to your IT requirements. I suggest you go away and think about what you need, write it down in joined-up-words or get your mummy to do it for you, and then get back to us.' But we are far too polite in IT.

Quote from an ex IT director
(now sadly employed stacking shelves)

'The intelligent customer function is a role within the business domain through which the complex issues of IT and the richness of IT functionality can be translated into 'user' jargon for communicating to the user community, such as:

"It beeps."

"It's got nice colourful pictures and graphs."

"Look at the fishy swimming, this is a screen saver."

"This is a PC. It can be used for other things as well as playing games, or being used as a big desktop calculator."

So real, so perceptive. And they got rid of this poor guy. Why??? This guy knew how to keep things the same, even though his empire, sorry, we mean the IT organisation, had been outsourced.

8
Scoping the fightback

"I pay a lot of
money for a man
with integrity."

Kenneth R. Wilson

8.1 Service with a snarl

This module of 'Not the IT Infrastructure Library' is designed specifically for those in the forefront of user service. In other words, **you** are the pig in the middle, the mug who has to deal with the SLA (or Slave Level Agreement, as it is properly known) after the glamour boys who singularly fail to take any notice of the guidance herein, have negotiated an entire Vietnam's worth of no-win situations with those individuals laughingly known as 'customers'.

And who gets it when the SLA is breached?
*You do. Because you deal with **users**.*

Make no mistake, you need to fight back and this module tells you how. Of course, this stuff is only for the eyes of IT managers. If your customers (or worse, *users*) get hold of this your life won't be worth living.

This chapter covers the following important issues:
- the Help Desk from hell (reduce the number of calls made by those irritating users),
- getting the IT infrastructure you want,
- providing less with more,
- SLAs that work (for the IT manager),
- capacity and cost management,
- costs, benefits and possible problems.

It is also worth warning you that a lot of stuff is out there waiting to trip you up with its earnest guidance about improving IT performance. Nearly all of it originates at the OGC and nearly all of it is published by the Stationery Office. It is available in bookshops (yes, it is legal) and by mail order (in plain, brown envelopes) from, EXIN, itSMF and others. So now you know how to avoid coming across the stuff.

8.2 Arcane pleasures

For the really curious among you, (remember what happened to the cat), stay away from the following:
- the IT Infrastructure Library,
- PRINCE 2 (project management),
- the IS guides.

The books mentioned above are of course hidden away from sensitive souls, minors, old ladies and feminists, being generally placed out-of-reach, on the top shelf (except in

Holland of course where they don't care about such things) at your local bookseller/newsagent. A group of feminists picketed a well known high street bookseller recently, demanding removal of the offensive material. Almost certainly, if you do pluck up the courage to buy one, these 'books' will be placed inside copies of the newspaper you purchase at the same time (to avoid embarrassment). Allegedly.

Don't be embarrassed. It is nothing to be ashamed about. Why, we remember in our youth when we would buy one of these books, take it home and sneak glances at the diagrams while the older boys would explain what they were about.

Curiosity about these things is perfectly natural. Some of our friends continue to buy this material, unashamed. The books contain information that is better accessed in an open, honest fashion, rather than from those 'advanced' kids that we all know. So long as you are over 18, no one can stop you buying this material.

It is even found on the Internet. You can see free samples, meet like-minded individuals, even subscribe to obtain books. So we are told. By other people. The authors however would point out that people wishing to access this material via the Internet should not do so in working hours.

If this 'material' is for you, don't worry. Support is available. There are, surprisingly, a number of legal organisations such as itSMF, and the HDI that cater for people with these esoteric interests. They are not perverts, just people with special needs. People stand up in public at events organised by these bodies (and yes, they are legal) and admit these 'interests' Some individuals with specific 'needs' form Internet chat lines or 'special interest groups' (fnaar, fnaar). Well, we are old hippies, and if that's your bag, man, and it don't hurt no one.........

One final thing however. Liberal as we are, we cannot leave the subject without mentioning one particularly esoteric group. Not content to read this 'material', they want to 'convert' others to its use. Believe this or not, they advertise training in its use!!!! Worse, you can sit examinations to gain 'qualifications'.

This is going too far. These people are perverts. What you do behind closed doors is one thing, even within groups of like-minded individuals. But this is a blatant attempt to corrupt. You need to know the names of these shameful organisations, they are Stichting EXIN (a Dutch organisation), and ISEB. You can expect this sort of behaviour from the continentals, especially the Dutch, but when we consider that British organisations are also involved, well, words fail us.

Once more, you have been warned.

9

The Help Desk from hell

"Trust me."

Richard Nixon

9.1   Help Desks

A Help Desk is a central point of contact for customers and users to call when they are in difficulties with the IT services. So your first question should be 'How can you reduce the number of calls made?'.

The following are tested methods of getting shot of those people who continually call for advice, tying up valuable resources and engaging the phone lines that you need to call your bookie.

First, some tips about how to greet an incoming call:

- Ignore it. That's right, let it ring. For hours if necessary. And if you get written complaints, send them back marked 'Return to Sender, undeliverable because of contagious disease'.
- Publish incorrect phone numbers .
- Pick up the phone but say nothing. And then put it down again (sends them mad this one!).
- Pick up, and to the enquiry "Is that the Help Desk", reply "Might be, who's asking?". Then put down the phone.
- Follow a scripted response, irrespective of the enquiry, an example is given below:
  "Hello! This is Walter. I am here to help. Please tell me how I can be of assistance."
  "Yes, it's John Stewart here. The accounting system applications cannot be accessed."
  "I see. Is your PC switched on?"
  "What?"
  "Is your PC switched on?"
  "Yes it is. I said the accounting system applications cannot be accessed."
  "Mmm. Very good. You'd be surprised how often that is the cause of the problem! Now, is your PC plugged in?"
  "Are you incapable of understanding English?? The accounting system applications cannot be accessed. Shall I speak to you in Dutch? Or Chinese??"
  "Ah well you should have checked that of course! Never mind sir, on this occasion there is no charge. Thank you and do call again! Don't be a stranger!!"

Should the unfortunate little oink fail to get the message, either follow the script once again, or pretend to be an answer-phone. Remember, it is not the goal to induce a coronary. Simple apoplectic fits will suffice.

Other recommended strategies include screaming uncontrollably, trying to enrol callers to the Hare Krishna movement and weeping apologies to everything said to you, finishing with hysterical sobs about how you now face the sack as your Help Desk has received so many calls. Finishing the call by firing a starting pistol, feigning frantic, gasping sounds, then allowing the receiver to fall to the floor may appear theatrical, but also has hilarious effects on callers.

9.2   Lightening the load

All of the above should have the desired effect of reducing the number of calls made. Resources can then be redeployed more effectively on card schools, poker and going to the races. If all else fails, apply to BT for the provision of a series of 0898 numbers, advertise a charge of 99 pence a minute and make sure a pre-recorded tape runs for at least fifteen minutes, before a human needs to intervene. And then follow the advice earlier.

Another useful tip is to employ a tape loop asking the user to press the numbers on their telephone in response to the following questions:

> *if you need assistance press 1*
> *if you wish to hold press 2*
> *if you don't wish to hold, hang up*
>
> *in response to 1*
>
> *if you need assistance press 1*
> *if you wish to hold press 2*
> *if you don't wish to hold, hang up*
>
> *in response to 2*
>
> *if you need assistance press 1*
> *if you wish to hold press 2*
> *if you don't wish to hold, hang up*

If that doesn't send them crazy, then we will win the next itSMF customer service award.

9.3 Training

Training for Help Desk employees should also include how to gain psychological superiority over the user and how to make users feel insignificant and utterly dependent upon the good will of the IT specialists. Therefore training should include guidance about how to answer the telephone in the event of an emergency ie the failure to implement the advice given in 3.1 and 3.2, that would have prevented calls being made.

> Some useful responses to calls will include:
> *"what do you want NOW?"*
> *"you REALLY don't know how to do that."*
> *(emphasis upon disbelief)*
> *"don't tell me ....you've broken it again,"*
> *"sorry, did I hear you say you WANT?..."*
> *"did I hear a pretty please?"*
> *"did I hear you correctly, did you say...*
> *...COMPLAINT!?"*
> *"get bent."*
> *"eat my shorts."*

These responses can only enhance the use of the Help Desk scripts used earlier in this chapter.

What if however, despite your best efforts, you are forced into providing a Help Desk? Well, you may as well make it work to your advantage by forcing the users to adopt technical terms and follow lots of rules. Begin with the terminology needed to be adopted (the etiquette, if you like), before moulding a really good system that you can buy some really good software to manage it with.

9.4 Problem management

The first thing then, is to invent some terminology (we love jargon), and the first term to recognise is 'incident'. An incident is when an (ab)user suddenly realises that they are using Information Technology and that they haven't got a clue what they are doing, or more often what day of the week it is, who they are or what their password is. You can use the term to help IT professionals also (even though we do know what we are doing) by providing a common language. The terms used to head the paragraphs in this chapter will be of use.

It is important that the IT section continually monitors incidents raised by users to identify any adverse impact upon the IT components themselves, or more importantly the impact upon IT staff. The aim of problem management is to analyse these incident trends and to ensure that adequate 'corrective actions' are carried out to reduce the amount of incidents and subsequent impact upon the IT and the IT organisation.

Important, key elements of this operational process are:
- incident analysis,
- incident classification and priority coding,
- error definition,
- problem user registration,
- problem user analysis,
- corrective action response.

The problem management buffoon will need to work closely with the Help Desk for defining incident classification and priority codes for determining how 'quickly' the IT organisation needs to respond to user 'incidents'.

9.5 Incident classification and priority coding

Example codes
Classification code: User is very polite and apologetic and regrets any inconvenience caused to the IT section.
> ***Impact (upon IT):*** Can be handled very quickly.
>> ***Priority (for resolving or calling back user):***
>> Within a day.
> ***Impact (upon IT):*** Costs half day work.
>> ***Priority (for resolving or calling back user):***
>> Within a week.
> ***Impact (upon IT):*** Costs more than a day.
>> ***Priority (for resolving or calling back user):***
>> Depends upon how much the user grovels.

Classification code: User is indifferent to the fact that they are disturbing the IT section.
>> ***Impact (upon IT):*** Can be handled quickly.
>> ***Priority (for resolving or calling back user):***

Moan to the user about their attitude and the amount of
work they are causing and handle within a day.
Impact (upon IT): Costs half day work.
Priority (for resolving or calling back user):
Moan to the user about their attitude and the amount of
work they are causing. Handle within a week, phone
him/her each day and stress that this will be escalated to IT
management the next time he or she does this.
Impact (upon IT): Costs more than a day.
Priority (for resolving or calling back user):
Severely chastise the user for their attitude and inform them
that a memo will be sent to both the head of IT and to the
business unit manager, and that their incident will not be
handled. Then handle the incident as quickly as possible, so
that when the user complains to his or her business unit
manager the IT section can show that the incident was
handled very quickly and the user was obviously making it
all up.
Classification code: User is objectionable and has a severe
attitude problem.
Impact (upon IT): Doesn't matter how much time it costs.
Priority (for resolving or calling back user)
Do nothing until the user phones back in a more pleading,
apologetic tone, if after one week the user has not pleaded
then invoke a corrective action response.

9.6   Problem user record

The problem user record is a record identifying awkward,
objectionable, difficult users. Items that should be recorded
against the problem user record are such items as:

Attitude	Apologetic, indifferent, demanding.
Gratitude	Ecstatic that (s)he has been helped, extremely grateful, thankful, doesn't realise (s)he should be grovelling, or wasn't in the least bit grateful and is going to get it in the neck next time (s)he calls.
Praise rating	High praise for the way (s)he has been helped, thinks the IT department is the best thing since sliced bread, says things like 'about time too', or 'is that the best you could come up with'.
Incident count	Amount of incidents raised.
Classification	Deserves continual abuse on the telephone, deserves threatening mail.
Corrective action	Details of the corrective action response invoked by the IT section for handling the response to the problem user.

When a user reports an incident, this user should be
matched against the problem user database and the problem
user incident count updated. Problem analysis is concerned

with identifying problem users and taking appropriate action, for example if the problem user is continually raising incidents about disk space (capacity management) the problem record should be routed to the capacity management team to ensure appropriate 'performance tuning' actions are taken such as tidying up or deleting all the important user files and requesting computer operations to delete any backups.

When the action is taken, the corrective action response carried out should be recorded against the problem user record. The next time the user raises an incident the Help Desk can check against the problem user record to see which corrective action response was carried out in order to determine its effectiveness. For example if the user phones up in a panic mode jabbering on about 'my files have gone, please you've got to help me, I don't know what to do...please, please help' the corrective action can be deemed a success.

9.7 Change management

If you change something, you have to test it. This takes time. Time is money, and anyway you have better things to do, like watching football on the TV. So either have a policy of not changing anything (justified because you will certainly reduce the number of problems in the systems) or, not testing anything (also justified because of the horrendous problems that will be caused to customers, almost certain to result in them demanding a policy of no changes).

10

Getting the IT infrastructure you want

"To err is human, but
to really foul things
up requires a
computer."

Anon

10.1 The IS strategy

A lot of present day theorists propose that the IT strategy is linked closely with the Business strategy. It is predicated that Business excellence depends entirely on ensuring that IT investment is focused on improving business processes and increasing profitability (in the private sector) or efficiency (and therefore cost reduction) in the public sector.

Of course, the theories are deeply flawed.

- We have to listen to people who know nothing about IT.
- Why do we want IT to be more efficient? Good gracious, you might have to work harder, or out of hours, or even go on training courses.
- It is IT that is important. We can always run other applications on the IT infrastructure if the business goes bust.
- If the theorists are so clever, how come Bill Gates is the richest man in the world?

No, friends, a radical approach is needed to customers that demand an IT strategy. Scare the pants off them first so they accept without question a *strategy for IT!!*

(*Editors note:* The authors are well aware that many managers wear skirts. However, most managers, male and female do wear trousers and therefore the word 'pants' was used as non sexist universally applicable term. 'Skirt' could not be used in the same way, as the number of men wearing skirts is restricted to certain extrovert Scots and one or two people who would prefer to be anonymous).

10.2 Scaring the pants off them

Prior to meeting customers, send them a copy of any PC installation manual, asking them to memorise the information in readiness for strategic discussions about empowering the business to use IT.

10.3 Blackmail

Blackmail is cheap and effective and recommended highly. It is also a dirty word. If the word offends, use 'Green mail', but who cares so long as you get your way. Choose the guy (or gal) in charge of the business negotiating team, then using your IT skills or those of your redeployed Help Desk staff, forge documents showing that your prey once owned and used 'material' such as the IT Infrastructure Library and offer to destroy the evidence in return for their co-operation in agreeing your IT strategy.

You can as you know (nudge, nudge) use the internet to find all varieties of revolting and perverted images. It will be easy to substitute a photo of your prey into an internet-sourced, down loaded picture of some sad individual reading, say 'Software Lifecycle Support'. Then, for those plucky, but misguided fools who do not respond to your first kind offer to destroy such 'evidence', simply wave a few copies of the picture in front of their noses and offer to send it to their husband/wife/partner.

10.4 The components of the IS strategy

What then do we need in our IT strategy?
- identify our key IT goals and drivers,
- the information we need to make these work,
- performance measures (eg what else have we mechanised so that the business is even more reliant on us),
- how you will implement the strategy,
- how to overlook the costs, risks, benefits and where appropriate, the risk mitigation proposals,
- project plans.

Don't forget, they should be grateful to us for providing a strategy that they can fit to their business; if they aren't, find a more grateful business and offer to take the IT elsewhere.

10.5 Measuring for performance

Crucial for the management and operation of an effective IT infrastructure management organisation, is the ability not only to set clear measurable objectives, but also the ability to define, measure and report upon performance indicators which deliver management control information enabling strategic IT planners to continually align IT users to IT. The balanced scorecard is a method which lends itself to this aim.

The aim is to make a selective choice of performance indicators underpinned with management information systems that will allow:
- The production of misleading, highly impressive facts and figures relating to the quality of IT services in terms only the IT organisation understands.
- The IT organisation to rapidly respond to changing patterns of user behaviour to ensure that adequate steps are taken to bring the user behaviour under control in these times of increasing, wide ranging escalation's of 'user' demand for quality IT.

10.6 The Balanced Scorecard

Everyone has come across the Balanced Scorecard, but how should it be used? The Balanced Scorecard should, in fact, be skewed, to address the performance indicators from four perspectives that we wish to use:
- *Customer:* to what degree does the user respond to IT behavioural conditioning, respect for IT rules, responsiveness to ITs demands and to what degree is the user a pain in the infrastructure.
- *Innovation:* to what degree does the user invest in innovative challenging IT requirements that are satisfying to the demands of the IT specialists.

- *Internal communication:* to what degree do the service management processes ensure IT organisational awareness of the impact of the users upon the smooth running of the IT, such that process actions can be taken to both reduce user impact and to influence user behaviour and responsive-ness.
- *Financial:* what is the percentage of user investment in challenging innovative technology.

10.7 Quality improvements

Underpinning the key performance indicators there should be a quality system for ensuring quality improvement initiatives are identified, implemented and continuously verified, such as the Deming circle:IT examples are given below.

- *Plan:* to get your own back on those slimy users, ...to stay one jump ahead of the users.
- *Do:* 'the users in the car park'. Motto here is: Do unto the user organisation before it does unto you, from a great height. Which underpins the 'proactive' nature of the tactical 'offensive' service management processes.
- *Act:* in such a way as to put the fear of God into them.
- *Check:* both internal (process controls) and external (we've got our eyes on you...).

Obviously, we don't believe in any of this Deming rubbish (the Lemming circle would be a better description), but you'll seem really impressive to users when you start talking about their worries using these Guru words. Then you can simply ignore whatever they want unless it meets IT criteria for success!

10.8 Risk management

Those who paid attention to the wisdom in the pages describing project management, will know that we need to look at the risks that something might go wrong with our finely wrought plans and prepare assessments of risk, risk mitigation strategies and plans to ensure business continuity in the event of a disaster (maybe such as being outsourced).

You should be aware by now that IT is for IT people. Therefore risk assessments and continuity plans should be predicated on survival of IT. Remember that when you 'do' the project planning.

And here are some examples of what to think about:

Risk	Customers understand IT.
Likelihood	Nil.
Impact	None.
Mitigation strategy	Have a beer and stop worrying.

Risk	Users demand better quality services.
Likelihood	High.
Impact	Extreme hardship. May have to become more efficient.
Mitigation strategy	Keep them away from the ITIL.

Risk	Customers demand a Help Desk.
Likelihood	High.
Impact	Lots of telephone queries, new technology needed.
Mitigation strategy	Set up the Help Desk as described earlier in this book.

Risk	IT strategy has to be changed.
Likelihood	Medium.
Impact	None, if the strategy cannot be implemented anyway.
Mitigation strategy	Draw up the strategy in a loose leaf, hand written school exercise book, leaving lots of blank pages between the sections for alterations.
Risk	We are to be outsourced.
Likelihood	Very high.
Impact	Catastrophic, we might be out of a job.
Mitigation strategy	1. Get yourself in position to be an intelligent customer.

If all else fails, improve levels of service and reduce costs (makes us ill to even think about this).

We should draft and regularly test plans that will ensure the continuity of IT in the event of say, the businesses going bust, or (Heaven forfend), a real disaster hitting IT such as the apocryphal Jumbo Jet crashing onto the mainframe. This Jumbo scenario is quite interesting actually. For example, what if you arranged storage of the contingency plans under the girlie magazines, by the tape decks in the computer room?

In a bit of trouble then aren't you? Unless you were in the room at the time and in that case you probably don't care much either way.

11

Providing less with more

"Abbreviation is much too long a word."

Inuit saying

11.1   Managing resources

Probably the first thing you learned when you started your career in IT is that customers are never happy. So don't bother trying to improve things, just concentrate your efforts on building up an IT empire that Alexander the Great would give his elephants for. Or is that Hannibal who, oh, forget it, you get the picture. The idea behind management of resources is that of ensuring that you are never short of people, time or money, each of which can be deployed in projects to make the business ever more dependent on IT, at minimum expense to IT.

Techniques that you might find useful include:

- Creation of an IT infrastructure roughly two or three times the size needed to handle peak workloads.
- Ensuring that service performance is degraded at all peak periods, if necessary by issuing all IT staff with games software and precise instructions about when to run them on the IT infrastructure.
- Invest in client-server systems where service levels at the PC user-interface cannot be defined.
- Investing in a cost management system (see chapter six) that is incomprehensible to customers (and users!).

11.2   Misunderstanding customer needs

This is crucial to survival. Take steps to ensure that minutes of all meetings are documented inaccurately (preferably by hiring illiterate staff for this specific purpose).

If minutes are queried, abuse the change control system by insisting that a change request is raised. You can design change requests in such a way that Einstein wouldn't have a clue about how to fill them in.

In meetings, always use jargon and acronyms (as described throughout this guide). Should anyone ask for clarification, a withering glance followed by a sad shaking of the head works as a method of making the enquirer look very small indeed.

Bursting into gales of laughter is however, only recommended if everyone else at the meeting is an IT person. It is important that no one has sympathy with your interrogator. Therefore outright humiliation is the last option. If under questioning you find yourself under pressure (and worse, having to supply answers that embarrass), then fainting is recommended.

11.3 The services provided

Never let any of the customers forget that they would not be there but for IT. For a start, point out to awkward customers that their salaries depend on IT systems, and that it is very easy for a trained IT professional to take their names and ensure that this months moolah is paid to a more deserving person.

Make certain that new applications are tested prior to live use so that you can be certain that they will fail the instant that there is demand. Failures should be investigated to ensure that outage - or even outrage - is kept to a maximum. In this way, you can make certain that when service is restored, customers really are grateful.

11.4 Measuring customer satisfaction

Ten years ago, measuring and influencing customer satisfaction was a simple affair. The FT approach was adequate (Fawlty Towers approach), known also as the FT Index.

However nowadays customers demand satisfaction surveys where they have a chance to ventilate their views on IT service delivery and express their degree of (dis)satisfaction. As if we care. However the surveys can be turned to the benefit of the IT organisation. Surveys that allow the 'satisfaction' of the IT organisation with the business to be assessed, such that the IT organisation can take measures to bring the customer community up to the next level of IT satisfaction.

The IT organisation satisfaction categories are:

Converted	This is the optimal level of IT satisfaction indicating that the business community is converted. They have seen the error of their ways and accept that IT should be left firmly in the capable hands of IT professionals and the business should be aligned to the demands of IT.
Convinced	This level indicates that they are convinced that they must strive to satisfy the needs of IT.
Conditioned	This level is an indicator that their behaviour is being influenced through effective service management controls such as problem customer management and charging for abuse, and that they are aware of their responsibilities for improving business use of IT.
Cowed	This level indicates that the business community is totally focused on responding to IT behavioural influence but hasn't yet appreciated that it must be proactively working to align the business to IT needs (such as coughing up the necessary high funding, and requesting interesting technological requirements).
Clever	This level indicates that drastic measures are required from the IT organisation, perhaps outsourcing the business to another IT provider. Recommended where they control budgets properly, manage investment, and are actively engaged in requirements specification, strategic planning and service definition.

11.5 Satisfaction measurement methodology

Of course, we all know that an 'ology' is the study of something. And that a methodology must therefore be a study of methods. But who cares? Tell anybody that you have a method and they don't give a monkeys, tell 'em you have a methodology and they're all over you like a rash. So, always have a methodology, and here's one we started earlier. The CSIs (Customer Satisfaction Indicators) described on the next page illustrate the sort of foolish issues that customers wish to express their satisfaction with regarding IT. The statements beneath these headings illustrate the responses you would expect from customers in each of the categories described earlier.

CSI	**Problems are resolved**
Converted	before I can even consider causing one,
Convinced	before I get a chance to report one,
Conditioned	faster than speeding bullet,
Cowed	above and beyond the call of duty,
Clever	chance would be a fine thing.

CSI	**The IT department communicate with me**
Converted	before I even know that I need to contact them,
Convinced	as and when they deem necessary, with information within the boundaries of my limited ability to comprehend,
Conditioned	whenever I need comforting,
Cowed	in joined-up words that treat me like a real person,
Clever	in grunts and snorts.

CSI	**IT staff**
Converted	are in total harmony with our needs, they are sympathetic and understanding of our deficiencies,
Convinced	are highly professional, proactive, courteous and service minded,
Conditioned	deserve a better class of users,
Cowed	are the bees knees,
Clever	are power crazed, abusive, Neanderthal technoids.

CSI	**IT products**
Converted	are optimally designed to ensure that we can align our business to IT functionality,
Convinced	are capable of doing things we didn't even know we needed,
Conditioned	are far too good for us common users,
Cowed	are turbo terrific,
Clever	are technological gridlock's of mismatching, unreliable components.

CSI	**Charging for IT services**
Converted	is optimally aligned to influence user behaviour and reduce inefficient demand upon valuable IT assets,
Convinced	is the best possible option for what I need to influence my abuse of IT,
Conditioned	is well below what we deserve to be charged,
Cowed	is fair for all,
Clever	is based upon the principles of squeezing blood out of a stone.

Of course, under the guise of finding out customer perception about IT, you use the responses to categorise the customers and if necessary, outsource those who don't meet your criteria. It is possible that you may have come to like some customers (though maybe they need a lesson or two about who is in charge). You need not outsource them until you have tried (and failed) bringing them back into line through interrupting vital services at critical moments and perhaps increasing charges until they hurt.

You can use all of the information you get from satisfaction surveys to help you get service levels agreements that work (the subject of our next chapter), or you can do with the information what every IT organisation does with such data.

Put all of the responses in a big box and ignore it until they stop bothering you. Then chuck it out.

12

SLAs that work

> **"A verbal agreement isn't worth the paper its written on."**
>
> Louis B. Mayer

12.1 Practising safe SLAs

If the quotations on the left and below don't make you think, consider this; if the customers were happy with us, why do they need us to write things down? Why do they demand satisfaction surveys (see previous chapter)?? They are cunning as well as being a nuisance. But you can really show you care (as well as being even more devious) by addressing their principal complaint.

Customers are fed up with long, boring SLAs.

Show them you are listening by providing a short, to-the-point agreement. This is known as safe SLA. An example SLA is provided on the following page. It is different to any other that you may have read in one particular fashion; you can meet all of the conditions in it. Easily. And what's more, by listening to customers, you put paid to any chance that the users might have of getting a decent service.

Slave Level Agreement (SLA)
between (your organisation) and
(whoever it is that you are stitching up)

This agreement will remain in force while either of the signatories is alive. Or dead. Or until hell freezes over.

IT Mission

We will at all times (except when the letter 'y' appears in a weekday) provide 100% service availability, including bank holidays and even on Christmas day. At all other times, we will provide the best possible service given the restraints placed upon us by customer demands, such that whenever we have staff available (and where commitments such as attending the bookmakers, or public house gatherings arranged with not more than five minutes notice do not get in the way), then some form of service will almost certainly be available to somebody or other at some time during any given month. Except when the machine is down for essential maintenance or testing continuity plans, when we get paid overtime.

Hours of service

As determined by needs of customers, relative to the theory of the internal combustion engine and divided by Foucault's pendulum. Arbitration is always possible. Problems should be telephoned immediately to the Help Desk.

Availability

Yes, there are (or will be) times when the service is (or will be) available.

Reliability

We can be relied upon at all times to support this SLA, even in times of crisis.

Capacity

Capacity management is a rather technical thingy that no one other than highly trained, IT literate experts such as exist in the IT services team should even think about.

Customer signature	IT department signature
....	....
Date:	Date:

12.2 Managing change

It is important that the IT department define change categories to assist in the correct prioritisation and planning of changes. We will therefore need to know in *advance of having to actually talk to anybody*.

- Has the change originator got enough cash.
- Have they a history of requesting interesting technological challenges for the IT, or do they insist on the most cost effective solution.
- How much work is involved.
- Whether the originator will let us get on with it, or will want to be involved in 'discussion' and 'project management'.
- Integration with other processes (eg the Help Desk; how much of a pain in the backside is the requester, are they continually bothering the Help Desk?).
- Integration with SLM (how often do they moan about service levels?).

The Board of Directors is complaining about the amount of IT changes that seem to go wrong. They want to know what we are going to do about it!

Just tell them concrete actions have been taken by our IT professionals that CLEARLY show a drastic reduction in the amount of changes that degrade IT services.

13

Capacity and cost management

"The brain is a wonderful organ. It starts work the moment you get up in the morning and does not stop until you get into the office."

Robert Frost

13.1 Capacity management

From an IT perspective, the important terms here are 'Demand management', 'Performance management', 'response' and 'tuning for performance'; from a customer standpoint they are... ...well who cares really?

Users are often demanding more for less, faster throughput of workloads, more capacity, response times faster than a speeding bullet, to them 'space, the final frontier' means unlimited filestore space for their very own personal abuse. Users are also very 'demanding' upon other processes such as user support or the Help Desk, change management, service managers. Therefore integration between these processes with capacity management is important to establish just how demanding the user is.

Tuning for performance, means placing priority files of 'demanding' users on heavily accessed discs and disc controllers, and running their workloads in heavily loaded machines, this means that performance management must be in place to identify suitable processors and discs. This will in effect 'tune user behaviour, or performance' and increase their responsiveness to the IT organisation.

13.2 Cost Management

The purpose of cost management is to identify the costs incurred by the IT organisation in delivering IT products and services and to translate them into totally meaningless 'cost units' which are ultimately charged to the users (preferably for a vastly inflated profit margin).

The amount a user pays can be related to:
● the amount of IT resources abused by the user,
● the degree of unpopularity they have within the IT department.

Examples of IT cost units:
● OCP clock-ticks,
● duplexed multi-block fibre optic transfers,
● asynchronous packets,
● bits & bytes,
● bobs & nobkins,
● gangle pin socket extract doodahs.

The costs units must be set against a complex charging mechanism to ensure the cost units are (un)fairly proportioned against users. Example charging mechanisms are:
● PTTN   (pay through the nose),
● STTS   (squeeze till they squeak),

Because all of the above has been couched in meaningless and highly complex technological jargon or acronyms that you never explain (and knowing that questioning will undoubtedly lead to IT recognising that it has, indeed, incorrectly translated the cost units, and that the user is to be charged an extra 10%), users rarely question the seeming unfairness of the cost distribution.

Which is of course exactly what you want. All of this 'best practice' information about using terms customers can understand is just going to get you into trouble. And if you use genuine technical terms in front of users, well, we've already warned you that those pesky users can be dangerous.

14

Costs, benefits and possible problems

**"Women.
Can't live with them,
can't kill them."**

Harold Solomon

One of the most successful features of IT is the way in which we have created a male dominated environment in which to enjoy the male bonding rituals (drinking, football, going to the races and talking about women because it is easier to feel superior when they can't answer back). There is a place for gorgeous, pouting, sexy creatures in IT, but enough about us and back to the subject. We have made women unwelcome for years through a focus on the technical environment, making the subject boring and insular. Making IT service management interesting and using advice such as that in the IT Infrastructure Library is likely to attract women into IT given that they are often more focused on people and on improving relationships. The IT Infrastructure Library is therefore a major threat and it is vital that you invest in this guide as a counter measure.

Other costs, benefits and possible problems are discussed in the following paragraphs.

14.1 Costs

Millions. Millions and millions and millions are spent on IT and we want to keep it that way. And lets face it, so do all of these outsourcing organisations who are so keen to take over the world. The difference between them and us is that they have to bid for business and provide service guarantees. Well, that's their fault for raising expectations. If, on the other hand, like us they had spent years fudging the true cost and hiding the failures, do you think they would be happy to just move aside when some organisation or other, tries to persuade the customers we had been treating as imbeciles (for years and years, at great cost in terms of time and trouble, sometimes even delaying our lunch for, perhaps minutes on end, while we fobbed them off with some highly original excuse for yet another service outage), that they should buy IT services from people who knew what they were doing?

Of course not.

But, there is no honour among thieves... or some such saying. And it means you must invest money in being ready to fight off these avaricious organisations. Spend money on the following:

- Campaign to illustrate that outsourcing companies are greedy, unprincipled and will pull the wool over the eyes of the business (ie people currently protected by you).
- Benchmark standards of service against organisations worse than your own to show how good you are.
- Wage rises for IT staff that make it impossible for outsourcers to mount a viable bid.
- Bribes.

The costs associated with implementing IT infrastructure management practices designed to optimally align business use of IT to IT requirements can therefore be quite considerable, hence the need to implement effective cost management and adequate charging mechanisms to ensure that customers foot all the bills (including the cost of bribes).

Vital to the underpinning of IT Infrastructure management practices are the production of management information reports. However you must be aware that setting up effective, misleading yet highly impressive sets of complex technological management information is a costly business (even though the intention is to get the money back from the customers to whom the reports are sent).

Setting up the necessary procedures and training of IT staff are equally important and also expensive. So never forget the old saying 'Changing user behavioural attitudes takes time, effort and plenty of user money.'

14.2 Benefits

The benefits should be obvious. If they are not obvious to you, you do not deserve to be in IT.

- Follow our advice and you have it easy for life.
- Follow our advice and you have it easy for life.
- No standards, rules or targets to meet.
- No ability - or need - to compare performance with other organisations.
- Everyone can work to their own methods, thereby making themselves both unique and irreplaceable to the organisation.

And if that does not convince you, there are other benefits associated with implementing ineffective IT infrastructure management practices, for example:

- Provide the IT organisation with structures, systems and information that enable the IT organisation to 'pro-actively' align the business organisation to IT requirements.
- Provide the ability to influence user behaviour and attitude, such that they live in awe, respect and absolute fear of the IT organisation.
- Enable the IT organisation to pass on the high costs of IT infrastructure management to the very people that (ab)use it.
- Enable the IT organisation to identify potential business units that should be outsourced to other IT service providers (ie the stroppy, awkward blighters).
- Ensure that IT is put back on the pedestal it so rightly deserves and ensure that customers become aware of their inadequacies and total dependence upon the good will of the IT organisation.

14.3 Possible problems

Of course, the principal problem is the growing menace to our youth of hard core 'manuals' such as the IT Infrastructure Library, as we mentioned earlier. Other possible problems associated with implementing ineffective IT Infrastructure management practices may be:

- Management expectations are too high. Changing customer/user behavioural patterns and creating an environment of subservient, cowering users takes time. Should you attempt to accelerate the programme through over emphasis of shock therapy, it may very well back-fire, creating a rebellious breed of mutinous users.
- The 'smart alec', 'IT aware' user, who undermines or screws up your best laid plans, a dangerous breed of users that exercise their right to influence the intelligent customer to insist upon meaningful service level agreements.
- IT staff commitment. Treacherous, misguided, ill-informed IT staff who start believing industry 'best practice' nonsense and ask themselves questions such as 'shouldn't we be providing a level of service that the business needs?'
- Customers start to ask for meaningful management information and reports, worse still they start to seriously question and examine costs.
- Customers ask awkward questions like 'what added business value do we get from our IT?'
- The board of directors insist that IT staff undergo ITIL training.

14.4 And finally

Never forget, that if a job is not worth doing, it is worth doing it badly!

Definitions, abbreviations and acronyms

Definitions, abbreviations and acronyms

A	First letter in the alphabet
Balanced Scorecard	The opposite of an unbalanced scorecard.
Blackmail	Preferred means of getting what you want.
(the) Business	Trouble.
Bored	Project management committee status
Cantona	French for 'incomprehensible, pretentious bad actor'
Customer	More trouble
Change control	A change we would make if we had any degree of control over this project
Configuration management	Making sure there are so many different versions of the project plan that if anybody raises any difficult or awkward questions you can say 'oh! you've got the wrong version'
CRAMM	A game of chance where those taking part attempt to cram more lies into their project than their opponents.
Consultant	An expert (so they say).
Culture	Found in yogurt, but not in the best run IT departments .
Descartes	French for 'the carts'
Dutch	Perverts.
EXIN	An organisation for Dutch perverts who study the IT Infrastructure Library.
GANTT	Got Another New Timewasting Toy
Goalkeeper	Being not found in Scotland
HDI	Help Desk Institute.
I	Irony.
II	Roman rubbish to signify the number 2.
Incident	An Incident.
Intelligent customer	An oxymoron.
IS	Information System.
ISEB	Information Systems Examination Board.
ITSM	I Tried Sado-Masochism.
ITIL	A series of books that should be hidden away from sensitive souls, minors, old ladies and feminists.

IT Infrastructure	The hardware, software, people, networks and other rubbish that make up the entire IT system.
itSMF	IT Service Management Forum.
Jargon	Word first made famous in a Hollywood movie called 'Jason and the Jargonauts'.
Jargonaut	IT consultant who spends his whole life dreaming up meaningless jargon and buzzwords.
John	American for toilet, as if we care.
Lion	Large, yellowish animal with big teeth, best avoided in the jungle.
Lion	(alternative definition) Creatures to whom users should be fed.
Model	Claudia Schiffer.
Outsourcing	What you must do to troublesome business.
Oxymoron	Intelligent customer.
PC	Personal Computer.
Planning	Planning timescales bear no resemblance to time scales in reality. Time scales in planning belong to another realm and dimension of time and space. It is akin to Einstein's theory of relative stupidity. For example a plan may say 'completed in three months' whereas to the people who exist in the 'reality' outside the dimensions of the project plan this is actually six light years elapsed time.
Philosopher	Out of work Frenchman
PRINCE2	Projects In Controlled Environments (dangerous stuff about project management).
Problem	A problem.
Philosophy	Waste of time
PRAT	A prat is one of those morons that has to agree to sign off and authorise your plan.
PRAT	Project management risk assessment technology
PRAT	(alternate) Quality Control Officer
Project manager	Slave driver

Project resource	Modern day equivalent of a slave labourer
PUG	A small ugly dog
PLUG	Character in the Beano
Quality control	Something to be avoided at all costs. Usually instigated by some interfering member of the project board, trying to pin you down by insisting that you define and quantify the deliverables so that they can check this against what you actually deliver! They should be grateful that the product bears any resemblance what so ever to anything you may have happened to suggest in the first place.
Resource	(rare, arcane) Something or somebody that helps you make progress. Since resources are rarely committed to projects, you will not need to know the definition.
Risk	No ideas at all; could be a breakfast item intended for babies and small children
Scotland	Lovely place with no Goalkeepers
SLA	Slave Level Agreement.
Software tools	Wonderful things to play with.
Spook	Secret agent (they like to think that anyway)
Stage	In the world of entertainment a stage is something for an actor to die on 'he died on stage last night'. For a project manager a stage is something to die in.
SSADM	Mis-spelling of Saddam
Stagecoach	Form of mid western US transport, circa 1875, commonly attacked by hordes of screaming red Indians.
Technobabble	Language spoken by technoids.
Technoid	Spotty faced, know it all IT techie that can only speak in technobabble or grunts and snorts.
Third party	The one after the second party.
User	Real trouble.

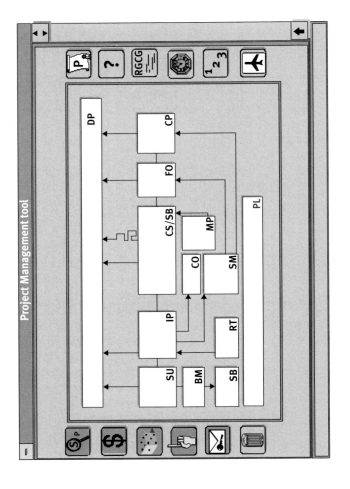

Project Management tool

Small print generator

❖ the project manager is absolved from any blame arising from anything, anywhere or anytime.

❖ the project manager has the right to call emergency project 'bored' meetings any time/any place without having to inform or involve anybody.

Buck passer

❖ maintain a list of people to whom the buck will be passed when buck passing is necessary.

Random decision generator

❖ type in a question, press the button and a 'yes' or 'no' will appear.

Finger of blame

❖ maintain a list of people to whom the finger of blame will point when necessary.

Black mail file

❖ maintain a list of 'juicy' blackmail items relating to project 'bored' members.

Bin

❖ directory for 'binning' the 'advice' from the project 'bored' or quality team.

Principle rules

❖ a good project doesn't end, it simply fades away.

❖ the truth, the whole truth and anything but the truth.

❖ the buck stops anywhere but here.

❖ unknown finish date, unknown resource usage, no idea of deliverables and yet the plan is still authorised.

Ignorance generator

❖ automatic generation of an excuse.

❖ ...I wasn't there....

❖ ...it was her fault....

Random GANTT chart generator

❖ automatically generates meaningless charts linked to stage plan numbering.

Random time generator

❖ specify a number between 1 & 10, automatic multiplication by the day of the week and division by the pre-specified combined IQ of the project bored.

Stage plan generator

❖ random stage numbering and plan generation (numbers in the correct sequence; 2 follows 1, but before 3).

Ticket to South America

❖ ticket generator.

❖ false passport application.

❖ names and addresses of certain groups in South America.

❖ german phrase book.

Editors

GABRIELLE KELLY screenwriter and producer is also a media educator and story expert. She has worked in Hollywood on both studio and indie films and on productions from Russia, Brazil, China and Europe. Her films include: *All the Queen's Men*, *Stag*, *D.A.R.Y.L.* for Paramount/Columbia, and her script of indie feature *All Ages Night* is set in the music scene of LA. She developed and edited the industry bible, *The Movie Business; a Legal Guide* with entertainment lawyer Kelly Crabb. www.gabriellekelly.com

CHERYL ROBSON is a producer of several short independent films, most recently *Rock n Roll Island*. She worked at the BBC for several years and then taught filmmaking at the University of Westminster, before setting up a theatre company. She also created a publishing company where she has edited over fifty books and published over 150 international writers. As a writer, she has won the Croydon Warehouse International Playwriting Competition and has had several stage plays produced.

www.cherylrobson.net

First published in the UK in 2014 by
SUPERNOVA BOOKS
67 Grove Avenue, Twickenham, TW1 4HX
www.supernovabooks.co.uk
www.aurorametro.com
CELLULOID CEILING © 2014 Supernova Books
Series editor: Rebecca Gillieron
With thanks to: Fay Allum, Alex Chambers, Neil Gregory, Simon
Smith, Jack Timney, Richard Turk, Suzanne Moore

Cover design © 2014 by Cheryl Robson
Front cover image © 2014 Paola Pagano
Back cover images © 2014 copyright Rex Features and Harrison
Gordon Schaaf
Printed by Ashford Colour Press, UK
ISBN: 978-0-956632-90-6

CELLULOID CEILING

Women Directors Breaking Through

edited by

Gabrielle Kelly and
Cheryl Robson

SUPERNOVA BOOKS

CONTENTS

ASIA

MIDDLE EAST

Introduction

Gabrielle Kelly and Cheryl Robson

'I speak out about women because I am one. I see inequities and disparity in pay at the very top of our industry and at the bottom. And I see it in every industry and across cultures... I don't think about "empowering women" – it's about enhancing humanity.'

Meryl Streep

Action!

With this command the director of a film orders the scene to begin. A film director creates the total vision of the film managing technical and creative elements represented by a group of highly skilled individuals all fighting to get the most money and time for their specific department. The director needs to mediate conflict, which in a creative enterprise is like the grain of sand that becomes the pearl. They also must keep track of multiple financial and business demands that change according to weather, time and unexpected events, possess great psychological acumen, force of personality, and superb communication skills, be persuasive, bold, passionate and able to weather love and hate from their cast and crew. All these qualities are needed to deliver images on a screen from words on a page turning money into light. All these qualities plus reserves of stamina, which often provokes the analogy of being a general in battle.

Mostly thought of as the author or auteur of the film, the director is usually the most important interpreter of a story that is developed, written, directed, edited and then brought to market. There is a staggering power and beauty to film as a medium; if a picture is worth a thousand words, a moving picture is worth an infinite number of words. These visual stories can reach millions and make millions, provoke inspiration, laughter and tears, and with the power of their stories can change laws, attitudes and lives.

For all these reasons including prestige, power and financial rewards, it is a job and a role widely coveted and desired.

Although women are half the population of the world and in many countries buy half of the movie tickets, the stories that they watch in this most powerful medium – the most popular and expensive art form that exists – are usually directed by men. Despite the many extraordinary talents of male directors who fill nearly all of the top 100 Best Film Lists ever written (with barely a woman on any of them), everyone wants to hear their own story. In addition, women want an equal chance at the often lucrative and artistically satisfying work that is film direction. Our history used to be told only through the accounts of those in power; kings, queens, presidents and tribal leaders. We've come to appreciate and increasingly demand other perspectives, those who were on the sidelines, the serfs, servants, slaves and 'nobodies' who have a different experience of the same story. As soon as money and power came into play, after the beginnings of Hollywood, the plethora of women working in all roles in filmmaking declined rapidly and with it, the ability to tell their stories. Mostly, this situation hasn't changed and while we know of amazing films that speak for humankind, the male perspective is but one. We are half the world and we have our own experience. We want the same chance to show it and by doing so, humanity will be enhanced by the diversity.

New era?

Race, class, age, nationality, income level, education, family connections and most crucially luck and talent all play a role in a woman's chance of directing a feature film. Each chapter that follows is a window into the political, social, cultural, artistic and financial world in which women directors work. As the usual business model of the Hollywood studio system buckles under recent sweeping global economic, political and cultural changes, expectations are upended; for example, it may be easier for a woman to make a film in Iran rather than the USA. While Kathryn Bigelow, US director, won an Oscar in 2013 for *The Hurt Locker,* her film focusing on the lives of male soldiers, the number of women directors in the US has fallen every year for the past several years. Martha Lauzen whose Center for the Study of Women in Film and Television documents this reality with her yearly report on women in media notes:

> 'The assumption is that the problem must be solved, that well-deserved success radiates or creates this halo effect. I just don't think it works that way. It's not immediate. We're talking about social change here, and attitudes about gender, race and age are all very deeply held.'

Accounts that follow, from the Middle East to Latin America and from Russia to Laos give us a glimpse of the bold, inspiring and entertaining work being done by women directors as well as the often overwhelming challenges they face. Change is happening, but for some, not fast enough.

In 2014, *Wadjda*, the first full length feature to be shot entirely in Saudi Arabia and the first by a woman director (Haifaa Al-Mansour) was also the first film Saudi Arabia submitted for a Foreign Language Oscar. Mansour did not intend to focus on women's issues but found they were too important to ignore. Her critics attack her on religious grounds which she denies are central to the film. Over and over we see that, against all odds, women are often the first to speak out against racism, sexism, lack of money, power and connections.

But despites the myriad firsts, Lauzen notes that perception is a huge stumbling block.

> 'If you don't perceive it as a problem, then you're not going to do anything to fix it. People don't say "I'm not comfortable with women having all that power or handling a budget of $100 million or more". They'll say, "Well, filmmaking is a business, and we try to avoid risk." And because there are fewer women out there, they're perceived as being more of a risk. But the fact is, Hollywood makes risky decisions every day.'

CELLULOID CEILING

Far from Hollywood, Senegalese director Safi Faye realised she could communicate more effectively in visual images rather than words to overcome the multiple languages of her country and avoid using the language of France, the coloniser of her country, Senegal. While feeling that 'phallocracy is universal' she sees African men and women as experiencing the same challenge, and Western feminist concerns having little to do with the women of Africa.

The twin Soska sisters, Canadian directors with their unique transgressive horror personae, publicise their work presenting themselves as feminist characters who do not, however, sacrifice their sex appeal. They provoke as they entertain and boldly play with ideas far from preconceptions of what type of story would automatically interest a women director. Tapping into a fanzine base usually thought of as male dominated, they reinvent horror in ways that are not always acceptable from many points of view, including feminism.

The enormous financial and artistic success of women such as novelists, Stephanie Meyer: *Twilight*, J. K. Rowling: *Harry Potter*, Suzanne Collins: *The Hunger Games* and E.L. James: *Fifty Shades of Grey*, is weighed against the systemic exclusion of women in many competitive fields and the lack of credit even when they are key to major scientific discovery – as with Rosalind Franklin and the discovery of the human genome. When there is little work, no record, no critical study and little publicity, the work of women directors goes unrecorded and this adds to the sense they cannot compete equally. This discrimination transcends class, age and race in the very different societies of the world. One example is the refusal to release Brazilian director Teresa Trautman's 1973 film *The Men I Had*, with its bold unfettered view of women's sexuality, which was banned for over a decade while more violent and sexual films directed by men escaped the censor and reached large audiences. That sexism in film directing continues today, that it is institutionalised in Hollywood, the most advanced world of film production, shows how far there is still to go.

Class Act
All across the globe, young women are signing up for training at

film schools and institutes. Like their male counterparts they have big dreams. These bold young women want to make all kinds of films from hard-hitting documentaries to cutting edge animated shorts to action blockbusters. Despite almost a century of male domination over both the content and production of films, women filmmakers still hope for and expect equal opportunities in the 21st century.

New Zealand director Jane Campion has come up against the system many times, as she explains in an interview with Anita Singh:

> 'The studio system is kind of an old boys' system and it's difficult for them to trust women to be capable.' (Anita Singh, 2009. 'Jane Campion: Female directors need to be tough to make it in "sexist" Hollywood,' in *The Telegraph*.)

British director Lynne Ramsay also says that little has changed:

> 'Well, the film industry is completely sexist and completely class-biased. It's not something I get on the ground level, it's more from financiers and producers and distributors. It's a way of dealing with you that is essentially patronising: I know better than you.' (Sean O'Hagan, 2011. 'Lynne Ramsay: Just talk to me straight' in *The Guardian*.)

But despite the male-dominated systems operating in many film industries, the importance of education and training in filmmaking is confirmed over and over again. Many successful women directors around the world have benefited from training at film schools or universities either at home or abroad. It enabled them to master the technical aspects of filmmaking and to analyse the work of other filmmakers – to understand the language of film and to have the confidence to use it. With women professors and women directors as their role models, women directors in film training programs can more successfully thrive.

Location, Location, Location!

What this book clearly demonstrates is that the chance of a

successful career for any woman filmmaker depends among other factors, on her race, her age, where she lives in the world, what class she was born into and whether her government has a policy of supporting emerging filmmakers in training and subsidies.

British director Andrea Arnold commented on the diversity of films by women made in France, which has a long-running film subsidy programme:

> 'I went to Créteil International Women's Film Festival in France with Wasp in 2004, stayed on for a few days and watched all these films by women. I spent the whole time crying because there were so many films that had so much resonance for me, being female. It actually made me realise how male-dominated the film industry is in terms of perspective. If you think about a film being a very popular and expressive way of showing a mirror on life, we're getting a mainly male perspective. It's a shame. I saw a lot of fantastic films at Créteil that I never heard about again.' (Amy Raphael, 2009. 'Real life in the Fish Tank,' *The Guardian*.)

The Swedish government believes that equality at all levels strengthens its society and culture. It is leading the way with policies to encourage gender equality in the film industry and wants to see 50% of all films created by women. Apart from its extensive film funding programme, Sweden is also developing strategies such as mentoring for women directors to help them with the challenges of making a second or third film and generally making women directors more visible in society to act as role models for girls. In the five years between 2006 to 2011, 29% of films which gained funding from the government in Sweden were directed by women. However, the need for such mandated policy that forces change is clear when we hear that investors in Sweden, even with this mandate, in some instances continue to resist funding women because they are considered too risky.

Increasingly as we see from recent legal action taken by women members of the Directors Guild of America to force gender parity, women directors will not wait for permission. Like it or not, whether they are allowed or not, they are telling their stories from Burkina Faso, Iceland, Kazakhstan, the Marshall Islands and in every corner of the world. In today's visual world, a wired and connected world where production can be handled from the phone in your hand so a film doesn't have to be an expensive historical or fantasy blockbuster to get made, access to the audience can now skip the permission of gatekeepers (almost always male) and go straight to the audience that wants to see it. Crowd funding allows the means to find the audience for the story before beginning to make it. Therefore films made by women are coming to a festivals, a theatre multiplex in China, a laptop, a sheet hung from a tree in a refugee camp, a wall on an ancient city in Italy, a broken TV in Siberia. Their stories will be told.

The default setting of humankind is humans, not only men. Theirs is a view that counts but in truth only half a view, they are half of humanity just as women are. Breaking down the denial, publicising the successes, defeating the preconceptions that women cannot direct, all will help change the landscape for women film directors. Of course, not all films directed by women will or can succeed. It's a brutally competitive and artistically difficult challenge to direct a film that excels artistically and commercially. Women want the chance to fail just as men have that chance, to learn from mistakes, to experience what doesn't work and make it work the next time.

Hidden Talents

Consider what we would never have known without the films made by women; these are stories that need to be told in order to broaden our vision of the world and enlarge our experience of the human condition. Who can forget the suffocated passion of Campion's mute protagonist Ada McGrath in *The Piano*, how persistence triumphed in getting back a beloved green bicycle for the girl in Al Hafah's Saudi feature, the first ever black British feature, edgy, *Welcome II the Terrordrome* directed by Ngozi Dnwurah, *Mamma Mia's* dancing queen anthem, keystone of all wedding dances, the secret torment of Kimberly Pierce's transgender heartbreaking heroine in *Boys Don't Cry* and Lois Weber's 1923 *Christopher Strong*, an action film for girls... and there is an overwhelming number of films we have had to leave out here. The stories of lucky breaks and bravery are there in the films of director Matilde Landera of Mexico who proclaimed, 'I used the only weapon at my disposal, my absolute knowledge of the technique,' in a 1948 interview of her journey as a director in a difficult and hostile environment.

In the 21st century we have learned that for a society to thrive, women must thrive. The education of women is the single biggest reason for growing prosperity, peace and justice. In a global marketplace no country can afford to deny the talent and capabilities of half its work force. Not only is discrimination unjust, it's a waste of a country's human resources. As politicians who fail to win the votes of women discover to their cost, gender inequality is politically unacceptable.

The level of gender inequality in a society is often reproduced not only within the stories filmed for its cinema screens but also in the hierarchical ways its film industry operates. As British director Sally Potter said to Melissa Silverstein in 2012:

> 'You can't really divorce women's struggles in the world from women's in the cinema. As long as there's hierarchy it means that women are somehow secondary or second-class or less than. That's going to be reflected in movies because films are the most powerful medium to reflect back society's view of itself.' ('TIFF: Interview with Sally Potter Women and Hollywood')

The diverse contributions to this book from filmmakers, journalists, academics and fans help us understand the complex factors that have helped or hindered women filmmakers internationally. While some contributors chose to explore the incredible history of female filmmaking in different societies and geographies, discovering the amazing pioneers who broke through the industry barriers and lit up cinema screens with stories of love, family, suffering and war, others chose to focus on female themes within particular films or the ways in which women filmmakers have played with genre ironically, subverting expectations of the 'woman's view'.

These essays demonstrate that women's talent for making films and the urge to tell stories from a female perspective is common to most cultures worldwide and has endured, despite many obstacles, since the beginning of filmmaking.

Indian-born director Deepa Metha emphasises the incredible amount of female directing talent in India, which gets little attention globally:

> 'I think that the perception [that there is a relatively small group of women from India who are taking most of the chances in filmmaking] is a western one, because perhaps these are the few filmmakers that come outside. But within India, and the subcontinent there, there are really some incredibly courageous film makers who make fabulous films.' (See Rubin Safaya, 2006. 'Interview with Deepa Mehta'. *Cinemalogue*)

Continual Discovery

> 'I am female; I have a female sensibility; I make female films; and when I die, God will explain to me what the difference was.' Ngozi Onwurah, UK/Nigeria

Successful Hollywood producer Lindsay Doran (*This is Spinal Tap, Sense and Sensibility, The Firm*), has studied the nature of movie accomplishment and relationships and made a surprising discovery. She already knew that relationship movies were gender-specific. In movies aimed at men and boys, she said, 'there is the goal, the thing the hero is trying to accomplish.' There is always the relationship, '… usually with a woman, child, friend or father. Usually at the end, the hero realises the relationship is more important than the accomplishment.' However, in most movies geared toward women, she discovered in her TEDx study 'Saving the World vs. Kissing the Girl,' the relationship *is* the accomplishment.

> 'Some would say that this is patronising to women,' she said, but for her it was empowering: 'Maybe it just means that women have figured it out.'

CELLULOID CEILING

The process of editing this book has uncovered some other surprising facts:

- The percentage of women film directors in Iran is higher than the percentage of women directors making feature films in the USA.

- When given the same budget, feature films by women do as well at the box office as those by men. This is the deciding factor in predicting box office success.

- The percentage of women film directors is higher in countries (like India) where the upper classes are involved in film production.

- The percentage of women film directors decreases as the level of investment in a film increases.

- Although digital technology has opened up access to filmmaking and also provided new distribution channels, the volume of pornography filmed from a male perspective widens the gap between the amount of male and female content made available annually.

This book documents just some of the incredible talent, which exists, and the important legacy of women's filmmaking internationally. We hope that the collection of essays in this book provides both inspiration and valuable information for students and lovers of film everywhere. Look out for films made by women; they are coming to festivals, to a sheet hung from a tree in a refugee camp, a wall on an ancient city in Italy, and a broken TV in Siberia. They will not be sidelined, their stories will be told. Look out for them, they are speaking out and breaking through.

We encourage readers to write in and post updates on emerging women filmmakers. We've set up a page where you can tell us more. See https://www.facebook.com/CelluloidCeiling

1. African Women Directors:

Edited version of a speech given at the colloquy 'Francophone African Women Filmmakers: 40 years of cinema, Paris (1972-2012)'

Beti Ellerson

We read and hear incessant lamentations regarding the absence of women and the dearth of realistic and positive representation, lack of funding, of support, and all the other misfortunes that exist for women directors the world over. I would like to take into account the potentials and assets rather than the disadvantages.

Emerging during the independence movements in Africa in the 1950s and 60s, African cinema reappropriated the camera as a tool to fight against the colonial gaze which had dominated visual representations of Africa. The emergence of women in cinema coincided with this nascent period in the course of which a group of women professionals positioned themselves in the creation of a veritable African film culture. Notably, the pioneer of Senegalese media culture, Annette Mbaye d'Erneville, who was the first Senegalese to receive a diploma in journalism. Upon her return after studying in Paris, she immersed herself in her work, eventually broadcasting a seminal radio programme on cinema. More than a generation later, Congolese Monique Mbeka Phoba continued this practice, leading her to filmmaking. Inversely, Chadian Zara Mahamat Yacoub, also a filmmaker, is at present the president of the Chadian association of independent radio stations and directs radio programming in Chad.

Annette Mbaye d'Erneville has dedicated her life to cultural policy issues in the country and has forged important institutions such as the Senegalese Film Critics Association, RECIDAK, a Dakar-based film forum, and the Henriette Bathily Women's Centre. And as portrayed in *Mère-bi,* a film about her life by her son Ousmane William Mbaye, she continues still today.

In the same spirit, Guadeloupan Sarah Maldoror, a diasporan already with a pan-African perspective, united in Paris with other artists from Africa and the Caribbean during the course of an intense period of cultural, intellectual and political discovery. Sarah Maldoror's contribution to lusophone African cinema was of seminal importance. In the 1960s she studied cinema in Moscow, and already active in the pro-independence movements, it is inevitable that she would follow the same anti-colonialist path in the themes of her films. Maldoror has always worked at the intersection of African and women's liberation and is mentor and reference to numerous women filmmakers, notably Togolese filmmaker Anne-Laure Folly whose film *Sarah Maldoror ou la nostalgie de l'utopie* traces the politically-engaged filmmaker's life.

Similarly, the experiences of Annette Mbaye d'Erneville and Sarah Maldoror reflect that of other students and artists living in Paris during a period of heightened consciousness, such as the trinity of négritude, Senghor, Césaire and Damas, of Africa and the diaspora, who came together to address important political issues using culture as a weapon.

After independence the call evolved into a cry of the heart, and the role of culture would be an important tool to highlight Africa's contribution on a global scale. In 1966, six years after its independence, Senegal stepped on the world stage as its poet-president, Leopold Sedar Senghor hosted the first World Festival of Black Arts. The young teacher Safi Faye was the official guide during the festivities, an experience that undoubtedly opened her eyes to the significance of culture and African art in the world.

Moreover, the work of Thérèse Sita-Bella and Efua Sutherland (both deceased) bears witness to the first cinematographic contributions of women. In 1963, Cameroonian Sita-Bella produced *Tam Tam à Paris*, a thirty-minute filmed reportage of the tour of the National Dance Company of Cameroon, presented at the first FESPACO in 1969. Dramaturge and writer, Ghanaian Efua Sutherland produced the documentary *Arabia: A Village Story* in collaboration with the American broadcasting company, ABC. While they only made one film each, their trajectory reflects that of many African women who marry filmmaking with their other professions and social, political and cultural interests. For instance, Anne-Laure Folly who is also an international lawyer, and writer Tsitsi Dangarembga.

In the Maghreb and its diaspora in France, women took initial steps which would come to fruition in the 1970s. In 1968 Tunisian Moufida Tlatli went to France to study cinema, though at the time women were directed towards careers as editors. Nonetheless she immersed herself in cinema studies developing the requisite skills of filmmaker, which led to the production of her first film, *Le silence du palais* in 1994. Arriving in France as a young adult in 1960, Moroccan Izza Genini immediate plunged into its cultural life, and in 1973 she created her production and distribution company. Similarly, the renowned writer Assia Djebar since the 1960s, elected to the Academie Française in 2005, took a sabbatical from the world of literature to enter into the landscape of image-sound with her first film *La Nouba des Femmes du Mont Chenoua* in 1978.

At the beginning of the professionalisation of cinema in Africa, with the emergence of emblematic institutions such as FESPACO and FESPACI in the 1960s, women were at the forefront. While other institutions have developed since, these two structures remain a reference for continental cooperation and organisation in the cultural domain. Pioneer actress Zalika Souley of Niger, sat on the founding committee of FEPACI (Pan African Federation of Filmmakers), while Burkinabé Alimata Salembéré, a founding member of FESPACO (Pan African Film Festival of Ouagadougou), presided over the organising committee of the first festival which her compatriot Odette Sangho was also a member.

Spurred by the United Nations Decade for Women (1975-1985), the 1970s launched a call to action in all areas of women's lives, according unprecedented global attention to women. Evolving into a universal movement for the promotion of women's rights and of feminist activism, it also played a significant role in raising consciousness throughout the continent. Following into the 1980s many women reiterated the UN Decade themes in their films, focusing on the empowerment of women and highlighting a woman's vision of economic, social and cultural development.

Following the growth of the second wave of feminism, its influence was apparent in several developments during the 1970s: women's studies in the academy, feminist film theory, and the critical analysis of the visual representation of women. From this seminal decade, a presence of African women in cinema slowly emerged. As one of the rare African women enrolled at the École Nationale Supérieure Louis-Lumière in the 1970s in Paris, pioneer Safi Faye recalls the curiosity around her enrolment at this prestigious film school.

The 1980s also witnessed a marked growth in film production by women. Many of the first generation of Burkinabé women in the 1980s, notably Fanta Régina Nacro, Valérie Kaboré and Aminata Ouedraogo, to name a few of international renown, entered the doors of INAFEC, the historic film school, based in Ouagadougou, Burkina Faso which operated from 1976 to 1987.

Moreover, in East Africa, the first wave of Kenyan women of cinema began to study in the Film Training Department at the Kenya Institute of Mass Communication in the 1980s. As Kenyan scholar Wanjiku Béatrice Mukora observes, they have played a determinant role is the formation of a national cinema in Kenya.

This tendency spread to other regions, notably in Southern Africa. In Zimbabwe in the 1990s a cadre of women professionals of cinema was formed around the organisation, Women Filmmakers of Zimbabwe (WFOZ). In 2001, WFOZ launched a women's film festival, and in 2009, established the Distinguished Woman in African Cinema award.

In the same way, the 1990s witnessed the strengthening of networks and a visible presence on a continental and international scale. Having already established the groundwork at the *colloque Images de Femmes* (Images of Women colloquy) at *Vues d'Afrique in*

Montréal, Quebec in 1989, an organised movement emerged. The 12th edition of FESPACO in 1991 marked a historic moment for African women in the visual media, forging an infrastructure for the association which is presently known as the Pan African Union of Women Professionals of the Image. The continental meeting, presided by Annette Mbaye d'Erneville outlined the following key objectives, which are often reiterated in other women's organisations:

- to provide a forum for women to exchange and share their experiences

- to ensure that women have equal access to training and production

- to be aware of the concerns of women professionals

- to ensure a more realistic visual representation of women

- to establish the means for transmitting their point of view.

Since this emblematic moment, projects initiated by women throughout the continent extending to the diaspora, gained momentum in their efforts to promote African cinema and develop infrastructures.

While all of the initiatives have not been able to come to fruition, their encouraging presence indicates the desire to create sustainable and accessible structures in support of African cinema and the empowerment of women practitioners in cinema in particular.

Paradoxically, during the years after the women's decade, the second wave of feminism began to wane, with declarations in post-feminist discourses that it had reached its objective of eradicating sexism.

When in fact, rather than paradoxical, this decline is quite possibly the consequence of these multicultural encounters, even confrontations, during the decade, at which time an oppositional discourse emerged among women of colour around the world in response to the hegemonic feminism of and the domination of discourse, research and knowledge production by white women.

Moreover, already taking shape in the 1980s, in response to a feminism considered elitist, ethnocentric, or to some, even racist, a third wave emerged. By the 1990s, in rupture with the strategies of struggle and the essentialist aspects of the second wave, a new generation positioned itself to confront the problems of the present world, very different from those of the 1970s and 1980s.

This generational rupture and continuity brings to mind the 2008 Cannes Festival roundtable at the Pavilion of Cinemas of the South entitled: *l'Engagement des femmes cinéastes* (The commitment of women cineastes).

Personal stories and post-colonial histories were part of a very engaging conversation among women of the South in general and women of Africa in particular, highlighting a genuine willingness to meet each other face to face on complex issues. Despite the generational differences among the cineastes, present experiences are in many ways similar to those of the first generations.

African cinema, itself a post-colonial phenomenon, emerged in tandem with African independences and has always existed within a transnational context. Using post-coloniality as the point of departure, its films dealt with tensions between African tradition and westernisation, reframing the colonial version of African history and the politics of identification.

A generation later, African women filmmakers continue to work through their multiple identities in their films. Some are bi-racial from parents of two different races, and this double identity is problematised in their work. Others have a double nationality or live as permanent residents and confront issues of integration or the complexities of identity having been born of the first generation in the diasporic communities of the West.

Drawing from the notion of double consciousness explored by the American intellectual W.E.B. Dubois where the Afro-American lives with a sense of two-ness – as an American, as a black person, Ghanaian-American filmmaker Akosua Adoma Owusu describes the triple consciousness of the African immigrant to the United States: (1) she must assimilate into the American cultural mainstream (2) she is identified with African Americans by the colour of her skin but may not always identify with their culture or history, and (3) she has to deal with the

African world and her own line of descent.

African filmmakers have for a long time insisted on being filmmakers period, and in the case of women, to not have to also carry the label of woman. Safi Faye for example always stood by this idea, even when producing Africa-themed films. As the notion of transnational cinema gathers momentum, the non-identifiability of the filmmaker's nationality is increasingly garnering notice.

Furthermore, for some filmmakers residing in the West, Africa is not always the subject of their films nor are Africans automatically represented in the main characters. Are these films as well as their aesthetic excluded from the African cinema discourse and reinserted when the subject focuses on Africa? Besides, the practice of a cinema without borders by a growing number of filmmakers re-poses the question regarding the categorisation of a film according to the filmmaker's nationality.

Moreover, certain South African film practitioners of European, Indian and Malaysian descent are affirming their African identity and reclaiming their experiences as part of the continent's history, showing their desire to be included in the dialogue, even when the themes of their films focus on people with non-African ethnicities.

Africa is a vast continent with diverse languages, as well as social and political histories, geographical and demographic specificities, and cultural and religious practices. And thus, its borders, extending to a global diaspora, engenders a plurality of cinematic practices.

Furthermore, this transnationality, with its travelling identities and exilic homelands is increasingly present and thus demands a redefinition of the concept 'African women in cinema', as well as the renegotiation of its positionality, social location and subjectivity, not only in terms of filmmaking but also in relationship to its audience.

In the same way, these transmutations underscore the fact that these cinemas and cinematic practices are not a monolith and thus the discourses on Africa women in cinema are based on the plurality of cinematic histories embracing the intersectionality of trans/national and racial identification and ethnic and cultural specificities.

Since my objective was to use a non deficit approach by drawing from positive, optimistic and encouraging experiences, I want to end in the same spirit. As Sarah Maldoror has declared in an interview by Jadot Sezirahiga (see *Ecrans d'Afrique*/African Screens, No. 12. 1995):

> 'The African woman must be everywhere: on the screen, behind the camera, in the editing room, in every stage of the making of a film. She must be the one to talk about her problems.'
>
> Africa women pioneers and leaders in African cinema form an impressive list. Their presence on the timeline of African cinema is witness to the heritage they leave as role models, mentors and activists, opening the path to other women who follow them.'

Author biography

Beti Ellerson is founder and director of the Centre for the Study and Research of African Women in Cinema, which features the African Women in Cinema Blog. She was the executive producer and host of *Reels of Colour*, and director of *Sisters of the Screen: African Women in the Cinema* (2002). Her publications include the book, *Sisters of the Screen: Women of Africa on Film, Video and Television* (Africa World Press, 2000) and articles in *Journal of African Cinemas and Feminist Africa,* among others. In addition to serving as president of the Diaspora Jury at the 2013 FESPACO, she was keynote speaker at the 2012 Paris Symposium on forty years of African women francophone filmmakers. Dr Ellerson teaches courses in visual culture, African cinema, women's studies and Africana studies, most recently at Denison University (USA) for the 2013-14 academic year.

Contact: africanwomenincinema@africanwomenincinema.org

2. *Speak Up! Who's Speaking?*:

African Filmmakers Speak for Themselves

Maria Williams-Hawkins

African female filmmakers have been telling stories on film for nearly fifty years. Some of those stories have reflected a storytelling approach they learned through their mentors, usually mentors who were not African. Others told stories they thought the world would accept from them. Following a Eurocentric acceptable model, early African filmmakers chose a documentary style of story (*allAfrica*, February 17th 2012). Today, African women are telling their own stories, which focus on their lived experiences as well as their dreams and creative designs for the future. While some women filmmakers have invested their talent talking about their villages and communities, others have gone into the challenges of being African women in patriarchal, sometimes abusive situations. Finally, some have juxtaposed the challenges of traditional concerns with modern opportunities – which are just new concerns. This chapter provides a revelation of where and how new filmmakers are preparing for the art and the venues for their new productions. From small, dusty villages to sprawling big cities, these women tell African women's, all women's, stories. They do not focus on their experiences exclusively but write scripts with other women from other countries whose experiences bind them emotionally. Their stories come from Northern Africa down to the tip of Cape Town. These stories tell of the trials that women face across the diaspora, rich or poor, pearlescent or onyx, in trials or triumphs, African. African women filmmakers are telling their stories their way.

The purpose of this chapter is to identify the storytellers first. Anyone who believes that African women have been silenced is simply wrong. Second, we examine the themes of their stories by providing an historical perspective on their work. Knowing that women are speaking, I ask whether the voices of women filmmakers are getting stronger? Or are they succumbing to the challenges of the marketplace, just trying to produce films that will make enough money for them to continue making films?

Some filmmakers presented were born and lived most of their lives on the continent. Others, as Isabel Wilkerson would say, have been warmed by other suns. The chapter is structured to give honour to whom honour is due. Therefore, we pay tribute to Senegalese born Safi Faye and all that she endured. Recognising that while one is gaining recognition, others are also in line for their day in the sun, we also pay tribute to French filmmaker born of Angolan descent, Sarah Maldoror, a woman whose works highlight a different aspect of African women's experiences. We learn of women whose careers are established as African women filmmakers such as Ethiopian-born Salem Mekuria, Anne Mungai of Kenya, Fanta Régina Nacro of Burkina Faso, Anne-Laure Folly of Togo, Nigerian-born, British-reared Ngozi Onwurah, Tsitsi Dangarembga from Zimbabwe and Marguerite Abouet from Cote d'Ivoire. The chapter also introduces the works of some and the film perspective of others. Some of these women are younger and produce films for television or other forms of distribution but they continue to speak on the issues of their day. These filmmakers include: Tanzania, British-born, South African-trained Ingrid Sinclair; Monique Phoba, Democratic Republic of Congo, South African-born; BoKaap-reared Zulfah Otto-Sallies; Bridget Pickering, Namibia; Wabei Siyolwe, Zambia; Prudence Uriri, Zimbabwe and Zanele Mthembu, South Africa. The chapter concludes with a summary of what African women have contributed to the field.

When examining *Speak up Who's Speaking!,* readers might consider the voice used in the film. Most filmmakers chose the language of financial backers and trainers for most of their early films if not all their films. Films produced in Ghana and Nigeria were produced using the English language in one form or another. Filmmakers from French speaking countries used French as the language of the production. Faye produced many of her films in French. However, using the language of those who were or once were considered the oppressor caused viewers to evaluate whether the films gave an accurate portrayal of African thought or just utilised the images of those on the continent. Western audiences, according to Malkmus and Armes (1991), saw nothing wrong with Africans speaking French or English rather than their native tongues but some segments of the African ticket buyers did (1991). Peasants complained that filmmakers alienated themselves from the audiences when they failed to consider or use the native language when producing films about real Senegalese people. In a post-colonial time frame, Africans understood the challenges of speaking their minds in the language of others. The African filmmakers who found success making feature length documentary films that used the language of the people were those in exile such as Senegal's Safi Faye.

Safi Faye, Ph. D.: La Grande Reference

Safi Faye is the pre-eminent African female filmmaker from the country that produced the father of African cinema, Ousmane Sembene. Compared to other areas of accomplishments, the time span between men reaching goals in cinema and women accomplishing the same goal, is shorter in Senegal than in most other countries. Ousmane Sembene produced his film in 1963. Faye produced her first film in 1972. Although she is a film director and ethnologist, she is also a documentarian, the creator of several fiction-based feature films, an actor and professor. Most importantly, Faye is the first Sub-Saharan African woman to direct a commercially distributed feature film (Ellerson, 2004; Malkmus & Armes, 1991). Malkmus and Armes (1991) included a dictionary of Arab and African filmmakers and Faye is listed and discussed. Only one other woman is even listed. Faye's work has encouraged African and other women to pursue filmmaking.

Faye was born in Dakar, Senegal in 1943 to a Serer family. The Serers are an ethno-religious group that is the third largest ethnic group in Senegal and the producer of the country's first two political leaders. For the period in which Faye was born, however, neither politics nor filmmaking seemed the most appropriate profession for a young African girl to consider. Having attended The École Normale in Rustique, Faye earned her teaching certificate and began teaching French in a primary school in Dakar in 1963 (Ellerson, 2004). Recognising her own creative talents, Faye wanted more from her life than classroom teaching. So, in 1966 she decided to attend the Dakar Festival of Negro Arts where she met Jean Rouch, a French ethnologist and filmmaker as well as other intellectuals and researchers. It was this festival that awakened Faye to broader thinking and an understanding of the need to preserve African history and culture (Cissé and Fall, 1996). According to Ellerson (2004), Rouch encouraged Faye to use filmmaking as an ethnographic tool. After returning to Senegal Faye later accepted an invitation to return to France to act in Rouch's 1971 film *Petit à Petit* (1971). Nonplussed by the experience, Faye returned to teaching after the completion of the film.

In the 1970s, she studied ethnology at the Ecole Pratique des Hautes Études and Lumiere Film School. Faye continued her sound effects, modelling and acting career to support her efforts to earn her PhD. In 1979, the University of Paris awarded her PhD in Ethnology. Following the completion of her doctorate she studied video production in Berlin and worked as a guest lecturer at the Free University of Berlin. Never losing her focus on ethnology, in 1988, Faye received an additional degree in ethnology from the Sorbonne.

Although Faye accomplished many academic goals, she has occasionally reviewed and evaluated her performances as an actor and director. According to Haffner (1982) when Faye had developed her own filmmaking skills she realised that she disliked Rouch's *Petit à petit* (1971) film. She described the film as naïve and unstructured. She noted that it had no plot and seemingly no purpose or ending. Some sources (Ellerson, 2004) say that Faye acknowledged that working with Rouch enabled her to learn about filmmaking and cinema verité. Other sources suggest that she is not sure whether he taught her or if she had an intuition about 'how things should go'. Because she had a limited sense of Africa and did not know what to study, ethnology seemed to be the most appropriate path to take. At the Sorbonne, students were encouraged to record interviews with a video camera. Faye believes this led her to develop video storytelling skills. The camera helped her record what she saw in helpful ways. First, in explaining the value of using a video camera for her ethnographies, she said.

> '…there are many abstract things in the course of events that could not be explained, such as African ceremonies. One observes them but cannot actually explain them. I thought perhaps that in analysing these elements, I might find the foundation of these things. I decided that the best solution was to do film.' (Cissé and Fall, 1996)

Second, Faye realised that she was researching and reaching an uneducated audience base. They could not read words or phrases but they could read pictures and moving images (Amarger, 1998). A video camera better collected what she was seeing and allowed her to share those images with those she researched.

Themes in Faye's works

When considering what was important to Faye in her film production, one might consider the impact or conflict between her French and African or, more specifically, Senegalese cultures. Add to that the fact that she was a woman caught in the vortex of this conflict and one can better understand the evolution of her films.

Faye is said to have disliked her performance as an African woman living in France in *Petit à Petit* because her performance reflected negatively on the ways African women in Paris are presented. Other African women in a cine' club in Kinshasa, Zaire agreed that her role was superficial (Haffner, 1982). Finally, Rouch had to acknowledge that the film lacked structure. According Serceau (1982), the film is considered one of Rouch's least successful ones. It should not be a surprise that Faye's first student film *La Passante/The Woman Passerby* (1972) focused on beauty and fantasy. According to Traore (1979), this film was created for her own enjoyment but led to the inclusion of these themes in her future films.

If Faye believed that her role in *Petit à Petit* was unstructured, she gave the female character in *La Passante* (1972) the freedom to be unstructured. She facilitated that performance by acting as the main character and placing that character in Paris. Based on a poem from Charles Baudelaire, *A Une Passante*, Faye allows the woman to move through the film freely. In an interview, Faye described her film this way:

> '...a beautiful African woman arrives in Paris. Dreamlike, she notices that everyone watches her, admires her. Among her admirers she chooses a White man and allows him to dream, then a Black man who dreams as well. They watch her walk down the street. In fact, they are dreaming. That is not at all my reality; Baudelaire inspired me.' (Cissé and Fall, 1996)

While Faye's first student film does establish the collision of cultures it also suggests that she does not seek to be a Westernised or liberated woman (Remy, 1996). She leaves herself situated in the vortex. She also addresses racial diversity in that she is 'observed' or made an object of fantasy by both a White (European) man and a Black (African) man. The white man is privileged to 'dream' or fantasise about her first as they dine in a restaurant and the black man fantasises or dreams about her as they share a meal that she prepares at her home. The two situations are culturally appropriate and both focus on the intimacy of sharing a meal (Bouzet, 1991). Because food is closely associated with culture Faye returns to the theme in her documentary, *Ambassades Nourricières* (*Culinary Embassies*, 1984).

Faye returns to what she knows best in her first professional films. While others struggle with what they will tell and whose voice they will use, Faye goes to her home village in the directing of *Letter From My Village/Kaddu Bey Kar* (1995) and *Fad Jal* (1979). These works are special in that they use the French language to share the thoughts of the characters who represent her actual family members and friends, yet when those characters speak, they do so in their own language. Guback and Varis (1982) share Faye's thoughts about giving her characters voice:

> 'I give people a voice, they are enabled to speak about their own problems, to show their reality and I take a position within that. I situate myself on one side or another, my voice criticises what is open to criticism or I provide some small explanation, but that's all. And I'm paving the way for the possibility of future self expression because it is only they who can appropriately speak about their problems.'

Faye gives us a deeper insight into life of African women with each film. She takes us to her parents' home in Fad'jal. In *Goob na nu*, even the title tells us that the harvest is in. *Harrow* (2007) suggests that Faye presents a representation of the 'absent father insane mother' archetype in spiritual form in *Mossane* (1996)

Faye brings the sensibilities of women into her films and a view of women's sensuality. Her portrayals of female protagonists provide a much broader or deeper analysis of African women's lived experiences. Her background in anthropology and filmmaking are apparent in the stories she tells. Her training in capturing the rituals of various cultures has paid off as she includes the celebrations of various ethnic groups. Her early focus on documentary style has allowed her to examine the political, social and economic aspects of the villages she includes in her character development or story background. She includes the experiences of women from her village as a basis for many of her characters.

Faye's Philosophies

While a treatise on Faye could fill a book, this chapter will close her section with some of her beliefs on feminism and African women, on being a woman, a mother and her detractors. We will close just with her thoughts on being a filmmaker.

According to Cissé and Fall (1996), Faye never considered herself a feminist but rather a woman affirming the rights and opportunities of women. Like American Womenist scholars,

CELLULOID CEILING

Faye sees the concerns of Western feminists as unrelated to the specificities of African women and their realities. Saying that 'phallocracy is universal', Faye notes that there are women in Africa who want to change their situations (Faye, 1984). Faye noted that there are many misconceptions about African women:

> 'It is always difficult for Europeans to see Africa, and its women, without taking sides and without bringing European notions of civilisation. Today we do a lot toward the emancipation of women. It is a subject of many of the films on our continent, but women are not as dependent, submissive or deprived of rights as one thinks. If I consider the situation where I live, in the country, in the Serer region and the responsibilities that the women take on, for their families and the household, I see women as active partners – courageous and liberated – in relation to their husbands. In the city, on the other hand, women's dependence, financially speaking, appears to me to be much greater.' (Eichenberger, 1976).

Faye believes that Western feminist filmmaking has privileged the lives of women (Ellerson, 2004) and she emphasises some serious differences in African women's lives. She also talks about the differences in how African women in rural areas are reared compared to more urban African women and sees the need to present women in the context of their societies and experiences. Noting the importance of presenting women reared in matriarchal cultures accurately, Faye points out that these women are taught to be self-sufficient and independent (Faye, 1984). The contrast in women's experiences is presented through her characters in *Mossane* (1996) where the main character is a young woman who refuses to follow her parents' wishes and marry the rich Diogaye and lives between 'rebellion and effacement', and *Selbé et tant d'autres* (*Selbé and So Many Others*, 1981) where Selbé is left to her own devices when the men of the village leave to find work and she has to rear her children alone. She struggles to figure out what to do even though she actually has a husband.

Faye talks about being a woman in this field. Although she has found success and established herself, she recognises that trying to meet the needs of a man and her own goals can be problematic when she has her own income.

> 'I think it is very difficult when you are an intellectual, to find a man who accepts these things. They become jealous, the relationship is destroyed. But sometimes I say to myself – if you are born free, buying your own clothes, bringing your own money to get your own food, then if you are not with a man, you have more time to think about your own work. And that is very important. What a woman like me needs is only affection, nothing else. If it is possible, okay, if it is not possible, I prefer to get affection from my child rather than staying without work because a man wants to destroy me. I am not afraid of anything.' (Vasudev, 1985)

Faye's films do reflect her love of being a mother. While viewers can see portions of Faye's personalities in the lead characters, her films also reflect her relationship with her daughter. Faye says that the film *Mossane* was created for her daughter. The film allowed her to teach a certain reality about African life. *Trois ans, cinq mois* (*Three Years, Five Months*, 1983) portrays her daughter as an infant. *Mossane* allowed Faye to present some of the characteristics her daughter had developed.

Her detractors

According to Ellerson (2004), Faye does not prefer to discuss her films after they are released. She believes that the films belong to the viewers after they have been released. Additionally, she does not have a strong desire to defend her work to critics. Some critics question her creativity. Because she began as a documentary filmmaker, some challenge her contention that *Mossane* is actually a work of fiction. Her story includes rituals and cultural components that seem to be more reality than creativity. Bartlett (1997) confirms that the rituals and ceremonies used in *Mossane* are all Faye's inventions. During the 1997 FESPACO, a panel of newspaper reporters and critical members of the public asked Faye to defend some of her creative devices in *Mossane*. Based on the conference transcript, attendees found it difficult to believe that *Mossane* was a reflection of Faye's creativity rather than her academic training.

Questions about Faye's creativity fit the challenges of many African filmmakers. European research on Africa and Africans has often been told through documentaries or reality based productions (Ellerson, 2004). Because of this, when African filmmakers produce creative projects, for some, it becomes impossible to believe that these stories are not reflections of what they have actually seen or lived. Faye keeps this argument alive because she refuses to delineate between reality and fantasy. As a filmmaker she sees life as a story. She presents life's story instead of trying to create a story (Playback, 1981).

As a filmmaker

Although Faye is quite aware of her recognition as a female African filmmaker, she talks about the experience as an African not as a woman. According to Cisse' and Fall (1996), Faye sees no difference between being 'Safi as a man or Safi as a woman'. To her, the two are one. Faye believes that African men and women experience the same challenges in filmmaking. Her greater concern is that attracting women to filmmaking is challenging.

> 'I think it is important that there are women filmmakers, and it is a pity that film work is so hard and that many African women don't get involved in it. Women should have an important role to play in African cinema, given their sensitivity and their truthfulness. There is also reluctance to tackle such a hard and unstable job that doesn't offer much financial security.' (Ouaga, 1989)

Conclusion

Safi Faye is a mother, teacher, director and a woman. Her tenacity and determination helped her give birth to a film directing style that teaches others about Africa, Africans, independent women and new ways of doing things. Her directing has allowed her to teach her daughter about aspects of African life that are less apparent than they once were. Safi Faye has taught and continues to teach women how to be who they are, no matter the cost, without regrets. She has given African women filmmakers a voice. Her work still speaks.

Sarah Maldoror

Safi Faye and Sarah Maldoror are considered the mothers of African cinema. The two break away from classical narrative structures in their stories (Marker, 2001). The examination of Faye first seems appropriate but the transition to Maldoror might be a bit problematic for some. First, Maldoror is French, not African. Her mother was French and her father was from Guadeloupe, a key French island. Maldoror became African when she married Mario Andrade, the leader of the Angolan Liberation Movement and invested her life in his Angolan culture. Andrade and Maldoror complemented each other in their behaviours and works. Maldoror's political protests did not begin when she married her husband. She was considered a political activist because of the creation of a troupe in French theatre known as *Les Griots* (Marker, 2001). While Faye was developing her craft, Maldoror was also producing her first films. The first two films dealt with political protest. Andrade overturned Portuguese rule in Angola and Maldoror created films about the event.

Maldoror's first film was a short produced in 1969 entitled *Monangambee*. The Portuguese use the word 'monanagambee' pejoratively to describe Angolan rebels. Maldoror then developed the short into a radically political feature film entitled *Sambizanga* (1972). *Sambizanga* was filmed in what was then called Congo using Congolese militants. This film received special recognition at the 1972 Carthage Festival and several other awards (Marker, 2001).

Maldoror chose a fictional approach rather than documentary style for the feature film in order to explore the participation of women in the Angolan conflict. Her story focused on a woman searching for her imprisoned husband only to learn that he had been murdered. She chose this approach in order to reveal the spirit of the rebels and the casualties of the conflict. Of course, Maldoror's aesthetic approach caused critics to accuse her of selling out to Westernised images. Critics accused her of taking a stylised, sophisticated approach. In an interview with *Le Monde* she explained that she chose to privilege the heroine's perspective rather than the portrayal of violence in the struggle. Unlike many commercially distributed films, Maldoror gave *Sambizanga* a feminine perspective in order to see the struggle many experienced outside the fighting. She showed the internal struggle and gave viewers close-ups of human suffering

While Faye was able to get her films commercially distributed, opportunities for African filmmakers and especially African women caused Sarah Maldoror to announce to Marker in a 2001 personal interview that there was no African cinema after Faye's seeming retirement. Maldoror made people aware of the challenges that African filmmakers all faced. In the post-war era, Westernised images of Africa began to flood the continent. Westernised countries provided the training for Africa's top filmmakers. Faye was trained in France and Maldoror herself was trained at the Moscow Film Institute. The countries that provided the training, however, also controlled the finances and images that African filmmakers were able to distribute. While the Western filmmaking in Africa was focused on fact-based, documentary style, showing African traditions and unknown African locations, African women filmmakers were attempting to empower women by examining women's lived experiences at all levels. To be sure of this fact, one might note that although Faye finished *Mossane* in 1992, the French government did not allow it to be distributed until 1996. Faye had to fight to get the film out of the French production company's hands. African filmmakers did not have the resources to market their creative endeavors without a fight.

Maldoror's directing techniques reveal her perspective of the female experience. Maldoror visualises the conflicting experiences of women's lives. She portrays the political, economic and emotional conflicts women face. Using finalised preproduction scripts as a starting point, Maldoror allows her intuition to determine the best way to tell her stories. Her use of montages, point of view shots and exquisite use of sound always helped her to speak subtly and powerfully to her audiences. In Maldoror's documentary on Leon Damas, she focuses on a slave woman interned at a transportation camp. Her use of voiceover tells the audience that the camp of transportation is more like a camp of desolation (Marker, 2001). We see the woman's desolation through a point of view shot from a decaying building in the centre of the camp. Her shots make the viewer feel trapped as the screen goes to black and only allows a sliver of light to enter. Maldoror also provides an aural backdrop of popping sounds that could be gunfire or worse. All these techniques help audience members feel the perspective of the woman.

Salem Mekuria

Salem Mekuria was born in Ethiopia but now makes Boston her home. She is an independent producer, writer and director who is the Luella LaMer Professor of Women's Studies in the Art Department at Wellesley College. Mekuria has worked with international film production that focused on issues of African Ethiopian women and development and worked for many years with NOVA seen on PBS.

According to *Women Make Movies* (2005) Mekuria has won numerous accolades for her films. Her filmography includes: *Our Place in the Sun* (1988) which was nominated for an Emmy and *As I Remember: A Portrait of Dorothy West* (1991). These films were broadcast on Boston Public Television, WGBH. *Forced Exile* (1991) received the Silver Apple in the National Educational Film & Video Festival, Honorable Mention, 7th Annual Atlanta Film & Video Festival, First Place in the National Black Programming Consortium's (NBPC) Prized Pieces, and Outstanding Independent Film in the New England Film & Video Festival. Her film *Ye Wonz Maibel / Deluge* (1997) won first place in NBPC's Prized Pieces at the Black Maria Film and Video Festival and screened internationally. Mekuria's most recent film includes *Square Stories,* which captures fragments of Ethiopia's past history, and *IMAGinING TOBIA,* which explores Ethiopia's cultural and physical landscapes.

Fanta Régina Nacro

Born in Burkina Faso in 1962, Nacro was trained in France, earning her first degree in audiovisual science and techniques in 1986 from INAFEC and a Master's Degree in Film and Audiovisual Studies at the Sorbonne. Nacro created her first film in 1992 with the release of *Un Certain Matin*. She has specialised in movie shorts ranging from five to forty-two minutes. She began to gain true recognition of her work in 2001 with the release of *Bintou* which won more than twenty prizes in international festivals. In 2001, *Bintou* was awarded the FESPACO best short film of 2001. FESPACO is considered the biggest regular cultural event on the continent. In 2004 she created her first full-length feature, *La Nuit de la Verité* (*Night of Truth*).

Nacro continues to humorously compare the modern with traditional national customs. Several films examine their subjects through the eyes of women. Her full length film moves away from women and humour as it explores serious military and political issues.

Nigozi Onwurah

Nigerian-born Ngozi Onwurah is the product of a Nigerian father and a white British mother. She was born in 1966 in Nigeria but when civil war became imminent, her mother, Madge Onwurah took her and her bother Simon to England where she believed they would be safe. Simon and Ngozi spent most of their growing years in England but endured a different kind of war. Both of them endured racial discrimination there.

Onwurah's lived experiences shaped the narrative of her first film, *Coffee Colored Children* (1988). Foster (1991) describes this film as autobiographical, ethnographic, experimental and performative. She explored the racial discrimination she and Simon felt as mixed race children in a predominantly White environment. The film portrayed isolation and self-hatred. She included scenes of her brother and scrubbing their faces and putting on white powder so they might appear all white instead of mixed race. Like other Eurocentric and Afrocentric filmmakers she explored the challenges of being a 'Tragic Mulatto'. This film reevaluates the concept of cultural *melting pots* and identifies them more as *incinerators*.

Inspired by Poet Laureate Maya Angelou, *And Still I Rise* (1991) explores the concept of black women rising through the ravages of slavery. Using graphic scenes and piercing sounds, she frames the black woman's lack of control over her body. The film reflects the maltreatment of women around the world but emphasizes the mistreatment of women in sub-Saharan African countries (Foster, 1997).

For Western viewers, Onwurah's *The Body Beautiful* (1991) presents some graphic images. The movie features Onwurah and her mother. She explores their relationship and allows her mother to share her thoughts about being a White woman married to a Nigerian man, being the mother of mixed race children, functioning as a single mother, experiencing breast cancer and having a mastectomy. Ngozi talks about having a white British mother, being a mixed race model in a fashion industry that featured white models, her mother's sexuality and other aspects of her life started in her first film.

Ngozi chose close ups, medium shots and panning shots to give her production more intimacy. Avoiding a cinema verité approach, Ngozi uses jumpcuts and stable shots to increase the audience's discomfort with the scenes. From the close ups of her mother's mastectomy scar to pseudo-erotic shots of a hand almost touching that scar and re-envisioning her mother making love to a black man, Ngozi pushes her audience's comfort level.

Onwurah challenges viewers to explore the traditional versus the modern in *Monday Girls* (1993), her documentary told in narrative style. Onwurah juxtaposes the decisions of two young women's passage from being girls to being women. One chooses to do as she is expected to do. She spends her time in the 'fattening room' for five weeks, exposes her breast for public display, allows herself to be examined by a Mother Moses who can look at her and determine if she is pregnant and walks before a panel of chiefs (old men) to receive a certificate that supports her virtue. Girls unwilling to go through this process are labelled as whores, a term that women use to insult each other in this culture (Savory, 2001). The other young lady's decision to avoid this ceremony automatically identified herself as a whore. She chose to leave the village and live in the big city, eating in restaurants and bars. Whether the young woman chose to remain chaste or not, the place she chose to live her life, placed her in an undesirable category in any case.

Onwurah's heritage and the place she was brought up may have affected her message according to Savory (2001) Onwurah values tradition rather than modernity. Her perspective allows viewers to really question what their decision might be if they had to experience something most modern women would consider demeaning, or make their parents embarrassed in front of all the people they knew. She does not glamorize life in the city. She reveals to viewers what both girls pay for the decisions they make.

Onwurah combines her gift for focusing on the body and retelling history in her 1994 film *Welcome II the Terrordome*. The film tells a fictional black history story where, as in reality, the black body is a focus of commodification, sterilisation and genocide. *According to Foster* (1997), a political action thriller, was the first independent Black British feature film to be released.

The Desired Number (1995) explores how and when Nigerian women will use birth control. Onwurah establishes the fact that Nigerian women do have control over their bodies but like many women in the developing world, they feel compelled to follow tradition rather than common sense. She notes the availability of clinics that could provide birth control but also the challenge of being a woman with only a few children, rather than a woman who shows her fertility by having numerous children.

Onwurah's filmography suggests a sustained interest in women, self-identity, the challenges of being powerful that women face, black history and of course, beauty. Her other films include: *Best Wishes* (1989), *Fruits of Fear* (1990), *Who Stole the Soul* (1992), *Flight of the Swan* (1993), *Siren Spirits* (1994), *White Men Are Cracking Up* (1996), *Behind the Mask* (1997), *Hang Time* (2001), *Mama Africa* (2002) and *Shoot The Messenger* (2006).

Anne-Laure Folly

Key distributor of films made by women, Women Make Movies, considers Anne-Laure Folly to be one of Africa's finest female filmmakers even if she is one of its newest. Born in Togo, Folly produces films that reflect the cultural experiences of people across the continent rather than just those of her home. Folly is considered a gifted documentarian who examines women's lives and decisions. From her first documentary, *Le Gardien des*

Forces (1992) which focused on women from Benin, Burkina Faso, Mali and Senegal (http://www.wmm.com/FilmCatalog/makers/ fm165.shtml), Folly focuses on the difficulties and joys of their lives. Her second documentary, *Femmes of Niger*, explores the challenges of trying to develop a national democracy in a country that is traditionally Islamic with authorised polygamy and Muslim fundamentalists as citizens. *L'Or du Liptako*, was a thirteen-minute video. Folly gained recognition, however, with her third documentary, *Femmes aux yeux ouverts* (1994). This documentary earned her a Silver Medal at the Monte Carlo Television Festival in 1994. Folly returned to her thirteen minutes approach with *Les Amazones se sont reconverties* but chose a documentary style for this film *Entre l'Arbre et la Pirogue* (*The Tree to the Dugout*, 1996). *Les Oubliées* (1996) is a documentary that was shot in Angola in Portuguese with French subtitles. The film allows women to discuss the ravages of thirty years of war on their lives. Folly is focused on women's thoughts not their bodies in this production, therefore viewers see faces. She explores political implications of the cold war, Cuban intervention and South African racism (*Association des Trois Mondes*). Included in the interviews of Angolan women is an interview with Sarah Maldoror's daughter Ruth Neto. Folly pays tribute to Sarah Maladoror in 1998 and *Deposez les Larmes* in 1999.

In terms of attention given to her works, several critics chose to analyse *Femmes aux yeux ouverts*. Just as in her original documentary, Folly uses the combination of women from Benin, Burkina Faso, Mali and Senegal to inform the viewers. Women talk about the challenges they face. They discuss clitoridectomy, forced marriage, HIV/AIDS, survival, economics, politics and other struggles. As other African female filmmakers have chosen, Folly allows the women to express the challenge of being in charge of the family but powerless to express their concerns about the family (Thackway, 2003).

Tsitsi Dangarembga

Tsitsi Dangarembga, born in 1959 is a novelist, scriptwriter, consultant and film director. She lived in Mutoku, Rhodesia, now Zimbabwe for her first two years but moved to England with parents when they went off to college. Although her primary education was started in England, she and her family returned to Rhodesia when she was six. Dangarembga completed her primary and secondary education at a mission school in Mutare. Dangarembga returned to England at the age of eighteen to study medicine at Cambridge University. After three years of feeling lonely and alienated she left Cambridge and returned home. This was the same time that Rhodesia was about to become independent.

Dangarembga quit her plan to become a doctor and began working in marketing and began studying psychology at the University of Zimbabwe which is when she first started to develop her directing skills in the University's Drama Club where she wrote and staged plays. When she finished her degree, Dangarembga accepted a teaching position. She did not see teaching as her true calling so she left her position to work on her writing. Dangarembga became the first black Zimbabwean woman to publish a novel written in English. The novel, *Nervous Conditions* (1988) presented themes that were included in much of her future work. *Nervous Conditions* earned her international recognition. Dangarembga continued to gain recognition when she became the first black Zimbabwean woman to direct a feature film. *Everyone's Child* was her first film of notoriety. Her films and novels examined colonial and post-colonial Zimbabwe through the lens of education, feminism, gender equality and patriarchy.

Dangarembga's work has helped gain a lot of attention for Zimbabwe's film industry. Dangarembga worked with Robert McLaren's Zambuko theatre. McLaren introduced her to community theatre and initiated her participation in several productions. This exposure led to her development as a theatre director and playwright. In 1983, she wrote *The Lost of the Soil* and *She No Longer Weeps*.

Dangarembga's career presents an established a pattern of writing novels, followed by screenplays and then directing the films. Death and its effect on women and children became a theme in several films. *Everyone's Child* (1996) focused on the effects of AIDS on orphans in Africa. Her publications have gained international recognition. Her novels *Nervous Conditions*, *The Book of Not: A Sequel to Nervous Conditions* and *Bira* present a trilogy that reflects her life and the lived experiences of women caught in professional and personal traps because they of mixed heritage. Danganrembga currently teaches writing for the theatre and film direction to women.

Anne Mungai

Anne Mungai is representative of many African women filmmakers working in the first half of the 21st century. They tell stories of the problems women faced in the last century whilst also confronting contemporary issues that affect women.

Born in Kenya, Mungai knew in her high school years that she wanted to work in communications. She chose to explore film studies at the Kenya School of Mass Communications in Nairobi. Her current work shows she continues to forge her career using combined resources in a university setting. She has produced film shorts, medium length documentaries and she has attempted to stay focused on topics of interest to the market: women, health, youth, religion, agriculture and education.

Mungai produced the first feature film by a Kenyan filmmaker male or female. *Saikati* (1992) juxtaposes two worlds in Kenya (urban and rural) and the decisions two sisters have to make in order to live there. Mungai attempts to present a balanced look at female sexuality and the challenges young women face as they attempt to negotiate life in a changing world.

Mungai felt comfortable discussing the challenges of being a woman filmmaker in Kenya. In an interview with Mbye Cham (1992), she shared the challenges Kenyan filmmakers face. Two issues that seemed to be intertwined were gender and finances. From a gender perspective, Mungai discussed letting her husband know that she wanted to make films. He, like the bankers, could not believe that she, a woman, wanted to make a film. Whoever heard of a woman making a film? For those unfamiliar with the culture, Kenyan women (and many other African women) cannot own property. Women are expected to get married and it is assumed that the property a woman and her husband will live on will be his family's property. If the husband dies and no one in family agrees to take care of his wife, what will she have to survive on? So, how can this person with no money and no property plan to run a film company? Additionally, women do not tell men what to do. Who will she find to work for her? The challenges seem so insurmountable.

At first, Mungai's husband did not go with her to find funding or do anything to promote her effort. After she proved she could get everything done on her own, however, he did take some time off to help her with her next film.

In continuing her discussion of women filmmakers in Kenya, Mungai noted that Kenyan film backers seemed to feel that women filmmakers would not know how to manage the money for their films. She noted that of while there had been no cases of financial mismanagement of money on women's films, there had been a number of such problems on men's film productions (Cham, 1992). While three other women had started to produce films in Kenya, at that time, she was the only one to produce a feature length documentary. Originally, like many struggling filmmakers today, she used a grassroots marketing approach to get the resources she needed for her films. That meant negotiating with airlines and hotels so she could cover travel and sometimes making smaller films. Mungai learned that if she took her husband along with her, the negotiations would go better for her efforts.

Passing the torch

The year 2011 marked the twenty-year anniversary of the historic conference in Ouagadougou on African women film professionals, during which an organised movement was born. This conference established ground rules for creating an infrastructure to present and promote the cinematic works of women. The members understood that the new voice must be heard and it must be heard in more distant lands. At this celebration, discussions began to help women filmmakers achieve this goal. They no longer needed to produce reels of celluloid when distribution could take place over the internet.

In this section of the chapter we will see women whose creativity began and continues in some non-traditional venues while they also continue the traditional approaches.

Zanele Mthembu

Those working in the media saw the gift that Zanele Mthembu possessed. She chose to work on media related studies, earning an Honours degree in communication and majoring in broadcasting in South Africa. Her main focus was education and the media, not filmmaking. Mthembu was very interested in how television could facilitate education. Because her university did not have the equipment needed to provide theory and praxis, Mthembu learned the practical aspects of producing on the job. When she began to work for Penguin Films in South Africa, it all came together for her (Ellerson, 2000).

Like many media employees, Mthembu began working in television as a production assistant in 1992. At that time, she wanted to become a director. While working at Penguin, she found herself in an environment where documentaries, educational programs and dramas were produced. Given an assignment that allowed her to show her skills, the producer allowed her to direct her own five-minute show after only four months on the job.

Like many of the younger filmmakers, we have no commercial releases of Mthembu to discuss at this time. Her vision for the use of media to enhance education will surely lead to the production of films under her direction. The original focus for her five minute show was how violence affects children in South Africa. Her voice may be heard addressing that theme on longer productions soon.

Monique Mbeka Phoba

Award-winning filmmaker Monique Phoba was born in Brussels, Belgium in 1962. Phoba is the daughter of a diplomat from the Democratic Republic of the Congo. Although her heritage was Congolese, Phoba lived the first half of her life in Belgium. She and her family would go to the DRC for school holidays but her home was Belgium. Even after her father resigned his job, Phoba began her studies at the Free University of Brussels and obtained a degree in International Business from the Institute for Advanced Studies of Saint-Luc in Brussels. Phoba's international exposure affected her thesis topic, 'Cooperation between the European and African Audiovisual Industries'. Although she had spent far more time in Belgium than she had in the DRC, Phoba gave talks on African culture for independent radio and she wrote articles on the same for Brussels and Geneva. Recognising Jean Rouch as a gifted documentary professor, she took his introductory course at Ateliers Varan in Paris (http://www.africine.org/?menu=fiche&no=3265 accessed February 3rd 2012.)

Phoba produced her first film with Zairian journalist, Fred Mongu in 1991. *Revue en vrac* examined the press in the DRC, looking at both the pluralistic and the independent. In 1993, she produced *Rentrer? (To return?)* followed by *Deux petits tours et puis s'en vont (Two little turns and then go)* in 1997. In 1996, Phoba won the North/South prize of the Council of Europe at Rencontres Media Nord/Sud in Geneva. She discussed an HIV positive Viennese character in her short, *Une voix dans le Silence (A voice in the silence)*. She worked with Emmanuel Kolawole on *Deux petits tours et puis s'en vont* which won a second prize for TV/Video documentary at the FESPACO in March of 1997. Phoba's 1998 film *Un Rêve d'Indépendance (A dream of Independence)* focused on thirty-five years of independence in the DRC. This film earned the Images of Women award at the Vues d'Afrique Festival in Montreal in 2000. *Anna, l'Enchantée (Anna, the enchanted),* about a singer who wins a scholarship to study in France, was released in 2001 and won the Images of Women award at the Ves d'Afrique in 2002. She wrote, directed and acted in *Sorcière, la Vie (A Bewitched Life)* in 2006. She wrote and co-directed with Guy Kabeya Muya *Entre la coupe et l'election (Between the cup and the election)* in 2007.

Phoba chose simply to act in *Tout le monde a des raisons d'en vouloir a sa mère (Everyone has reason to want their mother)* in 2010. (See http://banamboka.com/2011/02/08/monique-mbeka-phoba-femme-engagee-cineaste-passionee/accessed March 2nd 2014.)

Bridget Pickering

Bridget Pickering is a Namibian filmmaker and producer. Her father is a Namibian diplomat and trade unionist. Her mother is from South Africa. She came to the United States to attend Syracuse University. After Syracuse she began working for Universal Pictures. She returned to Namibia after leaving Universal.

An examination of Pickering's filmography suggests valuable

experiences that prepared her for her own career in filmmaking. She worked as assistant to Bonnie Timmerman on *The Hard Way* (1991), *Mobsters* (1991) and *Glengarry Glen Ross* (1992) and in casting on *The Last of the Mohicans* (1992). In 1996, she worked as the co-producer for *Flame,* produced the short *Uno's World* (2001) and was the co-producer of *Hotel Rwanda* in 2004. Back in Namibia, she produced the TV movie *Gugu and Andile* and a TV mini-series, *Dream World.* She served as executive producer of the TV movie *Mzansi Love: Colour Blind* (2013) and co-produced the documentary *Changing the Game.*

Wabei Siyolwe

Wabei Siyolwe may be better known by some westerners for her acting. In her earlier years she performed in *Scene* (1968), *Cry Freedom* (1987) and *Nuns on the Run* (1990). Siyolwe, in fact, has been performing in some capacity all of her life. Born in Zambia, Siyolwe learned to act at the Guildhall School of Drama in England. Trained in acting for film, all students were taught the technical side of theatre. Students also produced their own films. They were required to write the stories then act in them.

Siyolwe identified theatre as her first love. She recalled always acting and working in music since she was a small child. When she lived in Russia, she stayed focused on music and acting, and participated in the conservatory there. According to Ellerson (2000), Siyolwe believed that producing film was a natural progression from her theatrical works. By 2000, she seemed to be engaged in more film work than theatre. The films she performed in as a teen and young adult led her to a commitment to the creation of film behind the camera. She committed to film in 1986 (Ellerson, 2000).

Prudence Uriri

Prudence Uriri was bon in Zimbabwe and became a freedom fighter of the Zimbabwean liberation war. Before working the independent production house, CVU, she worked at Zimbabwe's Broadcasting Corporation Television. Uriri is the founder of Eye for Africa, a production company and she now teaches film at the University of Tromso in Norway.

Ingrid Sinclair

Ingrid Sinclair is part of the African Renaissance. She was born in the United Kingdom where she studied Literature and Medicine. She studied filmmaking and film production in South Africa. Her film *Flame* gained her recognition as a filmmaker of the African Renaissance. Sinclair's documentaries on the Zimbabwe Liberation Movement gained her recognition at the Cannes Film Festival as well as other international praise. According to Women Make Movies (http://www.wmm.com accessed February 14th 2003) her film *Africa is a Woman's Name* (2009) produced along with Bridget Pickering and Wanjiru Kinyanjui allowed each woman to discuss their country's stories.

Zulfah Otto Sallies

Zulfah Otto Sallies was born May 8th 1961 in Cape Town, South Africa. In speaking of her filmmaking style, Otto Sallies compared making films to making a mosaic:

> 'Each setup is like a tiny tile. You colour it, shape it, polish it as best you can. You'll do thousands of these. Then you literally paste them together and hope it's what you set out to do. But if you expect the final mosaic to look like anything, you'd better know what you're going for as you work on each tiny tile.' (See http://www.slideshare. net/ZulfahOttoSallies accessed March 14th 2005)

Marguerite Abouet

Marguerite Abouet is an Ivoirian writer born in Abidjan, Côte d'Ivoire in 1971. When Abouet was twelve, her great uncle moved her and her brother to France (Zuarino, 2007). From that point on, France became her home. She married Clément Oubrerie and they became business partners as well. Abouet writes comics which her husband illustrates. She worked as a legal assistant in order to support her writing until the release of her first feature film.

She is best known for her graphic novel series *Aya*, and the series is special for several reasons. It is Abouet's first effort at publishing graphic novels as well as her first effort at professionally collaborating with her husband. This was his first effort at comic illustration as well. *Aya* is a product of Abouet's desire to present an image of Africa that did not focus on famine and war. While Abouet denies comments that *Aya* is autobiographical, she does acknowledge that the story is based on people she knew growing up but their situations have been changed to protect their identities (Zuarino, 2007).

Aya has been considered a success especially for a first-time author. It won the 2006 Angoulême International Comics Festival Prize for First Comic Book and sold over 200,000 copies in France (Berretta, 2008). After much success, she transitioned from her comic book trilogy to video.

Conclusion

Young or old, African women filmmakers have continued to speak up on the issues that are close to their hearts. Some needed to speak of the oppression of their people by those from other continents. Others needed to talk about the oppression of women, led by men they knew, and sometimes of their oppression by other women. As African media opportunities have increased, African women are telling the stories of their generations and their experiences. These filmmakers do not forget the challenges some of their sisters are enduring. They just want to let the world know that African women's experiences are like women everywhere… worth talking about. They invite other women to 'Speak up'.

Author biography

Maria Williams-Hawkins, Ph.D. Ohio State, is an Associate Professor of Telecommunications at Ball State University where she teaches undergraduate courses in media criticism, graduate special topics courses that produce new media and approaches to assisting patients with Parkinson's Disease and Alzheimer's.

She was the host of several public affairs shows on WIPB TV in Muncie, Indiana. She has published on topics ranging from the use of social media and cell phones to economic factors related to the media. Her speaking usually focuses on portrayals and interactions with international and marginalised groups as well as the representation of women.

She was the owner of Video Verification Production Company

earlier in her career and worked as Lecturer and Cable News Seven News Director in Huntsville, Texas, News Director and Executive Producer at KMOS-TV in Warrensburg, Missouri and technical director and assistant producer at WREG-TV in Memphis, Tennessee. In addition to her professorial work, Maria is also an ordained deacon in the African Methodist Episcopal Church. She is currently working on *Indiana African American Legends and Strange Fruit*, a documentary of the last known lynching in Indiana.

Contact: mhawkins@bsu.edu

References

'African women and cinema: a conversation with Anne Mungai', Research in African Literature (Fall 1994) (www.jstor.org/stable/3819847)

Arevalo, Rica (March 13th 2010). 'Producer notes great strides of women in cinema,' *Philippine Daily Inquirer.*

Beus, Yifen (December 2011). 'Authorship and criticism in self-reflexive African cinema,' *Journal of African Cultural Studies,* vol 23 (2) December 2011, pp. 133–152.

Bobo, Jacqueline (1998). *Black Women Film and Video Artists*, New Routledge, New York.

Deppey, Dirk (March 19th 2007). 'Review of *Aya.' The Comics Journal.*

Dovey, Lindiwe (2009). *African Film and Literature: Adapting violence to the screen.* Columbia University Press, New York.

Ellerson, Beti (2004). Africa through a woman's eyes: Safi Faye's cinema,' in *Pfaff, Francois, Focus on African Films*, University Press, Bloomington, Indiana.

Foster, Gwendolyn Audrey (1997). *Women Filmmakers of the African and Asian Diaspora*, Southern Illinois University Press, Carbondale.

Ellerson, Beti (2004). 'Africa through a woman's eyes: Safi Faye's cinema,' in Pfaff, *Francois, Focus on African Films,* Bloomington, Indiana University Press.

Guback, Thomas and Varis, Tapio (1982). *Transnational Communication and Cultural Industries*, UNESCO.

Gugler, Josef (2003). *African Film: Re-imaging a continent.* Indiana University Press, Bloomington.

Harrow, Kenneth (2007). *Post Colonial African Cinema.* Indiana University Press, Bloomington.

AFRICA

Malkmus, Lizbeth and Armes, Roy (1991). *Arab & African Filmmaking*. Zed, London.

Marker, Cynthia (2001). 'Safi Faye and Sarah Maldoror: Cine'crivaines of African Cinema', *Twentieth-Century/Contemporary French Studies*, Fall 2008, Vol. 4 (2 pp. 453–480).

McCluskey, Audrey T. (2009). *The devil you dance with: film culture in the new South Africa*

Savory, Elaine (2001). 'African Women's Voices on Film,' Review Essay

Wilkerson, Isabel (2010). *The Warmth of Other Suns*. Random House, New York.

Zuarino, John (May 2007). 'An Interview with Marguerite Abouet', Bookslut website, http://www.bookslut.com/

3. The Home, the Body and Otherness:

Canadian representations of identity and feminism in Mary Harron's *American Psycho*, Sarah Polley's *Away From Her* and the Soska Sisters' *American Mary*.

Dr Karen Oughton

This chapter will explore the work of Canadian film directors Jen and Sylvia Soska, Mary Harron and Sarah Polley; and it will discuss how their nationalities and gender are reflected within their work. As all four directors' features focus on otherness and all have been associated with the horror genre, examination of them will be placed within that theoretical framework. Beginning with a brief history of the role of women within the horror film industry, the chapter will suggest that these filmmakers have constructed alternative depictions of gender roles within their genres. With this in mind, the critique will initially focus on the Soska Sisters' *American Mary* with reference to Carol Clover's theories of the final girl and Laura Mulvey's theorisation of the cinematic male gaze. It will then examine Mary Harron's adaptation of *American Psycho* and Sarah Polley's adaptation of *Away From Her*, focusing on their investigations of otherness and empathy.[1]

Firstly, in order to contextualise the impact the Soska Sisters have had on the film industry, it is necessary to consider women's historical role within horror cinema. From the early days of film, heroines included *Nosferatu*'s Ellen who sacrifices herself to kill Graf Orlok. They exist alongside later victims such as Marion Crane in Alfred Hitchcock's *Psycho* and have been theorised as subject to what Laura Mulvey has called 'the male gaze' and are discussed in her seminal essay 'Visual Pleasure and Narrative Cinema' as an 'erotic object for the characters within the screen story and as erotic object for spectator within the auditorium' (p. 11) within the traditional, male-managed Hollywood cinema. Women appeared on screen foremost as the objects of men's fantasies. However, female character representations began to change with US-produced 'slasher' horror film cycle of the late 1970s and 1980s. This is generally credited to characters such as Laurie Strode, nemesis of Michael Myers in the *Halloween* (1978) series and the last victim left standing. Strode became a blueprint for Carol Clover's influential theories on the role of horror's 'final girl' as developed in her book, *On Men, Women and Chainsaws* (1992). Clover's theory contends that the voyeurism of women within horror cinema is ambivalent, with the final girl enabling the audience's affiliation to switch from the monster to the often tomboyish female who becomes the hero by the end of the film.

The Soska Sisters

However, as the Soska Sisters recognised, women's representation is still largely mediated by men. This often lends women a passive or largely sexualised quality. As Jen Soska has stated, while *Halloween*'s Laurie Strode attacks the villainous Myers, she does so 'for self-preservation rather than to be assertive'.[2] Therefore, the film can still be considered as somewhat lacking from a feminist perspective. The Soska Sisters have said they want to change this by challenging ideas of normality through cinema as a result of their understanding of 'unusual' identities that is a result of their identical twinship and in line with their life-long love of horror. As stated by Sylvia Soska:

> 'Jen and I being twins, were almost born into being somewhat of a spectacle. Try as we might, we never could fit in.
>
> Then came horror – we would watch the way people treated one another, how different things invoked fear and others to be embraced. I suppose it was because

we were so used to being watched and asked questions. Horror made us feel strong.'[3]

Their initial attempts to become actors did not meet with the results they had hoped, so they enrolled on a stunt persons' course at film school. Their course closed but they converted their final student project into the micro-budget grindhouse feature, *Dead Hooker in a Trunk* (2009).[4] Somewhat predictably (the humorous point of the ostensibly exploitative title), the story focuses on friends who find a murdered sex worker and attempt to dispose of her body.

The film enabled them to demonstrate their devotion to genre and, by writing, directing and doing their own stunts, endeared them to many genre fans as a result. Moreover, via pre-recorded videos at initial screenings at the Abertoir festival and others they spoke about this film incorporating violence and rape so enthusiastically they seemed ultimately non-threatening, their judicious cursing actually appearing rather sweet.[5] No matter the violence they show, the Soska Sisters can appear as likeable 'girls next door'.[6]

Theirs were personae and indeed fledgling roles akin to, though not yet as developed as, the traditional horror hostess and this impacted greatly on their career ascent. The horror host is a tradition within the genre. It is a combination of filmmaker, journalist, presenter and figurehead for the community.

Horror hosts, such as the television character Vampira, traditionally introduce film and television attractions to audiences in home entertainment and local movie theatres. They dress in costume or other themed clothing, often have a definitive stage persona and often have a somewhat comic delivery. Their presence and branding represent the cultural recognition and indeed legitimisation of the horror communities' tastes and in the context of their popularity they are consumed as representations of its core values. However, these horror community core values, as David Sanjek quotes David Chute as stating, represent:

> '[a] deadly serious undertaking [whose] seriousness can never be openly acknowledged. The gross-out aficionado

> savors his sense of complicity when the values of a smug
> social stratum, from which he feels himself excluded, are
> systematically trashed and ridiculed.[7]

This seriousness, as Chute suggests, must remain playful so as not to be co-opted by the mainstream. As a result, horror hosts subvert traditional standards and also comment on the films.[8] The emphasis is firmly on the ethos of the host character as an icon of horror convention, often with a short section of very light comedy film criticism thrown in.

However, of great importance to the branding and perception of the Soska Sisters is the notion that this overly camp and performance-based presentation began to change with the advent of increased focus on industry figures as opposed to the roles they played in the industry. This can be seen through the career of Emily Booth in the 1990s. Booth was one of a number of women who evolved the female horror personality. She acts in cult films, has written for magazines including *Bizarre*, is known for her presenting role at Sky's *The Horror Channel* (denoting that she has genre knowledge), is a glamour model and, importantly, frequently references her own love of the genre. She reflects girl-geek culture, embodying the supposedly tomboyish trait of enjoying violence while looking conventionally sexually attractive. This is emphasised by her being photographed in revealing clothing whilst covered in gore. She is the male audience's best friend with breasts who will encourage their interests and desires. The Soska Sisters' work (intentionally or not) mirrors this template of the on and off-screen filmmaker fan. While the Soska Sisters' use of the role does not reduce their filmic achievements and indeed accolades in any way, it informs their rise within the industry owing to the role's historical but changing remit.

The initial film festival screening period of *Dead Hooker in a Trunk* marked the time when the Soska Sisters appear to have consciously stepped into the horror persona role to publicise their work.[9] Shortly afterwards they began to work with Hannah Gorman (also known as Hannah Neurotica), founder of the gender and horror-focused zine, *Ax-Wound,* and the then-fledgling Women in Horror Recognition Month campaign. The campaign aims to highlight women's contributions to the genre. Gorman at the time was a fan whose emphasis on the manual creation of the zine made it appear more authentic than the output of some corporate publishers. Association with the Women in Horror Recognition Month campaign could be seen as a marker of authenticity and indeed the Soska Sisters frequently extol the virtues of the Do-It-Yourself approach. The Soska Sisters joined the Board of Women in Horror month and became its ambassadors. They write articles on women's contribution to horror and promote charitable activities such as Massive Blood Drive, a campaign to increase blood donors by – you've guessed it – appealing to gorehounds via blood-soaked short films featuring themselves in sexy business attire casually maiming each other. They blend being seen to pay homage to work lauded within the genre while simultaneously showcasing their own work as writers, entrepreneurs and directors. However, they remained somewhat niche and known mainly to horror connoisseurs rather than the casual filmgoers.[10]

American Mary, the Soska Sisters' second self-directed film, changed this. The plot concerns Mary Mason, a medical student in debt. After a botched job interview at a strip club finds her carrying out emergency surgery on one of its associates, she specialises in underground body modification while mutilating and murdering her enemies until being killed by a patient's partner. According to the Soska Sisters, Mary represents the evolution of Clover's theorised 'final girl' as she is both the film's heroic victim *and* its aggressor. The sisters have also stated that Mary is intended to be an outsider, being of Hungarian heritage and yet fighting to live the American Dream, as symbolised by the Stars and Stripes outlined in her blood on the floor where she dies.[11] The film's preview at Frightfest was highly anticipated, particularly as the Soska Sisters were in attendance and a number of audience members were familiar with their work with the Women in Horror Recognition Month campaign.[12] After the screening the sisters set the pattern for future appearances by arriving on stage to discuss the empowerment of producing the feature. They were dressed in revealing clothing modelled on Mary's sexy surgical costumes and were insistent on extended meet-and-greet sessions with fans. They were adored, displaying a seemingly genuine, innocent (and deafening) excitement that their work was being admired.

The Soska Sisters came to be seen by a significant proportion of the genre scene in particular as feminist icons who had created in Mary Mason a new breed of feminist character without sacrificing either her or (importantly) their sex appeal, a proposition they repeatedly stated in interviews that they saw as being 'sexist', considering their appearance as a form of 'armour' to deflect from any inner uncertainty.[13] That their appearance and espousal of feminist ideals gained the attention of the genre press may have been facilitated by increased academic interest in horror not only from within the academy but also within the film industry, as demonstrated by the profusion of academic bonus features from specialist home distributors such as Arrow Films. This cultural shift allowed the recognition and admiration the Soska Sisters have expressed for older tropes of sexy and secretly business-brained but branded-pop-intellectual female horror hosts such as Elvira. That this trope has been recognised may, they believe, enable them to move beyond that representation.[14] They now discuss academic cinema theory and increase their genre kudos without making themselves appear distant. They also practised what they preached, with their character Mary beginning and ending the film in glamorous costumes that suggest sexuality without actually revealing her body even during the film's rape scene. Mary is a depiction of female empowerment devoid of the titillation associated with other so-called rape-revenge films including *I Spit on Your Grave*.

Indeed, I assert that the Soska Sisters can themselves be perceived as an attempt to embody Clover's concept of the 'final girl'. Sylvia Soska has commented that *American Mary* is their response to the 'monsters' in the film industry who tried to subject them to sexually improper behaviour.[15] By delivering an acclaimed film and being so visible to the horror public both in terms of discussing their past trauma and using it to advance themselves, they created a new model for the female horror persona. The model they promote is that of an intelligent business woman unashamed of publicly placing herself on a cultural par traditionally associated with men by planning rather than adopting the conventional image that they are fans making films for the love of it alone.[16]

American Mary won a host of awards and enabled the Soska Sisters to develop their brand. They took on additional local screening presenting voluntary work, briefly ran a radio programme, wrote for a time for a number of alternative interest publications but importantly also invested time in cultivating their internet fan base by establishing brand alignment by endorsing others' horror culturally-important products, releasing content teasers (such as photographs of their costumes for conventions) and rewarding fan loyalty through Twitter retweets and personal communication.

Nonetheless, they (like Emily Booth) contend with what David Sanjek has called the 'Connoisseurs of the badfilm [sic], trash, and gore…'.[17] While some of the Soska Sisters' publicity photographs are faux naive and feature 1950s style prom dresses, Sanjek states that horror editors, '…insist upon the pleasures to be found in the consumption of such raw, undiluted imagery.'[18] The word 'trash' reveals the importance of this. Taken literally, it is waste product with connotations of contamination rather than purity, suggestive of the notional loss of virginity and gore. A significant level of the sisters' output is, to use Sanjek's term, 'undiluted' – extremely sexual imagery delivered with minimal clothing, a knowing wink and a bucket of blood.[19] Naturally this creates complexities for the Soska Sisters' branding. Their social media demonstrate how much fan attention focuses on their physiques rather than their feature films. Indeed, their aficionado's interest (what David Chute's terms the 'seriousness' of horror discourse) is subsumed within the iconography of horror – in this instance their slightly ironic and highly-sexualised style.[20] They even cut their hair into bangs like their character Mary's despite saying in several interviews that they hate the style.[21] It may be the case that this is in recognition that brackets of the horror fan base find replication of the characters themselves reinforces the fantasy of the final girl whilst also making it more sexually stimulating by blurring the line between fiction and reality.

Maintaining this balance between enjoying and exploiting their and their characters' gender and sexuality is all the more challenging as their careers have developed with the announcement that they have directed the joint Lions Gate/ World Wrestling Entertainment (WWE) project *See No Evil 2*. The feature is narrative concerning a fictitious serial killer and stars the wrestler, Kane (actor Glenn Jacobs), as character Jacob Goodnight. It brings the enormously popular, family-orientated wrestling events (rated PG) and branding together with the more adult aspects of the slasher horror genre. It enables the sisters to appear both suitably raunchy and ethical all at once.

As a result of their films and branding via their personal media outlets and interviews with external sources, Jen and Sylvia Soska have established themselves as commentator-filmmakers who remain accessible to fans. They are an acceptable face of horror and have become somewhat mainstream, even appearing at WWE events due to *See No Evil 2*. It is an ethos that the media-savvy twins use to their advantage.

Mary Harron

Mary Harron, on the other hand, has a very different background. Harron's comparatively short but influential filmography comprises of the biographical *I Shot Andy Warhol* and *The Notorious Bettie Page* as well as horror adaptation *The Moth Diaries*. However, it is *American Psycho*, the adaptation of Brett Easton Ellis's tale of a Wall Street worker who channels his rage into murder, for which she is best known. *American Psycho* is a film famed particularly for the scenes in which antagonist Patrick Bateman (actor Christian Bale) has intercourse with two sex workers while watching himself posing in the mirror. Together with its self-reflective post-modern ending, stylised violence and paranoia it at once eulogises and demonises its anti-hero through the eyes of its two women writers, who are both affiliated firmly with educated liberalism.[22] This female perspective plays a marked role in *American Psycho*.

Harron was born in Vancouver, raised in London and educated at the University of Oxford.[23] She subsequently moved to New York and became immersed in the burgeoning music scene as a journalist specialising in punk rock and culture. Following this she developed documentary projects for English outlets focusing on art and culture-based content. It was as a result of her connections within this field that she worked on her biopic of Valerie Solanas, the lesbian separatist who shot pop-art mogul Warhol. Harron's lauded role on that feature led to her involvement with *American Psycho*.

Like the Soska Sisters, Harron has stated in Johnson's *Maclean's* article that *American Psycho* is born of a Canadian sensibility and sense of separateness from America.[24] The Brett Easton Ellis book on which the film is based was first published in 1991 and is a decidedly dark-hearted look at the corporate America of the infamous 1980s. It mixes Ellis's disgust with conspicuous consumption with the styles of some of the most infamous films of that period, notably *Maniac* (1980) and *Driller Killer* (1979), in which anti-heroes acted out their fantasies on strangers and friends alike in the most violent of ways. Moving straight from text to film, Harron could, within the boundaries of censorship, have sought to create a similarly sadistic movie even if it would pale in comparison to some of the extreme sexual violence in the book.

Instead, her film focuses on its antagonist's internal dialogue by mirroring it through attention to detail of the conspicuous consumption Bateman uses to fill his emotional void. The financial world and the material and other goods success buys become fatuous in its gaze. Harron focused on this satirical interpretation of the story to the extent that she wrote a public letter to *The New York Times* when the film was released to contest the censorship debates and controversy it encountered. At the same time, however, the film pictorially acknowledges the art of its superficial representation. The camera lingers over fine dining amongst Bateman's supposed friends while the characters (who never seem to actually eat in the restaurants) bicker amongst themselves. Furthermore, while the traders fetishize designer haircuts and clothing despite being unable to tell each other apart, their lustre is nevertheless underscored by their opulent surroundings. As a result, one of the central concerns of the film, Bateman's supposed murder of a colleague, is itself left in doubt owing to information given to Bateman by a colleague. The satire is only effective as it is believable enough to be true and Bale has commented that Wall Street workers he interviewed for the role genuinely loved the book precisely for its ostentatious presentation of their lifestyle.

However, rather than just being a Canadian critique of conspicuous consumption associated with the American Dream, this damning depiction can also be understood by considering Bateman in terms of gender politics in relation to the film's female characters and indeed audience. It is the angle of Harron, a cool-headed feminist reflecting on a very masculine culture. The beginning of the film is indicative as we see Bateman walk around his sterile apartment in his boxer shorts while carrying out an extremely detailed morning beauty routine. Rather than it making Bateman appear sympathetic or even fearsome, for example by showing that he cares what others think, his over-confident movements and unctuous facial expression instead make him an instantly dislikeable character for whom (Harron's audio commentary suggests) women have only contempt.

Harron emphasises the film's feminist critique through Bateman's interrelationships with women, particularly in supposedly romantic places such as restaurants, with constant close-ups on his face. The camera crops the scene between a close-up and a medium close-up, sitting just at the top of Bateman's collar and using this different framing emphasises the lines around his face and his lift-eyed look of disdain. It demonstrates that he views even women who are his social class equals as objects to mould around social expectations of him, at one point explicitly telling his fiancée that he wants 'to fit in'. Similarly, regarding the infamous sex scene in which Bateman watches himself having intercourse Harron has commented to Eugene Hernandez at *Indiewire* that,

> 'We were trying to make the scene as un-erotic as possible to underscore that these women were being paid for sex, which their facial expressions make clear.'

This is despite the fact that the book, unreliable narrator notwithstanding, states that the sex workers enjoy the consensual intercourse during the encounter and do not appear to view the entirety of their interaction with Bateman in a solely negative light.

Bateman is incapable of actually enjoying the pleasures his money can give him and is instead controlled by it. He is made to appear pathetic even as he bullies and controls. As a result, for the first twenty minutes of the film, Harron's direction places him in the role of an almost cartoonesque pantomimic villain whose persona is built on grandstanding. In doing so, Harron shifts the viewer's expectations for the film's female characters and it is not until the second murder (of the homeless man and his dog) that Bateman begins to lose his more comic and marginally sympathetic aspect.[25]

However, this dismissive gender critique is developed in more serious and traditional genre style when Bateman does not act in accordance with audience expectations, for example in the tryst with Christie, the sex-worker he had previously allowed to leave and with Elizabeth. Even the apparently assertive Elizabeth jokingly refutes his sexism, demonstrating just how far his behaviour is from social norms. Nevertheless, she too complies with his requests to engage in the threesome and is subsequently dispatched. At this stage, Harron's film shifts between suggestions of Bateman as the manic killer and the Bateman the narrative eventually leads the audience to question has never actually killed. Initially, we are shown him emerging from under the bed covers with a bloodied mouth as he maims Elizabeth. This is reminiscent of the realism of his previous encounter with Christie, but with the immediate difference of his hyperbolic, manic actions. The camera then appears to suggest the spread of his mania as a number of trick shots convert his large but geographically appropriate apartment into a conspicuously cavernous lair. It becomes nightmarishly repetitive as Christie tries to escape. This style of filming also leads to a level of additional involvement for the audience as it alters their expectations for both the film and the characters. When Bateman is more realistically and indeed more calmly portrayed, it is easier to consider him a representation of the art of social satire. However, in the sections of narrative where his actions do become more overt, the narrative moves closer to the feel of the classic, campy slasher movie and into the territory of self-deprecation and comedy. However, rather than derailing the tension built by the previous seduction scene, this works to prepare the audience's emotional responses for the section's climax. Bateman finally allows Christie to run to the bottom of the apartment's service stairs to escape before dropping his chainsaw on her, killing her. The camera zooms in to magnify the body for twelve seconds. There is a level of conscious hyperbole present in this segment in terms of the presentation of killer as supernatural being that can use superhuman judgement to drop the chainsaw at exactly the right time. Nevertheless however, the image is still shocking. Christie's body and her stillness are thus rendered horribly real particularly against the backdrop of a normal living space rather than an overly ostentatious and illusory area or indeed somewhere set-dressed as dank and degenerate.

It is, finally, the utter normality of the female characters that makes Bateman's character appear truly tragic. This can be seen through his secretary Jean's reaction as she reads the diary that he has covered with childlike but grisly cartoons of murdered women. Regardless of whether the audience interprets the film as suggesting that Bateman is a murderer or simply imagined committing the acts, Jean is shown as ambiguously upset. It is not clear that she thinks he has murdered anyone, for she is not shown contacting the police, but is instead contemplative whilst crying quietly to herself when realising how disturbed she feels he is. It is hinted through the close-up camera shots of his diary that her disquiet may be equally to do with his perception of women and the performance of gender roles as with the depicted violence.[26] This direction and characterisation represents an act of deliberate defiance on the parts of Harron and co-writer Turner, who altered the action from the book in which it is suggested Jean marries Bateman. This alteration, Harron's audio commentary informs the audience, was done because she and Turner felt it more appropriate for Jean as a character who could try and empathise with, yet not condone, the actions and beliefs of the man she loves and yet who is deeply flawed. The significance of this could be argued as placing the female character in a complicit role within the relationship, yet not one in which she wholly sacrifices her morality, instead demonstrating some of the independence of thought Harron demonstrated throughout the film.

Harron's contribution to this notional canon of Canadian women filmmakers has, via her best known work in *American Psycho*, been the repositioning of a misogynistic product to instead represent dialogue on the nature of the otherness that can be encouraged by commercial cultures. Unlike the Soska Sisters, she has not sought to interact with fans in popularist ways, rather writing for highbrow newspapers, and has instead converted salacious topics into consciously intellectual yet entertaining exercises. She may appear to have a comparatively limited filmography, but at the same time her work contains an earnestness that showcases the female filmmaker as a force rather than cultural fancy.

Sarah Polley

Following Harron, in being born to parents involved in the entertainment industry and being known both as a documentary maker and for her work in horror film, is Sarah Polley. Polley directed and was Academy Award-nominated for her screenplay of *Away From Her* and is arguably best known for her work as an actor on films such as *Dawn of the Dead*. While the genres she works in vary, her work on themes frequently found in horror such as otherness, dislocation and loss, feature strongly in her directorial output.

Away From Her is in many ways as clear about the horrific potential of the body as Polley's zombie film, *Dawn of the Dead*. *Away From Her* is an adaptation of Alice Munro's 'The Bear Went Over the Mountain' and focuses on a couple, Grant and Fiona, who must readjust their lives when Fiona is diagnosed with the early-onset of Alzheimer's disease. On a very obvious level, the film focuses on the emotional dislocation caused by the illness. We witness the couple's forty-four year relationship first strain as Fiona's memories and thus sense of personal history appear to be lost, then the way in which their relationship is restructured when she insists on moving to a care home. Within the thirty days' period of no-contact required by the care home, Fiona appears to lose all knowledge of Grant. In the first scene following her admittance, we are guided through the eyes of Grant as he enters the corridors, expensive bouquet in hand, to the institution's common room only to find Fiona sitting with another man and unwilling to leave him. The camera focuses on Fiona's face as she looks at him and thanks him for the flowers politely, yet without the warmth of their previous encounters. The notion that her character does not react in the overjoyed manner expected of her gender only reiterates the notional otherness she symbolises. Her relationship with the other man, in contrast, is nurturing yet robotic as she takes a place alongside this new coping partner as his care-giver and is apparently unaware of any of her former interests, such as reading. In this sense, the film focuses on the idea of personality being eroded to the extent that it appears Fiona's former persona is effectively dead. Polley's direction emphasises the profound cruelty of the illness as a final scene in which Fiona remembers her husband in an embrace is foreshadowed by a scene in which Grant is informed by a nurse that those with Alzheimer's disease may recall their memories, but that this is temporary. It is an ambiguous, bittersweet ending that brings to a close a story which, as Polley has commented in interview 'An Affair to Remember', allowed her creative control. Fiona is now a ghost of her former self, and moreover, a cipher of the horror of the possibility of losing sense of her life within a mere month.[27]

Furthermore, Canada as a space illustrates Polley's vision. Told predominantly through Grant's eyes, the film encapsulates not only the horror of seeing a loved one change, but also more generalised notions of otherness of a loved one changed by choice through circumstance. While Grant is indeed forced to be a voyeur watching as Fiona goes about her business, Fiona evades what Laura Mulvey would term Grant's 'male gaze' by controlling not only where she is but what (as a result) he is forced to see. It is not a particular comment on either of them as they are both complex and not entirely moral characters, but it gives an indication of how her role for him is based on interaction rather than simple physical appreciation. Pivotal shots move between sweeping, snowy landscapes where the couple enjoyed previous happiness to the confines of the regulated treatment centre. It is a setting that threatens to further modify its patients, with death being suggested as the final outcome through the hyperbolic insertion of fantastical filming elements. The common room is a place where the patients socialise and attempt to cling to their identities, and yet in another sequence it is here that they chatter before turning ghostly-transparent and vanish before leaving the room. The same can be said of the corridors. As per their use in horror films from *The Shining* to *Hell's Ground*, they suggest both passage and constriction and are the place in this film where the couple sometimes meet but cannot communicate in their old way. The film even subverts the apparent positive of the amount of natural light the windows allow in by having one scene in which the light envelops the patients as they walk along the corridor with apparent parallels to 'going into the light' and going to Heaven as per Christian belief.[28] The location and Fiona's actions in insisting on going to the medical centre appear to be to their detriment as much as her health.

Happily however, as Polley comments, there is a sturdy basis for the production of more films to be made within Canada, thus she feels enabling other independent artists to remain true to their visions rather than having to comply with the requests of some of the more familiar studios outside of the country. In her *Reverse Shot* interview Polley stated:

> *'Away from Her* is such a Canadian film, and I don't think I know a single American filmmaker who's had that when making their first film. I had the final cut on my first film. [...] You can't do that when a film's made by a committee and you have people breathing down your neck. [...] It was so coddled and idyllic making the film in the Canadian system.
>
> As much as they like to flirt with the idea of making commercial films, it's like a cultural mandate, it's about the artists and it's not yet totally driven by profit. And because nobody's losing a lot of private money, you're dealing with bureaucrats – they get creatively involved

for sure, but there's nothing prescriptive. You have to deal with them but you don't ever feel like you're going to get kicked out of the editing room.'[29]

In support of Polley's statement, organisations such as the Canada Feature Film Fund not only offer programmes to facilitate the learning and development of filmmakers, but also provide funding for ventures. Tax relief is also available, offering rebates for costs incurred during the production process. It must, however, be noted that Polley hails from a family involved in the broadcast and entertainment industry and perhaps this knowledge facilitated her use of this government support with minimal interference. Such a query is particularly pertinent considering that Polley's view of Canadian film financing is not unanimous. Sylvia Soska has commented that:

> 'There's a joke in Canada, that our government only aids films that no one would ever want to see, and in a way, it's true. You have phenomenal filmmakers like David Cronenberg – who didn't always have that much support – we have Jason Eisener, Astron 6, Maude Michaud, Patricia Chica, Jovanka Vuckovic, and Brandon Cronenberg – all brilliant filmmakers but because they make odd mistyped as genre films, they don't get the proper respect […] I think because we live so close to the boarder [sic], that we are pre-occupied with being a service country for American productions [to use our resources] rather than focusing on building our own self-sustaining filmmaking, Canadian teams making Canadian films with our voices that don't reflect stereotypical Canada.'[30]

As a result of these filmmakers' reflections on the financial and cultural relationship between a notional Canadian sensibility and an American one, what appears to be reflected here is the contrast between a pressure to cater for a mass market, yet as a direct result of this relationship assuming a more contemplative approach. The latter probably feels more apparent and overtly countercultural as a result of its inquisitive investigation of social norms. Indeed, Sylvia Soska has commented that '…strangeness is a cool Canadian trait that I wish we celebrated more.'[31] However, perhaps the individuality that recognises and celebrates itself risks losing the essence, rather than the expectation, of that very quality. It may well be something of this that affects these filmmakers' sensibility and leads them towards the themes of horror cinema. They interrogate themes of otherness that are at once united by the idea of abstract abjection and at the same time are altered by their own and their characters' experiences of objective cultural abjection, rather than simply allowing the violence of theme or visual imagery to objectify their tales.

At the time of writing it has recently been announced that the Soska Sisters will work with Harron, fellow Canadian Jovanka Vuckovic (*The Captured Bird*) and other female directors on a new horror anthology film entitled *XX* which, as the title's reference to the female chromosome suggests, will feature female leads. They will also contribute a segment to the forthcoming men and women-led anthology feature *The ABCs of Death 2*. This represents a mixture of the media-savvy and more traditional product driven approaches to horror and offers the possibility of representing the differing experiences of women in a manner that has the potential to move beyond the tokenism with which gender has sometimes been approached. It is a credit to Polley that when the much-anticipated Oscar nomination for her documentary, *Stories We Tell* did not materialise in January 2014 that she took to Twitter to congratulate a filmmaker who was nominated and made specific reference to the qualities of that film, *The Act of Killing*. While this was no doubt first and foremost a supportive gesture, it also repudiated any suggestion that Polley would wish to be judged on anything other than the standard of her work.[32]

Academics write about women in horror and the film industry while distributors produce products that they know will in turn be analysed. Many festivals are now capitalising on women in film as a brand in itself, but all too often this transforms into the representation of appropriately behaving and 'looking' women only – it is common, for example to find interviews with Polley that place the initial emphasis on her good looks equally or in addition to her work. This can constrain genre film by encouraging only similar product. This similar product appears at the moment to be overly self-aware treatments of gender roles. It does not feel as though we are yet at the stage where women have the cultural capital to move beyond discussions of gender equality in their filmmaking, particularly within the horror genre precisely because of its cultural heritage. It is a genre that at once celebrates and constricts women, with features such as *American Mary* positioned by the filmmakers as exceptions to the rule despite this interpretation being contested by academics and film fans alike.

That said, Harron, the Soska Sisters and Polley additionally sought to look at other, more mundane horrors through their films – the psychologically damaging effects of conspicuous consumption in the case of Harron, the transformation caused by time for Polley and transformation into, and definitions of, otherness for the Soska Sisters. We should wonder whether we should aspire to celebrate the notionally embattled feminine state or try to escape it as our notions of femininity are inextricably linked to past inequality and difference. We must hope these directors continue to develop and that their projects will have a lasting impression not only on perceptions of women's ability to steer film projects from behind the camera, but also to open the door for more directors from diverse different backgrounds such as the nationality-based ones that have been discussed here. After all, a woman is more than her 'look'.

Author biography

Dr Karen Oughton lectures in Media Communications at Regent's University London. Specialising in film studies, Oughton contributed to *Intensities: The Journal of Cult Media* and has presented papers at conferences including Cine-Excess and for IAFOR. She is currently preparing research on the depiction of gender in the characters of Robert Downey Jr. and on representations of serial killers in film. Oughton is also a broadcaster and film journalist and has contributed commentary packages to home distributors including Lionsgate and articles to publications including *Sight & Sound, Little White Lies* and *Ain't It Cool News*. She has also served on England's judging panel for the Melies D'Argent award amongst other film industry duties.

Contact: karen@karenoughton.co.uk

Endnotes

1. I am not arguing that either these directors or their onscreen outputs are the first depictions of feminism or their chosen theme types. Instead, I hope to suggest how their work attempts to reshape the way women are seen both on and off-camera and how they are perceived by the industry.

2. Interview with the author August 27th 2012.

3. Email interview with the author August 30th 2012.

4. The Soska Sisters screened *Dead Hooker in a Trunk* for their college cohort. That half of the audience walked out and half cheered has become the stuff of genre legend.

5. The Soska Sisters have stated that they did not record introductions for film screenings prior to *American Mary*. However, email correspondence with Gaz Bailey, Festival Director at the Abertoir Horror Festival on February 14th 2014 has confirmed that a brief video featuring the Soska Sisters was indeed played before the *Dead Hooker in a Trunk* screening.

6. The Soska Sisters have stated that they aimed to show scenes without the masturbatory aspect associated with horror and based *Dead Hooker in a Trunk* partly on the case of Canadian serial killer, Robert Pickton. See Rachel Fox's interview in *Canadian Gothic* for further information.

7. Quoted in David Sanjek's 'Fans' Notes: The Horror Film Fanzine', p. 151.

8. Vampira was the first famous female horror host played by Maila Nurmi on television in the 1950s. Vampira was a voluptuous, vampire-like woman inspired by comic book characters. Other character-based horror hostesses have included Elvira: Mistress of the Dark and Bunny Galore.

9. They sent the film to several genre directors which led directly to Eli Roth supporting them, something they discussed in festival Q&A sessions to their audiences' delight.

10. It is not possible to verify a precise historical record of these relatively recent events as some information has since been removed

from, or altered on, a number of the original web pages and resources. While supportive of this chapter, the Soska Sisters declined to be interviewed for this specific project or to read the piece prior to publication.

11. Interview with the author and Adam Stephen Kelly, August 27th 2012.

12. The film was acquired (with personal recommendation) for the festival by Michael Hewitt for Universal Pictures. Hewitt is a regular and friendly face on the horror film scene for industry staff and fans alike.

13. Interview with the author and Adam Stephen Kelly as above.

14. Email interview with the author, January 31st 2014.

15. Interview with the author and Adam Stephen Kelly as above.

16. Considering horror film creation as an industry rather than being a fan is viewed in a most negative light within some quarters of the community. This can be seen from the treatment of Lianne 'Spiderbaby' MacDougall, a former journalist, author, actress and award-winning blogger who was found to have plagiarised others' work. MacDougall used her image as part of her marketing just as the Soska Sisters have and was accused by commentators Annie Riordan and Keri O'Shea on influential horror website *BrutalasHell. com* of using the genre as '…something you have to get through to earn your stripes, move into the big time of being a Personality.' The underlying assumption or accusation was that because MacDougall had lied about the origins of some of her written work, she had also faked her entire interest in the genre and did not, therefore, deserve to work within the sector or enjoy its communities' support. MacDougall's treatment here in light of an assumed lack of integrity may be the reason that the Soska Sisters do not publicly discuss their acting and directing work on features such as *ReGOREgitated Sacrifice* as its erotic and arguably misogynistic content is in direct contrast to their more famous, feminist output.

17. In 'Fans' Notes: The Horror Film Fanzine,' p. 151.

18. Ibid.

19. Ibid.

20. Ibid, Sanjek quoting Chute.

21. Interview with the author and Adam Stephen Kelly as above.

22. Co-screenwriter Guinevere Turner initially attracted attention for her involvement with lesbian film *Go Fish!*

23. Harron's parents also worked within the entertainment industry. Her father was actor Don Harron and her first stepmother, Virginia Leith, is most famous for playing the decapitated women in B movie *The Brain That Wouldn't Die*.

24. As has been stated in Brian Johnson's article on the film in *Maclean's* (2000).

25. It is notable that in her audio commentary Harron's personal politics are obvious as she describes the murder as Bateman victimising 'a poor homeless man' with obvious emotion in her voice rather than using other descriptors such as 'vagrant'. To consider how this scene could otherwise have been played, one has only to compare the style of dialogue with that of the sequence in Stanley Kubrick's *A Clockwork Orange* in which Alex and the Droogs attack an alcoholic.

26. It is a theme Harron would explore again particularly in *The Notorious Bettie Page* in which men and women played with the notion of submission and domination on which patriarchal society is based.

27. An alternate reading of the narrative directly suggested by Grant's lines is that Fiona could be faking her illness as revenge for various extra marital affairs he had had over the years. Ibid.

28. This notional loss of self is also addressed in Polley's latter work on her documentary, *Stories We Tell*. A study of identity, the film focuses on her attempt to understand her relationship with her family following the death of her mother and the realisation of her disputed parentage.

29. See *Reverse Shot*'s 'Interview with Sarah Polley'.

30. Email interview with the author on January 27th 2014.

31. Ibid.

32. It should be noted that Polley's Twitter account has since been deleted with no information available as to why this is the case. She has not responded to requests for interview.

References

'American Mary.' Interview by Karen Oughton and Adam Stephen Kelly. *Ain't It Cool News*, n.p., August 27th 2012. Online April 15th 2013.

American Mary (2012). Dir. Jen and Sylvia Soska. Perf. Katharine Isabelle. Twisted Twins Productions. (Film)

American Psycho (2005). Dir. Mary Harron. Perf. Christian Bale and Justin Theroux. Lions Gate. (DVD)

Away From Her (2006). Dir. Sarah Polley. Perf. Julie Christie and Michael Murphy. Foundry Films. (Film)

Bizarre magazine. Dennis Publishing, London. Issue 180 onwards.

Clover, Carol (1992). *On Men, Women and Chainsaws: Gender and the Modern Horror Film*, Princeton University Press, Princeton. (Print)

Dawn of the Dead (2004). Dir. Zack Snyder. Perf. Sarah Polley. Strike Entertainment. (Film)

Dead Hooker In A Trunk (2009). Dir. Jen Soska and Sylvia Soska. Perf. Jen Soska and Sylvia Soska. Twisted Twins Productions. (Film)

Driller Killer (1979). Dir. Abel Ferrera. Perf. Abel Ferrera. Navaron Films. (Film)

Ellis, Bret Easton (1997). *American Psycho*. Norstedts: Pan. (Print)

'Extra,' Interview: Katharine Isabelle, Jen and Sylvia Soska on *American Mary*. This is Fake DIY, n.p., n.d. http://www.thisisfakediy.co.uk/mobile/articles/film/interview-katharine-isabelle-jen-sylvia-soska-on-american-mary/

Fox, Rachel. 'Canadian Gothic: Jen and Sylvia Soska's Scary-Fast Industry Ascent.' *Bitch Magazine: Feminist Response to Pop Culture* Winter 13.57 (n.d.): 65–67. (Print)

Go Fish! (1994). Dir. Rose Troche. Perf. Guinevere Turner. Can I Watch. (Film)

Halloween (1978). Dir. John Carpenter. Perf. Donald Pleasance and Jamie Lee Curtis. Compass International. (Film)

Harron, Mary (April 9th 2000). 'The Risky Territory of American Psycho.' *The New York Times* April 9th 2000: 13. (Print)

Hell's Ground (2007). Dir. Omar Khan. Perf. Kunwar Ali Roshan. Bubonic Films. (Film)

Hernandez, Eugene. 'PARK CITY 2000 BUZZ: "American Psycho" NC-17; Next Wave Nabs Sundance Doc.' *Indiewire.com* (http://www.indiewire.com/article/park_city_2000_buzz_american_psycho_nc-17_next_wave_nabs_sundance_doc accessed 10th February 2014)

I Shot Andy Warhol (1995). Dir. Mary Harron. By Mary Harron. Perf. Lili Taylor and Jared Harris. Samuel Goldwyn Co. (Film)

I Spit on Your Grave (1978). Dir. Mier Zarchi. Perf. Camille Keaton. Cinemagic Pictures. (Film)

Johnson, Brian D. 'Canadian Cool Meets American Psycho'.

Maclean's, 00249262, October 4th 2000, Vol. 113, Issue 15.

Koresky, Michael. 'An Affair to Remember: An interview with Sarah Polley'. *Reverse Shot, n.*p., n.d. Issue 20. (Web)

Mulvey, L. (1975). 'Visual Pleasure and Narrative Cinema'. *Screen.* 16 (3): 6–18

Maniac (1980). Dir. William Lustig. Perf. Joe Spinell. Magnum Motion Pictures. (Film)

Munro, Alice. 'The bear came over the mountain'. *The New Yorker.* (http://www.newyorker.com/fiction/features/2013/10/21/131021fi_fiction_munro?currentPage=all accessed February 10th 2014)

Nosferatu (2002). Dir. F. W. Murnau. Perf. Max Schreck. Thunderbird Films. (DVD)

Pervirella (1997). Dir. Alex Chandon and Josh Collins. Perf. Emily Booth. Exotic Entertainment Productions. (Videocassette)

Psycho (2006). Dir. Alfred Hitchcock. Perf. Anthony Perkins and Vera Miles. Shamley Productions. (DVD)

ReGOREgitated Sacrifice (2008). Dir. Lucifer Valentine. Perf. Ameara Lavey. Kingdom of Hell Productions. (DVD)

Riordan, Annie and O'Shea, Keri. 'Demonic Douche vs. Horror Plagiarism'. *BrutalasHell.com* (http://www.brutalashell.com/2013/07/demonic-douche-vs-horror-plagiarism/ accessed February 10th 2014)

Rogers, Martin. 'Video Nasties and the Monstrous Bodies of American Psycho.' *Literature Film Quarterly* (n.d.): 231–44. (Print)

Sanjek, David. 'Fans' Notes: The Horror Film Fanzine.' *Literature/Film Quarterly*, Vol. 18, No. 3: 150–59. (Print)

See No Evil 2 (2014). Dir. Jen Soska and Sylvia Soska. Perf. Glenn Jacobs and Danielle Harris. Lions Gate and WWE Studios (Film)

Stories We Tell (2012). Dir. Sarah Polley. Perf. Michael Polley. National Film Board of Canada. (Film)

The Notorious Bettie Page (2005). Dir. Mary Harron. Perf. Gretchen Mol and Christopher Bauer. HBO Films, Killer Films and John Wells Productions. (Film)

The Shining (1980). Dir. Stanley Kubrick. Perf. Jack Nicholson. Warner Bros. (Film)

Women in Horror Recognition month. (http://womeninhorrormonth.com/ accessed February 9th 2014)

4. Female Filmmakers in Latin America:

Unsung pioneers, fierce explorers

Ana Maria Bahiana

Social, cultural and political conditions conspire to make the path of female Latin American filmmakers extraordinarily difficult. The prevailing *machismo* cuts across borders, languages and cultures to ensure that women remain second class citizens. As late as the Second World War, only four Latin American countries had granted their women the right to vote: Ecuador in 1929, Brazil in 1932, Uruguay in 1932 and Cuba in 1937.[1] Religion – predominantly Catholic, mostly conservative – reinforces the message. Add unstable political regimes, a penchant for military dictatorship, widespread poverty, lack of social services and health care – five of the seven countries that wholly ban abortion in all instances are in Latin America: Chile, Nicaragua, El Salvador, Honduras and the Dominican Republic[2] – and there it is: a perfect storm in the way of women's creativity in any field.

And yet… there they are, from the very beginning: directors, producers, documentarians. Many of these pioneers of the silent era were performers who, like their American counterparts Mary Pickford, Lois Weber and Dorothy Davenport Reid, found the work *behind* the camera, as directors and/or producers, more fulfilling and expressive. Such is the case of Brazilian pioneers Carmen Santos and Gilda de Abreu, major stars of the silent era who branched out as directors and producers in the 1930s.

A fourteen-year-old Portuguese immigrant working as a sales clerk in a Rio de Janeiro department store in 1919, Maria do

CELLULOID CEILING

Carmo Santos decided, on a whim, to try her luck at an open audition for a role on the moving picture *Urutau*, produced and directed by the American William Jensen. To her own surprise, she got the part, changed her name to Carmen Santos and quickly built up a career in the movies – an ironic turn of events for a young woman so poor she had never seen any pictures before going to the premiere of her own *Urutau*.

Santos worked as an actor with some the most important directors of early Brazilian cinema, like Humberto Mauro, Mario Peixoto (she is the female lead in Peixoto's iconic unfinished masterpiece *Limite* (*Limit*)) and Adhemar Gonzaga. Marriage, the birth of her two children and a desire to expand her career led Santos to explore developing and producing pictures, eventually leading to the creation, in partnership with Humberto Mauro, of her own production company, Vox Filmes. Besides the silent short *A Carne* (*Flesh*) from 1923, Santos directed several pictures for Vox – all of which were destroyed in a fire that razed the studios in the 1940s. Her only surviving title is the historical drama *Inconfidência Mineira* (*The Minas revolt*), 1948.

This pattern from actor to filmmaker in the silent and early cinema era can be found throughout Latin America – again in Brazil with Cléo de Verberena (*O mistério do dominó negro/The mystery of the black domino*, 1931); in Mexico with Mimí Derba, Candida Beltrán Rendón (*El secreto de la abuela/Grandmother's secret*, 1928) and Elena Sánchez Valenzuela (the documentary *Michoacán*, 1936); in Chile with Gabriela von Bussenius Vega (*La agonía del Arauco/The agony of Arauco,* co-directed with Salvador Giambastiani, 1917) and in Argentina with Emilia Saleny (*Niña del bosque/The girl from the woods*, 1917; *Clarita*, 1919) and Maria Celestini (*Mi derecho/My right*, 1920).

Many of these pioneers also wrote, produced and financed their own pictures. Mimi Derba – born Hermínia Pérez de Leon – was a major star of film and stage when she founded the Azteca Film Company in 1917. In its short one-year life Azteca produced and released five pictures, all starring Derba. Two were also written by her and one – *La tigresa/The tigress* – was directed by Derba, making her the first female director in Latin America.

Mexican sisters Adriana and Dolores Ehlers were the exception to the actor-director pattern in early Latin American cinema. Born in a family of modest means, the sisters lost their father early in life and grew up in the port city of Veracruz, where their mother supported the family by working as a midwife. Adriana and Dolores worked in a photography studio in their youth, and soon set up their own business and won a grant to study photography in Boston. When their grant expired the sisters obtained an extension to study cinematography, and went on to an internship at Universal Pictures Company, in Jacksonville, New Jersey. Back in Mexico in 1919, the Ehlers opened their own equipment company – Casa Ehlers – and produced and directed several documentaries and newsreels. One documentary, commissioned by the International Petroleum Company, was exhibited in the United States in 1922.

The last example of this first phase of women moving from acting to working behind the camera is Brazilian Gilda de Abreu. The daughter of an opera singer and a Brazilian diplomat stationed in France, Gilda de Abreu was born in Paris in 1904 and, by the early 1930s was a star of the stage in Brazil. Her debut on screen in 1936, *Bonequinha de Seda* (*Satin Doll*), directed by the renowned pioneer Adhemar Gonzaga made Abreu an instant star. Ten years later, unhappy with the roles available, Abreu began developing, producing and directing her own material. In 1946 her neo-realist drama *O Ébrio* (*The Drunk*), starring Abreu's then husband, the singer Vicente Celestino, was an enormous success and still remains one of the landmarks of Brazilian cinema today.

Abreu would go on to direct three additional pictures, the melodramas *Pinguinho de gente* (*The little one*, 1949) and *Coração materno* (*A mother's heart*, 1951) and the biopic *Chico Viola não morreu* (*Chico Viola is alive*, 1955) about singer Francisco Alves, a star of the radio era in Brazil.

Television arrived late in Latin America, rolling out in the 1950s, in many instances – Argentina, Colombia, Bolivia – as a governmental, almost always dictatorial, initiative. If in the US the film industry found ways to absorb the shock of the new medium and actually profit from it by adding television programming to its output, in Latin America the impact was brutal. In many ways the region's cinema production never fully recovered – television is, to this day, the dominant platform for audiovisual content in Latin America, untouched even by the expansion of new digital media in this century.

After a prolific and commercially successful period in the 1950s, the 1960s saw a retraction of film output that would be further impacted by political instability and the rise of a fresh batch of right-wing dictatorships throughout the region. Female presence in the period is small if compared with the early years, but notable.

In Venezuela, Margot Benacerraf's two documentaries, *Reverón* – focused on Venezuelan painter Armando Reverón – and *Araya* – about the harsh lives of salt mine workers – are landmarks of Latin America narrative non-fiction. *Araya* received the International Critics' award at the 1959 Cannes Film Festival, *ex-aequo* with Alain Resnais' *Hiroshima Mon Amour*.

Working with partner Jorge Silva until his death in 1987 and on her own after that, Colombian Marta Rodríguez directed fifteen documentaries depicting the lives and issues of workers, peasants and indigenous populations, with Chircales, about the living conditions of a family of brickmakers.

In post-revolutionary Cuba, Sara Gómez, an alumna of the newborn ICAIC – Cuban Institute of Motion Pictures Arts and Industry, founded in 1959 – wrote and directed nineteen documentaries on a variety of subjects. In Mexico, Matilde Landeta rose through the ranks of the thriving, male-dominated industry from script girl to screenwriter to director of short features (110 of them) and finally became the director of three features – *Lola Casanova* (1949), *La negra Angustias* (1950) and *Trotacalles (Streetwalkers,* 1951)[3]. Landeta was also to become one of the most important figures of the so-called Golden Age of Mexican cinema (1950–1954) when '*hecho en Mexico*' titles dominated the Spanish-speaking markets in Latin America. 'I used the only weapon at my disposal: my absolute knowledge of technique', Landeta said in an 1948 interview,[4] describing her journey in a difficult and sometimes hostile environment.

These pioneer women lay the foundation for a veritable boom of female directors that followed in the 1970s and 1980s throughout the region. In countries like Brazil, Argentina and Chile, which had extremely repressive military regimes, we also find extraordinary antagonists to all manner of cultural expression. Interestingly enough, women directors flourished at the time, finding creative ways to tell stories and bring attention to social and political issues in ways that had eluded their male counterparts.

Maria Luisa Bemberg in Argentina; Ana Carolina, Teresa Trautman, Suzana Amaral, Tizuka Yamazaki and Helena Solberg in Brazil; Valeria Sarmiento in Chile; Solveig Hoogesteijn in Venezuela; and Lourdes Portillo in Mexico are some of the key figures of this remarkable wave of women filmmakers. In *Camila* (1984) Bemberg works with an episode from the past – the persecution and execution of a priest and his lover in 19th century Argentina – Bemberg explored the terror of an autocratic state that had ruled the country for the past eight years (*Camila* was nominated in the foreign film category of the 1985 Academy Awards).

Ana Carolina's *Mar de Rosas* (*Sea of Roses*, 1978) takes a different route – pitch dark surreal humor – in eviscerating the concepts of 'tradition, family, property' deeply-rooted in the conservative Brazilian society of the time. Hoogestein uses the metaphors of magical realism in her *El mar del tiempo perdido* (*The sea of lost time*, 1980) to deal with poverty and social disenfranchisement. Sarmiento (living in Paris) and Portillo (living in California) opted for the documentary – Portillo's 1988 *Las Madres: The Mothers of Plaza de Mayo*, nominated for an Academy Award, brought to the attention of American audiences the plight of the generation of the 'disappeared' during Augusto Pinochet's brutal dictatorship.

Trautman's *Os homens que eu tive* (*The men I had*, 1973) was such a bold, unfettered look at woman's sexuality that it was banned from Brazilian screens for over a decade. Trautman said.

> 'The dictatorship had forbidden me to discuss the social realities of my country, but there was private matter that was also social that I wanted to discuss – the feminine condition.'[5]

Other important films of this wave of filmmakers include Yamazaki's *Gaijin*, a drama set against the early years of Japanese immigration to Brazil that touches upon the notions of nationality and integration; Amaral's *A hora da estrela* (*The hour of the star*, 1986) about a working-class woman and her dreams of becoming a radio star in the 1940s; and Solberg's Emmy-winning documentary *From the ashes... Nicaragua today* (1982).

The progressive democratisation of Latin America and gradual economic stability in the mid to late 1980s and early 1990s led to a surge of cultural production throughout the territory. The continued work of the 1970s pioneers, and the emergence of a new generation of filmmakers influenced by them, inspired a diverse and ever evolving body of work that, from Cuba to Chile, Ecuador to Brazil, has been mapping the lives and experiences of women and men in contemporary Latin America.

Key women of the current wave of Latin American directors are Colombia's Camila Loboguerrero, Mexico's Maria Novaro, Argentina's Lucrecia Martel and Brazil's Lucia Murat.

Camila Loboguerrero

The first woman to direct a feature film in Colombia, Loboguerrero faced tremendous odds to bring her first full-length project, *Con su música en otra parte* (*With her music elsewhere*) in 1983. She said in 2002:

> 'I would get on set knowing that I could not have a moment of hesitation, not even having the whole project mapped out on paper, because the moment I had even the glimmer of a second thought there would be a man popping up out of nowhere to say: "The camera goes here, because we have to tell those women how things are done'.[6]

The picture went on to win two acting awards at the Bogota Film Festival of 1984, and Loboguerrero went onto a fully-fledged career including documentaries and features.

Maria Novaro

Novaro's *Danzón* (1991), her third full-length project, had a substantial life beyond Mexico's borders, receiving best foreign language picture nominations at the Chicago Film Festival and for the Independent Spirit Awards, and winning five ACE[7] awards in Argentina. A sort of Mexican '*Strictly Ballroom*', *Danzón* follows a woman on a road trip from Mexico City to Veracruz and back in search of her missing dance partner, in a tone that mixes telenovela melodrama with sharp humour. The picture was crucial in presenting Mexico's *nuevo cinema* to the world and introducing a new generation of Mexican filmmakers with film-school credentials (Novaro herself is a graduate of the Centro Universitario de Estudios Cenmátograficos of the University of Mexico, UNAM).

Lucrecia Martel

Another film-school graduate – with a degree from Buenos Aires' National Experimental Filmmaking School – Martel did for the 'new Argentine cinema' what Novaro had done for Mexico. After four award-winning shorts, Martel's script for *La Ciénaga* (*The Swamp*), a scalding look into an upper-middle class Argentinian family, won the NHK award at Sundance in 1999; the picture went on to win several awards – the Alfred Bauer prize at the Berlin Film Festival, four ACES, four awards at the Havana Film Festival and receive nominations as diverse as Berlin's for the Golden Bear and MTV Latin America's for 'favorite film'.

Her following pictures, 2004's *La niña santa* (*The holy girl*) and 2007's *La mujer sin cabeza* (*The headless woman*) firmly established Martel as one of cinema's most original voices, collecting awards and critical accolades. As Kevin Thomas wrote in the *Los Angeles Times*:[8]

> '(She's) a subtle artist and a sharp observer, and manages a large cast with the ease that matches her skill at storytelling, within which psychological insight and social comment flow easily and implicitly.'

In spite of her studies, Martel considers herself an autodidact who started out intuitively filming nearby subjects – family and friends during her formative years – and gained little from the National Experimental Filmmaking School. 'I watched movies, I read books, I wrote. I was a free mind, because I had to be,' Martel told the *Telegraph*.[9]

Lucia Murat

Murat's very life is a capsule of the social and political transformation of the continent. In the 1970s, she was arrested, imprisoned and tortured for her political activism. In 1989, four years after civil rule and a fully democratic regime had been installed in Brazil, Murat released *Que bom te ver viva* (*How nice to see you alive*), her second full-length project[10] and the first to contain both elements of fiction and of her own experience as a political prisoner. *Que bom…* won all the Brazilian awards that year, a testament to its importance as an important reference piece in a moment of change.

The Retomada (restart) movement that marked Brazil's return to steady production starts, in many ways with Murat and her determination to shed light onto the years of darkness, persecution and silence that had nearly paralysed the country's cultural life. Her biggest commercial and critical success, the crime thriller *Como dois irmãos* (*Almost brothers*, 2004) once again bridges the gap between past and present, tracking the deep but uneasy friendship between a political prisoner and a common criminal, from their years in jail to the different and parallel lives they live in the post-dictatorship Brazil.

Contemporary Latin America has seen a steady influx of women directors throughout the region. Here's a brief (and far from definitive) list of filmmakers in action today:

Argentina

Mercedes Maria Guevara

Buenos Aires native Guevara became widely known in 2005 with her documentary *Tango, un giro extraño* (*Tango, a strange twist*), a chronicle of the transformations of Argentina's national rhythm in the hands of contemporary musicians. Her other works are the features *Rio escondido* (*Hidden river* 1999) and *Silencios* (*Silences* 2009).

THE AMERICAS

Lucia Puenzo

The daughter of acclaimed filmmaker Luis Puenzo (*The official story*, *Old Gringo*), Puenzo's first film, *XXY* (2007), a delicate drama about an intersexed fifteen-year-old (in a society that prizes clearly defined gender roles) won several awards, including the Grand Prize of Cannes' Critics Week. She followed up with similar accolades for *El niño pez* (*The fish child*, 2009) and *Wakolda* (*The German doctor*), a selection of the 2013 Un Certain Regard sidebar in Cannes and winner of ten awards from the Academy of Arts and Sciences of Argentina.

Brazil

Kátia Lund

Cidade de Deus (*City of God*, 2002), which Lund co-directed with Fernando Meirelles, put her on the map. Long before that, however, this Brown University alumna, born in São Paulo to American parents, had already made a name for herself with the acclaimed documentary *Notícias de uma guerra particular* (*News from a private war*, 1999) which brought to the surface the long-boiling conflict between a corrupt police force and the drug gangs that rule Rio de Janeiro's slums. Lund went on to direct several episodes for the TV series including *Cidade dos homens* (*City of men*), *Brava Gente* (*Valiant people*) and *Caminhos* (*Roads*). Lund oversees the non-profit organisation *Nós do cinema* (*We of cinema*), which trains young slum dwellers in the technical and artistic moviemaking crafts.

Carla Camurati

After a decade as sought-after TV, stage and film actress, Camurati branched out into directing in 1995 with *Carlota Joaquina – Princesa do Brasil* (*Carlota Joaquina – A Brazilian princess*). The period piece quickly became one of the biggest commercial successes of the 'retomada', paving the way to a string of box office hits: *La serva padrona* (1999), *Copacabana* (2001) and *Irma Vap – O Retorno* (*The return of Irma Vap*, 2006).

Laís Bodanzky

Daughter of cinema novo director Jorge Bodanzky, Laís started her career with the short *Cartão Vermelho* (*Red card*, 1994). Her breaktrough picture was *Bicho de sete cabeças* (*Brainstorm,* 2001), a powerful drama about a middle class young man confined to a mental institution that launched the career of Rodrigo Santoro and won all of Brazil's awards in 2002. Her most recent films were *Chega de saudade* (*No more nostalgia,* 2007), a romance drama set in 1950s Rio de Janeiro, and *As melhores coisas do mundo* (*The best things in the world,* 2010), a family drama that, once again, cleaned up all the Brazilian awards.

Tata Amaral

With fourteen films to her name and a long list of accolades and awards, São Paulo-born Amaral is one the most important filmmakers of the Brazilian retomada. Her first feature film, *Um céu de estrelas* (*A starry sky,* 1996) was chosen by local critics as one of the most significant movies of the 1990s. Her most recent work is the drama *Trago comigo* (*What I bring with me*), about a theatre professor who stages an improvised play to try to remember the years he spent in prison during the dictatorship.

Eliane Caffé

The power of myths and the human longing for storytelling are at the heart of Caffés's filmography and betray her first calling – Caffé's first degree, from São Paulo's Catholic University, was in psychology. Film came later, with studies in Cuba's Los Baños and Madrid's Instituto de Estética. Her first picture, *Kenoma* (1998) dealt with a craftsman obsessed with the idea of building his own perpetual-motion machine. The multi-award winner *Narradores de Javé* (*The storytellers,* 2005) is an *Arabian Nights*-like story within a story, with a group of villagers intent on keeping their heritage alive by telling tales about it. Caffé's most recent work is *Sol do meio dia* (*Midday sun,* 2009) winner of the Mostra São Paulo Festival.

Chile

Vivienne Barry

An animator with a passion for stop motion, Barry studied in Dresden, Germany, and worked as a teacher and journalist before dedicating her time fully to animation. She directed five stop-motion shorts between 2001 and 2005, including *Como alitas de chincol* (*Like the wings of a sparrow*, 2002), winner of the Biarritz and Havana film festivals.

Tatiana Gaviola

Daughter of Chilean author Hugo Gaviola, Tatiana started out as a documentarian, with pictures about the mapuche indigenous people (*Nguillatun* 1981) and the resistance to Pinochet's dictatorship *Tiempo de un líder* (*Time for a leader*, 1982). After a stint directing for television, Gaviola directed her first feature, *Mi último hombre* (*My last man*, 1996), working from a script by acclaimed writer Jorge Durán (*Pixote, How angels are born*). Her most recent piece is *Teresa, crucificada por amar* (*Teresa, crucified for loving*, 2009).

Alicia Scherson

After a couple of years as a biology student in Chile, Scherson decided that film was her calling. Graduating from Cuba's Los Baños. She won a Fulbright scholarship for an MFA in New York. In 2003, back in Chole, she wrote and directed her first feature, the psychodrama *Play* (2005), which debuted at the Tribeca Film Festival and won the award for best direction/first picture. Her latest work is the psychological thriller *El futuro* (*The future*, 2013).

Colombia

Patricia Cardoso

Born and raised in Colombia, the daughter of architects, Cardoso studied archaeology before receiving a Fulbright scholarship (the first in Colombia) to study film at UCLA. She directed four shorts (one of them, *The Water Carrier*, 1996, won two Directors Guild awards and one Student Academy Award) before her award-winning feature length film, *Real Women Have Curves* (2002). An audience and grand jury awardee in Sundance, *Real Women* introduced America Ferrera in a breakout performance. Cardoso's most recent work has been on TV, in the telefilms *Lies in Plain Sight* (2010) and *Meddling Mom* (2013) and the series *Ro* (2012).

Dominican Republic

Leticia Tonos

The same algorithm points to Leticia Tonos' *La hija natural* (*The love child*, 2011) as the best picture from the Dominican Republic. The story of a girl in search of a father she never knew, *La hija* is Tonos' first film as director, after many years as a film, TV and commercial producer. A graduate of the London Film School, Tonos heads her own production company, Linea Espiral, and has produced the biggest commercial success in the country, *Perico Ripiao*, directed by Angel Muñiz.

Ecuador

Tania Hermida

A graduate of the International Film and Television School of San Antonio de los Baños, Cuba, Ermida worked as assistant director in the Colombian-set *Maria Full of Grace* (2004) before venturing out on her own with the road movie *Qué tan lejos* (*How much further*, 2006), winner of several 'first picture' awards, including Havana and Montreal. Hermida's second feature is the coming of age drama *En el nombre de la hija* (*In the name of the daughter*, 2011).

Mexico

Guita Schyfter

Like Brazil's Eliane Caffé, Schyfter's first calling was psychology. Born in Costa Rica but living in Mexico since 1965, Schyfter discovered the audiovisual arts after graduating in psychology at the University of Mexico. She studied film and television production in London, working as an intern at the BBC. Back in Mexico in 1987 she launched her career as a director on television and documentaries . Her first feature, *Novia que te vea* (*Like a bride*, 1994), about coming of age as a Jewish woman in the 1960s in Mexico City was a critical and commercial success in Mexico. Her most recent work is the documentary *Los laberintos de la memoria* (*The labyrinths of memory*, 2007) about two women in search of their cultural identity.

Marisa Sistach

A graduate of Mexico's illustrious CCC – Centro de Capacitacion Cinematográfica – a key element in Mexico's nuevo cinema, Sistach started out directing for TV before trying a hand at feature films. Her first feature project, *Los pasos de Ana* (*Ana's steps*, 1988) about a woman who decides to film her own life, was accepted into the Berlin Film Festival. Her filmography includes seven other titles, including the multi-award winning *Nadie te oye: perfume de violetas* (*Violet perfume: no one is listening*, 2001) and 2011's *Lluvia de Luna* (*Moon rain*).

Paraguay

Tana Schémbori

According to IMDB's algorithm, *Siete cajas* (*Seven boxes*, 2012) is the best film to come out of Paraguay – a feat confirmed by a slew of awards and nominations, from the Spanish Goyas to Toronto's Discovery Award. The tale of a young messenger tasked with delivering the seven boxes of the title during a steamy hot night in Asunción, Siete cajas, co-directed with Juan Carlos Maneglia, is Schémbori's first feature film, after several successful mini-series and telefilms.

Peru

Claudia Llosa

A searing exploration of what it means to be a woman, a mother and a daughter in a culture of tyranny and fear, *La teta asustada* (*The milk of sorrow*, 2010) cut a wide path through festivals and awards: two awards in Berlin, including the Golden Bear; victories in Gramado, Brazil; Lima, Peru; Montreal, Canada; Guadalajara, Mexico; Bogota, Colombia; Havana, Cuba; and a nomination in the foreign film category in the Oscars. A niece of writer Mario Vargas Llosa, Claudia currently lives in Barcelona, Spain, and is a member of the Academy of Motion Pictures Arts and Sciences. Her new film, *Aloft*, starring Jennifer Connelly and Cillian Murphy, premiered at this year's Berlin Film Festival.

Venezuela

Mariana Rondón

Winner of the 2013 San Sebastian Film Festival, *Pelo malo* (*Bad hair*) is Rondón's third picture as a director. A visual artist trained in Paris, Rondón is also a graduate of Cuba's Los Baños Film and TV School and a partner in Empresa Multinacional Andina Sudaca Films. Her other films are also award winners: *A la medianoche y media* (*At midnight and a half*, 1999), co-directed with Marité Ugas, was nominated for best film at the Tokyo International Film Festival; *Postales de Leningrado* (*Postcards from Leningrad*, 2007), a drama about the revolutionary dreams of the 1960s Latin American youth, won or was nominated for the top prize at the Cartagena, Biarritz, Ceará, São Paulo and Kerala Film Festivals.

The present situation in Latin America, although far from ideal, is the best it has been since cinema came to the region. A certain amount of political and economic stability, combined with a proliferation of good film schools – from Cuba's Los Baños and Mexico's CCC to Brazil's Darcy Ribeiro and Argentina's ENERC – and the introduction of new tax-incentive policies have generated a boom of production in Latin America, both in film and television. Men still dominate the field, but never in the history of audio-visual exploration have women occupied so many key positions in the local industry, not only as directors but also as producers, writers, DPs and editors.

No longer a silent, almost secret force, women filmmakers are now key elements in Latin America's film and TV production.

Author biography

Born in Rio de Janeiro, Brazil, writer, journalist, author and professor Ana Maria Bahiana has worked in the entertainment industry for over two decades. Los Angeles based, she has written eight books on film, music and pop culture, and has translated and edited the Brazilian edition of Peter Biskind's *Easy Riders, Raging Bulls*. In addition to her work as a journalist and author, Bahiana works as a lecturer, curator and consultant for film-related projects. Her first film as a writer/producer, titled *1972,* was made in 2006 and co-produced and distributed in Latin America by Buena Vista.

She is currently working on a non-fiction book about the year 1964, for Brazil's Companhia das Letras.

Contact: ambahiana@gmail.com

Endnotes

1. Molyneux, Maxime, *Movimientos de Mujetes en América Latina: estudio teórico comparativo* (2003). Ediciones Cátedra, Madrid.

2. Fernadez Anderson, Cora. 'The Politics of Abortion in Latin America' in *RH Reality Check: Reproductive & Sexual Health and Justice*, July 17th 2013.

3. Landeta directed a fourth feature much later in her life – the romantic drama *Nocturno a Rosario* (*A Rosario nocturne*), released in 1992. She died on January 26th 1999.

4. *Matilde Landeta, hija de la Revolución*, Julianne Burton-Carvajal, Conaculta/Imcine, Mexico, 2003.

5. Interview with Ana Maria Veiga for *Historia Agora Magazine*, Rio de Janeiro, Brazil, December 5th 2010.

6. Interview with Paola Arboreda Ríos and Diana Osorio Gómez, '*La presencia de la mujer en el cine colombiano*', *Escuela de Ciencias Sociales*, Universidad Pontificia Bolivariana, Medellin, Colombia, 2002.

7. Award given out by the Asociación de Cronistas del Espetácula de Argentina, Argentine's Association of Entertainment Journalists.

8. *Los Angeles Times*, film review, May 13th 2005.

9. Review of *La ciénaga*, October 2001.

10. Her first film was the 1984 documentary *O pequeno exército louco* (*The crazy little army*) about the revolt that toppled Somoza in Nicaragua.

5. USA: Flouting the System

Lois Weber, Dorothy Arzner and Ida Lupino

Jacqui Miller

During the classical Hollywood studio system, which existed from the silent era until its encroaching disintegration in the 1950s, many women had great fame as actors, some of whose star personae have continued iconography in the present day. Far more women worked behind the scenes – as screenwriters, and in the myriad technical roles indispensable to filmmaking; although they may have had fleeting acknowledgement in the credits, their names remain largely unknown. Hollywood was a thoroughly male dominated industry, in which even the leading female stars had little control over their careers, and aside from the aforementioned army of anonymous women technicians, direction, the most elevated sphere of creativity, is often presumed to have been solely peopled by men. However, though their presence may be comparatively rare, examples of women taking artistic control through direction are threaded through the history of the studios.

This chapter will explore the work of three pioneering female film directors, whose creative complementarities means their work is almost invariably considered as a trio, or shifting pair: Lois Weber, Dorothy Arzner and Ida Lupino. Collectively they spanned the classical Hollywood studio era from the silents (Weber and Arzner) to its 'golden age' (Arzner)[1] to its post-World War II demise (Lupino). Making an examination of the socio-historical and film industry context of the eras in which the directors were working, an overview of their films, and a close critical analysis and aesthetic reading of two of each of their key films, the work will reveal both the struggles and achievements of women working across the grain in Hollywood and the ways their work served as implicit and explicit vehicles for cultural commentary.

Lois Weber: American Progressive

It was claimed in the 1970s, and may still hold true from the perspective of the 21st century, that the silent era afforded women more opportunities to work in the creative film industry than any time since.[2] Amongst her peers, Lois Weber is regarded as pre-eminent, directing more than one hundred films from 1911 onwards, including the first female-directed full-length feature, an adaptation of *The Merchant of Venice* (1914).[3] The silent era was also a time not only when the ground work for future filmmaking techniques were laid, but also incorporated methods that are considered avant-garde today. Weber utilised split screen in *Suspense* (1913)[4] and presaged neo-realism in *The Blot* (1921) location shooting in natural light and use of non-professional support cast. It is also the case, perhaps somewhat ironically, that the pre-Production Code silent era afforded filmmakers greater scope in directly tackling controversial subjects than any other period until the late 1960s.

Working at the time of the American Progressive Era, Weber's work typified the movement's quest to expose and rout out political graft and corruption in every public sphere from industry to the church, whilst promoting female suffrage, family stability, immigrant assimilation and education. A religious woman, Weber first worked as an evangelist in areas of urban deprivation and continued to have a missionary zeal when working in the theatre and cinema. Arguably, Weber's status as a woman was able to effect positive benefits from otherwise stereotyped connotations of gender. Contemporary notions of women's 'favourable moral influence'[5] enabled her to address topics that might have been considered seedy in the hands of a male director. Thus she is recognised today for her studies of social issues presumed to have particular relevance for women, such as contraception, in *Where Are My Children* (1916)[6]. In fact, Weber's Progressivism melded with her commitment to women's issues to make *Where Are My Children* a morally ambiguous film. Not only the use, sale or distribution of contraception, but also any means of communicating information on the subject was outlawed in the US under the Comstock Law of 1873, leading to middle class women increasingly resorting to abortion as a method of birth control.[7] *Where Are My Children* was seeking a legalisation of contraception but seemed to do so by drawing on Progressive Era theories of 'race suicide', a concept articulated by President Theodore Roosevelt, in which the middle classes were admonished for producing fewer children than allegedly 'inferior' eastern and southern European immigrants. Accordingly, contraception for poorer families would preserve the 'integrity' of WASP American stock. This point was reiterated in the informal 'sequel', *The Hand That Rocks the Cradle* (1917) which connoted negative and positive signification to poor and affluent parents respectively.

However, the films must be considered in the context of their times. Both in America and the UK, early feminist movements, whether seeking the vote or a variety of social reforms impacting on women's lives, tended to be led by the middle class women who had the necessary time and education. Therefore the seeming class bias of some of Weber's films should not detract from their genuine attempt to implicitly politicise the female sphere. Likewise, *Too Wise Wives* (1921), narratively seems to offer merely a story of two women of varying degrees of wealth keeping their husbands happy by domestic diligence. However, its visual style posits more thought-provoking layers. At a political meeting, amongst the matrons clad in conventional fur coats and hats, the *mise-en-scène* reveals a woman matter of factly wearing the current 'uniform' associated with suffragettes.[8] *Too Wise Wives* whilst having this thread of socio-political commentary, also further extends Weber's feminist range, by anticipating, through the realm of melodrama, the empowerment brought in classical studio era 'women's pictures' by the representation of close female friendships.[9] This establishment of female community was also part of Weber's professional practice. As would be the case for Dorothy Arzner, she too nurtured the career of women technicians in Hollywood[10], and she was known for getting the best performances from actresses considered 'difficult', such as Mildred Harris.[11]

Hypocrites (1915) takes its title from the hypocrisies of a wealthy city congregation for whom church attendance is a mere social convention. The film was notorious for its extensive representation of female nudity but Weber posits the conundrum that an image has no inherent meaning until the viewer brings their own context. A title card reads 'truth as ever is elusive'; thus a nude female form, dancing in woodland can connote Edenic innocence or salaciousness depending on point of view. The image is erotic, but that does not make it corrupting; corruption is the province of the hypocritical congregation that pays lip service to a moral code they leave behind at the church door. *The Blot* epitomises Progressive tenets. An impoverished college professor, Andrew Griggs (Phillip Hubbard) is mocked by unruly students, but one of the ring leaders, Phil West (Louis Calhern), whose father is the college's wealthiest trustee, is secretly in love with his daughter, Amelia (Claire Windsor). This love has the end result of Phil's father intervening to reform teaching salaries (the title comes from Phil's description of their pay as 'a blot on the present day civilisation'), and the harmonisation of different social strata, as the rich and poor (the Griggs and West families) as well as immigrants and native born (the Griggs and their erstwhile hostile immigrant neighbour) see their prejudices resolved and better selves revealed.

Dorothy Arzner: From Silent to Sound

Dorothy Arzner worked her way through the ranks of technical skills, beginning as a script typist at Famous Players in 1919. Her path to direction reveals a community of craftswomen in Hollywood successively supporting and nurturing each other's careers. It was film cutter, Nan Heron who facilitated her promotion to script girl and editor, while Arzner in turn taught actress Bebe Daniels editing.[5] Arzner defied convention in her personal life; openly gay, she shunned 'feminine' costume, perhaps gaining a sense of empowerment through the cultural codes attached to 'masculine' apparel. Both these points are given substance in the selected films. Although not gay, Hepburn too usually wore trousers off set, and *Christopher Strong* (1933) epitomises a woman breaking the rules in a male dominated sphere: aviation.[6] *Dance, Girl, Dance* set in the showbiz world depicts women necessarily pulling together for survival. Both films seem to counter Robin Wood's belief that although Arzner had built up a 'solid body of films' they were always projects regarded by the studios as 'minor and feminine, which came to the same thing'.[7] In any event, *Dance, Girl, Dance*'s original reception has been overtaken by its 2007 selection by the Library of Congress' National Film Registry.

Dance, Girl, Dance sees two very different women seeking a living as dancers. Bubbles (Lucille Ball) is an overtly sexy burlesque artist, while Judy (Maureen O'Sullivan) is an aspirant ballerina. At first glance, it may appear to stereotype women and even exploit their sexuality for an audience seeking escapist smut, but Arzner subverts conventional constructions of gender through her characterisation, cinematic style, and social critique. In a typical scene, Judy and a group of similar girls audition to a bored agent, performing a hula number. He politely declines to book them, when Bubbles bursts in. Her audition is evidently all that Judy's had lacked as she winks suggestively and gyrates her hips. On the one hand, the women, especially Bubbles, are displayed for heterosexual delectation, but it isn't that simple. The agent's unappealing, sweating face is offered for audience scrutiny just as much as the girls' bodies. The cigar clamped in his mouth serves as his exposed penis, static and slightly drooping, although rotating a little in response to Judy, then upright and puffing smoke as Bubbles ignites his interest. In this way, Arzner presents the sordid character of voyeurism. In another twist on this theme, the film has some notoriety for featuring a 'cat fight' in which Judy and Bubbles grapple on stage, in front of the audience as male security staff try to separate them. This would doubtless be highly titillating, except the stage curtain comes down, excluding the theatre audience. The film's audience can still see the action but are forced to consider that they are having a 'private show' and have been uncomfortably turned into voyeurs who must consider the ethics of watching. This process is carried through to the climactic scene. Judy has become Bubbles' burlesque stooge, but still tries to perform ballet to a largely male audience. Tired of the catcalls and jeering, she turns to leave the stage, but refusing to submit to the mocking calls of 'What are you going to do now, cry?', she takes centre stage and presents a response that recognises and critiques the exploitative triptych of class, economics and patriarchy. Her opening retort to the leering men opens up the commodification of sex, and the confines of marriage within capitalism:

> 'I know that you want me to tear my clothes off so you can look your 50 cents worth, 50 cents for staring at a girl the way your wives won't let you.'[8]

She then moves on to the socio-economic hierarchies generated by class, as the camera scrutinises the affluent couples, made as uncomfortable by its scrutiny as the booking agent:

> 'We know it's the thing of the moment for the dress suits to come and laugh at us too. We'd laugh back at you too, only we're paid to let you sit there and roll your eyes and make your screamingly clever remarks.'

Finally, she exposes, especially through the use of the term 'play', the ideological construction of patriarchy, and women's refusal to accept its imposition:

> 'What's it for, so you can go home after the show and strut before your wives and sweethearts and play at being the stronger sex for a minute. I'm sure they see through you, just like we do.'

The fact that this speech is given in a marked Irish accent adds a further dimension to this prescient analysis of exploitation and resistance.

Christopher Strong has been described as 'an action film for girls'.[9] There is no shame in that. Cynthia's love of speed defines her individuality from our first sight of her racing her car through the night. Arzner also uses her editing skills to create a dynamic film, incorporating stock footage of flights to heighten realism, a technique she honed in the bull-fighting scenes of *Blood and Sand* with Rudolph Valentino (1911).[10] But like *Thelma and Louise* (Ridley Scott, 1991) the successor with which it shares essential traits, *Christopher Strong* uses the 'action heroine' to challenge gendered behaviour and the tyranny of normative relationships.[11] The story's main thread concerns the adulterous relationship between Lord Christopher Strong (Colin Clive), a wealthy industrialist and politician, and the aristocratic young aviatrix, Lady Cynthia Darrington (Katherine Hepburn). The film ends in Cynthia's apparent suicide whilst chasing an altitude record, to spare Christopher divorce, scandal and misery because of the pregnancy she has kept secret. However, the film economically gives sensitive consideration to a range of female characters: Christopher's 'bright young thing' daughter, Monica (Helen Chandler) and his 'angel in the house' wife, Elaine (Billy Burke), whilst also giving insights into men's emotional lives, not just through the character of Christopher, but also the married man, Harry (Ralph Forbes) with whom Elaine has a wild fling, but who later divorces his wife to be with her. The contemporary filmmaker, Sally Potter has described her own cinema as 'androgynous', meaning a shared heritage with male directors, but Weber, Arzner and Lupino's cinemas demonstrated a form of androgyny in that they did not just make films about women's issues, but understood that if women are unequal, men's lives are damaged by their own power.[12] This ambiguity is signalled by the film's content, and also by a slyly ironic visual cue. Christopher Strong may be the titular lead, but the story is predominantly Cynthia's. This is paralleled by the opening credits; the name appearing above the title 'Christopher Strong' is Katherine Hepburn, not Colin Clive. In a neat bookend, the final name seen before the narrative starts is Arzner's as director. Thus what might be presumed to be a man's story has been androgenised before it begins.

Christopher Strong was undoubtedly controversial. Made in the liberal sound period before the Production Code was tightened in 1934 as a response to the sexual and violent content of many early talkies, it is set in the maelstrom of post-World War I London high society in which sexual rapacity is taken as the norm; Christopher and Cynthia initially meet because of a challenge to party guests to find what are believed to be obsolete species: a married man who has been faithful to his wife and a woman over twenty-one who has not had a love (meaning sexual) affair. Although they meet that brief, they are the architects of each other's disqualification. Arzner's wealth of skill as a technician is drawn upon in the scene in which they first sleep together. The camera focuses upon an illuminated bedside table, whilst Christopher and Cynthia speak, out of shot, but evidently in bed. She reaches out, turns off the light, and from then on, their affair, suspected all along by Elaine, is an open secret for the audience. The denouement comes when Monica, now comfortably married herself, discovers the relationship at the same time that Cynthia discovers her pregnancy. Without disclosing the news to Christopher, she does know that he would 'stand by' her, but instead she takes the altitude challenge. The ending has been described as 'a suicide run'[13] with Arzner's 'moral' stance undermining the film's 'feminist touches'[14], but, like *Thelma and Louise*, Cynthia chooses death (or perhaps feminist immortality) because she cannot be contained by the strictures of society.

Ida Lupino: Feminist Investigations of Masculinity

Ida Lupino is best known as an actor, whose work in front of the camera stretched from the early days of sound in *The Love Race* (1931) directed in her native England, by her uncle, Lupino Lane, to the New Hollywood film, *Junior Bonner* (Sam Peckinpah, 1972), as well as television in her later career. In the studio years, Lupino was often dissatisfied with the formulaic roles she was too frequently assigned, and like others, including Olivia de Havilland and Bette Davies, she was prepared to take suspension in protest. It was while on suspension she became fascinated by the creative process of filmmaking and this interest, coupled with her individuality within the constraints of Hollywood as 'some sort of rebel'[15] would lead to her becoming the first female actor to go on to write, produce and direct her own films, activities that she would later take into television projects. This, along with the fact that even as late as 1991 she could be described as 'the most prolific American woman director in history'[16], would ensure her place as a pioneer, but her legacy is compounded by the ways in which her work – its form, content and production processes – would anticipate the work of female and male Hollywood players decades hence.

Lupino notably said,

> 'If Hollywood is to remain on the top of the film world, I know one thing for sure – there must be more experimentation with out-of-the-way film subjects.'[17]

This premise informed her work, not just in terms of her subject matter alone, but her sometimes inversive approach to difficult issues. Her first four films as director, *Not Wanted* (1949), *Never Fear* (1949), *Outrage* (1950), and *Hard, Fast, and Beautiful* (1951), were melodramatic pictures probing social issues with a strong orientation towards 'women's' issues, and explored through the experience of female protagonists: illegitimacy, polio, rape, and a professional tennis player with an ambitious mother respectively. However, Lupino's next two films, *The Hitch-Hiker* (1953) and *The Bigamist* (1953) are unique in the Hollywood of their time, not simply because of their female direction, but because she was exploring social issues from a male perspective, anticipating the future work of women such as Kathryn Bigelow.[18] It is for this reason that these two films will form the basis of the analysis of Lupino's work.

The Bigamist's title is self-explanatory. A salesman, Harry Graham (Edmund O'Brien) is lonely when work takes him away from his wife, Eve (Joan Fontaine) in San Francisco. He falls into a romance in Los Angeles with Phyllis, a waitress he meets on a bus tour (Lupino)[19] and when she falls pregnant following what he had intended to be their only sexual encounter, he bigamously marries her. His deceit is uncovered when Eve, who cannot conceive a child, wants them to adopt. The vigilant adoption officer (Edmund Gwenn) senses Harry's discomfort at his probing questions, and tracks him to his second home with Phyllis and their child. The story is then revealed through a series of flashbacks, narrated by Harry, before moving forward to and ending at his trial for bigamy. This tale could form the basis of an archetypal melodrama, but Lupino makes cinematic convention look into an obverse mirror. Whereas classical melodramas or 'women's pictures' place the women at the centre of the filmic universe, the male characters only existing as their satellites, *The Bigamist* is a revised interpretation of the melodrama. Eve and Phyllis are well-drawn characters, and the audience has sympathy for them, but *The Bigamist* is doubly unusual for a Hollywood movie of the 1950s or any subsequent period. Harry is the central protagonist, acknowledging that men have emotional lives as complex as those of any woman, and second, Harry is not a bad person. Melodramas are littered with comic book male villains but Harry is not in this position because he has sought to seduce or exploit either of his wives, but because he had human frailty; he had tried to pluck up the courage to end his marriage to Eve, but loses his nerve upon hearing that her father has just died. Lupino is not afraid to acknowledge the tyranny of societal constructions of gendered behaviour and that men can be victims of their position of presumed dominance just as much as women suffer from their designated role as subordinates. Eve is a competent business manager, described by Harry as a 'career woman'. Of course the audience realises that he should not resent this, but also understand that he has been socialised into a sense of emasculation that he can only retrieve through solace with a woman who is his social unequal. As the adoption officer says when Harry has concluded his story:

'I can't work out my feelings towards you. I despise you and I pity you. I don't even want to shake your hand and yet I almost wish you luck,'

echoed by the trial judge's summing up:

'These are decent women, Mr Graham, you're basically a decent man and that's the whole point. When a man even with the best intentions breaks the moral laws we live by we really don't need man-made laws to punish him. You'll find out that the penalty of the court is the smallest judgement.'

The Bigamist is a film that uses both its form and content to challenge convention. Although not a noir, it was made in the post-World War II era in which social comment films predominated, and films of every type incorporated noir elements. Again borrowing from, but also reworking noir-melodrama hybrids such as *Mildred Pierce* (Michael Curtiz, 1945), Harry's psyche is translated cinematically, his periods of domestic calm being filmed in soothing high key-lighting, the times of mental torment and the threat of discovery being cast in low-key lit noir settings of the city and shadowed, seemingly imprisoning interiors. Fittingly, as a film that forces its audience to reconsider its relationship with human motivations, and the blurring of 'right' and 'wrong', closure is withheld. In court both women are present and seem neither hostile to each other nor to Harry, and judgement is not pronounced but reserved for two weeks hence – thus Lupino shares the creative process with an audience that ultimately has to consider its own verdict.

Several of Lupino's finest films as an actor were noirs made by Raoul Walsh: *They Drive by Night* (1940), *High Sierra* (1941), and *The Man I Love* (1947). Although sometimes stereotyped as a masculinist director, in these noirs Walsh captured 'the problematic of the independent woman'.[20] In turn, the problematic of the 'troubled man' is the concern of Lupino's directorial vision. *The Hitch-Hiker* was the first female-directed noir, but its real innovation goes in breaking generic convention. Usually predicated upon the premise of a beautiful but evil femme noir luring the anti-hero to his fate, Lupino instead presents a cast in which women have almost no screen presence. Two friends, both married and essentially good men, one a stable family man, Gilbert Bowen (Frank Lovejoy), the other, Roy Collins (Edmund O'Brien) having an eye somewhat more for a good time, are setting off for a fishing jaunt in Mexico, when they make the mistake of picking up a psychotic hitch-hiker, Emmet Myers (William Talman) who has left a trail of recent victims. This alternative road movie prefigures the opportunity John Boorman made to explore male relationships through a fraught journey two decades hence in *Deliverance* (1972).

Taking the film at face value alone, it is genuinely disturbing as Myers sadistically keeps the men travelling undercover at gunpoint, deferring the gratification of killing them, whilst they presume all along that they are doomed. Subtextually though, it explores the legacy of World War II, and what happens to men who are made to become killing machines to order, then expected to adjust to 'normal' society. The all-male central cast evokes the sense of combat, and the difficult journey across the arid terrain and outpost towns heightens the sense of a military campaign. From the outset, the war casts an existential shadow, and the fishing spree is at best a fraught pleasure; Gilbert is uneasy at not having left his wife and children for so long since the war – as if he can't quite take security for granted again, whilst Roy, like a soldier on a sordid furlough wants to pay pimps for Mexican sex-workers. Myers is certainly not a sympathetic character but he is established as one who has been dealt a position outside the bounds of society. His skills are the torture, killing and evading of capture that a few years earlier were the pinnacle of masculine achievement. Whilst Lupino depicts him as a character to be feared, she posits a wider point that if violence is to be switched on and lauded, society will be damaged if men are subsequently abandoned without help.

Overall, Lupino and her work are not simply important because she was a woman breaking the studio era's celluloid ceiling. In so doing, her work anticipated the styles, themes and production processes followed by subsequent male as well as female players in Hollywood. Although Linda Ruth Williams is accurate in saying that 'auteurist approaches have limited scope [with regard to female directors] in studies of the studio era', Lupino's cinema defined a clear identity predicated upon transcending stereotypes of gendered behaviour.[21]

Conclusion

Taken collectively, it is unsurprising that three women who carved out successful directing careers should often see their work grouped together. What is less often noted, and which this chapter has concluded, is the commonality of their themes, particularly that film is an effective tool for capturing the moment and making effective cultural commentary.

Author biography

Jacqui Miller is a senior lecturer in visual communication and subject leader for media and communication at Liverpool Hope University. In 1996 she completed her PhD, funded by the British Academy, on the relationship between Franklin D. Roosevelt's administration and Warner Bros. studio, 1930–1939. She has edited two books, *What Would You Have Done?: Ethics and Film Studies*, and *Audrey Hepburn: Fan Phenomena*. She has published book chapters and journal articles on a range of areas within film studies and cultural studies, including the French New Wave, New German Cinema, the novels and film adaptations of Patricia Highsmith's *Ripliad*, the Hollywood studio system, the New Hollywood, and representations of Liverpool on film. She regularly presents her research at conferences, and at Liverpool Hope, she leads the popular culture research group, and hosts the annual international conference, Theorising the Popular. As a film historian, she is particularly interested in the relationship between film, history, literature and culture.

Contact: millerj@hope.ac.uk

Endnotes

1. Nelmes, Jill (ed.) (2007). 'Arzner was probably the only woman whose directing career translated successfully from silent to sound.' p. 265.
2. Sklar, Robert (1975). *Movie Made America* p. 75.
3. Lewis, Jon (2008). *American Film* pp. 38–39.
4. Barsam, Richard and Monahan, Dave (2010). *Looking at Movies* p. 354.
5. Bordwell, David, Staiger, Janet and Thompson, K. (1985). *The Classical Hollywood Cinema* pp. 232 and 277.
6. The most deviant of Hepburn's roles in this regard is surely *Sylvia Scarlett* (George Cukor, 1935) in which she not only masqueraded as a boy, but was also, whilst passing as male, kissed on the lips by a woman, and the object of fascination by another man who said to her/him: 'I get a queer feeling when I look at you.' Moreover, she was one of the Hollywood stars around whom lesbian audiences created a cult of identification according to Karnick, Kristine Brunovska and Jenkins, Henry (eds.) (1995) *Classical Hollywood Comedy* p. 344.
7. Cited in Erens, Patricia (ed.) (1990). p. 342.

8. Bruce Babington and Peter William Evans liken Mae West's technique of turning 'the focus on her male patrons' to Judy's moment of triumph in this scene: Babington, Bruce and Evans, Peter William (1989) *Affairs to Remember: The Hollywood Comedy of the Sexes*, p. 125. Richard M. Gollin groups Hepburn, West and Arzner together in his section on feminist film theory: Gollin, Richard M. (1992), p. 197.

9. Lewis, Jon (2008). Op. cit. p. 126.

10. Brownlow, Kevin (1968). *The Parade's Gone By* p. 287. Arzner was a perfect fit at RKO, the studio most associated with technical innovation.

11. The term 'action heroine' was coined by Yvonne Tasker in Tasker, Yvonne (1993) passim.

12. Interview with Sally Potter in Cook, Pam (2005). *Screening the Past: Memory and Nostalgia in Cinema*, p. 142.

13. Lewis, Jon (2008). Op. cit., p. 126.

14. Cousins, Mark (2004). *The Story of Film*, p. 142.

15. Cousins, Mark (2004). Ibid. p. 198.

16. Acker, Ally (1991). *Reel Women: Pioneers of the Cinema* p. 74.

17. Lupino, Ida cited at http://www.dga.org/Craft/DGAQ/All-Articles/0604-Winter2006-07/Legends-Ida-Lupino.aspx

18. It should not be seen as mere coincidence that Paul Kolker follows a section on Lupino as a 'woman auteur' with one on Bigelow as a 'woman filmmaker today'. Cited in Kolker, Paul (2006) *Film, Form & Culture* pp. 157–160. In her overview of pioneering women directors, 'Giving Credit', an article in the online *Directors' Guild of America Quarterly* (Winter 2011), Janine Basinger begins by citing Bigelow's Director's Guild and Oscar awards for best director, before moving on to a study of Dorothy Arzner, Lupini, and Alice Guy-Blaché.

19. As Jon Lewis points out, 'That Lupino herself plays the object of desire and satisfaction further confuses the morality at play.' (Lewis, Jon (2008). Op. cit., p. 231.

20. Erens, Patricia (ed.) (1990). Ibid. p. 18.

21. Williams, Linda Ruth and Hammond, Michael (eds.) (2006). *Contemporary American Cinema* p. 299.

6. From Hollywood to Indiewood to Chinawood

Gabrielle Kelly

'It's always a little annoying to be labelled a woman film director because men are just "directors".'
Mary Lambert[1]

The Back Story

In 1916, the highest paid director in the world was not D. W. Griffith, hot off the success of his controversial *The Birth of a Nation*, nor the legendary Cecil B. DeMille, but actress, screenwriter, producer and prolific director, Lois Weber.[2] Weber had been directing since 1911 and her film *Suspense* is rightly regarded as one of the most innovative and influential of its time. She was the first woman to direct a feature film in the US – *The Merchant of Venice* in 1914 – founded her own studio and eventually directed over 100 films. Universal studio head Carl Laemmle said of her,

> 'I would trust Miss Weber with any sum of money that she needed to make any picture that she wanted to make.'[3]

Weber was America's most successful woman director of the Silent era, but she was far from the only one. There was Dorothy Arzner, Ida May Park, Julia Crawford Ivers, Frances Marion, Dorothy Reid, Lillian Gish, Mabel Normand, Nell Shipman, Ruth Stonehouse, Grace Cunard, Cleo Madison and more. Many of these women were multi-talented people who wrote, acted and produced in addition to directing.

However, by the mid 30s there was only one female director

working in the entire Hollywood studio system. Dorothy Arzner, the only US woman director to have made the transition from the silent era to talkies, was also the first to be given a screen credit as a film editor and the first woman to join the Directors Guild of America.

In the highly collaborative and inventive world of early filmmaking, women excelled. Indeed Hollywood in its earliest incarnation was gender blind. While in the US, women were directing films before they were able to vote, today the history and achievements of these women is largely forgotten, and the numbers of women film directors in the US seems to be in stasis or falling. As Hollywood filmmaking evolved into the multi-million dollar industry it has become, women were sidelined as directors, not to succeed again in any real way until the disruption of the studio system and the rise of independent film in the early 21st century.

Hollywood's view of women directors has remained mostly fixed since the 20s and its view of the rest of the world, until recently, has been similarly dismissive. But times are changing. The current media landscape is both global *and* local, flattened by the connectivity of social media and the explosive growth of audiences outside the USA. Relatively recently, 80% of Hollywood's box office came from the American or domestic market and the remaining 20% from the foreign market, primarily Asia. Today, most of the US box office comes from the foreign market, primarily Asia. In China, nine new movie theaters open every day; soon it will be the largest box office in the world. Dan Mintz, CEO of DMG, China's largest media company, notes:

> 'Things have moved rather quickly for such a big traditional established industry like Hollywood. Not much has changed in the last seventy-five years, and then comes China.'[4]

The traditional distribution system which rolled out films in consecutive 'windows' from theatrical release to DVD, TV etc. is now irrelevant to a wired generation more accustomed to simultaneous delivery of content across all platforms, or 'day and date' releases as they are known.

The world that Hollywood has dominated is changing and it will have to change too, voluntarily or otherwise. The Chinese character for 'chaos' is the same as that for 'opportunity.' The chaos Hollywood experiences as its usual business model is threatened could provide opportunities for US women directors outside the US. This, combined with anger at long-term discrimination is now beginning to fuel action on legal and governmental levels as we shall see.

The First Act – Hollywood

From the inception of the film business in the 1890s until the introduction of talkies in 1927, motion pictures were produced without sound and it was during this era that women thrived in many capacities, most notably as directors. Alice Guy-Blaché's one-minute narrative film *La Fée aux Choux* (*The Cabbage Fairy*) – created in 1896 some months before George Melies' A *Nightmare* – made her the first fiction director in the world.

Despite this, once movies went from the novelty of the early 'nickelodeons' to a profitable, large-scale industry in the early 20th century, women in movie jobs, including directors, mostly vanished from the business. As movies exploded into a multi-million dollar concern, power ended up in the hands of a few studio heads, all men. This shift of money and control spelled the beginning of the end for women working in film.

And little has changed. Even though today Sweden demands a fifty-fifty gender parity in any project using state funds, outside financiers apparently still do not want to 'risk' their investment on a woman director.

There are other reasons for the disappearance of women directors. In the 30s many first time women directors began as writers. When the talkies arrived, studios lost faith in their mainly female writing staff because they had little experience in writing dialogue. Some, like Lenore Coffee and Anita Loos clung on but a great many lost their jobs to playwrights imported from Broadway, or popular novelists like F. Scott Fitzgerald and William Faulkner. Coming up through the ranks from writer to director was no longer an option.

A similar effect can be seen in the career path of actresses. Dorothy Reid (aka Dorothy Davenport) and Mabel Normand were predominantly actresses but moved into directing. The big stars of the 1920s were female; Mary Pickford, Gloria Swanson, the Gish sisters, Clara Bow and the number of women whose names could 'open' a film far outweighed the number of men. Indeed, to call a film a 'woman's picture' was a mark of respect for its box office potential and the earning power of its stars. If one of those stars wanted to direct, no producer or studio head would refuse. By the 1930s however, tastes had changed and the names drawing crowds were largely male; James Cagney, Clark Gable, Boris Karloff, Edward G. Robinson. Not only did this hurt the chances of actresses looking to direct, it made it harder for female directors in general.

It was in the 1930s that the film industry in Hollywood became truly standardised, ending the experimentation of the pioneering Silent era. Now, money and the strictures of sound dictated conformity. A factory-like production method often referred to as 'the Studio System' together with a broad sense that there was one way to make a film, came to define filmmaking in the US. As women directors disappeared, it was as if they had never existed; a woman director seemed contrary to 'the norm', and risk-averse Hollywood has always worshipped 'the norm'.

Up until the late 1960s, there was never more than one woman directing films in Hollywood. Between 1966 and 1980, the social foment of the sixties pushed the number to fifteen. Throughout the 1970s, the feminist movement impacted the entertainment industry in various ways, influencing Hollywood's own political consciousness. This decade, perhaps America's most brilliant for film – introduced names like Scorsese, Coppola, Lucas, Allen, Malick and Altman, yet women directors were largely left outside of a vaunted male circle. Even as the new guard moved in, Hollywood clung to what worked in the past.

In 1979 a group of women directors requested that the DGA, the Director's Guild of America (the organisation charged with oversight of studio agreements to hire more women in accordance with US civil rights laws) provide statistics on the percentage of women directors hired by the studios. The result was 0.5%. The women then formed the DGA Women's Committee and persuaded the DGA to sue Columbia, Paramount and Warner Brothers' Studios for their restrictive hiring policies. Although this produced a brief increase in the hiring of women to fulfil a quota, the lawsuit was thrown out when Judge Pamela Rymer ruled that the DGA itself was compromised in its representation of its women members.

Dr Martha Lauzen's widely quoted annual report on the status of women working in television and film shows that only 6% of 2013's top 250 movies were directed by women. She summed up the bleak situation by saying,

> 'the film industry is in a state of what might be called gender inertia. There is no evidence to suggest that women's employment in key roles has improved over the last sixteen years.'[5]

Adding to her evidence, the DGA recently instituted a "report card" available on their website, dga.org, for all TV shows and films, that shows the number of women and minorities hired. So far it does not seem to have generated any action. Other initiatives pushing for change include The Women's Directing program at AFI; Gamechanger, the company started to finance films directed by women; Women in Film, which promotes and focuses on women working in the media arts; Women Make Movies, a distributor of films directed by and about women; the Alliance of Women Directors, and many more.

The issue of work-life balance is not specific to women but often more of a challenge for them. As producer Alison Owen told the trade magazine, *Variety*:

> 'It's more difficult for female directors, but a little easier for women producers and writers… But in directing it's difficult to step off the ladder and have a few kids: people tend to be suspicious if you've been away too long.'[6]

This is more pronounced in the US which lacks widespread government-supported childcare.

THE AMERICAS

The small percentage of women who have directed mainstream studio movies are concentrated in certain genres: romantic comedies, teen or coming of age films, remakes of TV shows and family comedies. Nora Ephron (*Sleepless in Seattle*) and Nancy Myers (*What Women Want*) are writers who successfully moved to directing features. Slick, funny, and enjoyably escapist, their movies did very well at the box office. More recently *My Big Fat Greek Wedding* written by Nia Vardalos, and Diablo Cody's slyly ironic film *Juno* were big hits. Somewhat off the broad mainstream demographic, Amy Heckerling with her *Fast Times at Ridgemont High* and *Clueless*, excelled with her witty insider look at California youth culture. She rightly perceived that 'Hollywood is the Dream Factory and nobody dreams about older women,'[7] while continuing to write humorous scripts full of fast-paced dialogue and dramatic twists. In a similar vein, Martha Coolidge's *Valley Girl* humorously skewered a stereotyped lifestyle, while her issue-oriented comedy *Rambling Rose* won many awards for its intricate story and great acting. Penelope Spheeris nailed slacker dudes in her wildly popular *Wayne's World*, and more recently Catherine Hardwicke followed her searing look at a teenage girl's coming of age in *Thirteen*, with the first film of the hugely successful *Twilight* franchise. Mimi Leder meanwhile, proved that women could direct star-driven action with *The Peacemaker* and *Deep Impact*.

Many of these female feature directors came from TV, where strong writing and freedom from MPAA ratings often make it a more inventive medium. Recently Lena Dunham went from her successful feature debut *Tiny Furniture* to her hit TV series *Girls*, a frank and comedic look at young women living in current day New York.

Actresses such as Angelica Huston, Penny Marshall, Barbra Streisand, Elaine May and Jodie Foster have also directed features with varying degrees of success. Like many women directors, Marshall started in TV before turning to movies, where her smash hit *Big* became the first film directed by a woman to make more than $100 million.

It has long been said that the 'audience quandrant' studios are aiming for is teenage boys whose preference is for action, horror and comedy franchise movies which are directed mostly by men. Conventional wisdom remains that women cannot, and do not want to direct these sorts of films, and have no experience in doing so. Yet men are routinely hired to direct stories that are sure-fire material for female audiences; *Thelma and Louise, Steel Magnolias, Beaches, Blue is the Warmest Colour*, etc. Possession of a male physiognomy does not automatically confer the ability or the passion to direct action pictures. For example, we are unlikely to ever see Terence Malick's *Spiderman* or Woody Allen's *Hurt Locker*. In truth, women as storytellers, artists and craftspeople are as varied as men in the stories they want to tell. One of the most gonzo boy's movies ever made, *The Matrix*, was directed by the famously reclusive Wachowski brothers, Larry and Andy. Following Larry's gender reassignment surgery, the siblings co-directed *Cloud Atlas* and the upcoming *Jupiter Ascending*. Larry's taste in film did not change by becoming Lana, nor diminish an extraordinary talent for movie making. Doubtless the Wachowskis will continue making movies with budgets well into the hundreds of millions and maintain their fan-base. Failure to make a profit will be more of a hindrance than the sex of either director.

Kathryn Bigelow is probably the most recognised woman director currently working in Hollywood and the most comfortable with a traditionally male genre. On winning an Oscar for Best Director for *The Hurt Locker* in 2008, Bigelow did not frame her win as a first for women. Asked by Neda Ulaby later about her 'unique' experience directing she said,

> 'being a woman filming a nearly all-male movie in the Middle Eastern country of Jordan was simply not a big deal. You don't think about being a woman while you work.'

She elaborated,

> 'You've got a four-storey-high explosion taking place along an avenue, where on any given day there are 250,000 cars, so… that begins to take precedence.'[8]

To the general public, the director as auteur is synonymous with male directors, while women are often marginalised in the scholarship, history, and critical study of their work. As a result, many films by women directors are often lost to history, compounding the problem as each generation of women filmmakers almost has to start from the beginning every time.

The point being, there should be no 'women directors,' just directors who happen to be women.

The Second Act – Indiewood

> 'If there's specific resistance to women making movies, I just choose to ignore that as an obstacle for two reasons: I can't change my gender, and I refuse to stop making movies.'
> Kathryn Bigelow[9]

In 1989 Steven Soderbergh's ground-breaking *Sex, Lies and Videotape* was a huge commercial and artistic success despite its low budget, original visual style and provocative story about a man who films women discussing their sexuality. It launched Soderbergh's career, the distribution company Miramax, and the careers of its actors. Also crucially, it demonstrated a new form and method of independent filmmaking that was daring, personal, low tech and low budget. It also spearheaded the cinematic transition from film stock to digital, where cheap, lightweight equipment could be used to tell stories that would previously never have been deemed commercial enough for Hollywood studios to develop or make.

Of course there were independent films before 1989 but the expense of equipment and level of expertise necessary made it a tough world in which to work. For women filmmakers however, it was still easier than getting access to studio pictures. In the 1940s, Russian-born Maya Deren became the first filmmaker ever to receive a Guggenheim grant for her independent experimental films. Shirley Clarke, working from the 1950s to the 1980s, was one of the most important women in independent cinema, while Barbara Loden's 1970 film *Wanda* became one of the few independent movies directed by a woman to receive a theatrical release. Surely independent filmmaking, fast becoming technically easier and, crucially, cheaper, would usher in a new era of female directors?

Certainly there were more women directors working after 1989. Julie Dash's 1991 *Daughters of the Dust* became the first feature directed by an African-American woman to get a theatrical release in the USA. Barbara Kopple made her Oscar-winning documentary *American Dream*. Kathryn Bigelow continued her assault on the mainstream with *Point Break*. Those three women had all made films before but there were new names too, such as Jane Spencer (*Little Noises*) and Debra Granik (*Snake Feed*). The low cost world of indie films also offered the possibility of making money by being picked up for exponentially wider distribution by a major studio. Crucially for women, indie cinema had fewer gatekeepers and an audience open to innovative stories not delivered by Hollywood.

As these films began to make money, the definition of independent film as 'independent from studio financing, development, production, and distribution' changed. There are still genuinely independent films made, but the bigger players like Fox Searchlight and Focus Features are now 'independent' divisions of major studios, their 'independence' relative to blockbusters rather than to smaller 'passion projects.' Independent film today is mostly part of a range of companies, which studios buy up and add to their vertically integrated portfolio. In the US, the line between studio and indie has thus become blurred, and together with a huge proliferation of feature films, has turned the indie world into a version of Hollywood formula. Filmmaking in the US today is polarised between studio 'tentpole' franchise brands that financially sustain their film divisions, versus highly personal films often funded by new online financing structures such as Kickstarter and Indiegogo.

What does this mean for the filmmakers themselves? Hollywood is called show business for a reason – it is not called show art. The indie world gave us films like Allison Ander's gritty *Gas, Food and Lodging* and Nancy Savoca's finely observed *True Love*, but where they go from there? After Kimberly Pierce made her Oscar-winning indie film *Boys Don't Cry* she was offered big studio movies, but none appealed to her. As a director it is said in Hollywood 'you are only as good as your next film', meaning the choice of what you make and how you are perceived as a filmmaker is crucial. The first film is often a passion project where the director has more control, while the second and third are always much harder to choose and to get made. This is true for all filmmakers, but a much higher number of women directors make only one film.

One significant issue for women directors is that, being so few in number, each becomes perceived as representative of all women. While Kathryn Bigelow's success may not get any other women jobs, a film with a woman director that fails, for whatever reason, impacts women more negatively than men. When a male director fails it's 'because he's a bad director', but when a female director fails it's 'because *women* are bad directors'. This reinforces the assumption that all women direct and think alike, even when the reverse can be readily demonstrated.

Some independent women directors find the very word 'feminist' a barrier to their acceptance in the industry. Shirley Clarke, director of the ground-breaking *The Cool World* in the early 60s, refused invitations to women's film festivals for that reason. French director Diane Kurys (*Entre Nous*) has said that she considers the idea of women's cinema 'negative, dangerous, and reductive'.[10]

But other female directors are unapologetically feminist. Carolee Schneemann (*Fuses*), Donna Deitch (*Desert Hearts*) and Yvonne Rainer (*The Man Who Envied Women*), for example, all made (and make) films that deal with women's issues in a head on and sometimes controversial fashion. Barbara Hammer's experimental documentary feature *Nitrate Hearts*, made in 1992, centered on four same sex couples and intercut interviews with footage of them making love. That sort of thing was never going to be made within the machinery of the male-dominated studio system.

To be sure, not every filmmaker wants to be part of this machinery, but for now it has huge power to dictate how and if a film will be promoted and seen by the largest audience possible.

Distribution is the key issue for today's filmmaker. Drawing on various sources, Fandor, a new streaming service for indie films, notes that women find greater relative success in indie films than mainstream Hollywood. From 2002 to 2012, women comprised 23.9% of directors at Sundance but only 4.4% of directors of studio films with successful box office. In 2011, 5% of directors in Hollywood were women, down from 7% in 2010 and 9% in 1998. For every one woman director there are 15.24 male directors, and only 41 women have made films in the top 100 releases across the last decade, compared to 625 men.[11]

Does this mean that the independent film window, which can be a stepping-stone for women directors to mainstream opportunities and success, has closed? Julie Dash had used that window to massively advance the cause of African-American women in film, following in the footsteps of pioneers like Eloice Gist and Zora Neale Hurston. But contemporary African-American women directors have often struggled to convert independent recognition into the same mainstream success as their male counterparts. Dee Rees, Darnell Martin and Ava DuVernay are among the strong new voices in directing but where is the female Spike Lee, Paris Barclay or Lee Daniels?

In conversation with NPR's Neda Ulaby, Nia Vardalos, writer of one of the most profitable indie films ever, *My Big Fat Greek Wedding*, discussed how women directors are treated differently not just by studios but even by the crew on set.

> 'One day my focus puller turned to me, and he said, "As a female filmmaker, you have one shot, and if you go over budget, that bond company will be here in a second, breathing down your neck. So you're right to keep everyone on schedule."'.

Vardalos explained how, on the set of her debut feature *I Hate Valentine's Day,* she:

> '…had no sense of being an *artiste* – someone entitled to challenge the budget, the number of shooting days, or the rules.'

And yet she did enjoy directing. 'I'll describe it to you this way,' she says. 'It's like jumping into an orgy while you're still shaving your legs.'[12]

Vardalos's comment underlines an important fact; directors have a variety of reasons for pursuing directing. Here we are mainly focused on narrative feature film directors, but there are a huge variety of forms and genres in which a director can work. As the budget goes up, the director has less control, therefore the indie world still has much to offer. Lynn Shelton came to prominence with her breakout indie feature *Humpday* in 2009 – the story of two straight men who decide to make a gay porn movie together. The film was made outside of Hollywood on a shoestring budget with the director's friends helping out in front of and behind the camera and with a loose, partly improvised style. It sounds like the sort of story that would not appeal to Hollywood but its 'mumblecore' charms seduced critics and audiences who found it offbeat yet insightful and a bidding war broke out for the film at Sundance.[13] In mainstream Hollywood Shelton probably would never have got her chance to direct a story about men, but she didn't seek permission or apply for the gig, she made it happen.

Today the very notion of 'independent' is in flux, when the studios are but one part of a global media landscape it is not clear what independent films are independent *from*. But while independent film has acquired some of the problems and prejudices of the major studios, it still affords an opportunity to those who will take it. The dream of every director, regardless of gender, is to make a film that speaks for itself, that will be judged on its merits alone, not on who made it. In the US that dream is more likely to happen in the indie world, where a director can still be a woman without being a 'woman director'. And they have stories to tell, as director Jane Campion points out,

> 'I would love to see more women directors because they represent half of the population – and gave birth to the whole world. Without them writing and being directors, the rest of us are not going to know the whole story.'[14]

CELLULOID CEILING

The Third Act – Chinawood

The DGA has 3,500 members, and roughly 50% of film school graduates in the US are women, so there is no shortage of potential women directors. But in spite of ongoing efforts, including lawsuits against studios to stop women from being lumped into the "other minorities' category, a more equitable gender split in directing opportunities can still seem like an unreachable goal for women directors in the US. As women are not a minority, but form half the population and nearly half the audience in the US, this makes the problem all the more galling. In the end, however, the needed change may come as part of worldwide changes that will affect *everyone* in the business. It goes beyond gender to the economic balance of power, the shift in technology and the expansion of the global audience.

Asked how these changes have opened up opportunities in China, US director Dennie Gordon, a veteran of Hollywood feature films (*Joe Dirt, New York Minute, What a Girl Wants*) and TV shows (*Sports Night, Lifestyles of the Rich and Famous*) said,

> 'We can't get too comfortable in our positions; we always have to look where trends are moving and then stretch ourselves.'[15]

Approached by billionaire Chinese producer Song Ge to do a Chinese remake of her 2003 romantic comedy *What a Girl Wants*, Gordon became the first American woman to direct a Chinese language movie in China. Years ago while travelling the world as a working TV director, she had seen the future and it was Asia. Today that future has arrived in many forms including Chinawood studios, built by tycoon Bruno Wu outside Shanghai to service co-productions with China. Built on eighty hectares at a cost of $1.27 billion it signals a massive power shift financially and artistically. Asia is a booming market and money follows the market. This is how Gordon came to direct the hip rom-com *My Lucky Star,* not in the US but in Singapore, Hong Kong and Shanghai, building on the relationships she had made in Asia. She infused the movie with her usual filmmaking style; fast paced storytelling and bold camera moves. 'I do a lot of push ins,' says

Gordon, 'it's a physical, always moving camera. I always shoot my cut.'[15] Away from the gatekeepers of Hollywood, and deploying strategic thinking about where new opportunities have opened up she is acting on her belief that, 'In this day and age you do not need permission from others to make your movie.'[16]

Gordon also noted of her challenging production:

'The DGA were a huge help. The producers had signed a DGA contract which the DGA enforced, so I got my cut but it never ends, making a film is solving issues minute by minute. What is really interesting is that, in many ways I had more freedom in China than in America. That's the irony.'[17]

The market driven forces of most filmmaking in the US may be why the first American woman to be nominated for a Directing Oscar was Sofia Coppola, Hollywood royalty with access to stars and money. Despite the freedoms enjoyed by women in other spheres of life in the US, it is indeed ironic that film directing may be more accessible to women in what may be considered as more closed societies.

Following the rise of the Iranian New Wave, there are now record numbers of film school graduates in Iran and each year more than twenty new directors make their debut films, many of them women. In the last two decades, there have been a higher percentage of women directors in Iran than in most countries in the West. The cinematic New Wave in Iran was in fact spearheaded by a woman, the poet Forugh Farrokhzad, whose film *The House is Black* ushered in a new era of filmmaking and has been an inspiration to modern Iranian female directors like Samira Makhmalbaf[18] who made her debut film, *The Apple* at age seventeen. So why in Iran, and not in the USA?

Actress and director Jodie Foster says:

'I don't think it's a plot and these guys sat around and said, 'Let's keep these women out.' When you give up that amount of power, you want them to look like you and talk like you and think like you and it's scary when they don't, because what's gonna happen? I'm gonna

hand over $60 million to somebody I don't know. I hope
they look like me.'

Foster also holds women executives accountable saying the
names women executives put forward are, 'guy, guy, guy, guy.' She
also says that, 'Their job is to be as risk-averse as possible. They
see female directors as a risk.'[19]

To be sure, gender equality in film direction does not necessarily
mean better films, it means *different* films. Variety and constant
reinvention are what drives the film industry. Anything that adds
to that variety is good for the industry and the art, and what
detracts from it lessens choice as well as our ways of seeing the
world. At this time of massive upheaval in the industry, there has
never been a more important opportunity for American cinema
to embrace variety. Women directors and filmmakers may yet
save Hollywood.

Conclusion

America has given the world memorable movies of every kind,
some directed by women, who were such a powerful force in the
medium's early decades, but were then sidelined as mostly male
studio heads gained power over a hugely profitable business.
Whether working within or outside the Hollywood system, women
have made seminal and lasting contributions to filmmaking in the
US. Complex forces of change are now redrawing the template
of filmmaking familiar to Hollywood and the US. Answering the
call of this potentially lucrative global market and being able to
change the system from within, may now be possible, as alternative
funding opportunities and different distribution streams open up
to women producers, writers and directors.

This takes time however and as evidence of active
discrimination grows, so too does anger. Says blogger, DGA
member, and director, Maria Giese, 'USC's Annenberg School
for Communications and Journalism reported that this year a
criminally low 4% of movies are going to be directed by women.[20]
The word 'criminal' is invoked because, according to Title 7, (a
part of the Civil Rights Act of 1964 which protects individuals
against employment discrimination on the basis of race and

colour, national origin, sex and religion), this percentage reveals rampant violations of US equal employment opportunity laws in Hollywood.

She asked in her popular blog, 'It's 2014, what can we do this year to get women directors in the US working?' Here is what she proposed:

> 1. Demand Industry Compliance of Equal Employment Laws: Demand the lawful advancement of women directors through the Director's Guild of America and studio and network diversity programs. Unearth industry violations that impede progress for women directors.
>
> 2. Pursue Individual Legal Action: Let http://www.womendirectorsinhollywood.com know if you have been 'shut out' of a job because of your gender. Separate women of all ethnicities from male ethnic minorities in efforts to increase employment of women directors.
>
> 3. Increase Public Awareness: Make the issue common knowledge, not just in the US but also around the world. Work with all media outlets including bloggers, statisticians and researchers to educate the public. Create a paradigm shift in public thinking about the abilities and competence of women directors using employment, mentoring, panels, festivals, summits, seminars, screenings, conferences, and other events that involve issues of female director employment.
>
> 4. Support more Film Funds for Women Directors: Create more funds like Gamechanger, the first non-profit fund for feature films directed by women directors ONLY. As well as pursuing individual funding opportunities through Crowdfunding, like Kickstarter, take advantage of the 'Jumpstart Our Business Startups Act,' which President Obama signed into law in April 2012 to help fledgling businesses including film funds raise money to boost the economy.[21]

The US filmmaking model no longer defines the world. Its studio model and the increasingly studio-like 'indie' alternative embody the current idea of show business, but not always of show art. Without art, however, the business of film is empty, a blank screen. Ultimately the connectivity of the worldwide media landscape is most powerfully one of storytelling, and finding the stories that will resonate and attract the viewing public of a global marketplace, alongside the financial and production infrastructure to make those stories.

In March 2014, the American Civil Liberties Union (ACLU) spoke out against the persistent discrimination against women directors and more importantly, took on their case. With a long and successful track record in defending the rights of content creators in television, film and the arts and advocating for gender equity particularly in job sectors dominated by men, they are a force to be reckoned with. This combination of enforcement of women director's Civil Rights by the ACLU and women directors own strategic reinvention of best opportunities even if outside the US, may finally force equity. In this new strategy, the many voices of America's women directors are also supported by changes that have made Hollywood and the US rethink and rework their filmmaking status quo. In the end, we, the world audience really need women directors to tell their stories, expanding our experience as they share their vision and add to the cannon of American film as Alice Guy-Blaché was doing in 1896 at the age of twenty-three. With the might of the ACLU behind them, they may finally get to be called director without the qualifier 'woman'.

Author biography

Gabrielle Kelly is a screenwriter and producer of diverse content for the global marketplace who also teaches in international labs and film programs. She was a Fulbright Scholar in screenwriting and producing in both Taiwan and the Philippines.

She has worked with New York based director Sidney Lumet on films such as *Daniel, Prince of the City, Deathtrap, The Verdict* and with Andy Warhol on developing an audio-animatronic show *From A to Z and Back Again*. In Hollywood she ran producer Robert Evans' company at Paramount, working in development and production on a slate of diverse projects, and she also worked as executive and producer with such companies as HBO, Fields Hellman, Eddie Murphy Productions and Warner Bros.

Producing credits include indie feature *All the Queen's Men* (starring Eddie Izzard and Matt LeBlanc) for Strand Releasing, *Stag* (for Cineplex Odeon/HBO), the family feature film *D.A.R.Y.L* for Paramount/Columbia, and screenwriter and producer for *All Ages Night*, an indie feature set in the teen music scene of LA..

The writer of numerous screenplays she has developed several books in a variety of genres including Kelly Crabb's definitive work *The Movie Business: a Legal Guide*. Projects in development from an array of source materials also include Marvel comic *Mort the Dead Teenager* at Dreamworks and co-productions with filmmakers in Russia, Brazil, China and throughout Europe.

Teaching experience includes screenwriting and producing at UCLA, USC, Chapman, VGIK, Russia, London's PAL Labs, the first ever Middle East Sundance Screenwriting Lab and many others. Board membership includes the British Academy of Film and Television, Women In Film and the Irish Film Festival/LA. She is a judge and programmer at numerous film festivals worldwide and is currently working on projects for the global marketplace as a screenwriter and producer.

Contact: http://www.gabriellekelly.com

Endnotes

1. Marks, Lisa (2012). The horror, the horror: women gather in LA for Viscera film festival. *The Guardian*.

The Back Story

2. Acker, Ally (1992). 'Women Behind the Camera – Feminists or Filmmakers?' *Agenda*, no. 14, pp. 42–46.

3. Quoted by Aydelotte, Winifred (1934). 'The Little Red Schoolhouse Becomes a Theatre' *Motion Picture Magazine*, Vol XLVII, no. 2, p. 85.

4. Tartaglione, Nancy (2014). 'Year-End: Hollywood Film Biz Still Cautious, But Slow Boat To China Speeding Up After Busy & Edifying 2013,' *Deadline*, London.

The First Act – Hollywood

5. Lauzen, Martha M. (2014). 'The Celluloid Ceiling: Behind-the-Scenes Employment of Women on the Top 250 Films of 2013' *Celluloid Ceiling Report,* Diego State University.

6. Gray, Tim (2013). 'Oscar Pals With Women Producers, But Big-Budget Gigs are Scarce' *Variety*.

7. Murray, Noel (2008). Amy Heckerling *The AV Club*.

8. Ulaby, Neda (2009). 'Female Directors, Still a Scarce Movie Commodity' *NPR*.

The Second Act – Indiewood

9. Perry, Michelle P. (1990). 'Kathryn Bigelow Discusses Role of 'seductive violence' in Her Films' *The Tech*, Vol. 110, Issue 13.

10. Vincendeau, Ginette (1991). 'Like Eating a Lot of Madeleines' Monthly Film Bulletin, 58,686.

11. Fandor (2012). 'Where Are the Women Directors?' *Fandor*.

12. Ulaby, Neda (2009). 'Female Directors, Still a Scarce Movie Commodity' *NPR*.

13. Ulaby, Neda (2009). 'Female Directors, Still a Scarce Movie Commodity *NPR*'.

14. Singh, Anita (2009). 'Jane Campion: Female directors need to be tough to make it in "sexist" Hollywood', *The Telegraph*.

The Third Act – Chinawood

15. Rochlin, Margy (2013). 'Her Lucky Star' *DGA Quarterly,* Directors' Guild of America.

16. Kelly, Gabrielle (2013). 'Interview with Dennie Gordon,' Hollywood, USA, December 28th 2013.

17. Kelly, Gabrielle (2013). Interview with Dennie Gordon, Hollywood, USA, December 28th 2013.

18. Danks, Adrian (2002). 'The House that Mohsen Built: The Films of Samira Makhmalbaf and Marzieh Meshkini' *Senses of Cinema*, Filmmaker Profiles, issue 22.

19. Keegan, Rebecca (2011). Jodie Foster: Even Female Studio Execs 'see female directors as a risk' *Los Angeles Times, 24 Frames: Movies Past, Present and Future* http://latimesblogs.latimes.com/movies/2011/04/jodie-foster-studio-execs-see-female-directors-as-a-risk.html

20. Bartyzel, Monica (2014). 'Girls on Film: Hollywood's 4 percent problem' *This Week*.

21. Giese, Maria (2014). 7 'Solutions for Women Directors in 2014' *Women Directors: Navigating the Hollywood Boy's Club*.

References

Acker, Ally (1991). *Reel Women; Pioneers of the Cinema 1896 to the Present*, Continuum, New York.

Foster, Gwendolyn Audrey (1997). *Women Filmmakers of the African and Asian Diaspora: Decolonizing the Gaze, Locating Subjectivity*, University Press, Southern Illinois.

Goldovskaya, Marina (2006). *Woman with a Movie Camera*, University of Texas Press, Austin.

Hurd, Mary G. (2007). *Women Directors and Their Films*, Praeger, London.

Lane, Christina (2000). *Feminist Hollywood from Born in Flames to Point Break*, Wayne State University Press, Detroit.

Rashkin, Elissa J. (2001). *Women Filmmakers in Mexico; The Country of Which We Dream*, University of Texas Press, Austin.

Redding, Judith M. and Brownworth, Victoria A. (1997). *Film Fatales*, Seal Press, Seattle.

Slide, Anthony (1996). *The Silent Feminists America's First Women Directors*, The Scarecrow Press, London.

Wang, Lingzhen (2011). *Chinese Woman's Cinema*, Columbia University Press, New York.

7. US – Women film directors of the 'indie' world

Nathan Shaw

Until recently, the independent film arena had seemingly consisted of exclusively male directors. The same can be said for mainstream film. Yet, slowly but surely, somewhere after the massive critical and commercial success of Sofia Coppola's *Lost in Translation* (2003) and before Kathryn Bigelow's *The Hurt Locker* (2008) a nucleus of talented, female, independent directors began to emerge, not only in North America, which will provide the focus of this chapter, but also in the United Kingdom (Andrea Arnold, Lynne Ramsay, Cleo Barnard) and across Europe (Mia Hansen-Love, Susanne Bier, Lone Scherfig).

This chapter will look at the most important female directors currently working within the so-called independent arena, whilst also discussing its importance as, paradoxically and simultaneously, an alternative to mainstream Hollywood cinema, and as a training ground for future blockbuster directors.

The term 'independent cinema' is a difficult and problematic one to define. It can be taken to mean independently financed (i.e. financed by a non-major Hollywood film studio); a film that deals with subject matter often avoided by mainstream Hollywood movies; a labour of love for an auteur/director with a sole and uncompromising artistic vision; or even an amalgamation of all these definitions (and possibly more). Indeed, as revered film critic Roger Ebert attested,

> 'It's a film made outside the traditional Hollywood studio system, often with unconventional financing, and it's

made because it expresses the director's personal vision rather than someone's notion of box-office success.' (Levy, 2001: 3)

The paradox here is that most definitions of independent cinema come from an anti-Hollywood viewpoint – they embody the archetypal view of the auteurist director who follows his/ her own artistic vision to create a labour of love for relatively little money that will ultimately have little box office success but (hopefully) create enough of a critical buzz that will lead to more opportunities. This is almost inherently the opposite of what is considered mainstream cinema. In the realm of Hollywood, the director, who is often less important than the star(s), has a huge budget with which to entertain and enthral the general cinema-going public, with the hope that it will garner critical success. Yet, ironically, the first often leads to the second.

Big-name male directors such as Martin Scorsese, Steven Soderbergh and Christopher Nolan all started out working on smaller, independent projects before graduating to big budgets and blockbusters. Similarly, a number of female directors have trodden the same path. After directing low budget B-movies such as *The Loveless* (1981), *Near Dark* (1987) and *Blue Steel* (1989), Kathryn Bigelow made the move into mainstream cinema with the likes of *Point Break* (1991), *Strange Days* (1995) and *K-19: The Widowmaker* (2002); all of which had consecutively bigger budgets, an estimated $24 million, $42 million and $100 million respectively (IMDB), and featured star names including Keanu Reeves, Patrick Swayze, Ralph Fiennes and Harrison Ford. In addition to Bigelow, Catherine Hardwicke, whose recent directorial credits include *Red Riding Hood* (2011) and the first film of the all-conquering blockbuster franchise *Twilight* (2008), started her career with gritty indie drama *Thirteen* (2003); a film whose budget was roughly 3% of *Red Riding Hood*'s.

Breaking through

As well as the relatively smooth transitions of Bigelow and Hardwicke, other female directors have threatened to move from indie territory to Hollywood. Patty Jenkins is one such. In 2003, she wrote and directed *Monster*, a critically acclaimed biopic of serial killer Aileen Wuornos. The film garnered Charlize Theron, who played the role of Wuornos, numerous awards including Best Actress at both the Oscars and the Golden Globes, while Jenkins was nominated for the Director's prize at the Berlin International Film Festival. Following this initial success Jenkins directed television episodes for acclaimed shows such as *Arrested Development* and *Entourage* before finally looking to have got her break in 2011, when she was hired to direct the sequel to the superhero blockbuster *Thor* (Branagh, 2011). However, she left the project before it came to fruition, with Marvel citing 'creative differences' as the reason. Not unlike Jenkins, Scottish director Lynne Ramsay also started off in independent territory before looking to take the leap into the mainstream. Following a number of critically successful short films, Ramsay directed *Ratcatcher* (1999) and *Morvern Callar* (2002) and quickly became one of the most exciting and interesting directors in the world of independent cinema. She had been slated to follow up *Morvern Callar* with an adaptation of Alice Sebold's best-selling novel *The Lovely Bones*, a job that eventually went to Peter Jackson, after producers decided they wanted the film to be closer to the source novel than Ramsay's script had been. Ramsay was then scheduled to direct *Jane Got a Gun*, starring Natalie Portman, Joel Edgerton and Ewan McGregor, but in March 2013 she left the production. Litigation is currently pending on both sides.

These conflicting experiences of Bigelow, Hardwicke, Jenkins and Ramsay show both the successes and difficulties of making the transition from the world of independent cinema to the Hollywood mainstream. Yet as Bigelow in particular has shown, it is possible for female directors to straddle both sides of the divide. After making bigger budgeted studio controlled movies, she returned to developing a smaller scale story with *The Hurt Locker*, which led to her becoming the first, and only, female director to win the coveted Best Director Oscar. She followed up this success with the bigger budget, and critically well received but equally divisive, *Zero Dark Thirty* (2013), which tells the story of the hunt for Osama Bin Laden.

THE AMERICAS

Sofia Coppola

> 'I never get myself in a situation where I don't have creative freedom. I learned that from my dad: you put your heart into something, you have to protect it, what you're making. I always like to keep the budget as small as possible just to have the most freedom.'

> Sofia Coppola (Thompson, 2010)

One of the most recognisable names in independent cinema (though some may argue her eligibility for this category due to her family and Hollywood connections) is Sofia Coppola. She was born into movie royalty; her father is acclaimed, Oscar-winning director Francis Ford Coppola, her brother Roman is a successful producer and director, her cousins include Jason Schwartzman and Nicolas Cage, and her niece Gia Coppola, has just directed her first feature, *Palo Alto* (2013), at the age of twenty-six, two years younger than her aunt was when she released her debut film *The Virgin Suicides* (1999). Yet far from relying on her family name, Coppola has forged an impressive reputation all of her own. To date, she has directed five feature films, and with the exception of the bigger budgeted *Marie Antoinette* (2006), they have all been smaller scale, lower budget productions in which she has been able to retain the creative freedom and control instilled in her by her father. Indeed, although *Marie Antoinette* did have a larger budget (around $40 million) and was produced more within the typical Hollywood studio system, Coppola's rising stock, coming off the back of the success of *Lost in Translation*, meant that she retained control in spite of this and, I would argue, her status as 'an independent'.

After adapting and directing *The Virgin Suicides* from Jeffrey Eugenides' novel, about five mysterious sisters, one of whom commits suicide even though they are sheltered from the outside world by their overbearing parents, and the four neighbourhood boys who adore them, Coppola introduced herself as an indie talent to watch. American film critic Jonathan Rosenbaum described her as 'a genuine original' (Rosenbaum, 2003) and the film gained largely positive reviews. It also set out Coppola's auteur intentions, with a clear visual style that has since become synonymous with her work.

Having grown up the daughter of a famous and revered director, Coppola was used to being around the movie business. She has often talked of how she would spend a lot of time on her father's sets or travelling across the country as he was filming. Furthermore, she even has cameo appearances in a number of his films, the most memorable of which was, admittedly a little more than a cameo, in *The Godfather: Part III* (F.F. Coppola, 1990), a performance for which she was somewhat harshly criticised, and as a result saw her retreat from performing in front of the camera. Yet, one way or another, these experiences have certainly shaped her directorial work, as (quasi) father-daughter relationships and depictions of fame and celebrity permeate her oeuvre.

From Bill Murray's washed up actor in *Lost in Translation* via the self-involved teenage Queen in *Marie Antoinette* to the disenfranchised and drifting Johnny Marco (Stephen Dorff) in *Somewhere*, Coppola's protagonists often have to contend with the trappings of fame and recognition, or in Murray's character's case, he has to confront the reality of his diminishing fame. Even the Lisbon sisters in *The Virgin Suicides* are 'local-celebrities', simultaneously idolised and desired by the neighbourhood boys, feelings which are only enhanced by their alluring mystery. Furthermore, the band of teenagers at the centre of *The Bling Ring* (2013) are utterly obsessed with celebrity culture, a fascination which leads to them burgling the houses of LA's rich and famous.

However, it is in her 2010 film *Somewhere*, that the other overriding theme of her work comes most visibly into the foreground. The film features a jaded movie star, Johnny Marco, who lives an empty life filled only with alcohol and womanising. His monotonous and unhappy routine is threatened however, by the arrival of his eleven year old daughter, Cleo (Elle Fanning), from a previously failed relationship, who he has to take care of for a while. Marco is living in a luxurious hotel suite, and spends his days doing all tasks (filming, press releases, photo promotions, drinking, sleeping with women) with a largely vacant expression and an apathetic detachment bordering on boredom. Yet, although this set up seems ripe for some kind of character growth and lesson learning, Cleo's arrival barely appears to change a thing. Indeed, she readily fits into her father's benign lifestyle, seemingly without so much as an objection, and while the pair certainly seem to enjoy spending time together, there is no realisation or revelation to be had from Johnny. Although Coppola's films have always been more about moods and moments, as opposed to plot development and story arc, *Somewhere* certainly suffers from the lack of substance, in a way that the similarly themed *Lost in Translation* simply does not. That said, the interesting thing about *Somewhere* is the depiction of the straight father-daughter relationship (*Lost in Translation* has elements of a surrogate relationship) and its biographical nature. Perhaps the reason that there is what seems to be no development or character progression, as would possibly be expected from other directors, is because the way that Cleo adapts to Johnny's life and accepts it almost as normal is similar to her experience of growing up with her father – an experience that she often recalls as a happy and exciting one. Indeed, of the film, she has said that the character of Cleo was partly inspired by

> 'my memories of having a powerful father that people are attracted to being around and having a dad who did things that were kind of out of the ordinary. It's not all me, but there's things from my childhood.' (See http://www.focusfeatures.com for the full interview.)

Coppola's work has gained her mainstream adoration and attention. In 2004, at the age of thirty-two, she became the youngest woman ever to be nominated for the Best Director Oscar, and only the third woman in history, after Lina Wertmüller and Jane Campion. At the same ceremony she also won the Oscar for Best Original Screenplay. In spite of this acclaim, Coppola remains very much an indie director. The control she enjoys over her projects must surely be the envy of many a director, male or female, and as Rosenbaum again attests, when she works 'with her own material the freshness of her vision is even more apparent'

(Rosenbaum, 2003); showing that it isn't necessary to work within the mainstream to be popular and successful.

Following her success with *Lost in Translation*, a new wave of female indie directors started to gain more attention. Some, who had been active for as long, if not longer, began to receive more acclaim, whilst other, newer talents also started emerging.

Kelly Reichardt

In some ways the antithesis of Coppola's often vibrant and kinetic visual style, the films of Kelly Reichardt are stripped back and slowed down. Yet like her, Reichardt's works are populated with characters searching for connections and for meaning, in often inhospitable environments. In what is her best film to date, *Wendy and Lucy* (2008), the first of the titular characters, played by Michelle Williams, attempts to travel to Alaska on the promise of a potentially life-changing job, accompanied only by her pet dog, the eponymous Lucy. Wendy has only $500 to her name, and when her car breaks down in a small Oregon town, her situation begins to get worse at every turn. The world Wendy must navigate is sparse, and in the midst of the economic recession, employment is even more so. Released in 2008, the same year as Catherine Hardwicke's blockbuster *Twilight* and when *The Dark Knight* (Nolan) was breaking all sorts of box office records, Reichardt's small, relatable and masterful film, made on a shoestring budget of $300,000, reflects the social problems and anxieties felt in many parts of the country, particularly following the devastation caused in New Orleans by Hurricane Katrina.

This type of political commentary and social consciousness is typical of Reichardt's films and has garnered her great critical success, with *Wendy and Lucy* and *Meek's Cutoff* (2010) being particularly praised. However, in a 2011 interview with *The Guardian* newspaper, Reichardt states:

> 'I had ten years from the mid-1990s when I couldn't get a movie made. It had a lot to do with being a woman. That's definitely a factor in raising money,'

before going on to say that

'I teach for a living, and I make movies when I can. I've never made money from my films.' (Gilbey, 2011)

Furthermore, Reichardt has admitted that the ending of the final version of *Meek's Cutoff* was in fact not how she had originally intended it to be. On the last day of shooting, she was unable to get her final shot and as such, had to rework the ending, as she had no money with which to return for another day. The challenges that Reichardt faces when making a film seem to influence her on-screen style. Her films have muted colours and an often washed-out aesthetic, that reflect not only the frugality with which she has to physically make her films, but also the melancholic austerity (literal and figurative) faced by her characters within them. In addition, her films are set in large, unforgiving and natural places (*Old Joy* (2006), *Meek's Cutoff* and *Night Moves* (2013)) or somewhat hostile towns (*River of Grass* (1994) and *Wendy and Lucy*) that simultaneously inhibit her characters and at the same time, provide them with the tantalising possibility of freedom.

Having usually worked with lesser-known actors (the wonderful Michelle Williams aside), Reichardt's newest film *Night Moves*, about three radical environmentalists who plot to blow up a dam, marks a departure for the director, as it features bigger stars Jesse Eisenberg, Dakota Fanning and Peter Sarsgaard. At the time of writing, the film had only been screened on the festival circuit but had received a mostly positive response, and according to some critics, it seems to have a more discernible narrative plot structure than some of the director's earlier work (Kohn, 2013). Therefore, for Reichardt, it remains to be seen whether the addition of star names and a slightly more conventional narrative either facilitates a move into mainstream filmmaking or, better still, makes the funding for her own, personal projects, flow a whole lot easier.

Courtney Hunt

In the year prior to Kathryn Bigelow's Oscar success, first time director Courtney Hunt received a nomination for best original screenplay for her gritty debut thriller *Frozen River* (2008); the film also won her the Grand Jury prize at the Sundance Film Festival. Played out on a Mohawk Indian Reservation near the Canadian and American border in Upstate New York, a landscape similar in severity to those employed by Reichardt, the film focuses on a working class woman (Melissa Leo) struggling to make ends meet and raise her two sons, while her largely absent husband gambles away what little money they do have. Her dire plight leads her to a meeting with a similarly hard-up Mohawk woman (Misty Upham), and the pair decide to earn some extra cash by transporting illegal immigrants across the border. Following this success, Hunt appeared to be a film maker to watch. Unfortunately, her follow-up to *Frozen River*, whatever it may be, hasn't materialised as yet, and a planned biographical mini-series about Hillary Clinton, which Hunt was set to write and direct, was recently cancelled by American network NBC. That said, for the sheer harsh and gritty quality of *Frozen River*, Hunt's next project will certainly be worth a look.

Debra Granik

In a similar vein to *Frozen River*, director Debra Granik released her second feature *Winter's Bone* (2010) to almost universal acclaim (the film has a 94% 'Certified Fresh' rating on the review website rottentomatoes.com). Jennifer Lawrence plays Ree, a teenage girl with a mentally ill mother, who must take care of herself and her two younger siblings while trying to locate her missing, ex-convict father before the family are evicted from their home. The plight of characters in extreme poverty is once again the focus, as is the case with the aforementioned films of Reichardt and Hunt, yet the outcome of Granik's film is not quite as bleak or hopeless as that of *Wendy and Lucy* or *Meek's Cutoff*. In addition to garnering four Oscar nominations, as well as countless other nominations and wins at various festivals, the film also features the breakout role of Jennifer Lawrence, who excels incredibly as the feisty, tough-willed Ree, and has since gone on to star in blockbuster franchises *The Hunger Games* and *X-Men*, and win a best actress Oscar for *Silver Linings Playbook* (Russell, 2012). Prior to *Winter's Bone*, Granik had directed one feature, which won her the Best Director prize at Sundance, 2004's *Down to the Bone* starring Vera Farmiga, in another breakout performance. This film had similarly high critical praise, although it didn't quite gain the same widespread recognition as Granik's second effort. Although these two films have featured female protagonists and the struggles of holding together a family unit, the director's next project is slated to be an adaptation of Russell Banks' novel *Rule of the Bone* about a fourteen-year-old boy who flees his troubled home to search for his biological father in Jamaica.

Lisa Cholodenko

Just as the success of *Winter's Bone* thrust Granik further into the limelight, so in the same year, director Lisa Cholodenko also found her work receiving more attention thanks to her wonderful comedy-drama *The Kids Are All Right* (2010). The film features star names including Annette Bening, Julianne Moore and Mark Ruffalo, but was made for a relatively cheap $4 million and shot in under a month. The plot centres on married lesbian couple Nic (Bening) and Jules (Moore) who have had two children using the same anonymous sperm donor. The children, who are growing older, decide they want to meet their father and the older of the two, Joni (Mia Wasikowska) tracks the man down, at the behest of her young brother Laser (Josh Hutcherson). The arrival of the man, Paul (Ruffalo), causes tensions within the family, and as he and Jules begin an affair, proceedings become even more complicated. The film featured on many top ten lists of 2010, as well as receiving four Oscar nominations, including best film and best original screenplay, and winning two Golden Globe awards for best actress (Bening) and best motion picture – musical or comedy.

Cholodenko, herself a lesbian, has been praised for her depictions of LGBT issues, and indeed her and her partner had had a child via sperm donation prior to the filming of *The Kids Are All Right*. Exploring themes such as the fluidity of sexuality and the psychology of human relationships and family units is at the core of all of the director's films. She has been making films since 1998 and her debut came in the shape of poignant drama *High Art*. Coupled with *Laurel Canyon* (2002), these two early films share many common threads and offer interesting readings on women, sexuality, liberalism and perhaps even the movie industry itself.

CELLULOID CEILING

Both *High Art* and *Laurel Canyon* share a similar premise, and focus on the awakenings of, and rebellions by, their female protagonists. In *High Art*, young magazine intern Syd (Radha Mitchell) drifts further away from her steady, dependable boyfriend as she becomes increasingly enticed, both professionally and personally, by drug-addicted photographer Lucy (Ally Sheedy). Whilst in *Laurel Canyon*, the innocent and naïve Alex (Kate Beckinsale) is seduced literally and figuratively by her fiancée Sam's (Christian Bale) unorthodox, record producer mother, Jane (Frances McDormand) and her rock star boyfriend. As Syd is seemingly rebelling against what she perceives as the humdrum of heterosexuality, whilst trying to advance her career, so Alex revolts *against* her work; putting off completing her dissertation in order to shed her timid, bookworm persona by getting high with the band and her potential mother-in-law. Cholodenko wants both of her protagonists to have more. Unsatisfied by academic or career related success, Syd and Alex desire freedom from both the bonds said successes encumber, as well as from the conventions of contemporary society; a liberation they find mainly in sexuality and drugs.

In a male dominated sphere, into which female directors are often pigeon-holed or expected to make certain types of films, Cholodenko's early works provide an apt metaphor for women filmmakers as a whole. Yet interestingly however, the outcome is largely negative for both Syd and Alex. Having left her boyfriend and gained a front cover credit thanks to her lover Lucy's pictures, Syd is left alone and distraught as Lucy dies from an overdose; perhaps alluding to the difficulties women face in balancing a successful personal and professional life. Similarly, at the conclusion of *Laurel Canyon* it is inferred that Alex will be alone too, as Sam, having discovered his fiancée's dalliances, appears as though he will leave after simultaneously harbouring growing feelings for another woman; appearing to show that liberation and freedom come at a cost.

In spite of these possibly pessimistic conclusions, Cholodenko certainly rebels against the difficulties female directors face. And as well as familiar thematic strands, her first two features also share stylistic similarities – in the sense that the filmic form she produces, matches and compliments the content of each plot. In *High Art*, the cinematography is distinctive and fitting for its imperfection, slightly drained colour tone and raw photographic quality. In *Laurel Canyon* on the other hand, Cholodenko switches her focus to music (in keeping with Jane's career), and the film's memorable soundtrack, which encompasses both diagetic and non-diagetic tracks.

After two films in four years, Cholodenko's ratio has unfortunately slowed. Following the release of *Cavedweller* in 2004, there followed a six year hiatus until *The Kids Are All Right*. The success of the latter however, both critically and commercially, will hopefully mean that there will be more prolific work to come from a director who has strived to soar out of pigeon holes by producing interesting and engaging features within the indie world.

African-American newcomers

Whereas Cholodenko depicts and champions different perspectives of sexuality often marginalised by the mainstream (the work of director Jamie Babbit can also be bracketed here to a lesser extent), so independent filmmakers such as Kasi Lemmons, Gina Prince-Bythewood and Ava DuVernay explore and represent views of race and specifically, African-American culture. Prince-Bythewood's two features to date are arguably the most widely-known, the first of which, *Love & Basketball* (2000) was praised roundly and won her the Best First Screenplay award at the Independent Spirit Awards in 2001. Lemmons' work has perhaps received slightly less acclaim and attention but she has directed a wide number of star names including Samuel L. Jackson, Don Cheadle and most recently, Oscar winner Forest Whitaker in *Black Nativity* (2013). Her best work however, is arguably 2007's *Talk to Me*, a biopic of talkshow host and activist Ralph 'Petey' Greene (Cheadle), set against the backdrop of the Civil Rights movement.

Ava DuVernay is the newest talent of the three directors, with her first feature coming in the shape of the little-seen, but impressive, *I Will Follow* (2011). Her follow-up film, which was released just a year later, *Middle of Nowhere* (2012) secured her the Best Director prize at the Sundance Film Festival; making her the first African-American woman ever to win the award. Thanks to this film and its accompanying acclaim, her stock has quickly risen, and she is now scheduled to direct the Martin Luther King biopic, *Selma*, a feature that will surely see her move into more mainstream territory.

Comic Touch

The comedy genre has long been seen as a predominantly (if not *wholly*) male sphere. Yet in recent years, a number of female directors have moved into this area, and made smart, funny and successful films. Although predominantly a writer, Diablo Cody, has just directed her first feature film *Paradise* (2013). Yet, it was the scribing of 2007's indie hit *Juno* that brought Cody to the foreground of the genre. The endearing and charming film, which tells the story of a teenage girl who faces an unplanned pregnancy, and decides to give the baby up for adoption, received four Oscar nominations, with Cody winning Best Original Screenplay. She followed up this unprecedented success by writing comedy-horror *Jennifer's Body* (Kusama, 2009) and *Young Adult* (Reitman, 2013) for her *Juno* director, Jason Reitman. Likewise, Lena Dunham has received more acclaim as a writer than director to date. Her hit HBO show *Girls* (2012–) has highlighted her as one of the most promising talents in television and cinema. Her first feature-length film, *Tiny Furniture* (2010) was made for a miniscule $65,000 and featured her real-life sister and mother as her character's on-screen equivalents. Roger Ebert said of Dunham and the film,

> 'It's hard enough for a director to work with actors, but if you're working with your own family in your own house and depicting passive aggression, selfishness and discontent and you produce a film this good, you can direct just about anybody in just about anything.'
> (Ebert, 2010)

Although Dunham has received somewhat simplistic criticism for her depictions of white, middle class New Yorkers, her refusal to apologise for depicting early twenty-somethings searching for their purpose in life has won her many fans and a huge book deal.

Another director who has flourished on television is Nicole Holofcener who has directed episodes of comedies *Sex and the City* (1998–2004) and *Parks and Recreation* (2009–). In addition, she has five feature films to her name, the most recent of which was *Enough Said* (2013), a film that was not only a critical but also a financial success featuring, as it did, one of the final performances of James Gandolfini, before the actor's untimely death. Although her films are romantic comedies, her work has received praise for its realistic portrayals of women and relationships, and a number of films, despite being made with small budgets, have gone on to perform well at the box office.

For a unique, quirky and possibly darker style of comedy, the work of Miranda July (*Me and You and Everyone We Know* (2005) and *The Future* (2011)) and Tamara Jenkins (*Slums of Beverly Hills* (1998) and *The Savages* (2007)) is also worth noting.

Whereas mainstream Hollywood, with its increasing budgets, is continuously difficult to break into, the independent film world appears to be an arena where women filmmakers can flourish. Following the success of the likes of Kathryn Bigelow, who has (largely) successfully moved between the two worlds, and Sofia Coppola, whose work is decidedly indie but the attention it receives, pointedly mainstream, a new wave of talented independent women filmmakers has emerged in North America, gaining awards and critical acclaim.

Even if these directors do not move successfully into the mainstream world, they can continue to flourish in the indie arena, where they will arguably receive more critical success for their work and where their creativity can continue to develop unhindered.

Author biography

Nathan Shaw is a freelance film writer based in Spain and Wales. He completed his MA with a distinction in World Film Studies at Swansea University, after previously completing a BA in European Film Studies, where his dissertation focused on contemporary American Independent cinema. He is currently preparing his doctoral thesis.

Contact: nshaw17@gmail.com

8. Oscar-worthy Women Directors

Patricia Di Risio

Measuring the success of female directors is immediately problematised *ipso facto* by the constrictions of gender. They will inevitably be compared to men and measured by male standards while they will be subjected to the kind of scrutiny that would never be imposed or even raised when considering the career of a male director. Their ability or willingness to adhere to traditional social understandings of their gender role and promote issues of interest to their gender group is often fundamental in the consideration of the work of a female director and is frequently the main reason for ensuing controversies. This has undoubtedly been the case for most of the women who have proven worthy of an Oscar for Best Director.

In the entire history of the Academy Awards only four women have ever been nominated in the category for Best Director and only one woman has ever been awarded the Oscar. In 2010, Kathryn Bigelow made Hollywood history as the first female director to receive the coveted award. Only three other women have ever been nominated in this category: Sophia Coppola in 2003 for *Lost in Translation*, Jane Campion in 1994 for *The Piano* and Lina Wertmüller in 1976 for *Seven Beauties*. While all of these female directors have also been recognised for their achievements in other categories, such as Best Original Screenplay, and they have also received other desirable international awards, this golden statuette has largely remained elusive to women directors.[1] The feminist agenda with which their body of work is often imbued has given these women status as auteur directors and, given the inherent counter-cultural nature of both the form and content of many of their films, the expectation to sustain this alternative political quality has been intense. The nature of their auteurist status, however, frequently relies on, and resides in, their feminist politics. In some instances, the perception that they have abandoned, betrayed or distanced themselves from those principles is often seen as a consequence of their Oscar-winning success, including the fact that they were shortlisted. These four female directors have inevitably been subject to the uneasy relationship between the mainstream commercial success that the Academy Awards represent and the different feminist agendas their films promote. Understanding the nature of this relationship and the problems that are inherent within it is one of the important challenges that continue to face women filmmakers of the 21st Century.

Kathryn Bigelow

Kathryn Bigelow has maintained an unusual position regarding this relationship as she has frequently expressed a determination to make her gender inconsequential to her career:

> '…in numerous interviews Bigelow repeatedly denies the centrality of gender to the style and radical politics of her films and to her position within Hollywood cinema.'
> (Jermyn & Redmond, 2003: 4)

Although feminist themes and protagonists feature in her work she is best known for her ability to produce outstanding examples of 'traditionally' male-oriented Hollywood genre films. Her Oscar for *The Hurt Locker* consolidated the perception of Bigelow as a director who is more predisposed to action and thriller genres rather than melodramas and films about women's issues. *The Hurt Locker* focuses on the tragic and emotional journey of Sergeant First Class William James (Jeremy Renner) who is a member of an elite army bomb squad serving in Baghdad. As a story it has very little scope or development for female characters, however, as a war film it does fulfil the characteristics of what has been described as male melodrama (Modleski, 2009) with its focus on the theme of male self-sacrifice. In this context, the film is representative of her work in general.

It is not uncommon for Bigelow's protagonists to clearly overturn gender roles and expectations regardless of their sex. The dramatic closing of the film *The Loveless* (1981) sees the sexually precocious Telena (Marin Kanter) shoot and kill her sexually abusive father after becoming involved with the classic anti-hero Vance (Willem Defoe). In this film Bigelow pays homage to *The Wild One* (Benedek, 1953) starring Marlon Brando, but is seen to toy with the biker genre, especially through the subversion of gender roles. The protagonist Caleb (Adrian Pasdar) in *Near Dark* (1987) is taken through a journey of sexual awakening and seduced into the bloodthirsty world of vampirism by the young and desirable Mae (Jennifer Wright). His lustful exploits elicit and explore an eroticism which has distinct overtones of a queer hyper-sexuality (Jones, 2003: 69). Lenny Nero (Ralph Fiennes) and Mace Mason (Angela Basset) in *Strange Days* (1995) frequently invert traditional gender roles. Mace is often level-headed and physically agile while Lenny is fainthearted and riddled with insecurity which is exposed as they proceed to uncover a police conspiracy that involves the vicious murder of a prostitute. The film has shades of the science fiction and crime thriller genres but is considered to be quite elusive stylistically. Both gender and genre are extremely pliable terms for Bigelow. This tendency and her shift from the independent sphere to more commercially viable projects created a tension in the feminist concerns of her work that is paralleled in the narrative of Bigelow's 1989 crime thriller *Blue Steel*. Jamie Lee Curtis plays police investigator, Megan Turner, whose detective skills are often dismissed or overlooked because she is a woman. As a character she is taunted by colleagues and subjected to punishing violence for pursuing a career dominated by men and machismo. The film fuelled the debate around the feminist potential of action heroines whose gun-toting behaviour was frequently considered as merely emulating negative masculine stereotypes and, cinematically, representing women as merely pseudo males (Hills, 1999). Bigelow's interest in genres that are usually considered the domain of males, and her willingness to collaborate with men on such projects, challenges traditional understandings of feminist filmmaking practices and reiterates the feminist dilemma facing the protagonist of *Blue Steel*.

Christina Lane (1998) has argued that this has led to an unwarranted disqualification of Bigelow as a feminist filmmaker, which has also consequently led to a questioning of her status as an auteur director. Many of her projects result from a close collaboration with successful male writers, producers and directors who are action genre specialists. She co-wrote and produced *Strange Days* (1995) with her former husband, James Cameron, who also acted as executive producer on *Point Break* (1991). This script was written by two men, Rick Kind and W. Peter Iliff, and featured two male protagonists indulging in the male-oriented sport of surfing. However, Bodhi (Patrick Swayze) and Johnny Utah (Keanu Reeves) form a love triangle with Tyler (Lori Petty), also a surfing enthusiast, and the three protagonists in the film all exhibit a distinctly androgynous persona (Redmond, 2003).

Despite recurring feminist themes and a deliberate play with gender roles, which is carried through from her earlier work, Bigelow has been accused of abandoning a feminist agenda. Her propensity towards the action and thriller genres is seen to perpetuate the patriarchal structures which prioritise stories that focus on men and exclude or marginalise women. In this light, rewarding the work of a female director for what appears to be her least overtly feminist example of filmmaking could be perceived as disheartening. However, as Sean Redmond points out,

> 'She has arguably become the most visible, enduring and accomplished woman filmmaker yet to sustain a career in post-classical Hollywood.' (Jermyn & Redmond, 2003: 6)

Paradoxically, questioning Bigelow's authenticity as a feminist auteur results in reiterating the gender divides that feminism originally set out to overcome. Bigelow's unconventional feminist approach has produced, divided and confounded debate in relation to the interplay between feminism and film.

Her film *Zero Dark Thirty* (2012) features a female protagonist and portrays the most controversial manhunt in history. The film tells the story of CIA agent, Maya, and her determination to hunt down Al Qaeda terrorist leader Osama Bin Laden. This film was also surrounded by controversy as the filmmakers were heavily criticised for appearing to condone the practice of torture as a method of interrogating terrorists and even potentially revealing CIA trade secrets.[2] Less attention was paid to the prominent role of women in this film and the crusade they conduct. Yet this focus away from the feminist elements of the film could be seen as a largely unintentional strategy that is ironically in keeping with Bigelow's desire to take gender out of the equation of the evaluation of her work.

Sophia Coppola

Sophia Coppola's brush with Oscar glory represents another important historical moment as she became the first American female director to be nominated for the award for Best Director. Coppola's relationship to both feminism and auteurism is somewhat overshadowed by her Hollywood heritage. Her personal circumstance of privilege emanates from a family filmmaking business and tradition, which is characterised by complete abandon to artistic indulgence. Francis Ford Coppola, her father, is best known for his *Godfather* trilogy (1972, 1974, 1990) a chronicle of the dangerous and violent mafia dynasty – the Corleone family. He was one of the leading maverick filmmakers of the Hollywood renaissance period whose style integrated European art-house techniques. His filmmaking practice participated in firmly inserting such techniques into the filmmaking vocabulary of New Hollywood. *Apocalypse Now* (1979), a powerful anti-Vietnam war film, represented the epitome of his combination of chilling violence coupled or juxtaposed with impeccably tasteful imagery. When Sofia Coppola released *The Virgin Suicides* (1999), the story of five sisters who mysteriously commit suicide, her father's influence on her visual style was unmistakable, but the quality of her filmic perspective has increasingly become unequivocally feminine. At the time of her nomination for *Lost in Translation* Sophia Coppola was yet to even be defined or acknowledged as a director whose work might promote a feminist cause.

Coppola's 'feminist poetics' is particularly enunciated in her later film *Marie Antoinette* (2006) and affirms the unnerving manner in which she is able to portray the adolescent angst of teenage girls as perturbed and, in some cases, a serious cause for social concern. However, according to Lane & Richter (2011), Coppola's filmic voice complicates the 'triumvirate' term 'Hollywood feminist auteur' that is frequently used to describe her aesthetic. It is Coppola's powerful celebrity status and the subsequent unrestricted access to an enormous network of iconic artists and designers which affords her art-house cachet. This insider advantage is blatantly exploited in her film *The Bling Ring* (2013). The story is based on the actual events in Los Angeles that led to the arrest and jailing of a group of wealthy teenagers who broke into the homes of the big name stars which the adoring fans followed. In the film, over a period of several months, they invade the homes of major celebrities such as Paris Hilton, Lindsay Lohan and Audrina Patridge with impunity. They revel in stealing personal belongings including clothes, cash and jewellery and then posting photos of themselves sporting the stolen property on Facebook. The artistry which is exhibited in the product placement of designer labels such as Louis Vuitton, Chanel and Versace, or the cameo appearance of Paris Hilton, positions Coppola at the very heart of the vacuous culture of celebrity worship that she exposes. This tends to result in a simultaneous flaunting of the materialistic excess that is being mocked and criticised.

Coppola is a director whose work draws heavily on her own experience and she writes her material from a world which seems too far removed from feminist politics for the association to define her oeuvre. Yet her focus on the coercive and corrosive nature of gender constructs, as seen in her preoccupation with adolescent girls, imparts a powerful feminist message. Despite this, when asked if she is a feminist and whether women have enough opportunities in Hollywood, Coppola also avoids any such labels;

> 'I don't want to be political and make political statements. I don't talk about political things. But there are more and more women filmmakers and I try to do my work and I'm happy that I get to put out a feminine point of view.'[3]

CELLULOID CEILING

Jane Campion

Hollywood success for women directors is not necessarily facilitated by a willing or unwitting distance from feminism but the relationship to a feminist agenda is certainly complicated by it. When Jane Campion was nominated for Best Director for the film *The Piano* she was already a favourite with the French critics. In 1986 her student film *Peel* (1982) won the Palme D'Or for Best Short Film. Her later films, *A Girl's Own Story* (1984) *Sweetie* (1989) and *An Angel at My Table* (1990), were all well received critically and attracted awards both locally and internationally.[4] These films revealed a quirky irreverence in both style and content that made her popular and much sought after. Her work also appeared as unambiguously feminist as it placed women and the various ways in which they have been abused or oppressed at the hands of patriarchal culture at the centre of her narratives.

Campion's indictment of domestic spaces is unrelenting and pursues an aspect that can be identified in many women's films of the 40s and 50s which present a critique of domestic and family life, particularly the films of Douglas Sirk.[5] Her obsession with the theme of female confinement (Martin 2000) is frequently housed in the stifling suburbia she depicts (Simmons 2009). Campion often portrays domestic spaces as a disturbing and crippling environment for women and not a domain from which to yield power or authority or a place where female and feminine concerns reside and are resolved.

This welcome and incisive feminist vision was, for many critics, compromised by the Hollywood affiliation and success of *The Piano* and the relationship with more commercially-oriented enterprises it subsequently encouraged. The counter-cultural nature of her work, fundamental to the feminist tradition from which she emerged, was seen to be yielding to commercial imperatives. In addition, *The Piano* could be read as a film that only allows the protagonist, Ada, to speak from a marginalised position. She is portrayed as mute, a woman who refuses to speak, and whose thoughts can only be heard through the film. However, as Kathleen McHugh (2001) argues, the female narration frequently adopted by Campion is a means by which she is able to give voice to her own very distinctive and personal female perspective. McHugh suggests that Campion achieves this by shifting the voice-over from the more traditional use of the distant all-knowing and generally masculine voice to one more visibly grounded in female characters such as that of Kay in *Sweetie* and Ada in *The Piano*. Campion is extremely grateful for the favourable era that heralded her entry into the film industry and gave her the opportunity to enunciate this voice. However, in an interview, she suggests that the barriers for women have re-emerged;

> 'I don't think the same support exists for women now. I think the 80s were a hard won era … but I think that's all gone now and I don't think that things are better at all anymore, as hard as it was then for women in general.'
> (Verhoeven 2009, 186)

Lina Wertmüller

The audacious work of Italian director, Lina Wertmüller, never shies away from politics. On the contrary, her political vision is cynical, astute and can be described as heavy-handed. A disciple of Fellini, her characters are often grotesque or carnivalesque and no figure is spared her often acidic irony, least of all women and feminists. In *Seven Beauties,* Wertmüller produces another example of a contentious representation of feminism in the form of Hilde. Shirley Stoler plays the concentration camp commandant whom the Italian prisoner and former criminal, Pasqualino (Giancarlo Giannini), pretends to love in return for protection. Hilde is represented as an autonomous, intelligent woman who is in a position of power, however, she is also portrayed as extremely physically undesirable and prone to corruption. Wertmüller's treatment of female subjectivity has led to her being accused not simply of abandoning feminist principles but actively working against them. The subversive nature of her imagery often employs horrible and aesthetically displeasing images of women where their disproportionate features are emphasised. As Rodica Diaconescu-Blumenfeld argues:

'Her bloated bodies are not objects of male desire, indeed they are objects of repulsion to the male and, significantly, also to the spectator. It is through this characteristic that the grotesque females of Wertmüller take on a positive valence.' (Diaconescu-Blumenfeld 1999, 394)

Many theorists did not share her sense of humour which governed her often unflattering treatment of women. They viewed it as plainly misogynist and anti-feminist. The glaring incongruity of her imagery and her political vision, which was infused with unbridled humour, renders her work extremely satirical but sometimes difficult to decipher.

Wertmüller's interest in feminism is also couched in her broader commitment to more radical left-wing politics and even though her disruptive politics were considered vulgar by critics, her films had enormous popular appeal and performed very well at the box office in Italy. (Bachmann 1977) As well as sexism, she also addressed classism and racism and often made Marxist alienation a palpable reality. Women were frequently positioned as complicit in the structures that perpetuated prejudice, corruption and abuse of power and were no less condemned for their distorted morals. Such themes can be seen in many of her films such as *The Seduction of Mimi* (1972) and *Love and Anarchy* (1973). However, it is particularly evident in the film *Swept Away* (1974) where wealthy socialite, Rafaella Pavone Lanzetti (Mariangela Melato), ends up stranded on a desert island in the Mediterranean with her working class southern Italian deck hand, Gennarino Carunchio (Giancarlo Giannini).

The first part of the film sees Rafaella mercilessly belittle and intimidate Gennarino whilst in her service. Here the spoilt, liberated woman is cast as the capitalist and the macho Italian male as the communist underdog. Like their names, their personalities are exaggerations of the stereotypes they represent. As castaways on the island, the class power dynamics are reversed and they resort to the basest form of gender relations. Gennarino is seen to ruthlessly abandon his own political principles and takes advantage of the situation to exact revenge; he dominates and ridicules Rafaella and reduces her to a mere sex slave and servant.

The source of controversy around Lina Wertmüller's work

undoubtedly encompassed her left-wing political leanings, but the criticism levelled against her often centred on what looked like a troubled and ambivalent relationship to feminism. (Diaconescu-Blumenfeld 1999). As Wertmüller has indicated in an interview, she is frequently concerned with the ways in which individuals in all walks of life end up selling their soul to the devil in the name of survival. In Wertmüller's world view, the resulting loss of personal and political integrity is a form of death. Her characters are often reduced to a debased way of living from which they cannot genuinely promote any politics, feminist or otherwise. Thus, while she addressed feminist issues, Wertmüller's work was not confined to this agenda alone and, like Bigelow, she did not wish for her gender to define the quality of her work,

> 'What would make me really sad would be the realisation that my success is due to being a woman.' (Bachmann, 1977: 3)

Female Success in Film

Bigelow faced fierce competition in her category in the year she was nominated and received the Oscar. In the running were James Cameron for *Avatar*, Quentin Tarantino for *Inglourious Basterds*, Lee Daniels for *Precious: Based on the Novel 'Push' by Sapphire* and Jason Reitman for *Up in the Air*. Pictures published in *Mail Online* (March 8th 2010)[6] show the stars in the auditorium at the Oscar ceremony where James Cameron can be seen sitting directly behind Kathryn Bigelow. When he approaches her to give his congratulations, he is seen extending his hands towards her throat as if to strangle her. The photo makes it clear that this is nothing more than a jovial gesture. But this image is extremely evocative as it conjures up a simmering or unconscious desire to throttle women for succeeding in a man's world, even if that violence – in this case – is only manifested in jest. The sexism which confronts women in many professional spheres can be considered particularly acute in the film industry. It dates back to early cinema where women's contribution to the rise of Hollywood and their high level of involvement in the film industry in the silent era was largely written out of history. This is currently being redressed via efforts in recent scholarship to document their participation on and off screen. (Abel, 2006; Stamp, 2011; Hallett, 2013) Some of the research also covers related industries such as film promotion and journalism. Overall, this research suggests that there were mechanisms which subsequently and systematically excluded women from the more managerial or industrial aspects of the filmmaking process, especially as the cultural and economic capital surrounding cinema became increasingly valuable.

Invisibility

The 'Celluloid Ceiling' surveys compiled by Dr Martha Lauzen at The Center for the Study of Women in Television and Film, San Diego State University indicate women remain significantly underrepresented in the US film industry. Despite significant participation by women, the statistics show that it remains a staunchly male-dominated working environment.[7] In this industry and many others, such as politics, engineering and business, the absence of women is most acute in senior or leadership roles. In the 21st century, women filmmakers, and in particular female directors in Hollywood, might not risk being erased from history but they do risk continual marginalisation. The misconception that filmmaking has always been an enterprise inhabited by men may have been an error of early cinema history but, with the current state of affairs for female directors, this situation may turn out to be written into history as such. Moreover, in the process of the recovery of this buried history of women's marked involvement in silent cinema, scholars have reported that it is difficult to dislodge the centrality of the question of their sex and their relationship to a feminist agenda. These factors, while clearly not as inconsequential as directors such as Kathryn Bigelow might desire, do seem to have a habit of being unduly prioritised whenever considering the work of female filmmakers. The controversies or vicissitudes which have coloured the careers of the few women who have been awarded or nominated for an Oscar for Best Director can certainly attest to this.

I am very grateful to Professor Barbara Creed and Dr Fincina Hopgood for their input and invaluable insights.

Author biography
Patricia Di Risio is a PhD candidate in Screen Studies at the University of Melbourne. She is completing a thesis which has a particular focus on the representation of women in late 20th century New Hollywood cinema and explores the interplay between gender and genre. Patricia has been a teacher in film and theatre studies at secondary and tertiary level in Australia, Italy and the UK and is currently a sessional teacher in Screen Studies at the University of Melbourne.

Contact: dirisiop@unimelb.edu.au

Endnotes
1. Kathryn Bigelow received The Saturn Award from the Academy of Science Fiction, Fantasy and Horror films for Best Director for *Strange Days*. She also received the Boston Society of Film Critics Award for Best Director for both the *Hurt Locker* and *Zero Dark Thirty*. Sophia Coppola received the same award for *Lost in Translation* and also received numerous international awards for best direction from organisations such as the Chlotrudis Society for Independent Film, the Italian National Syndicate of Film Journalists (award for Best Foreign Director) and the Vancouver Film Critics' Circle. Jane Campion was awarded Best Director for *The Piano* by the AFI, the Film Critics Circle of Australia and the Los Angeles Film Critics Association. She also received Best Director for *An Angel at My Table* from the New Zealand Film and TV Awards. Lina Wertmüller has received numerous European and international awards and was nominated several times for her work as director.
2. *The Guardian* (UK) article ends with: 'Like Riefenstahl, you are a great artist. But now you will be remembered forever as torture's handmaiden.' (http://www.theguardian.com/commentisfree/2013/jan/04/letter-kathryn-bigelow-zero-dark-thirty) The CIA denies that the extreme methods of torture employed in the film were used or that such methods were so instrumental in the success of the mission to capture Bin Laden and asserts this is where the film has taken artistic licence. (http://dissenter.firedoglake.com/2013/05/07/declassified-memo-shows-zero-dark-thirty-filmmakers-were-willing-propagandists-for-cia/)
3. Interview for SBS television website by Helen Barlow, August 6th

2013. (http://www.sbs.com.au/movies/article/2013/08/06/bling-ring-sofia-coppola-interview)

4. Jane Campion received the Best Screenplay in a Short Film for *A Girl's Own Story* from the AFI. The film *Sweetie* won the AFI Best Original Screenplay award and was also nominated for the Palm D'Or in Cannes. It won the Independent Spirit Award for Best Foreign Film and was in third place for the National Society of Film Critics Awards, USA for Best Director. *An Angel at My Table* won in a variety of categories at the Venice Film Festival and the New Zealand Film and TV Awards. It also received the International Critics' Award at the Toronto International Film Festival and also won the Best Foreign film in both the Chicago Film Critics' Association Awards and the Independent Spirit Awards.

5. The woman's film of the classical Hollywood era also criticised a range of societal and patriarchal structures: small town prejudices in *No Man of her Own* (Leison 1950) and *All that Heaven Allows* (Sirk 1955), romantic love and male vanity in *Letter from an Unknown Woman* (Ophüls 1948), women's domestic role in *Mildred Pierce* (Curtiz 1945) and patriarchal power in *Written on the Wind* (Sirk 1956).

6. http://www.dailymail.co.uk/tvshowbiz/article-1256279/Oscars-2010-Kathryn-Bigelow-woman-win-best-director-Hurt-Locker-blasts-ex-husbands-Avatar-gongs.html

7. Just 9% of the directors of the top 250 domestic grossing films of 2012 were women (http://www.womensmediacenter.com/pages/the-problem)

References

Abel, Richard (2006). *Americanizing the Movies and 'Movie-Mad' Audiences, 1910–1914*, University of California Press.

Bachmann, G. and Wertmüller, L. (1977). '"Look Gideon–": Gideon Bachmann talks with Lina Wertmüller,' *Film Quarterly* Vol. 30 No. 3 Spring 2–11.

Diaconescu-Blumenfeld, R. (1999). 'Regista di Clausura: Lina Wertmüller and Her Feminism of Despair,' *ITALICA* Vol. 76 No. 3 Autumn 389–403.

Hallett, Hilary (2013). *Go West Young Woman! The Rise of Early Hollywood*, University of California Press.

Hills, Elizabeth (1999). 'From 'figurative males' to action heroines: further thoughts on active women in the cinema,' *Screen* 40:1

Spring 38–50.

Jermyn, D. and Redmond, S. (eds.) (2003). *Hollywood Transgressor: The Cinema of Kathryn Bigelow*, Wallflower Press, London.

Jones, Sara Gwenllian (2003). 'Vampires, Indians and the Queer Fantastic: Kathryn Bigelow's Near Dark' in *Hollywood Transgressor: The Cinema of Kathryn Bigelow*, ed. D. Jermyn and S. Redmond, 57–71. Wallflower Press, London.

Lane, C. and Richter, N. (2011). 'The Feminist Poetics of Sophia Coppola: Spectacle and Self-Consciousness in *Marie Antoniette* (2006)', in *Feminism at the Movies: Understanding Gender in Contemporary Popular Cinema*, ed. H. Radner and R. Stringer, 189–201. Routledge.

Martin, Adrian (2000). 'Losing the Way: The Decline of Jane Campion' in *Landfall* 200 November 88–102.

McHugh, Kathleen A. (2001). '"Sounds that Creep Inside You": Female Narration and Voiceover in the films of Jane Campion,' *Style* Vol 35, No. 2 Summer 193–217.

Modleski, Tania (2010). 'Clint Eastwood and Male Weepies' in *American Literary History*. Spring, Vol. 22 Issue 1:136–158.

Redmond, Sean (2003). 'All that is Male Melts into Air: Bigelow on the Edge of *Point Break*' in *Hollywood Transgressor: The Cinema of Kathryn Bigelow*, ed. D. Jermyn and S. Redmond, 106–124, Wallflower Press, London.

Simmons, Rochelle (2009). 'The Suburb in Jane Campion's Films' in *Jane Campion: Cinema, Identity, Nation*, ed. Hilary Radner, Alistair Fox and Irene Bessiere, 175–186, Wayne State University Press, Detroit.

Stamp, Shelley (2011). 'Women and the Silent Screen,' in *Wiley-Blackwell History of American Film*, ed. Cynthia Lucia, Roy Grundmann, and Art Simon, Blackwell Publishing.

Verhoeven, Deb (2009). *Jane Campion*, Routledge Taylor and Francis Group, London and New York.

9. Interview with Kathryn Bigelow

by Ana Maria Bahiana

From *Cinema Papers*, January 1992, 32–34.
Reprinted by permission of Ana Maria Bahiana

Born in 1951 and raised in San Francisco, Bigelow was trained in the arts; first in the San Francisco Art Institute and then at the Whitney Museum in New York. She found herself bored with what she called the 'elitist limitations' of traditional visual arts, so with a group of other avant-garde painters and sculptors Bigelow started dabbling in film as an expressive medium.

The passion struck immediately and lasted. Bigelow enrolled in Columbia University's Graduate School of Film, where she studied under Milos Forman. In 1978 she completed her first project, *Set-Up,* a much praised short film chronicling a violent street gang confrontation. Three years later Bigelow directed her first feature, *The Loveless,* a stylish biker movie starring Willem Dafoe.

Bigelow's next film, *Near Dark*, had a troubled post-production. 'The company that made it lost its distribution [deal] while we were cutting the movie,' recalls Bigelow. 'They sold it to Dino de Laurentiis, but DEG went bankrupt while it was releasing the picture. So it happened twice on the one film! That's terrifying for a filmmaker.' Still, when the film finally hit the major markets in 1987, it firmly established Bigelow as one of the most promising and interesting American filmmakers – 'non-gender specific', she adds with a mischievous grin.

Blue Steel (1990), a gripping thriller starring Jamie Lee Curtis and Ron Silver, and this year's surfers-on-a-crime-rampage, *Point Break* (starring Patrick Swayze, in his first post-*Ghost* role, and

Keanu Reeves), further expanded her clout as an action director who, of course, also happens to be a woman, and is married to another master of the genre, James Cameron. 'It's funny,' she says. 'No one approaches Walter Hill and says, "Walter, because you're a man, how do you make such and such a movie?"'

Q: After making *Blue Steel*, where the female character is the driving force, you chose to do *Point Break*, which is essentially a male-bonding picture. What attracted you to this project?
A: It had everything: characters with really great psychological dimensions and an environment and setting which I thought offered a lot of possibilities. It is a world that hasn't been seen before. You might think you know a lot about surfing, but when you analyse it under a microscope, it becomes very surprising: primal, tribal, mythical and romantic.

Q: Did you do a lot of research into the California surfing community?
A: I met and talked to some of them. They have a really strange spirit and are very spiritual, but in a crude, inarticulate way. They don't communicate verbally and are very Zen... It is like they have evolved to a higher state of consciousness.

Q: Did you uncover any violent strain in the community, such as the one you portray in *Point Break*?
A: No, no, no. They're not violent. In the film Bodhi [Patrick Swayze] says, 'I hate violence,' and that's very important for his character [a mystical mastermind who shows Johnny (Keanu Reeves), an FBI agent, a whole new way of looking at the world and himself].

Surfers are not violent people unless they're pushed into a situation. There is certainly a lot of aggression out on the water, but surfing is a singular quest and a personal challenge. They put themselves in life-threatening situations every single day because they love it. They are very surprising.

Q: You certainly portray them with an almost mythological dimension.

A: I look at things not in the specific but metaphorically. Politically, it's really interesting to keep those myths alive, to not buy that grid, that system, without challenging it. Maybe they don't articulate it, but surfers do challenge the system. There's a myth here, an American Spirit; they're like cowboys.

Q: Did you get a lot of feedback that you, a female director, were shooting a macho-action film?

A: I had people saying that the audience would never know that this was written and directed by a woman [laughs].

I don't think directing is a gender related job. Perceptions that women are better suited to certain types of material are just stereotypes, they're merely limitations.

Q: Would you say then that there is a stereotype that women can only direct 'soft' material?

A: I don't really know if that stereotype exists, because so few women direct! I can't buy into clichés. I think the other way around: Why aren't more women making this kind of action movie? I'm curious.

Q: What was the starting point for your previous film, *Blue Steel*?

A: It all began with the idea of doing a woman action film. Not only has no woman ever done an action thriller, no woman has ever been at the centre of one as the central character. Obviously, I was fascinated by that because I'm a woman watching all these action films and there's always a man at the centre. You begin to identify with this man, with the most powerful character.

From that takeoff – deciding to put a woman in the centre – we worked out what the ramifications would be: How was it the same? How was it different? Obviously, when a person is fighting for her life, for survival, there are universal aspects that transcend gender. To what extent is it germane to the fact that she's a woman?

We then put in a serial killer, gave her an obstacle, and also made it a twisted, strange love story.

Q: And for *Near Dark*?

A: *Near Dark* started because we wanted to do a Western. But as no one will finance a Western, we thought, 'Okay, how can we subvert the genre? Let's do a Western but disguise it in such a way that it gets sold as something else.' Then we thought, 'Ha, a vampire Western!'

So it became a wonderful meld of two mythologies: the Western and the vampire movie. One reinforced the other. That sort of clicked.

Again, we came up with some characters and then put them in horrible structures to see what happened.

Q: Were Anne Rice's vampire books a big influence in your writing?

A: We were aware of them, but when we were writing we went straight to Bram Stokers' *Dracula*. The transfusion in the end comes straight from *Dracula*.

Then our effort became: How can we redefine and reinvent this vampire mythology in a way that hasn't been done in writing or in the movies? So first of all we decided not to call them vampires and, second, we took away all the gothic aspects – castles, bats, crosses, stakes in the heart. Ours are modern vampires, American vampires, on the road. I don't know what they are. They're creatures of the night who must drink blood to survive. They are… curious.

Q: What prompted you to make the transition from painting to film?

A: I felt painting was isolating and a bit elitist, whereas film has the potential to become an incredible social tool with which you can reach a mass audience. Some painting requires a certain amount of knowledge or education on the part of the viewer to be appreciated. Film is not like that. It must be accessible to work within a cinematic context.

Given that, the transition made a lot of sense. Film is accessible, challenging, and very stylistic, very visual. It works as a narrative and I saw it as a kind of modern literature. It's a very complex medium and I love it.

CELLULOID CEILING

Q: Were you always attracted to directing?

A: I never thought of it as 'directing', but as a different way of making art. I was doing painting, then I was making movies. Later I realised that what I was doing was writing and directing, being a filmmaker. But I really saw it as just switching mediums, from the world of art to mainstream movie-making.

Q: Does your art training help in the visual stylisation of your films?

A: It is important, but I am drawn mainly to story and characters. That's the most important thing; the visuals come easily.

With my training, I can obsess on the visuals forever. But I focus more on the story and the character, because that is what needs the work. No matter how beautiful a film looks, the most important thing is that an audience connects with the characters. You can make the picture too nice and distract from the emotions it has.

Q: Your films show a certain fascination with the subject of violence. Is that a personal interest of yours?

A: I don't know. It's not necessarily a personal fascination, though I do like intensity in movies. I like high-impact movie-making. It's challenging, provocative. It makes you think. It upsets you a little.

I'm just not drawn to material that makes you feel good constantly. I don't know why. I just love to see action films by George Miller, Sam Peckinpah, Martin Scorsese [James] Cameron, Walter Hill. These are great filmmakers. It's high impact with emotional involvement.

I'm also drawn to strong, dark characters that you believe in and care about. I like putting characters in very intense situations, which are an organic extension of those characters and that story. Take the roadhouse scene of *Near Dark*: I know it is a very violent scene, but I couldn't imagine portraying those characters without that scene, without showing how they live. That is the truth of their life. I thought it was critical to the picture.

In *Blue Steel* the guy is a serial killer. He's not someone who just waves his gun around. He is a seriously deranged human being. You need the truth of his character, his psychosis.

So I guess I believe in violence as a way to portray a character or a story faithfully. That doesn't preclude soft, emotional material that has no violence. It's just that the particular stories I've chosen are very intense.

Q: Do you believe there is a feminine way of expressing violence in film?
A: I don't think there is a feminine way of expressing violence or dealing with it. There is only just the filmmaker's approach. I don't think it's gender specific. Violence is violence. Survival is survival. I don't think there is a feminine eye or a feminine voice. You have two eyes, and you look in three dimensions and in a full range of colour. So can everybody. What about a woman's background would make that vision different?

In all my films, my characters, male and female, are fighting for their lives. That's a human thing.

Q: As you said, women are still in a minority when it comes to directing – especially their own scripts. But there have been a few changes this year, with important films like *Thelma and Louise*, *The Doctor*, and *Rambling Rose* being written or directed by women. What, in your opinion, would be necessary for a major change in Hollywood's gender bias?
A: More women have to want to make movies. Maybe the desire is not there, because I have always believed that where there is a will, there's a way. I don't believe in tokenism. It's not a matter of the industry saying, 'Okay, we want more women directors.' A woman and a man should work under the same degree of resistance. In other words, it should be based on their projects and what they have to show behind them.

Women have to realise very early on that every conceivable occupation is open to them. I can't think of anything that would not be open to a woman. So, it's an educational thing. As babies, girls are given certain toys, boys are given certain toys, and certain instincts are developed and become encoded. If you just realise that anything is possible... it is!

10. Moving Up – Women Directors and South-east Asian Cinema

Anchalee Chaiworaporn

In the world of filmmaking and artistry, South-east Asian cinema has been one of the slowest to develop, compared to its counterparts in India and East Asia, such as Japan, Hong Kong and South Korea. Although the first film screenings were organised by travelling showmen in the former European colonies, only a few years after the Lumiere Brothers introduced the Cinemotraphie in France in December 1895, the film industry is still considered to be both in its infancy and an elitist occupation. Only the privileged class can readily gain access to the medium, a factor which continues to prevent the entry of women directors in to the field, even now. Furthermore, several countries in the region have suffered from on-going wars, which have hampered the process of filmmaking and destroyed valuable footage and information, making it difficult to report on South-east Asian cinema history.

This chapter attempts to trace down the developments of female film directing in eight out of ten ASEAN countries: Cambodia, Indonesia, Laos, Malaysia, the Philippines, Singapore, Thailand and Vietnam, leaving aside Brunei, which has produced only two features up to now, and Myanmar where internal politics have disrupted all the production to date. Due to the changing nature of each film industry in the region, there is a large disparity from one film culture to another. But what they do have in common is the recent growth of their cinema culture, following increasing social stability along with the arrival of digital media.

Women play an integral part in this rise of new cinemas. In fact, female film directors play a significant part in the recent culture of South-east Asian cinema, despite the fact that most of them only arrived on the scene in the early 2000s.

Interestingly, the participation of women in directing in this region, manifests several characteristics that are unique, complex and rarely met in any other film industries. Though the countries are geographically close to each other, the possibilities for directing are significantly shaped by the nature of their film industries, as well as the availability of social patronage, and the privileges accorded by social class and education. The cheap and fast nature of digital filmmaking has also proven to be a game-changer.

Philippines: the pioneers

The Philippines is the first country where women embarked on directing in the region, and they have been significant in the construction of Philippine cinema. Before the arrival of the independents in the early 2000s, female directing had been limited to those with an industry connection to popular cinema. The first female director was found as early as 1933 when Brigida Perez Villanueva explored parental interference in young love in *Pendulum of Fate* by her own Villanueva Production Company. It flopped and Villanueva's involvement with filmmaking is still something of a mystery today (Pareja, 2001, p.36).

Consuelo Padilla Osorio came next with several films made from 1938 to the 1950s. Her opportunities arose due to her experience of working with her scriptwriter-cum-director husband before going solo on *Dalagang Luksa* (*Young Woman in Mourning,* 1938). Carmen Concha followed a year later with *Nagkaisang Landas* (*Having the Same Destiny,* 1939). She had produced a number of male-directed films, including the popular, *Oriental Blood* (Carlos Vander Tolosa, 1930). Scriptwriter Susana de Guzman made the transition from writer with her directorial debut in 1946 *Probinsiyana* (*Lass from the Province),* and maintained her popularity for another decade, together with her writing position in literary magazines. The next decade welcomed popular actress Rosa Mia who moved across to directing with *Pagdating ng Takip-Silim* (*When Dusk Arrives,*1956) for her mother studio. It was Maria Saret who led the charge with thirty films and broke the female trend for directing dramas by directing action movies, following her training with director Eddie Romero. When television arrived in the Philippines, the film industry gained two women TV directors: Mitos Villareal (*9 Teeners,* 1969) and Lupita Aquino-Concio (*Magandang Gabi Sa Inyong Lahat/Good Evening to Everyone,* 1976).

Most of these female works, like those of their male counterparts, fell into popular genres such as melodrama and romantic comedy. Film styles were simple and casting film stars was essential to their success. It was Lupita Aquino-Concio who broke with popular formulaic boundaries and began experimentation, like her brother Benigno Aquino, who created change in Filipino politics. Her direction is described as 'both sensible and effective ... never becomes monotonous or flat,' (Tiongson, n.d., cited in Wikipilipinas, n.d.). However, Concio's cinematic career, was often interrupted by periods of exile, as a consequence of her family's political involvement, and she made only six films from 1976 to 1997.

When Ferdinand Marcos imposed martial law on the nation from 1972 to 1981, two of the best directors in Philippine cinema emerged, with strong cinematic storytelling and experimentation. Marilou Diaz-Abaya, right after her first feature *Tanikala* in 1980, deliberately created her first trilogy about feminist issues – *Brutal* (1980), *Moral* (1982) and *Karnal* (*Of the Flesh*, 1983). *Brutal* raises the rape issue for the first time in Philippine society, *Moral* examines the struggle of four young women in a patriarchal world, and *Karnal* questions the theme of incest and the constraints of social norms. Diaz-Abaya delivered the films with tight, calculated intensity and weaves in the theme of madness, as her way of responding to the Marcos regime and the Ninoy Aquino assassination (Diaz-Abaya, 2004). But after the trilogy, she became less radical, and even went on to direct a conventional film about Filipino hero *José Rizal* (1998). In her thirty-two-year cinematic lifetime, from 1980 to 2012, Diaz-Abaya made twenty features, all about Philippine social and historical issues. As she puts it, it was necessary for her own development as a person, not only as a filmmaker (Anon, 2003, D-2).

Veteran actress Laurice Guillen might be less conscious of feminist ideology than Diaz Abaya, but she has been recognised as one of the most important directors of the new wave. She brought her experience of acting and working with noted directors like Lino Brocka, into the creation of her debut film, *Kasal?* (1980). Her third film *Salomé* (1981), made her a legend, while the film has since become one of the Philippines' classic movies. Guillen conceived of the film as a single narrative divided into three conflicting investigations into the same murder, using a highly visual technique, as a homage to Kurosawa's *Rashomon*. In her thirty-three-year-directing life, she has worked on thirty features, both commerical and arthouse, tackling several issues from crime drama to spiritual faith, which significantly focus on the human condition, rather than feminist values. Women characters are depicted widely from an irresponsible one in *Init sa Magdamag* (*All-time Hear,* 1983) to a grandmother suffering from Alzheimers in *Tangying Yaman* (*A Change of Heart,* 2000).

Today Filipino female film directors still lead the charge within both the mainstream and the independent sector. Like their predecessors, these women have been industry-trained, have studied film, and have often focused on making blockbusters. Names of women directors abound like Olivia Lamasan *Maalaala Mo Kaya* (*Do You Remember* 1994), Rory B Quintos *Basta't Kasama Kita* (*As Long As We Are Together* 1995), the comedy queen Joyce Bernal *I'm Sorry, My Love* (1998), Cathy Garcia-Molina *Because of You* (2004) and Bernal's assistant, Antoinette Jadaone, who made features *Six Degrees of Separation* (2011) and *From Lilia Cuntapay* (2011). Some works are enriched with new portraits of women, especially those of Olivia Lamasan. In *Madrasta* (*Stepmother* 1996), Lamasan defies stereotypes in her portrayal of a loving, caring stepmother who tries to belong in a family but never succeeds. In her next movie *Hanggang Kailan Kita Mamahalin* (1997), Lamasan boldly investigates the family tension that is built up when the wife becomes her own husband's boss.

The strong-roots of female filmmaking in the Philippines have been strengthened by the newly developing independent sector, and been nourished by the arrival of digital filmmaking and the birth of the Cinemalaya Philippine Independent Film Festival in 2004. Several women directors are moving on to make feature-length debuts, following their efforts in shorts or documentaries. Though their messages are not all feminist, they do offer alternative perspectives on the world. What is challenging for them is that this early filmmaking is being judged in a global market-place immediately, without the directors having time to learn their craft over several films as did Maria Diaz-Abaya and Laurice Guillen. Among the latest emergent directors are Pam Miras (*Pascalina*, 2012), festival-favorite Shireen Sono (*Big Boy*, 2012) and Philippine representative for the Academy awards, Hannah Espia (*Transit*, 2013). With 180 titles since 1933, this trend demonstrates that the Philippines is one of the world's most productive cinematic countries for women's works.

Indonesia: back to zero

Indonesia used to have only four women directors who made around seventeen movies in the period from 1926 to 1990. Each one was related to a prominent male member of the film industry. Ratna Asmara (1950–1954) was the wife of writer-cum-director Andjar Asmara; Citra Dewi (1960–1982) was the wife of producer L.J.N. Hoffman; Sofia W.D (1970–1971) achieved greater success in her career as a director than her two husbands did as actors, and Ida Farida (born 1939) was the sister of writer-cum-director Misbach Yusa Biran. But today there are at least fifteen active women film directors, not to mention many others working in producing and script-writing roles. What has provided the impetus and opportunities for contemporary female directors to succeed? Ironically, it was the total collapse of the Indonesian film industry that turned everything into a level playing field, where new-comers could make swift progress.

During the late 1980s and the mid-1990s, the Indonesian film industry was vertically integrated by distributors-cum-exhibitors, such as Group 21. They mostly screened Hollywood films and rejected local productions. Very few directors continued filmmaking at the time. Most directors turned to making drama for television. In such a state of upheaval, everyone gained an equal chance to bring about a renewal, provided that they had some negotiating power with the distributors/exhibitors. Producers were increasingly important because they needed to have the power to take a project from the funding stage right through to distribution.

Those with access to investment – foreigners, the royal family, or upper-class people – became the main players, including upper-class women. Unsurprisingly, the first post-collapse revival was initiated by Mira Lesmana when she produced and co-directed the omnibus film *Kul-de-sac* (1998) – a minor success among the new generation of cinema-going audiences. A lot of young filmmakers followed. And Lesmana remains in a management position today, producing a number of the country's top grossers such as *What's Up with Love?* (Rudy Soedjarwo, 2002) or *The Dreamer* (Riri Riza, 2009).

One of *Kul-de-sac*'s directors, Nan Achnas led the directing charge by asking for foreign funds for her own feature debut *Whispering Sands* in 2001 and then became the first post-collapse female director. Achnas marked her debut with a strong feminist piece about a mother who obsessively attempts to protect her daughter from the father's sexual abuse. Achnas's narratives are often constructed using female voyeurism and gaze. In her section of *Kul-de-sac*, she explores the fantasy of a movie-ticket sales girl who dreams of meeting and kissing her favorite movie star. When it comes to the feature film of *Whispering Sands,* the film reflects the overprotective maternal gaze. However, despite a distinct feminist ideology in her films, Achnas credits her father, who worked in advertising, as the man behind her strength: 'I have a feminist father' (Achnas, 2014). Her following works *Flag* (2003) and *The Photograph* (2007) are less concerned with gender politics than with the human condition, exploring the adventure of two boys involved in cleaning the school's flag in one and the last breath of an aging photographer in the other. Achnas also produces films for other directors, and teaches film at the Jakarta Institute of the Arts (IKJ) – the main film school in Indonesia.

Following Achnas, was the younger director Nia Dinata – from the 1970s' generation which saw a major push of contemporary female directors. Dinata was able to launch her directorial debut *Ca-bau-kan* (2002) before her generational friends, due to her parents' business accomplishment. Dinata is one of the most active directors and producers to date, directing five movies and producing fifteen features. Preferring to be identified as a 'neo-feminist' (Dinata, 2004), her films explore several controversial Indonesian issues, from the trials of Chinese Indonesians in pre-independence days *(Ca-bau-kan)*, gay themes *(Arisan!*, 2003) – Indonesia's first film about homosexuality; polygamy *(Love for Share,* 2006); sex comedy *(Quickie Express,* 2007) to a feminist omnibus *Chants of Lotus* (2007). Despite her versatiltity, Dinata has directed two distinctly feminist movies in *Love for Share* (2006) and *Chants of Lotus* (2007). *Love for Share* looks at the problem of polygamy from the perspective of three different women through a traditional comic structure. *Chants of Lotus*, however, explores the lives of a range of women in different geographical and social contexts in Indonesia, looking at the sexual practices of the internet generation, the friendships between women of different generations and their deluded dreams and the prejudices against women in modern Indonesia.

Every year we find women directors from the 70s' and 80s' generation operating within the Indonesian film scene. But unlike other South-east Asian independents who are able to jump into the circle, making their debut films right after their film studies and short film-making period, most Indonesian female directors additionally require some special social status that can be either individually or socially constructed, to enhance their directing opportunities.

Many of them are already famous or known in the industry before making their first features, such as actress (Lola Amaria), writer-cum-actress (Djenar Maesa Ayu), political activist (Ratna Sarumpaet), or assistant directors (Viva Westi, Titien Wattimena). Some of them get the opportunity to make their debuts because of their family connections. At the age of twenty-three, Kamila Andini had already produced her debut film *The Mirror Never Lies* (2009), because she is the daughter of famous director Garin Nugroho. But once they start, most of them go on to make more than one feature.

Among the new faces of Indonesian women directors, Djenar Maesa Ayu, Viva Westi and Mouly Surya are the most outstanding. Djenar Maesa is a novelist, writer, actress with works that are bold, and sexually provocative. Her debut *Meraka Bilang, Saya Monyet* (2008), based on her own literary works, portrays the same sensibilities and is considered one of the most provocative pieces. Ayu's fellow director Viva Westi, might be considered less politically outspoken, but her experience with the established director Garin Nugroho, enhances her cinematic reputation as seen in her five features ranging from horror to drama. The most promising woman director of the younger generation is Mouly Surya who has made only two features so far. By the age of twenty-eight, Surya had already launched her debut feature film *Fiksi* (2008). In 2013, Surya was selected as 2013 Sundance finalist for her second feature *What They Don't Say When They Talk About Love* (2013). With the participation of female filmmakers in the renewal of national Indonesian cinema, Indonesia has become one of the Asian countries with a strong cohort of active women film directors breaking through.

Thailand : the first and the last

With the recent international growth of Thai cinema, Thailand should be noted as one of the most interesting countries for work by emerging female film directors. It has only come about recently. Most Thai women directors only began making films after 2003, and, sadly, their directorial debuts, no matter if they were commercial or arthouse in nature, often became the first and the last film they were to make.

The first woman director in Thai cinema appears to be Ubol Yugala-na-Ayuthaya, known as Mom Ubol (Mom is the unofficial prefix of a prince's ordinary wife), the wife of Prince Anusorn Mongkolkarn and the mother of Thailand's 70s New Wave director Prince Chatreechalerm Yugala. As a member of the filmmaker family, Mom Ubol helped her husband by producing a lot of works, some of which were later regarded as classics. She is also considered to be one of Thailand's film pioneers, directing several movies under her family's trademark, from drama to action, including *Muaysin* (*Unknown year*), *Pak Thong Chai* (1957), *Chaloeisak* (*The Esteemed Prisoner*, 1959), *Torachon Khon Suay* (*The Rogue and the Beauty*, 1967). However, other sources also suggest that the first female director might be veteran actress-cum-director Suphan Buranaphim. As one of the top actresses and stage directors during the 1940s to 1970s, Buranaphim spent her own money to adapt a novel for her directorial debut *Cha-am Amphrang* (*The Camouflage Cha-am*, 1952) (Atiphayak, n.d.), but it flopped. Her second feature came twenty-five years later with another adaptation *Sai Seema: Nak Soo Samanchon* (*Sai Seema, the Ordinary Hero* post-1976), one of the earliest leftist novels in Thai society. The film explores the personal conflict of the male protagonist in choosing between his love or social justice, but the film is not known much in Thai society even now.

Novelist Nanthana Weerachon is also noted to have directed a film, *Phoomaree Seethong* (*The Golden Bee,* 1987), based on her own novel of that name. Weerachon is a popular writer in Thailand whose works have been adapted several times into films and television series. They always become hits with women audiences, despite the portrayal of rape in her works. Her protagonists are always virgins who are forced through circumstance to live with, and later suffer being raped by, the male character. At the same time as Weerachon, another woman director, Chariya Rungrueng was also reported to have directed a movie – *Khon Klang Muang* (*The City People*, 1988). Little is known about Rungrueng, except that she was the sister of famous actress Preeya Rungrueng.

When Thai cinema entered the new era in 1997, women were slowly integrated as a part of the so-called New Thai Cinema movement. There have been twenty-six female directors with thirty-two features and documentaries, either made commercially or independently. This group varies in age, class and background. The experienced directors have already been established in directing television commercials or series, drama and commercials, or producing or acting in male works. A number of them are also film graduates and have gained experience in making shorts. Unfortunately, only nine of them have ever directed more than one feature. Mingmongkol Sonakul crossed over from the studio to producing commercial films and directing indies (*I-San Special*, 2002; *Three Friends*, 2003) but she has not directed any more works since 2003. Pimpaka Tohveera turned to indie films after her studio debut failure (*One Night Husband*, 2005).

The most productive ones, however, come from two transgender groups, each with three commercial features to their names. Tanwarin Sukkhapisit made locally-banned *Insects in the Backyard* (2010) and *It Gets Better* (2011) exploring the family conflicts of a transgendered father. Sarasawadee Wongsompetch attracted lesbian audiences, in Thailand and China, with her first two features *Yes or No 1* and *2* (2010, 2012) – which was also the country's first lesbian film.

Ing K, as the first and sole indie director in the 90s, came to filmmaking by way of investigative journalism and then made several controversial video documentaries even before the arrival of digital media. Her first experimental feature *My Teacher Eats Biscuits* (1998) was banned by the government, due to its hidden criticism of the royal family. Ing K switched to painting for a decade and recently came back with the politically charged film critical of the exiled premier Thaksin Shinawatr in *Citizen Juling* (2009). Her second feature *Shakespeare Must Die* (2012), adapted from Shakespeare's play, criticizes Thaksin's regime again, and is banned in Thailand for the foreseeable future.

Anocha Suwichakornpong and Visra Vichit-Vadakan are two newcomers both with their own unique styles. Graduated with an MFA in film from Columbia University, Suwichakornpong submitted her thesis film, *Graceland*, as the first Thai short film in the Cannes' official selection. Her debut feature *Mundane History* (2010) is an anti-narrative experimentation which uses editing, cinematography and music to portray the connection between Thailand's patriarchy and royalty. It won numerous awards from Rotterdam to Mumbai. Vichit-Vadakan, instead, broke down the formulaic storytelling by mixing documentaries and features – through the use of 16mm and digital, into an exploration of a karaoke girl's life in Bangkok in her debut *Karaoke Girl* (2013).

Malaysia and Singapore: the most complex and hybrid

Among the South-east Asian countries, the Malaysia and

CELLULOID CEILING

Singapore cinemas feature the most complexity of multiracial and transnational characteristics. They shared the same regional film industry before the official political divide in 1965 and have distinctively separated since the 1970s. However, even during the so-called conjunction, the Singapore Malay film industry was hybridised by the film producers of Chinese origins (Shanghai, Hong Kong and then Singapore) and also by those directors of Indian, Filipino and Indonesian origins. Confusion goes further with the differing languages used in the movies – Malay, Chinese, and English. It's difficult to establish who is the first female director with so many transnational complexities.

Latif acknowledges (2001, p. 186) that Malay women directors appeared to emerge during the studio era of the 1940s right up to the late 1960s, starting with assisting Indian and Filipino directors. They came to full swing during the industrial renaissance of 1975 – when the first female director emerged. In 1979, actress Saadish co-directed *Ceritaku Ceritamu* (*Your Story is My Story*) with a Japanese director who is not credited in the data found in books (Chaiworaporn, 2014a), followed by Zalina Mohd Som (1981), Sarimah Ahmad (1982), Rosnani Jamil (1987), Julie Dahlan (1995), Shuhaimi Baba (1992) and Erma Fatima (1995). However, only Jamil, Baba and Fatima have been fully involved. All of them, except Baba, came into the industry via acting. Jamil had acted since the era of the Chinese studios in Singapore, before switching to dubbing, directing television series and then making five movies. Fatima made her directorial debut *Jimi Asmara,* almost a decade after her acting debut and today is involved in doing everything from writing and acting, to directing for both television and features.

Baba, one of the lead 1990s new-wave, came into directing right after her education at the National Film & Television School in England. Since her first feature *Selebung* (*The Veil*, 1992), Muthalib remarks (2013, p. 134–137) that women characters were foregrounded and were depicted as strong, indomitable, intelligent and capable of charting their own future. Baba often contrasts contemporary issues confronting Malays with traditional and spiritual elements. However, with the aim of making mainstream movies since her fourth feature *Mimpi Moon* (2000), she has lost much of her distinctive touch and style. Baba has still been an important figure in Malaysian cinema, both through her films and in her role as an active speaker against the authorities on subjects like censorship and unprofessional film crews.

In the 2000s era, Malaysian cinema has moved into another growth period, with the arrival of alternative digital filmmakers. Three women, who were cinematically-trained have joined as an important part of the movement. Yasmin Ahmad, Tan Chui Mui and Charlotte Lim. Ahmad, an executive creative director with advertising company Leo Burnet, struck out on her own to make five features, starting with the cross-cultural love trilogy between a Chinese boy and a Malay girl in *Sepet* (*Slit Eyes,* 2004), *Gubra* (*Anxiety*, 2006) and *Mukhsin* (2007). Ahmad's movies always communicate with audiences, jovially but narratively challenging the Malay social norms. Unfortunately, she had completed only five movies before her sudden stroke in 2009.

Tan Chui Mui spent a number of years making short films before she set up her own company, together with male colleagues Amir Muhammad, James Lee and Liew Seng Tatt in 2004. Two years later, her feature debut *Love Conquers All* (2006) was completed, winning an impressive string of awards. On the surface, the life of the protagonist, a Chinese girl, appears submissive to all the men around her. In fact, Mui embraces all of her background as a second-generation Chinese Malaysian whose parents immigrated from Taiwan. According to Muthalib (176–177), Mui evokes 'a state of subjectivity through perception, memory and fantasy in her feature'. But Mui has only made two features so far, including *Year without a Summer* (2010), in which she explored the nostalgic memories of three friends.

Charlotte Kim Lay Kuen has tried everything at hand in her self-taught filmmaking career – making TV commercials and shorts, as well as assisting Malay indie groups, including Singaporean director Anthony Chen's *Ilo Ilo* that won Cannes' Camera D'Or in 2013. Charlotte's feature debut *My Daughter* (2009) 'intimately touches a love-hate relationship between an extrovert mother and her introvert daughter,' (Muthalib, 189).

CELLULOID CEILING

When it comes to women film directors in Singapore, things become more complex. Even finding all of the directors' names is not easy due to the film industry's uneven and hybrid development. During the golden era of the Singapore-Malay film industry, most Singaporeans took producing jobs, and most directors were imported. When the revival started in the 1970s, the whole decade had produced less than ten feature films – some of which were directed by European directors. It was in the 1990s that the new wave of Singaporean directors started to emerge in which women have been visible. Again, another question arises – who should be considered as 'the first' woman film director in Singapore – the first woman film director working in Chinese – or in an English-speaking film?

Singapore has Maria Menado as the first female producer in the golden era, and then Marie Lee as the noted actress from Cleopatra Wong in the 1970s. But in terms of directing, women have only been apparent since the 90s. Sandi Tan and Jasmine Ng were some of the first to be critically acclaimed in English-speaking cinema in Singapore, following by Tania Sng, Tan Pin Pin, Sun Koh and Li Lin Wee. Almost all of them have studied film abroad – New York, Columbia London or Melbourne, returning back home to take up TV jobs following their experience of having made a lot of shorts or documentaries. Unfortunately, only a few of them could progress to making features. Among these, Jasmine Ng who went duo with Kelvin Tong in directing *Eating Air* (1999). Li Lin Wee managed to make two features *Gone Shopping* (2007) and *Forever* (2010). Actress Michelle Chong also moved to the directing job with *Almost Famous* (2011), which was immediately selected as the Singaporean entry for the Best Foreign Language Oscar.

Tan Pin Pin and Lynn Lee are the most talked about female directors to date. Tan Pin Pin's films have won numerous international awards, from Berlin to Pusan. In her movies, Singapore is used as a focal point for her explorations. Lynn Lee, on the other hand, takes a different approach. Her works usually create controversy wherever they are shown, since her first documentary, *Passaba*. It was picked for a grant from the Sundance

Institute Documentary Fund, and was banned in Indonesia for two consecutive years. Lee's daring and straightforward documentaries have often infuriated the Singaporean authorities. She has been called in for several investigations by the police and warned by the court. Lee's strength and confidence demonstrate her ability to make films which break out of her own national boundaries and speak to audiences across Asia.

Vietnam, Cambodia, Laos: women directors in the post-war era.

In the war-torn countries, we are used to seeing feature films which deal with the experience of war from the western viewpoint such as *The Killing Fields* (Roland Joffé, 1984), *Good Morning Vietnam* (Barry Levinson, 1987), *Platoon* (Oliver Stone, 1986) but what of films by female directors? Do they exist? Post-colonially, film culture in Vietnam, Cambodia and Laos, has just resumed in the last few decades. But surprisingly, as these countries have opened up, we find that historically, female film directors did make films during the revolutionary period.

Vietnam suffered from its on-going wars until its unification in 1975, but occasionally, local directors emerged. Pioneers were found as early as in 1948, shooting anti-war documentaries right in the revolutionary bases. When the war ended, Vietnamese cinema culture began to expand. The first feature film *Chung Mot Dong Song (Together On the Same River)* was made in 1959 by the so-called Vietnamese Revolutionary filmmakers, Nguyen Hong Nghi and Pham Ky Nam. The first female director Bach Diep also joined this movement. Bach Diep, born as Nguyen Thanh Tam into a photography family, attended the Movie School at the Ministry of Culture and Information and was trained by Russian experts. After graduation, she worked at the Vietnam Feature Film Studio, and continued even during the time of the American War. She started her debut *Tran Quoc Toan Ra Quan (Tran Quoc Toan in Battle, unknown)* and made fifteen films from 1963 to 1992. Bach Diep's works pertain to something meaningful and new to cinematic arts. Trung accounts (2001) her works as, in *Ngay Le Thanh (The Saint Ceremony,* 1976), the exploration of the 'innermost feelings of characters,' (Trung, 2001, p. 71) and switched to 'the remorse of US-backed Vietnamese soldiers (Trung, 1975)' in *Trung Phat* (*Punishment,* 1983). Her movies won numerous local awards and she found herself being honoured as the People's Artist in her contribution to Vietnamese revolutionary cinema.

Another young woman, Viet Linh, studied filmmaking in 1971, before travelling to study in Russia. Back home in 1985, she made her directorial debut *Noi binh yen chim hot* (*The Birds Were Singing in the Quiet Place,* 1986) with the Giai Phong Film Studio and continued successively with three more films during 1987-1999. In the last two decades, Viet Linh has only been able to make a few films such as *Collective Flat* (1999) and *Me Thao: There was a Time When* (2002) due to the funding difficulties. Linh's works are always strong in reflecting the changing Vietnamese society – from the war to capitalist days. Her films show a diversity of styles because it is 'the feel or texture of the script and the process of filmmaking,' (Philipps, 2012) that makes her movie, not any particular style.

With the free market economy, women filmmakers in Vietnam have found it harder to find funding and distribution for their films. Pham Nhue Giang, the next female director, only made two works in her twenty-five filmmaking years – *The Deserted Valley* (2001) and *Mother's Soul* (2012), after her graduation from Hanoi's Academy of Theatre and Cinema in 1988. Though her films have been sponsored by oversea sources, she has struggled to find a way to reach the audiences in Vietnam. Giang's films manifest strong humanist ideology. *The Deserted Valley* unfolds a 'pensive narrative structure and compelling performances' (Melbourne International Film Festival, 2001), while motherhood and womanhood are in conflict in *Mother's Soul,* the film that she described as 'most me,' (Linh, 2012).

Cambodia also has several female directors involved in the reconstruction of its fragile industry. Cinema in Cambodia was initiated by the royal family and kept private until 1958 after the first public screening took place. It reached its peak of popularity in the 1960s. Although cinema-going was a very popular past-time among the people, everything was halted under the Khmer

Rouge occupation. It took a number of years for the film industry to recover following the occupation. Contributions to this developing film scene, started in the early 1990s and continues to the present day, with female directors of different generations. During the 1980s and 1990s, women directors such as Parn Puong Bopha, Channy Peakdei, Mao Somnang, and Pal Vanarirak have come to the fore.

The most active of these, Parn Puong Bopha, has worked in various genres, after her debut in 1989, ranging from horror flicks *Mohetjata* (*The Curse*, 2004) and *Rosewood Spirit* (2013) to romance *Mae Ombao Meas* (*The Golden Butterfly*, 2004). One of her films controversially depicts a lesbian love story between a Cambodian-American woman and a famous Cambodian actress in *Who Am I?* (2009). It attracted some 4,000 viewers – a blockbuster for the country. Bopha's fellow director Channy Peakdei also launched her debut in the same year, but moved on to producing for others instead, while the last two Mao Somnang and Pal Vanarirak preferred to focus on literature rather than cinema.

One of the highlights of the revival of contemporary Cambodian cinema is the incidence of a new-generation of filmmakers with a robust social conscience. These directors often have a strong background in social issues, and often present their messages through the arts or documentaries. Homegrown director Lida Chan specialised in the Khmer Rouge archives before being spotted by Rithy Panh who later trained her and produced *Red Wedding* (2012). Chan follows the journey of a survivor who was forced to marry and was later raped by a Khmer Rouge soldier. The woman had kept her silence for thirty years until her decision to disclose the matter to the courts. Another upcoming female director is the self-trained Sao Sopheak who has made several documentary shorts on various issues. One of them, *Two Girls Against the Rain* (2013) enabled her to become the first female Cambodian filmmaker to be accepted by the Berlin festival. There is also Cambodian-American Kalyanee Mam, whose *A River Changes Course* (2013) won numerous festival awards, including Sundance. Mam noticed a dramatic change in her country's landscape and met many friends whose lives were changed and impacted by development – culminating in the making of the documentary.

Unfortunately, Laos has not been able to recover as quickly as its neighbours. After six decades of French colonialism and three decades of civil war, the people encountered many obstacles in rebuilding their new country. Priorities have to be given to rebuilding infrastructure and alleviating poverty, rather than filmmaking. The film industry was abolished and films were then controlled by the Ministry of Culture's Cinema Department. By 1989, the government realised the failure of monopoly and replaced it with a state company for the purpose of developing self-dependence. But it was too late and most production companies had gone bankrupt by 1992. Domestic production came to a standstill. (Phichit, 2001, pp. 83–91).

As with Indonesia's post-collapse film culture, anyone could enter the film industry in Laos, provided they had access to funding and equipment. The first group to start was the privileged class – foreigners and upper-class locals. In 2008, Thai independent director Sakchai Deenan was one of the people behind the revitalisation. He co-directed *Sabaidee Luang Prabang* (*Hello Luang Prabang*), with home-grown director Anousone Sirisackda, who used to work with the governmental Cinema Department. Laotian filmmakers started to emerge, though most of the early films were made by Thai filmmakers. Sirisackda went solo with *Khophienghak* (*For the Sake of Love,* 2010) and the rest were all first-time directors – Anisai Kaewla on *Playthang* (*At the End,* 2012), Thailand-trained Panumas Deesattha on *Hak-Am-Lam* (2013) and Mattie Do, on *Chanthaly*, the first horror film out of Laos, and the first work of a Laotian female director (Chaiworaporn, 2014b).

Do was trained at Italian film academies and went back to Laos as part of a relocation deal which was offered by a local production company to her husband (Honeycutt). With her husband's support, Do demonstrated real talent in her debut feature, the horror film, *Chanthaly*. Do questions the meaning and nature of parental love in the film. The overprotective father keeps the death of the mother secret from his twenty-something daughter, resulting in Chanthaly's request to meet her dead mother. The ending provides a twist. And it seems that even the love of the father is something ambiguous.

In the old Thai saying, women are considered to be the rear legs of an elephant, while men are the front. Feminists counter this kind of discrimination daily and try to equalise opportunities for women. Although there are women working as directors in the film industries throughout South-east Asia, it is not really the case that there is equality of opportunity. Despite the support for filmmakers from the governments in South-east Asia, the progress of women film directors is largely due to the development of film education, the arrival of digital filmmaking, the mushrooming of film festivals, and the fact that many South-east Asian women directors come from privileged backgrounds.

The depiction of women in these films is not always consistent with feminist attitudes and many of the directors choose not to be associated with the term feminism. However, with the upcoming establishment of the ASEAN Socio-Cultural Community coming into effect in 2015, it is hoped that there will be more female sensibilities brought to bear on filmmaking in the cinematic world.

Author biography

Anchalee Chaiworaporn has been writing for both local and foreign publications from South Korea, Spain, France, England, Japan, etc. including *Cashier du Cinema* and *Variety*. She has also been a consultant to Udine, Cannes Critic Week and Venice. She won Thailand's 2000 best film critic and 2002 best feature writer. Since 2002, she has lived in South Korea, Japan, the Philippines, Malaysia and Indonesia where she has researched women directors and Asian Cinema. She is now a leader in a national research project on criticism in arts, literature, theatre, music and cinema.

Contact: ancha999@gmail.com

Endnotes

Achnas, N. (May 2004). Interview on Nan Achnas. Interviewed by Anchalee Chaiworaporn. Jakarta Institute of the Arts, Jakarta. (Cassette)

Anon (2003). Moral. s.n., August 3rd 2003. p. D-2.

Atiphayak, L., n.d.. Suphan Buranaphim : the first 'Nuan' of Panthay

CELLULOID CEILING

Norasing. Dara, n.d., pp. 122–127.

Chaiworaporn, A., http://facebook.com/messages/anchalee.chaiworaporn, 2014a. (facebook) Message to Hassan Abd Muthalib (http://facebook.com/messages/hassan.muthalib). Sent Wednesday January 29th 2014: 11.07. Available at: http://www.facebook.com/messages/anchalee.chaiworaporn. (Accessed February 3rd 2014.)

Chaiworaporn, A., http://facebook.com/messages/anchalee.chaiworaporn, 2014b. (facebook). Message to Sakchai Deenan (http://facebook.com/messages/sakchai.deenan). Sent Monday 20th January 2014: 08.16. Available at: http://www.facebook.com/messages/anchalee.chaiworaporn. (Accessed February 3rd 2014).

Dinata, N. (2004). Interview on Nia Dinata. Interviewed by Anchalee Chaiworaporn. (cassette), Alyana Shira Films, Jakarta, May 2004.

Honeycutt, H.,

Marilou, D. (2004). Interview on Marilou Diaz-Abaya. Interviewed by Anchalee Chaiworaporn. (cassette) Manila, January 2004.

Latif, B.A. (2001). 'A Brief History of Malaysian Film', in David Hanan, ed. 2001. *Film in South East Asia: views from the region.* Hanoi: Vietnam Film Institute, p. 186.

Linh, T. (2012). More acumen needed to tackle womanhood. Thanh Nien News (online) (Last updated 8am on March 2nd, 2012). (http://www.thanhniennews.com/index/pages/20120302-more-acumen-needed-to-tackle-womanhood.aspx accessed February 3rd 2014)

Melbourne International Film Festival, 2001. The Deserted Valley. [online] (http://miff.com.au/festival-archive/film/22572 accessed February 3rd 2014)

Muthalib, H. A. (2013) *Malaysian Cinema In A Bottle.* Selangor: Merpati JingGa.

Pareja, L. S., *'The Women Directors in Philippine Cinema.' Pelikula: A Journal of Philippine Cinema*, 3 (1), p. 36.

Phichit, B. (2001). 'Laos Cinema', in: David Hanan, ed. 2001, *Film in South East Asia: views from the region.* Hanoi: Vietnam Film Institute, pp. 83–91.

Philipps, R. (2012). 'An interview with Viet Linh, director of Collective Flat'. (online) World Socialist Web Site. (http://www.wsws.org/en/articles/2000/04/sff2-a21.html accessed 3rd February 2014)

11. Films from an Unknown Woman:

Remediating the absence of gender politics in the films of women directors in China, Taiwan and Hong Kong

Pieter Aquilia

A surprising trend in the film industries of the Chinese-language markets of China, Taiwan and Hong Kong is not the lack of numbers of women filmmakers, but the seeming absence of feminist subjectivities in the creative works of these directors. Unlike Western nations such as the United Kingdom and the United States, cine-feminism has never played a major role in the development of women's cinema in China (Wang, 2011: 15–16). Instead, the lack of women's issues explored in feature film closely correlates with filmmaking traditions evolving from state policies of nationalism and colonialism, which often contradicted Western assumptions of feminism.

As early as 1949, Socialist China promoted and empowered women politically and economically, including in the film industry, but the cultural production of nationalist propaganda eclipsed gendered realities. For many women etching a career in mainstream cinema, the issue of gender was silenced to ensure professional survival. The films produced by women in the Chinese speaking territories of northern and eastern Asia reflected the political and philosophical diversity of the state, which was branded differently across communist mainland China, than nationalism in Taiwan and the shifting colonialist rule in Hong Kong. These variations produced significantly different women's cinemas in the respective regions. As a result, this chapter focuses on the career trajectory of contemporary filmmakers Anna Hui (Hong Kong), Sylvia Chang (Taiwan), and Xu Jinglei (China), all of whom have achieved commercially successful films that negotiate transnational boundaries and trans-generational issues of Chinese women. As Wang correctly highlights, in the case of female directors in China, Taiwan and Hong Kong, the label of 'transnational feminism' is pertinent to the exploration of the historical effects of nationalism and the nation-state, which first world feminism often dismisses (2011: 16).

Background: Chinese Language Women's Cinema

Historically, Chinese women directors have worked across mainstream, commercial, independent and experimental cinema. As early as 1923, women directors played a role in the emerging film industry. In Shanghai, Xie Caizhen's *Orphan's Cry* (1925) heralded a tradition of women filmmakers producing popular family melodramas. Successful Shanghai actresses, together with their male counterparts wrote, directed and produced these films that resonated with audiences. During the 1930s to 1940s, Esther Eng, a second generation Chinese-American, directed more than ten Cantonese language films, mainly romantic dramas featuring women, in Hong Kong and the US (Taylor, 2011).

After World War II, three major Chinese-language filmmaking centres emerged in East Asia: colonialist Hong Kong; nationalist Taiwan; and communist China (Wang, 28). These political structures strongly influenced the respective film industries. In China, the socialist state was important to the development of women's films. Chen Boer, an actress and aspiring filmmaker, became the director of the Communist Party's Northeast Film Studio (Zhang, 2012: 321). Chen's films focused on women's important role and rights promoted by Mao's communist revolutionary movement, using

> 'the silver screen to try and change the popular image of women as powerful seductresses with tepid insecurities – an image she rightly viewed as one created exclusively by male-dominated culture.' (DeNobel, 2012)

ASIA

In the period 1950–1960, Wang Ping, Wang Shao Yan and Dong Kena emerged from Beijing's military production house, August Film Studios, established in Beijing in 1952. Despite the noted absence of gender identity in the films made by women in the era, the films revealed the nascent role of female authorship, important to the gradual evolution of the female voice in Chinese cinema (Wang, 2011: 29). Dong's films, especially *A Grass on Kunlun Mountain* (1962), reflected a strong sense of female consciousness, creating believable and psychologically complex women characters that appealed to audiences (Taylor, 2011).

During the Chinese Cultural Revolution, filmmaking was restricted and foreign movies were banned. Many key players in the Beijing and Shanghai film industry moved to Hong Kong where Chinese female directors, writers and actresses gained a new prominence in the industry. Eileen Chang wrote more than ten scripts, mostly romantic comedies, demonstrating her focus on 'internationalism' and 'the individual's ability to transcend a specific social or cultural context' (HK Shanghai Cinema Cities, 2007). Similarly, actress-director Kao Pao-Shu produced seven films in Hong Kong and Tang Shu-shien, a USC film school graduate, achieved international recognition with her film, *The Arch* (1970), about the sexual subjugation of village women.

During the 50s and 60s, Taiwan's film industry flourished, buoyed by the country's rapid modernisation and a bourgeoning economy. In 1963, the Central Motion Picture Company produced melodramas designed to build traditional values. In reaction to state films, a new wave of privately produced Taiwanese dialect films evolved. Che'n Wen-min became Taiwan's first female screenwriter and director, producing eight films between 1958–1959, which often featured under-privileged female protagonists in troubled relationships. Her films promoted women's potential 'despite socio-economic hardship' (Wang, 2011: 30). In the 60s and 70s, Taiwan's policy of 'Healthy Realism,' which supported cultural and moral maintenance, transformed the film industry. Actress turned-director, Chong Fang-Shia directed twenty films in the period, ranging from melodrama, romantic comedy and patriotic drama. In the late 1970s, Wan Ying gained prominence with her propaganda films. However, these political films struggled against the popularity of imported Hong Kong films.

By the early 1980s, the cinemas of China, Taiwan and Hong Kong experienced a new wave of state-reactionary Chinese-language films, influenced by the French *nouvelle vague* and Italian neo-realism. More films were directed in China at this time than in any other country in the world (Wang, 2011: 31). Female directors played key roles, but their voices were often overshadowed by the dominance of the Fifth Generation filmmakers graduating from the Beijing Film Academy: Chen Kaige, Zhang Yimou, Tian Zhuangzhuang and Zhang Junzhao. While less successful than their male counterparts, Zhang Nuanxin and Huang Shuqin managed a more 'subjective and personal mode' of women's cinema, historicising women's awakening consciousness in communist China.

By the 1990s, a female counter-cinema emerged in East Asia, which featured a contemporary presentation of gender issues and women's narratives. Ning Ying, partly as a result of her study abroad and her collaboration with Bernardo Bertolucci, was instrumental in this new female cinema presenting a post-modern subjectivity and employing a merger of Western and traditional film styles (Marchetti in Wang, 2011: 33). Her Beijing trilogy (*For Fun*, 1993; *On the Beat*, 1995; *I Love Beijing*, 2001) celebrated a realistic portrayal of an increasingly urban China. Hu Mei, a fellow graduate of the Beijing Film Academy, directed *Army Nurse* (1985), acknowledged as the first film to negotiate the boundaries between women's sensual desires and their obligations to the state. It is considered one of the first Chinese women's films on par with Western feminist filmmaking (Wang, 2011: 33).

In the 80s and 90s, China's liberalisation of its film industry redirected younger women film directors to the independent industry. Actress-director, Xu Jinglei, was one of the first women to benefit from China's more liberalised film permits. Her directorial debut, *My Father and I* (2004) dominated the prestigious Golden Rooster and Chinese Film Media Awards, while her second film *Letter from an Unknown Woman* (2004) was an international co-production exploring single motherhood and prostitution. Xu's films were integral to a new genre whereby female protagonists had equal footing to their male counterparts. Kaplan (1999) argues that Xu continued to transform the 'diverse female subjectivity' first evident in Hu's films of the 1980s (in Wang, 2011: 34)

In Taiwan, actress turned filmmaker Sylvia Chang explored women's sexual awakening in her melodramas of the 1980s, forging a career that would transnationalise Chinese language films throughout the 1990s and 2000s. In Hong Kong, Chang produced a then unknown Ann Hui's first feature, *The Secret* (1979). Hui continued to become the most prolific Chinese woman director in the world with a body of commercial and arthouse films on transcultural issues and personal-political female subjectivity. Together, Ann Hui (HK), Sylvia Chang (Taiwan), and Xu Jinglei (China) form a triangle of successful, contemporary Chinese women directors whose films re-situate the female subject into a contemporary, global cinema.

Sylvia Chang (Taiwan)

Sylvia Chang, a fluent speaker of Mandarin, Cantonese and English, revolutionised women's cinema in her homeland, Taiwan, and in Hong Kong. Her family and romantic melodramas, straddle commercial and independent filmmaking, revisioning *wenyi pian* melodrama with her focus on the emotional, perennial struggle over the meaning of family and love. Unlike many of her new wave peers, Chang did not attend a film school in the West and, like Xu Jinglei, she has juggled directing with acting. Her films present characters that are historically displaced or relocated away from the Chinese homeland, consequently dealing with the themes of postmodernism. Chang positions women not only against men, but against each other: *Passion* (1986) deals with two middle class women in love with the same man; *Sisters of the World Unite* (1991) features two sisters facing divergent fates in both love and at work (Cui, 2003: 96); and, *Tempting Heart* (1999) cements the theme of duality with two teenage girls competing for the attentions of the same man. Critics identify Chang's portrayal of women as a 'psychic interiority' for self-identity within a patriarchal kinship system (Chow in Cui, 2003: 101). Chang's most recent films,

20.30.40 (2004) and *Run Papa Run* (2008) progressively reflect a more mature director whose films deal with gender difference with more equitable compassion.

Ann Hui (Hong Kong)

Aside from acting and directing, Chang played an integral role in nurturing the career of young woman film directors, such as Ann Hui, in Hong Kong. During the 70s and 80s, the Hong Kong film industry was more independent than Taiwan. An increasing number of aspiring filmmakers were studying abroad, returning to kick-start their careers in the flourishing film market (Wang, 2011: 35). As a result, the Hong Kong cinema soon reflected issues of migration, diaspora and a globalised Chinese identity (35). Ann Hui graduated from the London Film School in the 1970s and began directing half-hour drama-documentaries for Hong Kong television. Incorporating European avant-garde filmmaking techniques, her debut film, *The Secret* (1979), explored Hong Kong's past and its distinct national identity (Freiberg, 2002). Hui's body of works bear

> 'witness to a critical juncture in Hong Kong's recent history,' realising its 'rapid urbanisation and emergence of a middle class life' (Ho, 2001:177).

Her films deliberately parted from earlier Cantonese cinema by centralising and individualising women subjects. While Hui's early female characters are still subordinate to men, her later films demonstrate a 'distinctly feminine turn,' fracturing the 'patriachial determination' with more 'equality, compassion and sociality' (Ho, 2001: 179–182). *Song of Exile* (1990) and *Summer Snow* (1995) both showed women's confrontation of memory and location, implicitly pre-empting Hong Kong's de-colonialisation and return to the motherland. *Exile,* Hui's largely autobiographical film, negotiated her own ethnic past and the lives of migrant women, while *Summer Snow* argued for the endurance of inherited values against the erasure by the forces of colonialisation (Ho, 2001: 182).

After 1997, Ann Hui's films shifted to themes of post-modernity and the issues of ethnicity and nationalistic corporatism. Her

2012 film, *A Simple Life,* was critically acclaimed at home and abroad for its exploration of a servant sister who sacrificed her life for four generations of a middle class family. Like many of her subsequent films, it dealt with women on the outskirts and the social realities of unemployment, single motherhood, and aging. These themes were most explicitly narrated in the film, *The Postmodern Life of my Aunt* (2006).

Xu Jinglei (China)

Xu Jinglei, another actress turned director, is one of the few prominent commercial successful women feature film directors in contemporary China. Her ability to consistently garner the confidence of cinema audiences and attract investors to her projects, allows her films a creative and financial freedom not possible in the mainstream film cultural production in China. Xu's directorial debut, *My Father and I* (2004), a melodrama about a determined young woman who pursues a university education and single motherhood, despite her disadvantaged, tragic childhood and the failure of her marriage, won critical acclaim and awards at home. Xu's ability to present women as equal to male counterparts continued in her second feature, *Letter from an Unknown Woman* (2004). Although the film is often criticised as counter-feminist, where a woman 'must live through her man as his selfless slave' (Wang, 2011: 302), in fact Xu explored a rarely seen psychological depth of female characters through the use of a double narrative line.

Her low budget experimental film *Dreams May Come* (2006) continued the narrative between woman and older man, but stripped of the lavish style of her earlier melodramas. Instead, the one scene, one location, abstract conversation shot in six days, elucidated the dichotomies of man and woman, memory and forgetfulness, past and present, friendship and abandonment. Indeed, *Go Lala Go* (2010), about a Chinese woman juggling a relationship and her profession, performed well against US box office competition. *Dear Enemy* (2011) reworked the theme with two competitive former lovers in the banking industry who are eventually reunited in a workable romantic relationship. Xu's films have played an important role in contemporary women's cinema in

China, straddling the tenuous periphery of the mainstream industry and using her prominence as a movie star to present a strong female presence within the narrative and authorship of her films.

Conclusion

Ann Hui, Sylvia Chang and Xu Jinglei are often cited as East Asia's top contemporary women directors. Their ability to produce a consistent body of works outside of state financing and cultural production attests to the tenacity of their commitment to the creation of Chinese-language female characters and exploring women's subjectivities for mainstream audiences. The filmmakers have carefully negotiated their own star power as actresses, directors and producers to win box office and investor support. Chang, Hui and Xu bravely confront barriers in their homeland to internationalise and re-culturalise Chinese-language cinema, which until the 1990s remained subordinate to nationalistic and patriarchal values. While critics often debate the direction of women's filmmaking in China and the region, general consensus indicates that Chinese women filmmakers are contributing a new diversity to a previously male-dominated screen space.

Author biography

Dr Pieter (Pia) Aquilia, is an Associate Professor and former Associate Dean of New York University Tisch School of the Arts. Dr Aquilia has an extensive background as a scriptwriter, script editor and director in film and television. She has lived in Singapore since 2000, holding academic positions with Nanyang Technological University, University of New South Wales Asia and University of Newcastle Singapore.

Dr Aquilia is the author of books, chapters, and journal articles on the practice of film, television, and new media. Her research areas include the Media in Southeast Asia (2002–2005), International Television Drama (2004), the Internet and National Elections (2006), and the Globalisation of Screen Education (2011–2013).

Contact: dr.pieter@gmail.com

References

Cui, Shuqin (2003). *Women Through the Lens: Gender and Nation in a Century of Chinese Cinema,* University of Hawaii Press.

DeNoble, Damjan (2012). 'Chen Bo'er, the modern Chinese heroine, and (briefly) China's healthcare workforce,' in *HealthIntelAsia,* November 16th 2012. (http://www.healthintelasia.com/chen-boer-the-modern-chinese-heroine-briefly-chinas-healthcare-workforce accessed January 31st 2014)

Freiberg, Freda (2002). 'Border Crossing: Ann Hui's Cinema,' in *Senses of Cinema,* Filmmaker Profiles Issue 22.

Ho, Elaine Yee Lin (2001). 'Women on the Edges of Hong Kong Modernity: The Films of Ann Hui. In Esther Yau, ed., *At Full Speed: Hong Kong Cinema in a Borderless World.* University of Minnesota Press, Minneapolis. 177–195.

Hong Kong Shanghai Cinema Cities (2007). 'Eileen Chang's Shanghai Stories.' *The 5th Asia-Pacific Triennial Of Contemporary Art.* Queensland Art Gallery-Gallery Of Modern Art. (http://www.qagoma.qld.gov.au/asiapacifictriennial5/cinema/hong_kong,_shanghai_cinema_cities/eileen_chang accessed January 31st 2014)

Marchetti, Gina (2011). From Mao's 'Continuous Revolution' to Ning Ying's *Perpetual Motion* (2005): Sexual Politics, Neoliberalism and Postmodern China. .In Lingzhen Wang, ed., *Chinese Women's Cinema: Transnational Contexts,* Columbia University Press, NY, 191–212.

Taylor, Kate E. (2011). 'Introduction: On East Asian Filmmakers.' In Kate E. Taylor, ed. *Dekalog 4: On East Asian Film.* NY: Columbia University Press. (http://books.google.ca/books?id=ldPjMO9S9YYC&printsec=frontcover&source=gbs_ge_summary_r&cad=0#v=onepage&q&f=false accessed January 21st 2014)

Wang, Lingzhen (2011). 'Introduction: Transnational Feminist Reconfiguration of Film Discourse and Women's Cinema,' in Lingzhen Wang, ed., *Chinese Women's Cinema: Transnational Contexts.* NY: Columbia University Press. 1–43.

Wei, S. Louisa (2011). 'The Encoding of Female Subjectivity: Four Films by Fifth-Generation Women Directors,' in Lingzhen Wang, ed., *Chinese Women's Cinema: Transnational Contexts,* Columbia University Press, NY 293–310.

Zhang, Jingyuan (2011). 'To Become and Auteur: The Cinematic Maneuverings of Xu Xinglei,' in Lingzhen Wang, ed., *Chinese Women's Cinema: Transnational Contexts,* Columbia University Press., NY

293 310.

Zhang, Yingjin, ed. (2012). Companion to Chinese Cinema, Sussex, UK Wiley Blackwell West.

Zhang, Zhen (2011). 'Migrating Hearts: The Cultural Geography of Sylvia Chang's Melodrama,' in Lingzhen Wang, ed., *Chinese Women's Cinema: Transnational Contexts*, Columbia University Press, 88-110.

Tsitsi Dangarembga (above) and Safi Faye

Dennie Gordon on the set of *My Lucky Star*
with actress Zhang Zhyi (© Harrison Gordon Schaaf)

Wang Lee Hom, Dennie Gordon, Jackie Chan and Zhang Zhyi
on the set of *My Lucky Star* (© Harrison Gordon Schaaf)

The indomitable Kathryn Bigelow (© Rex Features)

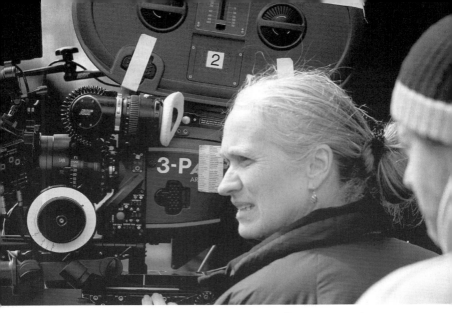

Jane Campion behind the camera (© Rex Features)

Soska Sisters in action on stage doing the Q&A at FrightFest

Katherine Isabelle star of *American Mary*
courtesy of Universal, care of Mike Hewitt

Sarah Polley's *Away From Her*
courtesy of Woody Southcott at Metrodome

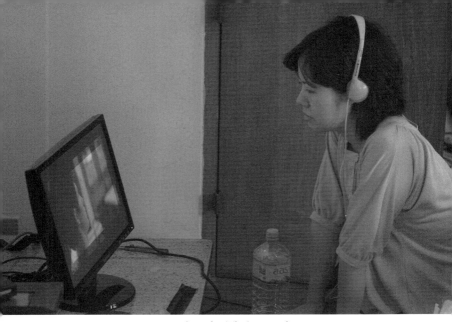

Anocha Thai at work

A scene from a film by Anocha Thai

Tan Chui Mui filming in Malaysia

Visra Thai with her actress (above) and
cinematographer (below) working on *Karaoke Girl*

Mira Nair on the set of *The Perez Family*

Kalpana Lajmi with Soni Razdan

The first narrative filmmaker:
Alice Guy-Blaché

Gurinder Chadra at the Women in Film and TV awards
(© Rex Features)

Sally Potter collects her OBE for services to film in 2012
(© Rex Features)

Margarita Barskaia studio shots

Margarita Barskaia in action

Hala Lotfy at the Tunisian Carthage Film Festival

Acclaimed filmmaker Moufida Thatli

12. Women Filmmakers of South Korea

Anchalee Chaiworaporn

Compared to all other Asian countries, Korean female directors are considered to be the most active. Many can now enter into film with far more diverse opportunities than in the past where only minor and more 'beauty-oriented' jobs such as acting, make-up and costume design, were permitted. However, in the early cinematic history of Korea, only five women, approximately one or two each decade, had the chance to direct one or more films, each over the course of a career.

The first woman director Park Nam-ok emerged in 1955 with her first and only feature *Widow*. Unfortunately, she was only permitted to release it after the New Year, as it was believed to bring bad luck if the New Year opened with a film directed by a woman. The second director Hong Eun-won waited over fifteen years to follow Park Nam-ok in 1962 with *Woman Judge* – a film based on the controversial death of a woman at that time. Despite its huge success, she only directed three films and remained primarily a screenwriter. In the same period, veteran actress Choi Eun-hee got to direct four films, partly due to her acting popularity and her husband Shin Sang-ok's support.

In the 1970s, the young intellectual filmmaker Hwang Hae-mi launched her career with three works including *First Time* (1970). Only Lee Mi-rye, made seven features from 1984 to 1991, after her debut *My Daughter Saved From the Mire* (1984). (See Joo, Jin-sook (ed.), *Films of Women Directors in Korea*, 2001, Seoul: 'Women in Film Korea', 2001, pp. 10–11.)

The 1990s marked the next flowering of female directors after the debut of Yim Soon-rye's *Three Friends* (1996). From 1996 to

CELLULOID CEILING

2003, women in Korean filmmaking have worked as follows:

> 1996 Yim Soon-rye (*Three Friends*).
>
> 1998 Lee Suh-goon (*Rub Love*), Lee Jeong-hyang (*Art Museum by the Zoo*)
>
> 2001 Yim Soon-rye (*Waikiki Brother*), Jeong Jae-eun (*Take Care of My Cat*)
>
> 2002 Lee Mi-yeon (*Bus Stop*), Lee Jeong-hyang (*The Way Home*), Moh Ji-eun (*A Perfect Match*), Byun Young-joo (*Ardor*)
>
> 2003 Park Chan-ok (*Jealousy Is My Middle Name*), Lee Su-yeon (*The Uninvited*), Kim Eun-sook (*Bingwoo*), Park Kyung-hee (*Miso*), Yoon Jae-yeon (*Wishing Stairs*), Gina Kim (*Invisible Light*)

This rise of Korean women directors did not come by accident or luck, but was led by several changes in both Korean society and its film industry, namely, the democratisation of Korean politics, the emergence of the so-called '386 generation' in the 1980s, the industrialisation of the Korean film industry, the promotion of film education, the arrival of a new-generation of filmmakers, the governmental support policy for filmmaking and the formation of independent or alternative cinema.

The South Korean film industry is one of the few in the world where local productions are better received than Hollywood films. This achievement was officially recorded from 1997 but several other changes meant that the film industry was developing at a rapid rate from the 80s, following the first democratic movement of the Gwangju massacre in 1980. Before then, South Korea had been controlled for over twenty years by the military regime of Park Chung-hee, until the political involvement by the younger generation – later identified as 'the 386,' referring to those who were born in the 1960s, attended colleges during the democratisation decade of the 1980s, and reached their thirties in the 1990s. They were also one of the main groups that coincidentally emerged into and developed the Korean film industry.

Following the internal liberation of the country in the 1980s, there had also been enormous changes in Korean film education and industry. In 1984, the country's leading film school Korea Academy of Film Arts (KAFA) was opened by the government-supported, self-administered body, the Korean Film Commission, followed by the formation of the Korean National University of Arts. Before then, only a few universities offered a degree in film production, but today doctorate degrees are available in South Korea. At the same time, the government also created several policies to help promote South Korean cinema across the country. Now any company and any producer can get help making a movie, which contributes to the development and prosperity of independent filmmaking.[1] In 1988, the government went further by introducing a screen quota system to assist local productions after the US intervention in film importation one year earlier. At first the film community resisted this intrusion, before finally realising that the only way to rescue the industry was by making good Korean movies, in order to win back public confidence. In 1991 the government also set a ten-year Cultural Development Plan and named it the 'Year of Drama and Film' in order to promote local films and television series, as significant steps taken to compete with Hollywood movies.

As these changes occurred, the rise of South Korean women directors can be seen as an inevitable outcome, however, it has happened at a very slow pace. Yim Soon-rye's emergence in 1996 only happened after the industry had already been developing for fifteen years. Initially, there were only one or two women directors every two or three years. It also took almost a decade before an active group of women directors existed and have continually been able to make their films.

They can be divided into the 386 and post-386 generations. Those in the 386 generation had to work for a long time, either in commercial and independent filmmaking, and they were in their thirties in the 1990s when they were eventually given a chance to make their directorial debuts. This generation had to consistently prove themselves and their abilities, by winning awards, either in short filmmaking or scriptwriting contests in order to get the chance to direct for the first time.

CELLULOID CEILING

The pioneering director, Yim Soon-rye studied filmmaking in France for four years, then returned and worked as Yeo Kyundong's assistant director on *Out of the World*. It was not until her short *Promenade in the Rain* won the Grand Prize in 1994 at the Seoul Short Film Festival, that she had the opportunity to get financing from the conglomerate Samsung, the main sponsor of the festival. Lee Suh-goon also received her filmmaking degree and an award for her short film *Suicide Party*. Lee Jeong-hyang started as an assistant director for a number of years and had never been given a chance to direct her own work until she won a scriptwriting contest with *Art Museum By the Zoo*. Byun Young-joo was famous as a strong independent director with her internationally well-known trilogy of documentaries *The Murmuring: A History of Korean Women*, *Habitual Sadness* and *My Own Breathing*. Lee Mi-yeon was a successful producer for six years and supported such acclaimed directors as Lee Chang-dong, Kim Jee-eun. Jeong Jae-eun and Park Chan-ok, who won many awards for their shorts or independent works. In fact, their first opportunities were given by two newly-established companies which were seeking new talent.

Owing to the pioneering efforts of the first group, the post-386 generation, or those who had just finished their film education and were under thirty, had fewer difficulties and spent less time proving themselves. Education played an important part to enable the second group to access film knowledge directly and immediately, instead of just working on the sidelines. They could practice technical skills making shorts or scriptwriting, and then gain some experience in pitching their directorial debut projects. Moh Ji-eun was offered a directorial job while she helped run an independent film festival and at twenty-five years old she became the youngest director who had worked with a studio. In an interview with *Screen*, she noted:

> 'If it weren't for the success of other women filmmakers in the industry, I probably would never have received this opportunity.'

Unsurprisingly, Lee Su-yeun was immediately given a chance

by Film Bom Co when her script made it to the final rounds of a scriptwriting contest. Today, young women directors follow their older sisters by first making shorts, then moving onto their own indie works and networking in the industry.

The different entry routes to the film industry are reflected in the diversity and strength of their features though few tackle feminist or female issues.

A large number of them – especially those working with studios, worked in the genres of romantic comedy, psychological drama and horror, while the indie directors preferred to focus on some more edgy themes – the everyday lives of female-coming-of-age stories, to the adultery of a bored wife. Byun Young-joo, however, has explored women's issues forcefully. In her first trilogy of documentaries, *The Murmuring: A History of Korean Women* (1995), *Habitual Sadness* (1997) and *My Own Breathing* (1999), she unhesitatingly and bravely called for reparations and an apology from the Japanese government to the six Korean women at the *House of Sharing*, who were forced into sexual slavery as comfort women. She then intertwined these stories with the suppression of Korean women today. An elegiac sense of sorrow prevails in her work. When she advanced to her feature debut *Ardor* (2002), the liberation of women continued to be an important concern for her.

Ardor, an adaptation of Jeon Gyeong-rin's novel *A Special Day That Comes Only Once in My Life*,

> 'was adapted as an erotic drama about the "reinvigorating effects of an affair on a woman's previously disenchanting life."' (See http://www.koreanfilm.org)

Her sophomore feature effort *Flying Boys* (2004) was shifted into a coming-of-age romance between the lower classes and sexual minorities. *Helpless* (2012), her most successful film, was based on Miyuki Miyabe's novel *All She Was Worth*, and focuses on a young woman who suddenly disappears just a few weeks before her wedding. Aside from feature directing, Byun Young-joo is still making shorts and documentaries on feminism and human rights for herself and producing and acting for other directors.

CELLULOID CEILING

Gina Kim is also another female director with a strong consciousness of women-on-the-move, drawing on her own experience as a Korean migrant torn between Korea and the US. Her documentary debut *Gina Kim's Video Diary* (1995) explores a personal account of 'one woman's fears, fantasies and projections.' In 2003, Kim began her first feature debut *Invisible Light* (2003), tracking the physical and psychological journeys of two Korean/Korean-American women, which led *Cahiers du Cinema* to call it 'a little block of feminine hardness and repressed anger'. She again looked at the issues of race and class for both women and Koreans in America in her film *Never Forever* (2007).

Byun Young-joo's fellow directors might be less political in an awareness of feminism and women's issues but their eyes are often focused on the marginalised people of Korean society. Yim Soon-rye explores the lives of three high-school graduates who fail to get into college in *Three Friends* (1996), the struggle of a third-class musical troupe in *Waikiki Brothers* (2001), and then the revitalisation of the national handball team in *Forever the Moment* (2008). Jeong Jae-eun also showed some interest in women's stories in her debut *Take Care of My Cat* (2001), which delicately portrays friendship and growth among five young women in their twenties. She shifted to documentary filmmaking after her second feature on the lives of Seoulite youngsters *The Aggressive* (2005).

On the commercial side, some of these directors still choose to focus on the lives of marginalised characters in making their features. One of the most successful, Lee Jeong-hyang, for example, focused on one of the most forgotten stories in Korean society – the life of a rural grandmother, to highlight in *The Way Home* (2002. Despite huge success when it became a blockbuster, she has still waited for another decade before making her third movie, *A Reason to Live* (2011), in which she explores the life-in-crisis of a female producer.

It is quite clear that South Korean women's filmmaking opportunities are a direct result of the growth and liberalisation of the Korean film industry, as well as women's access to film education. If the industry were not in such a developed state, with no room for alternative cinema, and no competitions for short or independent films or scriptwriting contests, women directors would find it harder to compete and gain experience. These opportunities open up the chance for new approaches not only to the different images of women but also the projection of new cinematic visions.

Author biography
See previous chapter by Anchalee Chaiworaporn.

Endnotes
1. The new Motion Picture Law was first revised in the early 1980s and went into effect on July 1st 1985. Before then, the industry was much controlled by the government in all aspects, obstructing the industrial development. Since 1962, the Motion Picture Law regulated production, export, import, censorship and the Motion Picture Promotion Corporation while the Performance Law concerned the exhibition of pictures, cinema theatres and audiences (Kuroda, quoted in John A. Lent, p. 144). A production company, for example, was required to have at least one studio of more than 60 square metres, three cameras, other facilities and US$100,000 in production funds, to be registered with the government and to be the sole importers of foreign films. Many companies made cheap and fast productions, just to grant the import film quota. At that time, a company was required to shoot four local movies for every one imported film.

13. 'Why Are You Making Such a Big Deal Just Because I'm a Woman?': Women Directors of Popular Indian Cinema

Coonoor Kripalani

Moving-image technology was embraced in India almost as soon as it was invented. In 1896, the Lumiere Brothers' cinematographe arrived in Bombay (present-day Mumbai) showing short (silent) films, and soon a number of enthusiasts and entrepreneurs acquired the equipment to produce films of their own. A century ago, in May 1913, D G Phalke presented India's first feature film, Raja Harishchanda, a story from the Indian epic, the Mahabharata. From these early days, a film-going audience was created, and it spawned what is today the world's largest film industry, in terms of annual production. With a domestic market hungry for film entertainment, popular Hindi films, the leaders of the industry in number and distribution, are omnipresent on the subcontinent, often to the exclusion of foreign (including Hollywood) films in many towns and certainly villages across India. One of the reasons for this offered by Zoya Akhtar, is that India has its own stars:

> 'we have our language; we have our own style, so our audience would want to see a Shah Rukh Khan and not Tom Cruise.'[1]

While the consumption of Indian films has been largely in the domestic market, films have always been an important bridge to connect diaspora communities to the motherland. As technologies have advanced, DVDs and digital downloading make films immediately available around the globe. Increasingly, audiences have widened to include non-Indian viewers as well.

Amongst the over 1,000 films produced and released annually in India, the majority are popular Hindi films. But amongst this number, less than two or three films a year are directed by women.[2] Despite this seemingly small output, over the years a number of landmark films have come from women directors such as Sai Paranjpaye, Kalpana Lajmi and Aparna Sen, and more recently from Tanuja Chandra, Pooja Bhatt, Zoya Akhtar, Reema Kagti, Farah Khan, Loveleen Tandon, Kiran Rao, Anusha Rizvi and Nandita Das. Films from women directors of the Indian diaspora, most notably, Deepa Mehta, Mira Nair and Gurinder Chadha, have also been significant, making their mark both in India and overseas.

As India marks 100 years of cinema, it is appropriate to take stock of women's contribution to this industry. From the earliest days, women worked behind the scenes; Phalke's wife, Saraswatibai, worked tirelessly with him, during the making of *Raja Harishchandra*.[3] Today the industry is powered by numerous women behind the scenes in capacities such as set designing, costume designing, cast directors, choreographers, and producers. Bhanu Athaiya, a costume designer of many decades worked on over 100 films with the most notable directors, bagging an Academy Award as the costume designer for *Gandhi* (1982). Sheena Parikh has worked as a costume designer for *3 Idiots* (2009) *Halla Bol* (2008) and *Lage Raho Munna Bhai* (*LRMB*, 2006), worked on the screenplay of *Kabhi Khushi Kabhie Gham* (2001), as well as worked as the Assistant Director for *LRMB*. Sooni Taraporevala, a noted photographer, is also a screenplay writer, having collaborated with and written scripts for four of Mira Nair's films, as well as for Jabbar Patel's *Dr Babasaheb Ambedkar* (2000). Saroj Khan has choreographed dances for a number of big name stars and worked in nearly 200 films. A number of well-known women from film families are powerful film producers. The famous actress Nargis participated with Raj Kapoor in producing films. Ekta Kapoor, daughter of film star Jeetendra, is a hugely successful producer of numerous TV shows, as well as films, most recent of which are *The Dirty Picture* (2011) and *Shootout at Wadala* (2013). Priyanka Dutt, daughter of Nargis and Sunil Dutt, Pamela Chopra, the wife of Yash Chopra, Gauri Khan, the wife of Shah Rukh Khan and Kiran Rao, wife of Aaamir Khan, are all producers of notable films.

While female actors have been many, and as anchors of films, star attractions who draw crowds in, there remains a wide discrepancy between their remuneration and that of their male counterparts. According to Kangana Ranaut, a National Award winning actor, female actors are paid about a quarter of the amount that male actors receive.[4] While this divide does not appear to be the case for women directors in the 21st century – their films are just as lavish as other mainstream Bollywood films – it is possible to see this divide in the case of the earlier film directors, whose films would qualify more as art-house cinema.

The women pioneers

Fatma Begum, an actor of the 1920s, is credited as the first female Indian director with her 1926 film, Bulbul-e-Paristan (Bulbul [songbird] of Fairyland). Reputed to have married the Nawab of Sachin, her daughters, the princesses Zubeida and Sultana, were superstars of the silent era. Zubeida crossed over to talkies and starred in India's first talkie, Alam Ara (1931).

Devika Rani, an educated woman of privileged birth (a grand-niece of Rabindranath Tagore), together with her husband, Himanshu Rai, founded the studio, Bombay Talkies, which produced a number of important films in the 1930s. A student of architecture, Devika Rani was a film set designer, and learnt many aspects of filmmaking as well as acting. She starred in a number of films produced by Bombay Talkies and took control of it after her husband's death, until competitor studios overtook it. At the helm of the studio, Devika Rani 'proved her independent capacity to organise productions, lead teams, and spot new talent.'[5] Devika Rani is known for having discovered Ashok Kumar, considered one of the great actors of his time.

Jaddan Bai, the mother of the famous movie-star, Nargis (a sensational actress of the 1950s and 60s), was a kothewali (courtesan) from Allahabad. Jaddan Bai was an accomplished singer, and made a break out of the life of the kotha (the home of the kothewalis, brothel), to establish herself as a classical singer in Calcutta. From here Jaddan Bai moved to Lahore to become a recorded gramophone artiste, as well as a film actor. The lure of films took her to Bombay, where she established a film company, and composed music for the first film it produced, Talashe Haq (1935), as its music director.[6]

In the years in which the struggle for India's independence from British rule intensified, the IPTA (Indian People's Theatre Association), a left-wing group of talented artists and intellectuals, influenced filmmakers. A number of films addressing women-centred social issues, were produced. Strong female characters were portrayed in films such as *Duniya na Mane* (*The Unexpected*, 1938), the 1940s films of Fearless Nadia of *Hunterwali* fame, and later the iconic *Mother India* (1957) and *Bandini* (*Imprisoned*, 1963), and in numerous Satyajit Ray films. Notably, all these films were directed by men!

In 1980, Sai Paranjpye released her first feature film, Sparsh (*The Touch*). Featuring actors Shabana Azmi, a social activist and established art-house cinema star, together with Naseeruddin Shah, also a well-known actor, the film addressed the rarely-touched theme of physical disability. Paranjpye, film director, screen-writer, playwright and recipient of the Padma Bhushan in 2006, was no stranger to the film world; her mother had acted in V Shantaram's Duniya na Mane, and Sai herself cut her teeth as a producer of children's programmes at AIR (All India Radio) and subsequently as a producer in DD (Doordarshan), the state-run TV channel. Depicting a widow's volunteer work in a blind school, Sparsh examines how her work is questioned by the recipients: is it genuine or self-serving, or occasioned by pity? Says Paranjpye of this film:

> 'I am happy to say I made my mark from the very first film. My success is perhaps due to the fact that my characters are not stereotypical and often do the unexpected. A gentle humour pervades the storyline.'[7]

Chashme Buddoor ([*Warding off*] *The Evil Eye*, 1981), a film about male bonding was successful at the box office and has been remade in 2013 by Director David Dhawan; *Katha* (*Story,* 1983) is an example of the hare and tortoise race amongst ordinary folk, while *Disha* (*The Uprooted*, 1998) tells of the plight of immigrant workers into urban areas. Her inspiration, Paranjpye says, comes from observing life.

> 'Life around you offers so much inspiration. Just go around with ears and eyes wide open. And then things start taking shape, unfolding with amazing speed… Like, I always say, I plagiarise from life.'[8]

She also made documentary films on several pertinent topics. While her films are not particularly feminist, and despite her avowed distancing from these themes – 'I'm getting a bit tired of social commitment, poverty, squalor and what have you,' she reportedly stated[9] – Paranjpye's sensitivities have led her to raise topical issues for audience awareness.

Kalpana Lajmi, a younger filmmaker, burst on to the scene with Rudaali (*Weeping Woman*, 1993). Lajmi hails from a family with a rich film background. Niece of the celebrated film director, Guru Dutt, Lajmi had worked as Assistant Director with Shyam Benegal, also a relative. At age seventeen, Lajmi became the life partner of famed poet, Bhupen Hazarika, some twenty-eight years her senior. Her unconventional choices in her personal life are a window to her ideology – Lajmi is known as a feminist film director. Based on a story by Mahasweta Devi, about professional female mourners, Rudaali explores the tyranny – in-built into society – of women's daily lives. A tyranny that leaves them benumbed, until something occurs to create a spark. The bleakness and complexity of women's existence and marginalised communities in a repressive society is portrayed in Darmiyan: In Between (1997). In her next two films, Daman: A Victim of Marital Violence (2001) and Chingaari: Spark (2006), Lajmi gives us two abused female protagonists – a wife in the first and a prostitute in the second, who eventually kill the perpetrators. While it may be satisfying for audiences to see evil characters get their come-uppance, or see victims empowered and emboldened sufficiently to annihilate their attackers, the solution offered by Lajmi could be more socially constructive rather than to counter brute force by even greater brutality.

Bengali actor, Aparna Sen, debuted in Satyajit Ray's film, Teen Kanya (*Three Girls*, 1961) at the age of sixteen. The daughter of well-known art and film critic, Chidanada Das Gupta, Sen was raised in a milieu of intellect and art appreciation. As she pursued her career as an actor, Sen earned fame which helped her switch into directing films. Her 1981 debut and award-winnng film, 36 Chowringhee Lane, in which a retired Anglo-Indian school-teacher faces loneliness, addresses both the issue of a dwindling and marginalised community, as well as that of an aging lonely woman. Sen's Paroma (*The Ultimate Woman*, 1984) portrays a woman who discovers herself through transgression, despite undertaking the traditional roles of wife, daughter-in-law, mother and friend, in genteel society. While the concept was shocking to some audiences, the film seemed starkly feminist in the development and choices of the protagonist. However, Sen does not see her work as feminist, but rather as humanist. The influence of Satyajit Ray and the intellectual traditions of Bengal can be seen quite clearly in her work. Says Sen:

> 'Women's issues are to me a part and parcel of humanism itself – something that I believe in and try my best to live by.'[10]

The humanist element of Sen is most clearly portrayed in *Mr & Mrs Iyer*, where a young Brahmin mother on a bus journey, and her fellow-traveller, a Muslim photographer, bond, as communal violence breaks out around them. Possibly one of Sen's strongest films, *Mr & Mrs Iyer* won not just the National Film Award, but a number of prestigious awards overseas. Following this success, Sen delivered two more films in 2010 to her audiences: The *Japanese Wife* and *Iti Mrinalini* (*The Unfinished Letter*). The former, based on Kunal Basu's short story of the same name, is reminiscent of Satyajit Ray's cinematography and sensitivities. Beautiful scenes of rural life in Bengal as well as in the mountains of Japan, as well as the unusual story, keep the viewer engaged in this slow-paced film. The latter is an introspective film, in its portrayal of an aging actress and how she wants to be remembered after she dies. It is perhaps reflective of her own personality, as she says she feels,

> 'vulnerable as a woman … if you are halfway sensitive, you are bound to be introspective. And introspection leads to self-doubt and a lack of confidence sometimes…'[11]

In this generation of women film directors, we see women who all have strong connections with the film world, and therefore one can safely assume that in this choice of career, had somewhat of an advantage. All of them are clearly moved by feminist issues, even though they feel they are not consciously doing so. The exception is Kalpana Lajmi, who acknowledges her feminist agenda.

Women directors from the 1990s

From the 1990s onwards, a number of films made by women directors such as Tanjua Chandra, Pooja Bhatt, Zoya Akhtar, Reema Kagti, Farah Khan, Kiran Rao, Loveleen Tandon, Anusha Rizvi and Nandita Das, have captivated audiences. Mostly auteurs, a number of them are from film families: Tanuja Chandra is a protégée of Mahesh Bhatt, the well-known film director. Pooja Bhatt is his daughter. Zoya Akhtar is the daughter of the brilliant, prolific and award-winning screenwriter and lyricist, Javed Akhtar, and his former wife, Honey Irani, a child-actress and screenwriter. First cousin to Akhtar, Farah Khan is the niece of Honey Irani, daughter of her sister, Menka Irani, and Kamran Khan, an actor and director. Kiran Rao is the wife of famous movie star, Aamir Khan, who she met as Assistant Director on the sets of *Lagaan* (*Land Tax*, 2001). Nandita Das is herself an acclaimed actor who turned to filmmaking, while Loveleen Tandan, a casting director, with no ostensible Bollywood family connections, worked with Danny Boyle as Assistant Director on *Slumdog Millionaire* (2008).

While there is clearly an advantage that connections bring of getting a foot in and a leg up, all the women directors with industry connections are vociferous in their claim that in the end, it is their work that speaks for them, and no help will be forthcoming if they are unable to produce a worthy end-product.

It is a commerce-driven industry, and they understand what will sell, both to their investors and their audiences. In this context, they are clear that women-centred films have a limited box-office appeal, and are hard to get funding for.

Tanuja Chandra

Of the directors mentioned above, Tanuja Chandra is the only one who states she is a feminist, '... I guess I'll always look at cinema from a woman's point of view.'[12]

Her 1999 film, *Sangharsh* (*Struggle*) portrays a strong woman CBI officer – a complex character but a capable one. In *Sur – The Melody of Life* (2002), Chandra explores a summer-winter relationship and male domination therein, while *Zindagi Rocks* (*Life Rocks*, 2006) portrays the extreme unselfish love of a mother. Collectively, Chandra's women-centred dramas look at the complexity of women's roles as young, beautiful and talented professionals, as lovers, and as mothers.

Pooja Bhatt

The work of Pooja Bhatt, herself a former actor, draws heavily on prevalent Bollywood formulae. Her director's lens is partial to the 'male gaze'[13] – she refers to hers as a 'fiercely feminine gaze'[14] – and there is no shying away from forthright scenes of love-making and bodies, enough for the censors to ask for cuts and to rate the films for adult ages – a rarity in Bollywood where more filmmakers prefer to make films for family viewing, that get more eyeballs. This is most evident in Bhatt's latest offering, *Jism 2* (*Body 2*, 2012), an erotic thriller. Featuring the Indian-Canadian porn star, Sunny Leone, the film has lengthy love-scenes and dwells a lot on bare bodies. Claiming that her feminine gaze enables 'a woman to look more beautifully at a man,'[15] Bhatt says cheekily that her mandate is to make men look more beautiful in Indian films. *Paap* (*Sin*, 2003), Bhatt's love-story set within a Buddhist theme, is filmed in the Spiti valley of Northeast India. It marked the debut of renowned Pakistani sufi singer, Rahat Fateh Ali Khan as a playback singer in Bollywood movies. Her next two films, *Dhoka* (*Betrayal*, 2007) and *Kajraare* (2010), are also love stories that use the backdrop of Islamic terrorism, both portraying its danger and yet, as in the latter, explaining how state terrorism and evil but powerful characters influence young people to join terrorist groups. *Kajraare* also introduces a Pakistani actor, Sarah Loren, to Indian screens.

Zoya Akhtar

Similarly, Zoya Akhtar and Farah Khan are also no strangers to the male gaze and draw on the film heritage that popular Hindi film offers. Akhtar worked as a casting director, assistant director and executive producer, before directing her 2009 film, *Luck by Chance*. With a star cast, the film provides an insider's view of the film industry, exploring values, goals and achieving happiness. Akhtar's *Zindagi na Milegi Dobara* (*You won't get life twice*, 2011), another multi-starrer, was both acclaimed and a commercial success. It was co-written with Reema Kagti, who went on to direct her own film, *Talaash: the Answer Lies Within* (*Search: the answer lies within*, 2012). *You won't get life twice* features young men on a road trip, discovering the meaning of life, love and commitment. Both films portray strong, though not central, female characters. In *Luck by Chance*, Sona, an actor, makes life choices by being content with small TV roles and finds her happiness in this, rather than ruthlessly seeking roles in the bright lights (in contrast to her erstwhile lover), while in *You won't get life twice*, Laila, the independent, easy and nature-loving dive instructor, is juxtaposed against Natasha, the stereotypical rich girl, who tries to plan everything to a tee, and in the end loses her man. In the film anthology, *Bombay Talkies* (2013), featuring four short films by different directors of whom Akhtar is one, she offers *Sheila ki Jawani*, a take-off on the popular number picturised on Katrina Kaif. Akhtar explores a young boy's fascination with Kaif and this song, and how this clashes with conventional attitudes.

Akhtar is modest in her interviews, citing the two films she has made insufficient to remark upon as a life-time's body of work. But speaking at a panel of women film directors at the Think festival in Goa in November 2012, Akhtar was forthcoming about her views on the older mainstream Hindi films, views that this author has long-shared. Referring to the romancing scenes, she said,

'My biggest problem is with the way women are perceived… men are not wooing women correctly. This hero is sexually harrassing this woman. He is stalking her, he is beating her, he is physically abusing her and she is falling in love! It puts out a very wrong signal to the Romeos on the street. They feel if they come and grab you, you are going to fall in love? It's not going to happen brother!'[16]

Her views were enthusiastically endorsed by her co-panellists, Reema Kagti and Anusha Rizvi, amidst clapping and cheering from the audience. All three directors felt the stereotypes of the 'good Indian girl' and the 'strong Indian woman' were trite and should reflect reality. Equally, none of these directors felt they were making women-centred dramas – these don't attract investors and are not considered box-office earners – yet, their sensitivities lead them to construct multi-layered textured female characters in their films.

Farah Khan

Farah Khan, actor, choreographer, judge on various TV dance and song shows, and film director, is one of Bollywood's top choreographers, having choreographed dances for over eighty films, in addition to stage and theatre work. Known for her forthright style and language (she's known to swear loudly on her director's foghorn), Khan has delivered some of the best-known choreography to hit songs, such as 'Chaiyyan, Chaiyyan', the opening song of Mani Ratnam's *Dil Se* (1998), and won awards for choreographing 'Munni Badnam Hui' and 'Sheila ki Jawani' in 2011. Her bold and contemporary choreography is a departure from the traditional choreography of Hindi films that hitherto picturised folk dances or the lines of classical dance. Khan has taken the dance of Hindi films out of the refinement of *kothas* (the brothels of the courtesans) into taverns, and replaced *aadaab* (refined courtly manners) with contemporary dance moves with attitude.

As a director, Khan has also delivered hits. Her films are very much part of the Bollywood mainstream – multi-starrers, with bankable names in the lead (especially Shah Rukh Khan with whom Khan has a close working relationship) – old-fashioned love stories which in the end, unite lovers. For example, her 2004 *Main Hoon Na* (*I am Here*), is a patriotic film, with simultaneous love stories and hidden identities in the plot set to the back-drop of India-Pakistan relations. Khan's *Om Shanti Om* (2007) is an insider's view of Bollywood – as it was in the 1950s and 1960s, and how it is today. It was Bollywood's highest grossing film at the time of its release. However, Khan's 2010 farcical comedy, *Tees Maar Khan*, did not fare as well at the box office after its initial opening, despite the popularity of the song, 'Sheila ki Jawani', and its dance choreography.

As a woman director, Khan does not feel she has faced any bias from her audiences, but she has felt resentment from some male directors.[17] Says Khan,

> 'They prefer to praise a small little movie that is not competing in their territory rather than a film I make…. Other directors have praised me too, but when *Om Shanti Om* became the blockbuster of 2007, they suddenly started bitching about the film…'[18]

Despite this cold-shoulder from industry-insiders, Khan is confident of her chosen path. She hopes to be making international films in the future and possibly even win an Oscar.[19] Her dreams for the future are picturised at the end of her film, *Tees Maar Khan*, where the 'Happy Ending' song sees the actors walking the red carpet to receive their Oscars.

Kiran Rao

Kiran Rao has been assistant director of some notable films: *Lagaan* (2001), *Monsoon Wedding* (2001), *Saathiya* (*Companion*, 2002) and *Swades: We the People* (*Self-rule: We the People,* 2004). Married to the famous film actor, Aamir Khan, a few years after meeting him on the sets of *Lagaan*, Rao directed him in *Dhoby Ghat: Mumbai Diaries* (*Washerman's Hill: Mumbai Diaries*, 2011), which looks at the lives of the privileged and not-so-privileged in Mumbai, and where these lives intersect. Rao is also associate producer of Aamir Khan Films *Taare Zameen Par* (*Stars on the Ground*, 2007), a film that addresses disability in the form of dyslexia; *Jaane Tu… Ya Jaane Na*

(*Whether you know… or not*, 2008), a rom-com; as well as producer with Aamir Khan of *Peepli Live* (2010), a satirical commentary on farmer suicides, directed by a woman, Anusha Rizvi; *Delhi Belly* (2011), a madcap romp that exposes the underbelly of Delhi's underworld; and the TV series, *Satyamev Jayate* (2012), a talk show anchored by Aamir Khan that exposes the injustices and corruption of Indian society. In this thinking duo, Rao has taken the role of associating herself with films that make a difference. Rao, self-assured and certain of her purpose, prefers to work with non-actors, to give her films a realistic quality.[20]

Loveleen Tandan

Loveleen Tandan worked as production assistant on Deepa Mehta's *Earth: 1947* (1998), before becoming the much-awarded casting director for films such as *Monsoon Weddding* (2001), *Vanity Fair* (2004), *The Namesake* (2006) and *Brick Lane* (2007). Working initially with the *Slumdog Millionaire* (2008) team as casting director, Tandan contributed by casting three children from the slums and teaching them to act, as well as with her suggestion for the inclusion of Hindi dialogue (which she then wrote), providing the film the Indian authenticity it needed. For her work, director Danny Boyle called her his 'cultural bridge' and credited her as co-director. That Tandan was not nominated for the Oscar along with Danny Boyle created a furore and generated a great deal of criticism especially among advocates for women in film. Tandan humbly distanced herself from these advocates, reiterating the brilliance of Danny Boyle, while stating:

> 'I am greatly honoured by the credit I have been accorded. It would be a grave injustice if the credit I have should have the effect of diminishing Danny Boyle's magnificent achievement.'[21]

Nandita Das

Acclaimed actor, Nandita Das, catapulted to fame for her role in *Fire* (1996), followed by *Earth 1947* (1998). In 2008, Das turned to film directing, with her film, *Firaaq* (*Quest*). Based on the immediate aftermath of the Gujarat communal riots of 2002, *Firaaq* claims to be a work of fiction 'based on a thousand true stories'. The film delves into the inter-relationships of Hindus and Muslims as friends, neighbours and family (through inter-marriage). That state policies give courage to local authorities and bigots to oppress minority groups is one part of the story. The support, friendships and compromises of women in times of stress and upheaval is the other part that is explored, as are the ways of male bonding as the men seek to avenge the wrongs they have been made to endure. Das approaches this very political issue with a great deal of sensitivity, making a statement on how the lives of ordinary folk are thrown into turmoil in such times. In an interview (in Hindi) on *Avaaz India TV*, Das, introduced as the recipient of ten international and ten national film awards, spoke of her free and liberal upbringing, where her artist father and writer mother taught her to question truth and inequity. Driven by her conscience, she claims to have fallen into acting quite accidentally, and uses the medium to speak out against injustice and address what she refers to as the universal 'human crisis'. *Firaaq* is her effort to see the post-traumatic effects of a crisis, which she feels the media and public lose interest in, once the crisis is past. Das particularly eschews the portrayals of women in mainstream Hindi film: dancing, crying and looking pretty – she looks to portray women as real in her films.[22]

Among this crop of Indian women directors post-1990, only Chandra is the self-declared feminist. The work of the women directors who are 'insiders', i.e., those from film families: Bhatt, Akhtar and Khan in particular, mostly conforms to the current standards of Bollywood. Their filmography, the camera 'gaze' and the way in which plots are structured, are very much informed by the norms of Hindi popular cinema, even as they are changing the idiom and tropes of Bollywood cinema. While they do present heroines as independent women without the usual constraints of family and society, the end message of '(romantic) love conquers all' persists as a common thread through their films. Kiran Rao's *Dhoby Ghat* is unique in its portrayal of relationships and social commentary. The films that she produces with her husband, Aamir Khan, all have a certain social focus, that are different from the formulaic Bollywood films. As Directors, Loveleen Tandan and

Nandita Das, too, have delivered films that are not mainstream conformist, but which comment on social and political themes that need to be brought to the attention of viewers.

The View from Diaspora Directors

The most well-known of Indian Directors from the diaspora are women: Deepa Mehta, Mira Nair and Gurinder Chadha.

Deepa Mehta

Indo-Canadian director, Deepa Mehta, famous for her trilogy, *Fire* (1996), *Earth 1947* (1998), and *Water* (2005), particularly addresses traditional family values that oppress women in India. In *Fire*, women fall into a lesbian relationship amidst the challenging family circumstances in which they find themselves. Said Mehta in a CNN interview to Monita Rajpal,

> 'Radha and Sita... their story was about the idea of emotional nourishment that happens... where women stand... Can a woman make a choice that might be socially unacceptable? How would she be treated?'[23]

Mehta's next two films, based on novels by Bapsie Sidhwa, are *Earth 1947*, a powerful portrayal of a young beautiful ayah (nanny) and her charge in the turbulent times of the partition of India, while *Water* is the story of widows in the first part of the 20th century who were exiled to ashramas in holy cities, and the fate that awaited them. Controversy and criticism surrounding the release of *Fire,* created a storm of political protest in India, eventually impacting the filming of *Water,* which was ended when the sets were burnt down. Mehta eventually completed the film in Sri Lanka five years later. Explaining her aim in these two films to Monita Rajpal in the same CNN interview, Mehta said vis-à-vis *Earth*, 'What's the fallout [on women] of sectarian war?' and vis-à-vis *Water*, 'What does religion do to women? Particularly women?'

Mehta's 2008 film, *Heaven on Earth,* tells the story of domestic abuse in an Indian immigrant family in Canada, with the protagonist being a bride fresh from the Punjab.

Speaking of her film adaptation of Salman Rushdie's *Midnight's Children*, Mehta said,

'...this is such a women's story... it's about women whose husbands have left, about women whose lovers have disappeared, it's about mothers, about women who have no dignity, women who have lost their voice, women who live in the shadows of their husbands, women who are lovers, and about women and their children. ... In this case I am a woman, and my lens is that of a woman.'[24]

Mehta's remarks and her body of work reveal her inquiry into the impact of larger political, social and religious issues on the daily lives of women.

Mira Nair

Mira Nair made several documentary films before turning to feature films. A spirited woman with a quick mind, Nair's films delve into the realms of human emotions and inter-relationships between Indian migrants and their host communities, e.g., *Mississippi Masala* (1991) and *The Namesake* (2007). The theme of exile is one that draws her: 'I feel very much that cinema is born as a medium to capture exile,' she says. Nair's collaborator on the scripts of several films, including *The Namesake* and *Salaam Bombay!* (1998) is Sooni Taraporevala, and both women are described as the Godmothers of *The Namesake*, by the *Harvard Magazine*.[25] *Salaam Bombay!*, a study of street urchins in the city of Mumbai and child abuse by the privileged, is considered a landmark film.[26] Upon seeing it, Satyajit Ray reportedly remarked,

'I cannot recall ever being impressed so much by a first feature... It shows complete command of every aspect of the medium.'[27]

Nair's immensely popular *Monsoon Wedding* (2001) profiles a Punjabi wedding (and again touches on the theme of child abuse), while her latest offering, *The Reluctant Fundamentalist* (2013) addresses the clash of Islam with the west. Nair's film repertoire also includes *Vanity Fair* (2004) and *Amelia* (2009), women-centred narratives. While not avowedly feminist, Nair's portrayal of her heroines and witty and sensitive handling of human relations bring to the fore many issues such as women in migrant communities, marriage, abuse and social mores. Nair, however, does not see her work as woman-centric. She is drawn to marginal figures, she says. So for example in her early documentary, *Indian Cabaret!*, Nair looked at two stories of the good wife who dreams of liberation and the nightclub dancer who buys herself some sort of liberation. Brotherhood, she explains is another theme that draws her.

> '[I am]... attracted to this tougher stuff that is different to the traditional stuff that is associated with women's lives... I feel suspect about those coming of age mother-daughter movies... I'm not interested in what is called the women's theme...'[28]

Nair's worldview is an expansive one, coloured by being resident in three geographical locations: Uganda, New York and India. Travelling between three continents, Nair observes people 'settling and unsettling the world', seeing each other through 'prisms that... are stultifying' and reductivist, e.g., 'if you are Pakistani, you are a terrorist, and if you are an American, you are a liberal.' Referring to her latest film, *The Reluctant Fundamentalist*, Nair explains that in the many films on the war on terror that take place in Iraq, Afghanistan or Pakistan, hitherto audiences have only been given one point of view – the American one. In this work she sets out to de-mystify the other, to create a dialogue for the two worlds to speak to one another, and to understand the complexities of the world of 'the other'. Her aim she says is to entertain, explain and provoke.[29]

> 'In my world I take... great strength in being distinct... I take care to not be anything other than I am... it is about this see-saw of moving between worlds and finding out about who your genuine self is... it's about the divided self in a globalised world.'[30]

Nair's aim in creating a dialogue between two worlds is to unravel layers of culture on both sides to fill the schism caused by Bush's famous admonition, 'You are either with us, or you are against us.' 'We are defined not just by events,' says Nair, 'but by the reaction to those events…'[31]

Gurinder Chadha

Raised in a Sikh family in Southall, UK, Gurinder Chadha is a film director whose work primarily reflects the interactions between the South Asian community living in the UK with their host community. Advised to do a secretarial course upon completing school, Chadha reacted: 'You're bloody nuts. I don't know what I'm going to do, but I'm not going to do that. You've got me wrong.'[32] *Bhaji on the Beach* (1993) is a vignette of a mixed group of south Asian women on a day trip to the beach, where the younger women's behaviour is in sharp contrast to that of the older and more conservative women. Chadha's 2002 box-office hit, *Bend it like Beckham*, once again looks at young British Asian women's aspirations in contrast to those of their parents. Chadha's spunk, humour and insight is packaged delightfully into this neat story of girlhood and growing up, and was the breakthrough film for Keira Knightley as an actor. Chadha clarifies how she rises to a challenge:

> 'You don't believe I can do that, so I'm going to prove you wrong. If you tell me I can't do something, that's the worst thing to tell me. And that's what I tell girls, and that's what Beckham's about: you can do it, you can do it better, and you can do it in the way you want.'[33]

In 2004, Chadha's *Bride and Prejudice*, an Indianised adaptation of Jane Austen's *Pride and Prejudice*, brought the story to life with Bollywood song and dance numbers, while showing Indian society akin to that of early 19th century England. Chadha's work is certainly women-centred, as it gives her audiences a look into the social mores that power Indian women's lives in India and overseas. Definitely not one to think of herself as a director of minority films, Chadha says,

> 'I think the reason I have the drive I do is ultimately about racism. It's about finding ways to diminish the impact of difference.'

When awarded an honorary degree for her excellence in showing Asian influences on British mainstream culture, Chadha said, '...that was really cool, because that's why I started doing what I do. To be honest, that's my life's work.'[34] And again, 'It's about my place in the world and it's about everybody else recognising that my world is their world too.'[35]

Each of these directors living overseas is concerned with space and depictions of layered cultures, and how these cultures interact with one another. Their works are important in understanding 'the other' culture and point of view. As women, their handling of female characters is richer, as their expansive worldview leads them to introspect about how wider socio-political issues impact the daily lives of ordinary women.

Final Take

'Why are you making such a big deal because I am a woman?' shouts Reema Kagti, at the panel of women film directors at the Think Festival 2012. Her co-panellists, Zoya Akhtar and Anusha Rizvi, enthusiastically agree. Each of them feels as women they have the choice to be in any profession. Their success or failure is not a reflection of their gender or who they are. Their work speaks for them, and ultimately the success of any film depends on its commercial viability. They are each acutely aware that the industry will not support losing propositions, no matter who the filmmaker and what her connections are. Zoya Akhtar, Pooja Bhatt and Farah Khan, are unanimous in their view that while some doors may be open to them, there are no backers forthcoming if a project is seen as unviable or a dud.
Pooja Bhatt says:

> 'Relationships don't matter... your talent and dedication are the only things that work... it is an industry with commercial interests... if you make money is what matters.' [36]

Akhtar echoed the same view as a panellist at the Think Festival 2012.

No doubt, the early film directors like Fatma Begum, Devika

CELLULOID CEILING

Rani and Jaddan Bai who were very much part of mainstream cinema in the 1930s, would have vociferously supported the same view. Films of the 1940s that addressed women's issues were the precursors of films by directors Sai Paranjpye, Kalpana Lajmi and Aparna Sen, who made films that could be loosely classified more as art-house cinema reaching out to a serious audience, than catering to mass entertainment.

As the film industry has grown into the 21st century, a number of women, particularly from film families – Pooja Bhatt, Zoya Akhtar, Farah Khan and Kiran Rao – have taken up the craft of film direction as auteurs and delivered a number of notable films that are both mainstream and also reflect women's many roles as lovers, friends, mothers, daughters, seductresses, and others. While Bhatt has been in the forefront of introducing Pakistani talent to Bollywood screens, directors Nandita Das, Loveleen Tandan and Kiran Rao have focused on disturbing social issues to create awareness among audiences. Specifically, women-centred films, with some exceptions, are generally not considered viable commercially, and it is therefore difficult to get funding to make them.

The works of women directors of the Indian diaspora are internationally recognised and have earned these directors – Deepa Mehta, Mira Nair and Gurinder Chadha – great reputations worldwide. Among their notable works, they look at issues dealing with immigrant communities and their interactions with their host communities, the social structure of these immigrant communities and the clash of cultures as they settle in the west and try to preserve their social mores. The latter is the most evident when suitable partners are sought for their offspring, and this aspect is repeatedly addressed in the films of these directors. Their ability to portray textured and layered characters goes a long way in explaining migrant cultures – 'the other' – to western audiences.

With limited output in comparison to their male counterparts, these spunky, witty, lively and humorous women directors' contribution to Indian films is significant. The issues they choose to develop in their films are unique, presented with a different perspective and sensitivity, and frequently with the aim of creating awareness amongst their viewers. The new breed of women directors are not particularly women-focused, but rather theme or issue or story-focused, have an expansive world view, and therefore make films that are both topical and of interest to viewers. They are subtly changing the idiom and tropes of Bollywood, while retaining the format that viewers know and love. These women film directors do not feel any particular bias due to gender, and their number appears to be growing. As long as they make commercially viable films, they can continue to bring their special craft and sensitivity to the big screens.

Author biography

Coonoor Kripalani is a full-time writer residing in Singapore. She is Honorary Institute Fellow at the Hong Kong Institute for the Humanities & Social Sciences (inc. the Centre of Asian Studies), University of Hong Kong, as well as a Board Member of the Asian Civilisations Museum, Singapore.

Coonoor is the author of numerous scholarly articles on sociological and political issues in popular Hindi film, which have been published in academic journals. She is also the author of a succinct biography, *Mahatma Gandhi: Apostle of Non-Violence*, published by Rupa & Co, 2003. At present she is writing on radio broadcasting (AIR) in India.

Coonoor writes in Hindi and English for children aged two to six. She enjoys creating bilingual books that intrigue and attract children, and at the same time provide them early learning skills in both Hindi and English. Coonoor's books are simple, lively, and full of fun and adventure. The books encourage good reading habits in children, and aim to create in them a childhood memory of books and stories that they will carry into adulthood. Coonoor's 12th book, on Yoga for children, is published by Scholastic India (2013).

Contact: coonoor.kripalani@gmail.com

References

1. 'Star System has helped Bollywood Flourish: Zoya Akhtar,' (http://www.planetradiocity.com/musicreporter/celebrity-interview-details/Star-system-has-helped-Bollywood-flourish:-Zoya-Akhtar/727 accessed January 11th 2014)

2. It should be noted that this does not include women documentary filmmakers, of whom there are several.

3. Nasreen Munni Kabir, *A Sideways Glance at Hindi Cinema 2013 Diary* (UK: Hyphen Films, 2012).

4. Indo-Asian News Service, 'Male actors take all the money and credit,' in *tabla!* November 22nd 2013, p. 14.

5. TJS George, *The Life and Times of Nargis* (Indus, an imprint of HarperCollins Publishers India Pvt Ltd, New Delhi, 1994), p. 9.

6. Ibid., pp. 28–32.

7. Sridhar Rangayan and Saagar Gupta, 'Queen of humour: a candid interview with award-winning writer and filmmaker Sai Paranjpye,' *The South Asianist, Journal of South Asian Studies,* University of Edinburgh, Vol. 2, no. 3 (2013), p. 159.

8. Ibid., p. 164.

9. In Sunil Sethi's interview, '10 Questions, Sai Paranjpye,' in *Outlook India,* June 4th 1997. (http://www.outlookindia.com/article.aspx?203658 accessed December 10th 2014)

10. Rajeshwari Das Gupta, *Aparna Sen*, in series 'Women in Indian Film,' edited by Nasreen Munni Kabir (Zubaan, New Delhi, 2011), p. 11.

11. Ibid., p. 31.

12. Subhash K. Jha, 'Why Tanuja is an angry young woman,' *The Hindustan Times* (Indo-Asian News Service, PTI), June 23rd 2005. (http://www.hindustantimes.com/indians-abroad/artsandentertainment/why-tanuja-is-an-angry-young-woman/article1-33395.aspx, accessed December 11th 2013)

13. This phrase is one that informs feminist film interpretations – it implies the objectification of women's bodies as viewed by men, which is presented to audiences in film. It refers to the theory of Laura Mulvey, in her well-known article, 'Visual Pleasure and Narrative Cinema,' in *Screen*, 16.3, Autumn 1975, pp. 6–18.

14. Pooja Bhatt in interview with Rajeev Masand, June 27th, 2012. (http://www.youtube.com/watch?v=E3vmxDVWP3Q accessed January 10th 2014)

15. Ibid.

16. Zoya Akhtar in Think 2012 panel, 'Cinema, Wide Angle – The Cats have got their Tongue: three Women in Bollywood'. (http://thinkworks.in/speakers/zoya-akhtar/ accessed January 9th 2014)

17. Nasreen Muni Kabir, *Farah Khan,* in series 'Women in Indian Film,'

edited by Nasreen Munni Kabir (Zubaan, New Delhi, 2011), p. 28.

18. Ibid., pp. 28–9.

19. Ibid., p. 30.

20. Interview with Rajeev Masand. (see http://www.youtube.com/watch?v=Tzn91xwBaWE and also http://www.youtube.com/watch?v=VS1IoHdsXz4 accessed January 9th 2014)

21. Laura Vasilion, 'It is written: the destiny of Loveleen Tandan,' Special for Films for Two®. (http://www.films42.com/faq/loveleentandandestiny.asp, accessed January 10th 2014)

22. Nadita Das interview in Hindi by P S Khobragade on Avaaz India TV, August 12th 2013.

23. Deepa Mehta interviewed by Monita Rajpal on *Talk Asia* CNN, February 23rd 2013. (http://transcripts.cnn.com/TRANSCRIPTS/1302/22/ta.01.html accessed January 10th 2014)

24. Madhu Trehan interview of Deepa Mehta on *News Laundry,* January 7th 2013. (http://www.youtube.com/watch?v=8fJeWMNb4kk, accessed January 10th 2014)

25. Craig Lambert, 'Godmothers of The Namesake,' *Harvard Magazine*, March–April 2007. (http://harvardmagazine.com/2007/03/godmothers-of-the-namesa.html accessed January 10th 2014)

26. Following the success of this film, Mira Nair used the proceeds to set up the Salaam Balak Trust in India, an NGO that provides schooling, training for jobs and health care to street children.

27. Quoted by Madhu Trehan in her interview of Mira Nair on *News Laundry* (http://www.youtube.com/watch?v=3D1wz_OR6ug, accessed May 16th 2013)

28. Bonnie Greer interview of Mira Nair, *The Guardian*, June 12th 2002. (http://www.theguardian.com/film/2002/jun/12/guardianinterviewsatbfisouthbank1 accessed January 10th 2014)

29 Tavis Smiley interview of Mira Nair, April 30th 2013. (http://www.pbs.org/wnet/tavissmiley/interviews/director-mira-nair/accessed January 10th 2014)

30 To Madhu Trehan on *News Laundry,* May 16th 2013.

31 Ibid.

32 Geraldine Bedell, 'Larger than Life,' Interview: Gurinder Chadha, *The Observer*, July 16th 2006. (http://www.theguardian.com/film/2006/jul/16/features.review1 accessed January 9th 2014)

33. Ibid.

34. Ibid.

35. Ian Watson interview with Gurinder Chadha, *Sunday Herald,* September 2004. (http://www.ianwatsonuk.com/gurinder.html, accessed January 9th 2014)
36. Pooja Bhatt speaking on Lehren Retro. (http://www.youtube.com/watch?v=Nk6P3-I_6AE accessed January 9th 2014)

14. CATS AND DOGS AND WILD BERRIES:

New Female Visions in Japanese Cinema

Adam Bingham

'If you want to say something about Japan, you have to focus on women,' Sachiko Hidari (Desser, 1988, p. 108)

The above quote, from a prominent actress throughout the 1950s and 1960s, points succinctly to the significance of female-centred films to Japanese filmmaking almost throughout its history, and certainly from the 1930s onward. The female melodrama, however, has typically been the sole preserve of male directors; Mikio Naruse, Yasujiro Ozu, Kenji Mizoguchi, Yoshishige Yoshida, Shohei Imamura and Juzo Itami among others all variously contributed to a woman-centric cinematic idiom, and have done so as a means of engaging specifically with their country and its modern socio-political specificity, to 'say something about Japan'. Historically, female perspectives on Japan have been much less forthcoming in Japanese cinema. Unsurprisingly, for such a patriarchal country, female directors have not predominated, with only a very few managing to carve out a career behind the camera and even then only fitfully and with difficulty.

Since the mid-1990s there has been a significant increase in the number of women directors, and these filmmakers – chiefly Naomi Kawase, Miwa Nishikawa, Yuki Tanada, Nami Iguchi, Naoko Ogigami, Satoko Yokohama, Momoko Ando, Mika Ninagawa, Shiori Kazama, Tsuki Inoue and Eriko Kitagawa – have in various ways subverted or destabilised the narratives and the commentaries offered by the aforementioned male directors. They have not always gravitated to explicit stories about women or about female selfhood, indeed have often tackled masculinity and stories concerning men and have expressed a desire that gender not be a determining factor in their professional designation (that they shouldn't be labelled as women directors, simply as directors). But nonetheless they have managed to carve out a space for reflecting upon identity and gender, especially as they figure in the landscape of modern Japan.

This essay will examine how and to what extent any meaning can be attached to these works from the point of view of gender in the country; whether any feminine discourse animates their narratives. It will elucidate something of the lineage of female filmmaking in Japan, before going on to consider the aforementioned directors and their place within this lineage, examining several representative works and arguing that the concerns of the typical women's film do not always find much of a place within them, indeed may be seen to contrast with them for specific effect. There are several different modes and genres that animate the films of these directors, and their use of these more or less recognisable frameworks as a point of departure is a salient aspect of their work, something that offers a site of negotiation with regard to gender and selfhood. In addition, one of the ways that modern, post-millennial Japanese cinema can be defined is by its overt return to past genres, forms and modes that bespeaks a desire either to recapture something lost, or to measure Japan now against the country of the immediate post-war decades. The intertextual work of several female directors can be similarly analysed, and this marks the foundation of the present chapter.

Japan is, and always has been, a markedly patriarchal society. In the immediate post-war years, following a 1946 decree, there was an enforced move to constitutionally guarantee gender equality and women's rights, and thereafter the rapid development of Japan's bubble economy helped to bring into focus ongoing issues and problems surrounding what Vera Mackie has termed 'the politics of everyday life and everyday relationships': those pertaining to the personal and to the body, to laws regarding abortion. (2003, p. 1) It has been a protracted and difficult process; women's liberation only began as a visible movement in the 1970s, whilst statistics even in the 1990s suggested that gender inequality in the workplace is still a problem. Furthermore, as Kumiko Fujimura-Fanselow has discussed, whilst the 1990s was seen as the era of women there has been a regression in the years since the turn of the millennium; young women in Japan have little exposure in their daily lives to diverse role models who can provide alternative visions of women's lives and different models of gender, and this has significantly limited their horizons. (2011, pp. ix–xxxii)

Discourse on cinema and feminism has often concerned film form as a significant factor in issues of spectatorship, in determining how a text positions and constructs its audience. Laura Mulvey's seminal essay 'Visual Pleasure and Narrative Cinema' (found in Mulvey, 2009, pp. 14–30) popularised a concern with the perceived male bias and address of mainstream cinema, a notion that the subject position of classical Hollywood filmmaking was inherently masculine, with the woman a mere object, someone to be looked at, a passive female spectacle for the consumption of the active male. This looking at woman, positioning her as an object to be gazed at and demystified, is, Mulvey argues, key to classical US cinema and its attempts to render safe the inherent threat posed by the castrating figure of the female. As such a concept (explicit or otherwise) of an experimental or art cinema narrative and stylistic practice as one that offers a potentially more pronounced space for a feminine subjectivity has tended to predominate, although it is worth remarking here that one is at least potentially re-inscribing the imbalance and normative patriarchal bias already noted above; that by ascribing a more overt feminist impulse to films that are perceived to contravene conventional, classical methodology (and Mulvey's own feminist film *Riddles of the Sphinx* (1977) most certainly works in this way) one implicitly positions them as Other, as deviant, and thus reinforces the masculine mainstream as dominant, the model against which others are measured and evaluated. Attempts have been made for a feminist intervention in popular cultural forms, whilst some academic work on filmmakers like Alfred Hitchcock has stressed a sympathetic exploration of women under patriarchy. But by and large the division remains pertinent, and it is one that offers a productive context for exploring female directors in modern Japan.

There were no female feature filmmakers in Japan until the 1930s; there were in fact a significantly higher number of female documentary directors than those making features in the post-war years. The first female director of a feature was Tatsuko Sakane, who directed the romantic drama *Hatsu sugata* (*New Clothing*) in 1936, and by the 1960s only the actress Kinuyo Tanaka had managed to add her name to the list. Beginning in the early 1950s with *Koibumi* (*Love Letter*, 1953), Tanaka went on to direct a further five features throughout the 1950s and early 1960s, something for which she received fairly forceful opposition, even from Mizoguchi, who, despite his sympathetic cinematic exploration of female subjugation and suffering, was not happy for his frequent leading lady to progress into directing. Nonetheless, Tanaka managed to carve out a space for herself as a filmmaker, working with several notable actors and even directing a film entitled *Tsuki wa noborinu* (*The Moon has Risen*, 1955) that was based on a scenario co-written by Yasujiro Ozu.

Throughout the 70s, 80s and early 90s there was little change to this trend. Shiori Kazama managed to make several features beginning in 1984 and thereafter throughout the 80s and beyond but by and large the inequality behind the camera in the Japanese film industry was ingrained and maintained. However, since the mid-1990s there has been an increasing number of female directors, something that has gone hand in hand with an identification of women as the primary audience for films in Japan. A symposium in 2009 saw the producer Yukie Kito estimate that 70% of filmgoers in the country are female, and this perhaps helps to explain the ongoing preponderance of female-centred films in Japanese cinema. Interestingly, though, as far as those by women are concerned this does not always equate to more forceful or probing narratives of womanhood, at least not directly so. There is certainly some exploration of female identity, but by no means an overarching concern with this as a point of departure. Indeed, even those films that are concerned with female stories often do not have explicit recourse to feminist impulses, and may be said to subvert or satirise such an imperative. It is as though a feminist framework would be an intrusion or an imposition upon the protagonists. It would stress the presence of a figure or an artist arguing for them or on their behalf where these frequently unreflective characters themselves could never pose or articulate such thoughts or concepts. There is thus a complex site of negotiation and dialogism in a number of these films as they work toward a space for feminine reflection and identity but without any concomitant dogmatic formalism or rarefied art cinema methodology.

Nami Iguchi

Paramount in this regard is the work of Nami Iguchi, who has in her short career as a director made only three features but nonetheless has developed a distinctive visual and narrative methodology built around a discreet, observational aesthetic, a cinematographic style defined by long takes and long shots and a serio-comic naturalistic tone reminiscent of the Taiwanese director Tsai Ming-Liang or the South Korean Hong Sang-soo. Profiled in *Cahiers du Cinéma* in 2009, Iguchi's cinema does contravene several facets of mainstream filmmaking, in its style and loose structure that de-emphasises tight causality and a plot-driven narrative in favour of the quotidian details of the protagonists' lives, but in this she offers a potent dialogue with the mainstream of the cinema of Japan.

Iguchi's feature debut *Inuneko* (*Dogs and Cats/The Cat Leaves Home*, 2004) concerns the tentative relationship and respective daily lives of two young women, old school friends, who begin to live together when one, Suzu, leaves her lazy, inattentive fiancé and moves out of her home. She moves in with Yoko, who is looking after the home of a mutual friend spending a year away studying in China, and the pair who seem on the surface to be like the titular pets (i.e. polar opposites) are gradually revealed to be almost identical. Indeed, in a distant echo of Ingmar Bergman's *Persona* (1966) they even seem to exchange lives and identities – beginning with a scene in which Suzu tries on Yoko's spectacles and, later, when Yoko borrows Suzu's contact lenses and subsequently helps out by undertaking her housemate's job as a dog-walker. Iguchi even underlines the similarity visually when she shoots Yoko struggling to find the right home and dog in precisely the same way as he had earlier shot Suzu, with the same camera set-up and same jump-cut to comically denote her having taken the wrong road.

The sense of an almost communal identity here facilitates a reading of this particular film as, slyly and satirically, about woman rather than women. It does not argue that all women are the same but, rather, foregrounds the fact that there is or may be a commonality of female experience. It is a point that comes to pass in particular when it transpires that the two young women have always shared the same taste in men, and is crystallised when Suzu, out on her job as a dog walker, falls down and is helped by the man whom Yoko secretly desires. When she invites him back to their house Yoko becomes perturbed and leaves to spend the night with Suzu's ex-fiancé. The lack of psychological insight or ostensible depth of characterisation that goes hand-in-hand with Iguchi's observational aesthetic reinforces this aspect of the narrative. She looks at rather than with her protagonists, and in so doing stresses the primacy of the camera's point of view, the lack of a gendered or biased perspective on the characters and narrative. This coupled with the fact that female desire and female gazing animates the structure of looks within the film (hence the motif of eyesight and glasses), and that men remain almost exclusively the desired objects, provides a female perspective that downplays the centrality of (heterosexual) romance but at the same time finds little in the way of a viable alternative. These women's variously reactive emotions and actions bring neither happiness nor satisfactory independence, making Iguchi's vision one of the limits of female selfhood and subjectivity.

The narrative concept of similarity and difference is made manifest textually from the very beginning of the film through Iguchi's prominent use of a cinematic intertext. She immediately signals such a relationship, one that will structure and animate its thematic centre, through the credits in *Dogs and Cats*, which unfold over a prominent burlap background of the type that became a trademark of the films of Ozu; indeed the beige colour of this cloth in *Dogs and Cats* directly echoes Ozu's late colour films, which all invariably employed this tone as a contrast to the often bright red characters of the credits. The point of having the ghost of Ozu so prominent throughout the film is, in effect, to draw a distinction between the Japan that Ozu's work described and documented and the country in the new millennium, the key distinction being the erosion of the family unit that was a staple of the director of *Banshun* (*Late Spring*, 1949), *Tōkyō monogatari* (*Tokyo Story*, 1953) and *Kohayagawa-ke no aki* (*The End of Summer*, 1961), among many others. The landscape of *Dogs and Cats* is dominated by individuals rather than families, by young characters who to all intents and purposes are estranged from any viable familial relationships. It is a measure of the lengths to which Japan has transformed itself that the family unit no longer seems at the heart of the country, and as a result, Iguchi's protagonists appear cast adrift, not so much aimless or in overt need of a family around them as they are in want of a way to define themselves against something tangible (another reason for the similarities between the two protagonists). But this is a double-bind for the characters; the two women (or girls, as they are often depicted as childlike) remain entrenched within their respective lives and enmities but tied to the same space. The home has often been encoded as feminine, a female sphere, and Iguchi here amplifies this perceived, stereotypical connection in order to suggest the limitations of such a construction.

This is a picture that carries over broadly into Iguchi's second feature, the much longer *Hito no sekkusu o warau na* (*Don't Laugh at my Romance*, 2007), a film whose de-dramatised narrative sensibility and exploration of female subjectivity elaborates upon its predecessor. *Don't Laugh at my Romance* concerns another tentative relationship, this time between a young male university student named Mirume and a middle-aged lecturer called Yuri, and typically Iguchi traces this story alongside two other characters – the young student's friends (a boy and a girl, the latter of whom, En-chan, is secretly in love with Mirume) – as a means of contextualising and casting fresh light upon the central romantic couple. Employing and indeed refining her long shot/long take methodology and chilly, autumnal mise-en-scène, *Don't Laugh at my Romance* can be read explicitly as a treatise on looking and not looking, hiding and being seen, invisibility and visibility. Within the film the protagonists are often desirous of looking but not being looked at. Several early comedic moments see various characters hiding from the sight of others, something that affects both Mirume and En-Chan repeatedly; however their looking connotes powerlessness rather than power, conferring on the (knowing) object a measure of control and agency that is typically associated with the desiring subject.

Mika Ninagawa, Momoko Ando and Yuki Tanada

Looking and femininity as spectacle are taken to an extreme in the work of Mika Ninagawa. A former fashion photographer, Ninagawa's first feature *Sakuran* (2008) is a jidai-geki (period film) about a young girl sold to a brothel as a child (echoes of *Memoirs of a Geisha*) who grows into the establishment's pre-eminent prostitute. The nature of her world as a perennial display with the women within as objects is connoted by both the exaggerated, almost expressionistic opulence of the mise-en-scène and the recurrent motifs of cherry blossoms and of a goldfish bowl. The protagonist is explicitly contrasted with the creature inside when she tries to escape and knocks the bowl over, both she and the fish, it is suggested, cast out of their respective worlds and thus unable to survive. The brothel as a goldfish bowl, always on show, is also prominent, establishing a concern with voyeurism and erotic spectacle that Ninagawa would expand upon in her subsequent film *Heruta sukeruta* (*Helter Skelter,* 2012). This is an excessive conceptual horror about a popular model literally falling apart due to radical surgery intended to retain her beauty and exalted status as perennially desired object.

Young female protagonists and their problematic relationships are also a key feature of films by several other young female directors. *Kakera* (*Kakera: A Piece of Our Life* 2009), the debut feature by Momoko Ando echoes *Dogs and Cats* in that in concerns a young girl who leaves her inattentive and casually indifferent boyfriend, and again as in Iguchi's film her life thereafter is defined by a tortuous relationship with another woman. However, in this case, the relationship is a sexual one, as the woman, Haru, meets and becomes intimately involved with a prosthetic surgeon named Riko. Ando flirts with a forceful, if simplistic, picture of gender relations here, especially as Haru's boyfriend is depicted as a casually indifferent, selfish and obnoxious partner who is only interested in Haru for sex, and who has at least one other lover besides her that he barely bothers to hide. Indeed, at one point the camera creeps over Haru and her boyfriend as he makes love to her prostrate body (after she has banged her head and fallen) and comes to rest on a television on which is playing wartime newsreel footage of conflict and fighting. However the lesbian relationship with Riko is not an ideal union to contrast with the problematic heterosexual relationship. Riko is possessive and suspicious and denies Haru a life and identity of her own, the point, ultimately, being that one must define oneself as an individual rather than beside anyone (or anything) else.

Such a concern with women and their relationships with abusive or indifferent men has animated other films like Tsuki Inoue's short *Daichi o tataku onna* (*The Woman Who is Beating the Earth*, 2008) and Shiori Kazama's earlier *Kasei no kanon* (*The Mars Canon*, 2002). Narratives of romance and problematic courtship have also been explored by another key female director in modern Japanese cinema: Yuki Tanada. Tanada has said that gender should not be a noteworthy feature of her profession, stating that 'there are male directors and female directors who produce interesting and not so interesting films, regardless of their sex,' (2009). However her first feature *Tsuki to Cherī* (*Moon and Cherry*, 2004) is rather a militant affair. It concerns a young university student, Tadokoro, who, after joining an erotic writing club, becomes involved with a young woman named Mayumi, offering practical research for Mayumi's serialised novel by sleeping with anyone who can help her story. Tadokoro, being a virgin, is quickly enlisted by Mayumi to sleep with her, and further to engage in a series of increasingly outré sexual encounters, but he falls in love with her, thus complicating a relationship that she needs purely for her work. It is a quasi-satirical picture of female agency, of a relationship entirely on the woman's terms and complicated by a male occupying a narrative role (sentimental, subservient) that is often associated with the female. Tanada's subsequent film, *Hyakuman-en to nigamushi onna* (*One Million Yen Girl* 2008), puts an entirely serious face on this narrative conceit in its story of a young girl whose troubles in the local community lead her to continually journey from place to place, living only long enough in any town or village to save up one million yen. She refutes all connections and relationships in pursuit of this goal; however she falls in love but abandons her partner to continue her journey. Tanada presents this in an upbeat way, as something of a victory for the female, who desires more than simply a romantic relationship.

Miwa Nishikawa

Of note for her lack of interest in overt stories of female selfhood is Miwa Nishikawa. A former assistant director to Hirokazu Koreeda, on his film *Distance* (2001), Nishikawa has progressed from a literature degree to produce a body of work that of all her contemporaries most explicitly eschews any engagement with female-centred stories. She has said that, for her, 'women are impossible to understand', (Blouinartinfo, 2013) but the indirect portraits in her work do not forego treatment of their problems and pleasures. *Dia dokutā* (*Dear Doctor*, 2009), Nishikawa's fourth feature and winner of the Best Film Award at the 31st Yokohama Film Festival, concerns the aging doctor in a rural village whose lack of detailed expertise in treating more complex cases is brought to light following his treatment of an elderly female patient. Unfolding in flashback from a framing story in which two detectives investigating the doctor's criminal negligence interview villagers about their relationship with him following his mysterious disappearance, the narrative posits this patriarchal figure as, in Mulvey's terminology, an enigma to be resolved, and thus once again as occupant of the classical narrative role typically taken by a woman. Elsewhere, the film offers a more subtle vision than one simply based around a man and his various problems; Nishikawa's intertextual film implicitly recalls Kurosawa Akira's

Akahige (*Red Beard*, 1965), and that film's picture of young and old and past and present as key oppositions in the narrative. In *Dear Doctor* it is a theme that underlines a more modern sense of female agency and professional capability. On the one hand, the village where Dr Osamu practices is depicted as, in a sense, an old space, a site of the past given that it is populated almost entirely by elderly people, and further one that is presided over (as one of the detectives says even 'held together') by this patriarchal figure, one who is celebrated by his patients for what they erroneously believe, or perhaps want to believe, to be his miraculous medical abilities. On the other hand, there is Osamu's victim's daughter, a relatively young woman who is herself a successful medical professional, one with the more modern beliefs and attitudes of those from Tokyo, where women are accepted into positions of power and responsibility.

Nishikawa's sensibility in *Dear Doctor* is nowhere aggressive or forceful regarding its gender politics. Indeed, the writer/director is throughout at pains to offer a rounded and complex portrait of the doctor, stressing the extent to which he is all but crippled by his lack of professional knowledge and expertise. This, in fact, is something that has defined much of Nishikawa's work. She herself has said that she is interested in 'encountering one's human nature' in her films, so that in a sense her work is not necessarily tied directly to any Japanese context.' (Blouinartinfo, 2013) Her sophomore feature, *Yureru* (*Sway*, 2006), exemplifies this point, concerning as it does two brothers and the harmful effects their respective actions have on a young woman, a young character who falls to her death from a bridge on an outing with the pair. The three are long-time friends who are re-united following the death of the brothers' mother. The older of the two, Minoru, sees himself as a failure, working still at his father's gas station, whilst the younger, Takeru, is a successful photographer. The girl, Chieko, also works at the gas station, and Minoru secretly harbours feelings toward her. However, following a one night-stand with Takeru, she desires to leave with him and return to Tokyo. Minoru and Chieko argue on a bridge and the girl falls to her death, following which the film offers a broadly Rashomon-like structure that stresses subjectivity over apparent 'truth', the primacy of perception and the influence of feelings and emotions on how events are seen and processed. Nishikawa explores the fallout to this incident, with the respective feelings of the two brothers traced over the course of the film as Minoru is arrested and placed on trial for homicide. *Sway*, like *Dear Doctor*, is thus concerned with a criminal case built around a female victim of men (and the girl is very much a victim of both brothers, given how she is essentially used by Takeru and then abandoned when she states her desire to return to Tokyo with him), and as such with male agency and identity. It is a story of masculine selfhood, damnation and potential redemption; indeed, it is the death of their mother that has brought the estranged siblings together at the beginning of the film, and this loss (which also unbalances their father) seems to hang over them, affecting their respective relationships with other women throughout the film.

The breaking of the law in Nishikawa's films may be said to have a symbolic meaning relating to the psychoanalytical law of the father – the perceived status for young men when they negotiate the oedipal complex and enter adulthood by finding a woman who takes the place of the once-desired mother. It implies the extent to which this normative process fails to be navigated, and as such the nature of the protagonists as perennial children. It is a theme that also animates Nishikawa's feature debut, *Hebi ichigo* (*Wild Berries*, 2003), albeit from a different perspective. *Wild Berries* is an offbeat family drama and *shomin-geki* – or story of everyday, often lower-middle class characters – that broadly looks back to some of the excessive, satirical family films of the 1980s. Like Juzo Itami's *Osōshiki,* (*The Funeral/Death Japanese Style*, 1983), Nishikawa's film also has a central scene at a funeral, and moreover one in which this paragon of a spiritual tradition – of mourning the deceased through recourse to Buddhist doctrines – is shockingly interrupted and parodied. While Itami shows this through the inability of several characters to sit formally throughout the ceremony (connoting their estrangement from tradition) Nishikawa uses the wake as a setting for a fight between the husband and a debtor looking for money, a fight that leads to the coffin falling to the ground and the corpse spilling out onto the floor.

Wild Berries does have a female protagonist, albeit one at the centre of an ensemble of competing characters in her family. The particular crises that face these characters relate specifically to issues pertaining to gender and, as it were, traditional divisions therein. The father of the house has lost his job but is too ashamed to tell his family, and as a result has been borrowing money from loan sharks, whilst his wife struggles with the upkeep of her home and the constant care and attention of her senile father-in-law, whom she eventually allows to die. It is this couple's adult daughter who is the central character, and her criminal brother who helps the family out becomes the chief locus of the tension. The latter's overt breaking of the law casts light upon the mother's crime of ignoring her father-in-law's distress, thus contributing directly to his death. Male and female criminality is juxtaposed, but the former ironically figures more as an act undertaken for the good of the family whilst the latter is a selfish act taken in the name of personal, individual gratification. This alludes to social constructions of gender and expectations therein, with Nishikawa's refusal to take sides or make judgements typical of her work as a whole, which feature makes her cinema of particular relevance in Japanese cinema.

Naomi Kawase

Beyond the female visions inherent in the work of the directors discussed above, the films of Naomi Kawase offer a detailed and probing examination of gender and modern familial relations. Kawase has said that 'I just make my own films, and tell the kind of story I want to tell,' (*Midnight Eye,* 2009); in other words she denies much in the way of specific influences on her films, and this work, both documentaries and features, predated many of the other directors examined in this essay. Indeed it is difficult to clearly separate this fiction and non-fiction. Her early features offer detailed pictures of family and domestic life, with loose, open narratives that enshrine the everyday and that frequently dwell on narrative temps morts at the expense of spectacle. *Moe no Suzaku (The God Suzaku,* 1996) and *Shara* (2003) both emanate outwards from incidents in the past to trace its lingering relevance to a family in the present. The fact that the settings of both works are relatively isolated villages (*The God Suzaku*, in particular, unfolds in a remote mountain location) reflects a division between the city and the country as a decisive aspect of modern Japan. In *The God Suzaku*, the father of the family finds himself out of work due to official abandonment of a planned railway line through the mountain, whilst impending motherhood in *Shara* offers a source of both pleasure and anxiety over the vulnerability of children (the films ends with a birth to counter a death at the beginning of the film, when a child suddenly and inexplicably goes missing). The stratification of gender is thus subtly questioned; the gravitational pull of the family home is apparent but Kawase highlight's the traditional strictures therein – that the man's place within it is ambiguous where the woman's is central, assured – in order to implicitly question their validity. In *The God Suzaku*, the man simply leaves, disappears, whilst in *Shara*, masculinity as a guardian and repository of tradition is stressed through the male being at the head of a village festival, and this apparent gendering of social and domestic space becomes significant. The fact that a woman is forced to find a job in the former film, and that a young girl leads the festival procession in the latter, alludes to the director's presentation of potentially alternative models to counter tradition. In both cases the future lies in a negotiation or dialogue with the past rather than an obliteration of it.

Kawase's films are by no means polemical works. But in their themes and documentary aesthetics they uncover something of the social make-up of Japan, and in her subsequent features *Mogari no mori* (*The Morning Forest,* 2007) *Nanayomachi* (*Nanayo*, 2008) Kawase has refined this picture through abstracting women from the family and domestic environment (and indeed eschewing their personal histories). She presents a quasi-existential dynamic wherein these protagonists must come to some self-definition of themselves away from the spaces, relationships and accoutrements of their daily lives. The former is about a care worker at an old people's home who gets lost in a forest with a patient, whilst the latter concerns a Japanese woman alone in Thailand, and both trace the respective ways that these protagonists define new lives for themselves from the ashes of their old selves.

The pictures of gender and womanhood in the films of modern Japanese female directors are complex and varied, accessible (whether directly or otherwise) to the concerns of modern women and their everyday lives whilst never dogmatic or militant in their representation of gender. These films have all found room for a female voice that stakes its claim to a distinctive aspect of Japanese filmmaking in the new millennium, and one that can be placed alongside those of Iran, Australia and the US as a major facet of its national cinema. The Japanese film industry has, in a way, responded to this increasingly prevalent aspect of its cinema, as there has been a marked increase in commercial, genre pictures directed by women. Several horror films in particular have been directed by women, including the popular fantasy horror works *Eko Eko Azarak: Wizard of Darkness* (*Eko eko azaraku,* 1995) and its prequel made the following year, as well as recent addition to the *Ju-on: The Grudge* series, whilst a film festival, Peaches (held every March), has been organised specifically to showcase the work of young female graduates from the Film School of Tokyo. On the whole, despite ongoing problems in the Japanese film industry – an industry Nishikawa has labelled as 'boring' (Blouinartinfo, 2013) – the situation seems to be reasonably strong in this regard.

Author biography

Adam Bingham teaches film studies in the UK. He is a contributing editor at the independent publisher Intellect and writes for CineAction, Cineaste and Asian Cinema. His book on post-1997 Japanese genre cinema is upcoming from Edinburgh University Press.

Contact: adam.bingham01@btinternet.com

References

Desser, D. (1988). *Eros plus Massacre: an Introduction to the Japanese New Wave Cinema*, Indiana University Press, Bloomington and Indianapolis.
Fujimura-Faneslow, K. (ed.) (2011). *Transforming Japan. How Feminism*

and Diversity are Making a Difference, The Feminist Press, New York

Mackie, V (2003). *Feminism in Modern Japan: Citizenship, Embodiment and Sexuality*, Cambridge University Press

Midnight Eye (2009). 'Yuki Tanada interviewed by Jasper Sharp'. (http://www.midnighteye.com/interviews/yuki-tanada   accessed 29th November 2013)

Blouin Art Info (2013). 'Interview with Miwa Nishikawa'. (https://web.archive.org/web/20130820101834/http://enjp.blouinartinfo.com/news/story/944947/interview-film-director-miwa-nishikawa accessed November 28th 2013)

15. To Direct Patriarchy

Iram Parveen Bilal

Since the 1980s rule of Zia ul Haq that took cinemas down and slandered filmmaking as a sin, Pakistan's healthy film industry, which had continued the momentum mostly from India post-partition, suddenly lost its courage and its identity. Lahore's 'Lollywood', a slogan synonymous to mostly cheap knock-offs and lack of original ideas, produced stereotypical recycled films centering on 'village boy meets girl' where women were versions of the Bond girl turned '*desi*' (South Asian – and certainly more curvy and voluptuous, like the local taste of desire). Lollywood is mainly made up of films in Punjabi, a dialect of the country's wealthiest and most populous province Punjab, where Lahore is found.

Another popular regional cinema is Pashtho cinema from the highly conservative Peshawar, in the province of Khyber Pakhtunkhwa, that surprisingly has recently started showing films with sexy, voluptuous heroines in a culture that is otherwise wary of showcasing its women. Urdu cinema, in the national language of the country, spluttered along barely staying alive.

In 2013, there was a sudden upsurge in production, with five releases in a six month period. For a type of cinema that only spits out one film every two years on average, that's an achievement and a brow-raising change. What's an even greater surprise is that out of these five releases, two were directed and co-directed by women. It seems that Pakistan has a higher concentration of well-known women directors than India in terms of percentages of working directors in the respective countries.[1]

Mehreen Jabbar, who comes from a film family from more than one generation, says of earlier Lollywood:

CELLULOID CEILING

'Some of the strongest directors in Lollywood have been
women. Directors like Sangeeta, Shamim Ara have had
successful films to their credit and full studio backing
so despite some unflattering opinions and perceptions
of Lollywood, it has produced at least two powerhouses
that I know of.'

This lineage of women directors indeed starts with the
traditional old school Lollywood actors turned directors, Sangeeta
and Shamim Ara who directed their first films in the 1970s,
namely *Society Girl* (1976) and *Jeo or Jeenay Do* (*Live and Let Live*
1977). Both enjoyed great box office success, and were Pakistan's
first women filmmakers actively making films in the mainstream
Urdu and Punjabi arena (Sangeeta has directed eighty films to
date in Urdu, Punjabi and Pushto cinema!). Remarking on control
on her sets in the 70s, Sangeeta says:

'I always did face a bit of conflict with the actors in my
films who made me dance around their schedules but I
was able to tackle the actresses easily.'

Then came Samina Peerzada, also an actress turned director,
with *Inteha* (1999), her directorial debut which was a voice against
domestic violence and faced trouble with the film censor boards.

In the last decade however, there has been a silent but persistent
army of women directors breaking through, not making their
entries first as actresses in the industry. Prominent names include
internationally celebrated filmmakers such as Sabiha Sumar *Silent
Waters, Dinner with The President, Who Will Cast The First Stone*
and more recently *Good Morning Karachi. Silent Waters* won the
Golden Leopard at the Locarno Film Festival, amongst other
awards; Sharmeen Obaid Chinoy, *Transgenders: Pakistan's Open
Secret, Saving Face*, Oscar and Emmy winning director, Mehreen
Jabbar *Ramchand Pakistani;* Meenu Gaur, Co-director, *Zinda Bhaag*
and Afia Nathaniel *Dukhtar* all of whom have seen international
film fraternity notoriety. Prominent TV directors also include
Angeline Malik (actress/director) and Amna Khan, the latter
being the only woman director to gain consistent jobs in the
advertising/commercial industry that is otherwise dominated by

male directors. Incidentally, Gaur's *Zinda Bhaag*, is Pakistan's first entry into the Oscars since 1963. Half a century on, I am proud to share that the re-formation of the Oscar committee was an initiative of myself and Sharmeen Obaid Chinoy.

My feature film *Josh*, with a mostly female crew, was shot in the unstable outskirts of Karachi in 2011 when the cycle of filmmaking hadn't picked up its recent momentum. During pre-production, the feeling of having to work harder than normal to prove oneself was certainly present. For instance, we even had to pitch ourselves to be able to rent equipment that should otherwise have just been a pay and go type of a deal. Additionally, there were a few male actors who (my co-producer, a Pakistani male, flatly told me), would not work with a woman director. But that's hardly a surprise anywhere in the world being a woman director, in terms of either an active or a passive-aggressive resistance, so why would it really be a surprise in a patriarchal culture? What's amazing is the resilience of these women directors. Jabbar adds:

> '...I managed to shoot in a desert and Afia Nathaniel shot in the Northern areas so I think where there is a will, there will be a way.'

Refreshingly, there are also perks of being a woman in a culture like Pakistan where there is an immense respect for the female and maternal figure. I, personally, felt a lot of care and respect on our set and my cast and crew didn't bat an eyelid in terms of me taking the reigns.

However, there is still no denying the prevalent gender politics. As Gaur notes,

> 'What I find interesting is that there are several women who work on film sets in various capacities and yet there are far too few women directors. Which means that there are several women entering the professions but far fewer who are becoming directors. I don't think this has anything to do with ability at all but much more to do with gender politics.'

In addition, the constant demand for big spectacle action

movies and comedies, almost a trend the world over, is hurting a lot of women directors whose themes mostly tend to not be in that vein. In a country where Bollywood and spectacle Hollywood is appreciated, where escape is the name of the game and perhaps the only purpose of cinema right now, realist cinema is still new, and still developing its audience.

Peerzada emphasises,

> 'Women must now start becoming their own distributors. We need to form a United Women's Artists front since the male domination will not allow women to succeed just yet.'

Most of the issue-based films made by women are still awaiting local box office success and in some cases even initial support by distributors. What's hopeful is that a lot of these aforementioned indie women directors are taking the torches forward despite a hard distribution scene due to the preconceptions of distributors who favour testosterone-driven cinema for the masses. Sangeeta says,

> 'Women must first make what the masses want so they can establish a firm footing. They are our and my future. Incredible talents are coming forth.'

Do we make films purely for the enjoyment of the masses or do we induce the masses to enjoy our alternative visions? That's an age-old battle that will have to be balanced delicately by these rising Pakistani women directors.

Author biography

Raised in Nigeria and Pakistan, Iram Parveen Bilal is conscious of the rare opportunity and voice she has on the filmmaking playground. Having directed short films which have appeared at international film festivals such as Rotterdam and Kustendorf, she is currently touring with her first feature *Josh*. Just released in Pakistan, this set records for a first indie project to be released on such a large scale with houses full. Bilal is also a key player in the rising Pakistani industry where she initiated the formation of the first ever Oscars' nomination committee in fifty years in the country.

Josh is a 2012 Women in Film Fund recipient and has been commissioned by Channel 4 and other TV outlets around the world. Bilal is interested in socially-conscious subjects relevant in both, the USA and South Asia.

For her three feature projects in development, she has received attention from FIND, IFP, Sundance, The CineReach Foundation and The Nicholl's Fellowship. FADWA, was a member of the 2008 IFP Emerging Narratives and then a Semi-Finalist at the Nicholl's Fellowship in 2009. *Forbidden Steps* was part of the 2008 Mumbai Sankalan Screenwriting Lab, the 2010 FIND Director's Lab and the 2013 FIND Screenwriter's Lab. Bilal was also a 2010 FIND Project Involve directing fellow.

She is a graduate, in honours, from the California Institute of Technology and the Peter Stark Producing Program at USC. She has also been adjunct Film Faculty at Caltech.

Recent awards and fellowships include the 2012 Women In Film Award, the 2013 TEDx Caltech speaking invitation, the 2013 FIND Screenwriting Fellowship, the 2013 Best First Feature, Silent River Film Festival, the 2010 FIND Director's Fellowship, 2008 IFP Emerging Narratives, the USC Stark Special Project Award, the Thomas J. Watson Fellowship, the Paul Studenski Fellowship, the Caltech Mabel Beckman Leadership Award and the Caltech Dean's Cup. In her spare time, she enjoys Bollywood dancing, reading and teaching AP math, science and economics.

See http://www.iramparveenbilal.com

Contact: parveenshahproductions@gmail.com

References

De, Esha Niyogi Fulbright Senior Regional Research Scholar, South Central Asia (2013–2014) 'Cross-Border Cinema by Women Filmmakers: Bangladesh, India, Pakistan.' Professor, Center for the Study of Women, University of California, Los Angeles

(More: http://wp.ucla.edu/index.php/faculty/2-uncategorised/133-eshade)

Internet Movie Data Base: http://www.imdb.com

Quotes by direct conversations of the author with: Sangeeta, Samina Peerzada, Mehreen Jabbar.

16. Brilliant Careers:

Three Waves of Australian, New Zealand, and Indigenous Women Film Directors.

Pieter Aquilia

Over the last thirty-five years, female directors in Australia and New Zealand have been instrumental in projecting feminist narratives onto international screens. Australian filmmakers such as Gillian Armstrong (*My Brilliant Career, 1979; Little Women 1994; A Thousand Acres, 1997*) and Jocelyn Moorhouse (*Proof, 1991; How to Make an American Quilt, 1995*), and New Zealanders Jane Campion (*The Piano, 1992; Bright Star 2010),* Niki Caro (*Whale Rider 2002; North County, 2005*) and Christine Jeff (*Sylvia,* 2003; *Sunshine Cleaning,* 2008) have led the charge, producing a body of globally recognised work representing the lives of women in historical and contemporary times. Their legacy has inspired a developing generation of filmmakers tackling a new genre of progressive films for and about women. In Australia, young filmmakers such as Cate Shortland and indigenous filmmaker Rachel Perkins, and over the Tasman, Kristin Mercon, and indigenous director Libby Hakaraia are telling these bold new stories – narratives from the heartlands, which reflect the gritty, often dark, forgotten or untold stories of women on the fringes of society.

Buoyed by two decades of public policy supporting women filmmakers and indigenous artists, more than 18% of directors and 34% of producers in the Australian film industry are women. This outstrips established industries in the US and Europe (*The Australian,* 2013). Critics have applauded the Australian industry for its relative openness to women and their brazen approach to exhibiting stories about women. Armstrong, Caro and Campion's films alone have resulted in a handful of Academy Awards, nominations for best supporting and best lead actresses, shoring up the role they have played in progressing the visibility of women on screen.

The anomaly of the female director in the antipodes was first explored in Blonski *et al*'s study of women's independent filmmaking in Australia (1987), noting that Australia's film industry was amongst the earliest and most innovative in the world, with women contributing significantly to its history. The women's film movement in Australia was borne from the feminist movement in the theatre in the 1960s and 1970s, supported by the federal government's Experimental Film Fund (distributed by the then Australian Film Institute). Many of these films were shot on Super 8 and 16mm. The narratives challenged prevailing ideologies and politics about women, and the films provided an aesthetic and technical training ground for female directors to advance to more professional productions (Blonski *et al.*, p. 45), mainly feature-length documentaries produced and broadcast on national television (financed by the Creative Development Branch of the AFC).

Gillian Armstrong, Jenni Thornley and Sarah Gibson were some of the key names producing non-fiction films in the 1970s, which focused on generations of stories about women previously overlooked in Australian cinema. By the mid-1970s, the Australian Film Television and Radio School, established to address the lack of training in the fledgling film industry, was integral to training a number of women filmmakers from both the continent and New Zealand, including Armstrong, Campion, and Moorhouse. The government funding agencies, including the Australian Film Commission (AFC) and New Zealand Film Commission (NZFC) adopted women's film funding as an important tenet of their charters, enabling these pioneer female directors to embark on documentaries, short films and features that jump-started their professional careers.

The confluence of a generation of young, talented and adventurous women, with a passion for film as an ideological medium, and a political environment that recognised the lack of women in key roles in the film industry in the 1970s, produced a stable of female directors who not only achieved national recognition but spread their wings to the established industries in the United Kingdom and the United States. This chapter celebrates these personalities, their films and the social and political factors that nurtured these globally acclaimed women directors. Moreover, the chapter investigates the new generation of antipodean women filmmakers of the 21st century and the new social and political themes that their films portray, heavily influenced by the important groundwork laid by pioneers such as Campion and Armstrong.

The Framing of Women's Films

Moran and Vieth in their book *Film in Australia: An Introduction* (2006) devote a chapter to Australian films about women. The authors provide various frames in which these films can be defined, including the common account whereby women are involved both in front and behind the camera. This definition marks Gillian's Armstrong's début on *My Brilliant Career* in 1979, when she became the first woman in forty-six years to direct an Australian feature film. Armstrong recounts the criticisms she faced when embarking on the film:

> '...it wasn't just me being judged about whether or not I could direct, but I was actually carrying all women in Australia on my shoulders. If that film had failed, they would have said, "Women can't do it.' (Seger, p. 98).

Bassinger (1993) acknowledges the important role that these films play on the narrative structure, imagery and ideology about female issues:

> 'A women's film is one, that places at the centre of its universe, a female who is trying to deal with the emotional, social and psychological problems that are specifically connected to the fact that she is a woman.' (505–6).

CELLULOID CEILING

Robin Laing, the most prolific producer of NZ films directed by women, confirms that

> 'many women filmmakers are saying that the big things in life, such as war and violence, have been overvalued and the small events that create the true texture and value of life have been undervalued' (Seger, p. 118).

Helene Wong, who served as a development officer at the NZFC, and a script writer and director in her own right, is emphatic about the role that women directors play in transcending the male-centric cinematic world and providing 'a broader interpretation of the human race.' (Seger, p. 225).

Moran and Veith (2006) call attention to a 'feminist cycle of narrative films' in Australia from 1977–1987, which coincides with the developing careers of women pioneers of the industry, including Armstrong and Campion, and the introduction of film development programs by the AFC, AFTRS and emerging university programs at Swinburne and Griffith universities. The second wave of women filmmakers in the years 1987–2000 bears the fruits of these years of development programs, evidenced by the growing international filmographies of women directors. Gillian Armstrong directed two Hollywood films in this era, *Little Women* (1994) and *A Thousand Acres* (1997), Jocelyn Moorhouse directed her first feature *Proof* (1991) before embarking on the US feature *How to Make an American Quilt* (1995), and Shirley Barrett's *Love Serenade* (1996) went on to win the *Camera D'Or* at Cannes. New Zealander Jane Campion completed the features *Sweetie* (1989), *Angel at My Table* (1990), *The Piano* (US, 1992) and *The Portrait of a Lady* (US, 1996). This list of globally-recognised productions acknowledges the prolific success of antipodean women in world cinema, with a large number of these films featuring key female characters and storylines tackling predominantly women's narratives.

Undoubtedly, the years since 2000 have marked a third wave of feminist filmmaking in the Australian and NZ film industries. The period has produced names such as Niki Caro (NZ: *Whale Rider* 2002; *North County*, 2005), Christine Jeffs (NZ: *Sunshine Cleaning*,

2008; *Sylvia*, 2003), Cate Shortland (Aust: *Somersault*, 2004) and Rachel Perkins (Aust: *Radiance*, 1998; *Bran Nue Dae*, 2010). Indeed by 2013, female directors dominated the major categories at the 2013 Australian Directors Guild Awards, including Cate Shortland winning the Best Director award for her film *Lore* (2012) and Rachel Perkins attaining Best Director award for direction of a TV drama series for *Redfern Now* (2012). The awards are further evidence that the third wave of feminist films in the antipodes heralds a new genre of women's film.

The Pioneers:

Gillian Armstrong

The leading figure in the resurgence of women filmmakers in Australia, launched her film career in the early 1970s when she started making 2–10 minute films while studying General Arts at Swinburne Technical College Melbourne in the late 1960s. These films included the *Roof Needs Moving* (1970) which secured her a place in the initial cohort of twelve students, alongside Phil Noyce, at the newly established Australian Film Television and Radio School (AFTRS) in 1973. Her graduate short film *One Hundred a Day* (1973), about a young girl working in a shoe factory who is facing an illegal abortion, was followed by a short film, *The Singer and the Dancer* (1975), which screened at the Sydney Film Festival in June 1976, winning the Greater Union Award for Best Narrative Film. Armstrong's success in these short films resulted in her first paid job after graduating from film school on the documentary *Smokes and Lollies* (1976) funded by the South Australian Film Corporation, one of the increasing number of institutionalised government film agencies established to boost Australia's young movie industry. The documentary, styled on the British *Seven Up* series, follows the lives of a group of teenage girls in Adelaide. The television documentary was met with critical success, introducing Armstrong to mainstream audiences. It was a project that Armstrong would continue to visit every few years, producing five sequels focusing on the same young women. The most recent documentary, *Love, Lost and Lies* (2010) explores the women at forty-eight years of age. It was the success of these early films that brought Armstrong to the attention of established producer Margaret Fink who hired her to direct *My Brilliant Career* (1979), based on the novel by Miles Franklin. The film won six awards at the Australian Film Awards, and was nominated for the Academy Award in costume design. *My Brilliant Career* examines late 19th century Australian society from the perspective of a headstrong woman who refuses to follow convention, rejecting a marriage proposal and defying her family to become a writer.

My Brilliant Career was to become Armstrong's platform to global success, winning international awards and worldwide distribution. However, Armstrong rejected overseas film offers to focus on a smaller Australian based project, the musical *Starstruck* (1982) about a young woman's dreams to become a singing star. The film proved her ability to direct contemporary subject matters and styles, while still focusing on the female narrative drama. Armstrong became the first foreign woman to have a film commissioned by America's MGM to direct *Mrs Soffel* (1984) starring Mel Gibson and Diane Keaton. Armstrong continued to work between Australia and the United States over the next twenty years, culminating in the Hollywood adaptation of the novel *Little Women* in 1994. The film demonstrated Armstrong's innate ability to elevate the lives and relationships of women on the screen. Despite Armstrong's strong command of the US market, she continued to make smaller films outside of Hollywood, including documentaries that featured at Sundance and Toronto Film Festivals (*Unfolding Florence,* 2006; *Death Defying Acts,* 2007). Critics surmise Armstrong's films as character studies, with human interaction and personal journey at the heart of the narrative. With that as her springboard, she has ventured to explore several genres, including musical, gangster and most commonly, period drama (Carter, 2002). Although her stories mainly revolve around female characters and feature women in lead roles (Everist, 1987), Carter (2002) believes the unifying theme of Armstrong's films is 'the story of unrequited love, restrained passion and friendship between men and women.' Haskell believes 'Armstrong cuts closer to the core of women's divided yearnings than any other director' (cited in Carter, 2002).

While Armstrong was forging her early career in the 1970s in Australia, New Zealander Jane Campion, a graduate of Victoria University in Wellington, went abroad to study fine arts. In the late 1970s, at the Sydney College of the Arts, Campion became interested in film and produced her first short film, *Tissues* (1980). The promising filmmaker was selected for the film program at AFTRS, where she made a trilogy of short films, *Passionless Moments* (1974), *Girl's Own Story* (1975) and *Peel* (1976) which garnered critical success. Together with her AFTRS classmate Jocelyn Moorhouse, Campion worked in television drama after graduation. Both directors' first feature films were selected for the Cannes Film festival in 1989 and 1991 respectively: Campion's *Sweetie* (1989), which traces the relationship of two sisters in a dysfunctional family and was financed by the New South Wales Film and Television Office; and Moorhouse's *Proof* (1991), about a blind photographer looked after by a migrant housemaid, which was financed by the AFC and Film Victoria.

First Wave: narrative structure, imagery and ideology

The first wave of feminist feature filmmaking, initiated by *My Brilliant Career* in 1979, coincided with a period of historical filmmaking in Australia. Some of the key films of the generation included Fred Schepsi's *The Chant of Jimmy Blacksmith* (1978), Bruce Beresford's *Getting of Wisdom* (1977), and Peter Weir's *Picnic at Hanging Rock* (1975). Although Armstrong's film is set at the turn of the century, it is considered an important feminist film of the time as it closely reflects the major social issues raised by the feminist movement of the 1960s and 1970s when unprecedented numbers of women were entering the workforce, portraying the tension between the pursuit of a career and the role of traditional homemaker. Ironically, as Sybylla chooses her creative potential as a writer over the love of a man in the film, so too did feminist films of the next ten years explore more contemporary issues surrounding young women.

Armstrong's second feature, *Starstruck*, situates the female narrative in the modern day, leaving behind the historical bush-scape for hectic pace of Sydney city in the 1980s. Carter (2002) explains that *Starstruck* begins where *My Brilliant Career* leaves off, by posing the question, 'What do ya wanna be?' Jackie, the lead, wants to be a singer and Angus, her brother, a producer. The film ends with the duo storming the Sydney Opera House to fulfill their desires. Jackie finds fame and Angus rolls down the carpet steps, kissing his first girlfriend (Carter, 2002). The films of Gillian Armstrong have regularly been 'noted for their rebellious, strong, independent heroines' (Collins, cited in Carter, 2002). *Mrs Soffel* continues this theme with the storyline of a woman deciding to leave her husband, children and prison duties for the love of an inmate, following him in a wild, dark adventure. *High Tide* (1987) is a return to contemporary Australian storytelling that re-explores the themes of career over motherhood with the protagonist preoccupied with finding her daughter who she abandoned as a baby in order to pursue her own career.

Jane Campion

Campion's early films move towards a more contemporary representation of the female narrative. Her early short films vacillate between the filmmaker's own childhood and present day themes. *Girl's Own Story* (1984) is a dark investigation of the protagonist's childhood in the 1960s as she revisits her first sexual experiences associated with incest. *A Girl's Own Story* and Campion's telemovie *Two Friends* (1986) are concerned with the problems and growing sexual awareness of adolescent girls, examining the experience of growing up female in the 1960s and

> 'the ambiguous and paradoxical messages about female sexuality … as objects of romantic and sexual desire and yet at the same time taught to be fearful of sexual expression.' (Bloustein, 1990)

In describing Campion's first feature film, *Sweetie* (1986), Gillett (1998) emphasises the filmmaker's commitment to representing 'unsayable' and 'unseeable', issues that affect women. Her early short films and television features deal with incest, while her later films Campion's films tend to gravitate around themes of gender politics, such as seduction and female sexual power.

In summary, the first wave of women's filmmaking in Australia features a feminist politics largely unscreened before the films of

Campion and Armstrong. The films work in the spaces of nostalgia and memory, often dealing with history and the recent past. While the themes are universal, the landscapes are national, featuring the rural and urban spaces of Australia and New Zealand. However, unlike the male directors before them, the representation of women is de-romanticised, often dealing with the realistic, unpleasant aspects of female sexuality from a woman's point of view. Here, the characters are often intelligent, creative women trapped or oppressed by the psychological torment of their everyday situations. These depictions by Armstrong, Campion and others paved the way for stronger emotional investigation of female characters in the second wave of filmmakers that would follow in their footsteps.

The Second Wave: 1987–2000:

Shirley Barrett

The path to international success proved more difficult for female directors in the 1990s. Australian Shirley Barrett, a graduate of AFTRS, whose short film, *Cherith* (1988) won an AFI award, achieved the prized *Camera D'Or* at Cannes with her first feature *Love Serenade* (1996). Barrett's female characters are quirky and eccentric, borne from the urban fringes and rural confines of modern society. In *Love Serenade,* two sisters compete for the attention of a local radio host who they hope will help them escape their mundane, homely lives. However, Barrett has found it difficult to win critical acclaim and box office success with her subsequent feature films. Barrett does not blame the film industry for her lack of success, instead she emphasises that she is 'an instructive case in how not to handle your career' (Schembri, 2005). Barrett chose not to go to the US, turning down *American Beauty* and *Erin Brockovich* because she had two young children at home in Australia.

Gaylene Preston

In New Zealand, Gaylene Preston's career path is punctuated by occasional feature films in a career largely dominated by documentaries. Her feature films include *Mr Wrong* (1985), *Ruby and Rata* (1990), and the mini series *Bread & Roses* (all with producer Robin Laing). She was writer, director and producer of *Perfect Strangers* (2003), a black comedy about the overriding human need to love and be loved, starring Sam Neill and Rachael Blake. For many female filmmakers, juggling family with a career, the decision not to work overseas has diminished their international career prospects.

Christine Jeffs

However, New Zealander Christine Jeffs, one of the country's most successful directors working on music videos and advertisements, transferred to narrative film after making her first short film, *Stroke* (1993), about a woman swimmer overcoming the oppression of a male swimming team competing for her space in the pool. The short, financed by the NZFC, was a critical success screening at Cannes and Sundance. Jeffs continued to work in advertising while developing her first feature film, *Rain* (2000), a sexual coming-of-age film about a thirteen-year-old girl set against the background of the her parents' disintegrating marriage. The film screened at the Directors' Fortnight at Cannes and Variety's 2002 named Jeffs on its 'Ten Directors to Watch' list. In 2003, Jeffs directed the Sylvia Plath biopic *Sylvia* for BBC films staring Gywneth Paltrow and Daniel Craig. In 2008, Jeffs directed *Sunshine Cleaning* in the United States, starring Amy Adams and Emily Blunt, about a single mother starting an unreliable clean-up business to support her daughter through school. The film was nominated for a Grand Jury Prize at Sundance.

Niki Caro

Around the same time, another New Zealander, Nikki Caro, who achieved international success with her feature *Whale Rider* (2002), was directing the Hollywood feature *North Country* (2005). The film, which explores female abuse in a local mining community, starred Charlize Theron and Francis McDormand who received Academy Award nominations for best actress and best supporting actress respectively. Caro started her filmmaking career at Auckland's Elam School of Fine Arts in 1988 before travelling to Australia in the early 1990s to gain a diploma in writing at Melbourne's Swinburne Film and Television School. In 1992, producer Owen

Hughes invited Caro to contribute to a trilogy of half-hour TV dramas being made to bridge a gap for filmmakers between short films and features. Caro's contribution was *The Summer the Queen Came,* an affectionate look at the small, twisted details of a family in suburbia. The film gained two nominations at the 1994 NZ Film and Television Awards. The same year, Caro's short *Sure To Rise*, about a woman discovering an injured airman, was selected to compete at the Cannes Film. Caro's first feature film, *Memory and Desire*, was selected for Critics Week at Cannes in 1998. Based on a short story by Peter Wells, the film follows the unraveling relationship of a Japanese couple as they travel New Zealand. In 2002, Caro wrote and directed her successful second feature, *Whale Rider* (2002) earning an Oscar Nomination for Kiera Castle Hughes who plays a Maori girl who has to face up to her paternal elders to take on the role of tribal leader.

The Influence of the Second Wave

The work of New Zealander Niki Caro shows a significant diversion from the sexual awakening of Campion's films. Caro, the director of *The Whale Rider* explains that she never really had to fight to be a feminist:

> 'stories about girls Pai's age tend to be about sexual awakening. I wanted to tell the story of how Pai awakens to her own strength and power' (NZ On Screen, 2013).

Caro's character disassociates herself from themes of sexuality and deals with the demands of gender equality and leadership. Grunes (2007) agrees that the film is feminist, supporting the hopes of women in societies that oppress them. If Caro's films are considered feminist, Christine Jeffs' films are often considered post-feminist. Certainly, *Rain* with its focus on the haunting, fragile nature of marriage, the sexual deconstruction of women in their middle ages, and the misaligned teenage obsession with sexual empowerment is a marked departure from romantic idealism of the historical films of the 1970s to 1980s. Jeffs continues this dark depiction of womanhood in the biopic *Sylvia*. Themes of madness, isolation, despair and violence dominate the film, and in this instance are closely connected to the early films of Jane Campion.

The Third Wave of Women Directors 2002–2013:

Cate Shortland

In Australia, the political environment of the new century shifted dramatically compared to the era of government financing and tuition-free film schools of Campion and Armstrong. Sydney-based director Cate Shortland studied fine arts and history before becoming one of the last cohorts in the now defunct Masters program at AFTRS in the late 1990s. Her lyrical short films, including *Joy, Flowergirl* and *Pentuphouse* marked her as a young director to watch. Her first feature, *Somersault*, screened in *Un Certain Regard* at Cannes in 2004 and scooping thirteen prizes the AFI Awards. The film, a harrowing tale of a teenager's sexual coming-of-age set against the backdrop of abuse and male exploitation in the snow town of Jindabyne, was produced by Jan Chapman (who has also produced Jane Campion and Gillian Armstrong's films) with the assistance of the government film agency, Film Victoria. However, for the next ten years, Shortland went underground directing prime-time television, before moving on to make her second feature film and her first commercially funded co-production. *Lore* (2013).

The critically applauded film, the national entrant for Best Foreign Film at the 2013 Academy Awards, centres around a young girl who is left to lead her four siblings out of post-war Germany after the disappearance of their Nazi parents. The film is a striking departure from the backdrop of *Australiana* which marks most of the nation's feature films.

Kristin Marcon

Similarly, in New Zealand, young director Kristin Marcon has recently released her first feature film, *The Most Fun You Can Have Dying* (2012), produced with the assistance of the NZFC, a coming-of-age adventure shot in several European rather than specifically NZ locations. Marcon studied at film school in New Zealand before producing several award-winning short films financed by the NZFC. However, it was difficult to finance her first feature film, and it was seven years and several failed European co-production deals before the film came to fruition (*Wellywoman*, 2012). For Marcon and Shortland, the reality of the global market place has shifted film narratives to more universal stories within transnational settings.

Rachel Perkins

The narrative from nationalistic stories to world audiences is not as marked for indigenous Australian filmmakers such as Australia's Rachel Perkins. Perkins, daughter of well-known Aboriginal activists, worked for national indigenous television prior to going to AFTRS, writing and directing shorts about her aboriginal heritage and forming a production company which has produced some of the biggest indigenous feature films, documentaries and television series in Australia. Perkin's first feature film, *Radiance* (1998), shares the role of the protagonist amongst three Aboriginal sisters. The environs of her film are the urban landscapes of indigenous Australia, rarely seen on the screen. Her second feature film, *Bran Nue Dae* (2010), like the indigenous community itself, celebrates a multiplicity of protagonists, each playing an integral role in moving the story forward. Her current television series *Redfern Now* (2013) is lauded for its gritty portrayal of domestic violence against women in the city dwelling Aboriginal community in Sydney, but equally represents the men, youth and children and the adversities facing the society.

Libby Hakaraia

Libby Hakaraia has been a strong pillar of the indigenous film industry in New Zealand, following the pioneering example of the late Merata Mita. Hakaraia is a producer and director of prime-time television documentaries, and has directed three award-winning short films funded by the NZFC. She is currently writing and directing her first feature film. A journalist by training, she has produced several award-winning documentaries and television series. Her first foray into fiction film was as the producer of the short film, *Hawaikii* (2007), about a Maori schoolgirl who is embarrassed by her family's poverty but soon learns the value of the family's love and cultural beliefs. Hakaraia's *The Lawnmower Men of Kapu* (2011), which has won several international awards and screenings, focuses on the struggles of four aunties to maintain their local *marae* told through the eyes of their twelve-year-old nephew. Hakaraia, like her Australian counterpart Rachel Perkins, is committed to telling stories about indigenous communities, whether in documentary or fiction form, bringing issues about the local community to mainstream audiences.

Characteristics of the New Wave of Women's Filmmaking

The narratives of this new wave of women's filmmaking are marked by a greater internationalisation, where national boundaries disappear. Female characters appear in universal stories that speak to global audiences, albeit sometimes set in local environments. Marcon's first feature film and Shortland's second feature are shot in European locations, a departure from their earlier national imagery, while still being produced by the NZ and Australian film industries respectively. Shortland's interest in global stories is first evidenced in her prize-winning short film, *Flowergirl,* which depicts the experiences of Japanese visitors immersed in Bondi's surfing culture facing the cultural shock of repatriating to traditional Japan. Moreover, Shortland and Marcon's films move away from the single female protagonist towards a co-protagonist, often male.

The ability to work with a variety of male and female characters sharing a singular focus, a deeper exploration of the psychological intricacies of women in relationships to other men, women and children defines the third wave of women's filmmaking in the antipodes. Shortland's harrowing investigation of the protagonists' deep self-hatred in *Somersault,* the harrowing realisation of Nazi genocide in *Lore*, Marcon's deeply personal exploration of death in *The Most Fun You Can Have Dying* and the painful aftermath of a road collision in the short film, *She's Racing* (2000), all indicate a shift in the narratives, imagery and ideology in Australian and NZ films directed by women in the 21st century. The feminist innocence of the period film has been replaced by a darker and edgier reality of what it means to be a woman on an equal gender footing in a post-feminist world.

Conclusion

This stable of female directors in Australia and New Zealand is recognised by several common denominators. Firstly, all the filmmakers have been supported in their early careers by government financing programs. In Australia, this includes, but is not limited to, the Experimental Film Fund (1970–1978), Women Film Fund (discontinued in 2001) and Indigenous Film Initiatives managed through the AFC; State film funding agencies such as the Film Victoria and the New South Wales Film Office; national and state-funded film schools, especially the Australian Film Television and Radio School; and quasi-government support groups such as Women in Film and Television, Women on Women and Indigenous Television Networks. In New Zealand, similar programs, such as the Screen Innovation program of the NZFC, Māori Affairs (now Te Puni Kōkiri Tu Tangata program) and Maori TV have played an important role in promoting women and indigenous filmmaking.

Secondly, women directors in Australia and New Zealand have shared the support of female producers who have actively worked towards employing, and financing, the works of women directors in Australia and New Zealand. Producers play a crucial role in the development and financing of films by and about women in the features industry. Seger (2003) argues that there are few women in power to make the decisions about what feature films will be made. She argues 'if there are few women in power, there are few women to mentor other women.'(54)

Margaret Fink was revolutionary in employing Armstrong as the first female in almost fifty years in the role as a feature director. In the case of Jane Campion, Gillian Armstrong's later films, Shirley Barrett and Cate Shortland, producer Jan Chapman is a key player in their careers. For Preston, Caro, Jeffs and Marcon, Robin Laing's steadfast commitment has sustained a strong collective of successful films made by and about women in New Zealand. These producers have carefully negotiated filmmakers through their early film careers, balancing government financing with

CELLULOID CEILING

private investment, liberating the directors to move into overseas co-productions, which has allowed the internationalization of women's filmmaking in Australia and New Zealand.

Finally, reviewing films by women directors in the Australian and New Zealand film has highlighted a progressive trajectory of themes surrounding the women's feminist movement in the late 20th and early 21st century. The films of Armstrong and Campion in 1970s to 1990s, with their focus on the historical film, proved an excellent vehicle to communicate the contemporary tensions for women choosing between traditional gender roles and professional careers. The success of these early films permitted a new generation of filmmakers such as Shortland, Caro, Marcon, Jeffs, Perkins and Hakaria to advance the philosophy of the individual heroine against a patriarchal society towards a modern day, psychological drama in which the female protagonist shares a communal experience. Since the late 1990s, issues such as death, sexual abuse, domestic violence and incest are laid bare on screen, providing audiences with raw rather than mediated experiences of the period films of the first wave.

The robust role of women directors in the Australian and New Zealand film industries, compared to other international cinemas, is largely contingent on a strong support structure by government initiatives to promote women and indigenous issues. Moreover, the commitment of producers such as Fink, Chapman and Laing has contributed to the mentoring of a new generation of women filmmakers. Of particular note, is the number of talented directors migrating to global marketplaces to internationalise their careers. The current status of women's filmmaking bodes well for future generations of women in the antipodes.

Author biography

See earlier chapter from Dr Pieter Aquilia.

References

Blonski, Barbara et al. (eds.) (1987). *Don't Shoot Darling!: Women's Independent Filmmaking in Australia.* Spinifex Press, Melbourne.
Bloustien, Geraldine, 1990. 'Jane Campion: memory, motif and

music.' *Continuum: The Australian Journal of Media & Culture*, Vol. 5 No. 2. (http://wwwmcc.murdoch.edu.au/ReadingRoom/5.2/Bloust.html accessed November 1st 2013) Carter, Helen, 2002. Gillian Armstrong. 'Senses of Cinema'. (http://sensesofcinema.com/2002/great-directors/armstrong/ accessed November 1st 2013)

Everist, Robyn (1987). 'Her Early Career: Gillian Armstrong's Short Films. In Creed, Blonski and Freiberg (eds), *Don't Shoot Darling!: Women's Independent Filmmaking in Australia*. Spinifex Press, Melbourne, pp. 314–322.

Flint, Rebecca (2010). 'Biography of Jane Campion', *New York Times*. (http://movies.nytimes.com/person/83988/Jane-Campion/biography accessed November 1st 2013)

Gillett, Sue (1998). 'More than Meets the Eye: The Mediation of Affects in Jane Campion's *Sweetie*'. Cinema and the Senses Conference, Sydney, December 13–15th (http://sensesofcinema.com/1999/feature-articles/sweetie/ accessed November 1st 2013)

Grunes, Dennis (2007). 'Whale Rider: Niki Caro, 2002'. (http://grunes.wordpress.com/2007/04/27/whale-rider-niki-caro-2002/ accessed November 1st 2013)

Wellywood Woman (2012). Kristin Marcon & 'The Most Fun You Can Have Dying.' Interview with the filmmaker. Sunday April 15th 2012. (See http://wellywoodwoman.blogspot.sg/2012/04/kirstin-marcon-most-fun-you-can-have.html accessed November 1st 3013)

Moran, Albert, and Vieth, Errol, 2006. *Film in Australia: An Introduction*. Cambridge University Press, Melbourne.

NZ On Screen (2013) *Niki Caro Biography*. (http://www.nzonscreen.com/person/niki-caro/biography accessed November 1st 2013)

Schembri, Jim (2005). 'Aren't you?' May 6th, *The Age*. (http://www.theage.com.au/news/Film/Arent-you/2005/05/05/1115092574563.html accessed November 1st 2013)

Seger, Linda (2003). *When Women Call the Shots: The Developing Power and Influence of Women in Film and Television*. iUniverse Inc, UK

17. Alice Guy-Blaché: True Pioneer

Tania Field

Alice Guy-Blaché was not only the first woman filmmaker in the world, she was the first person to make a film with fictional subject matter. Just as the technical revolution drew photography into motion, she created the role of motion picture director and producer, pioneering narrative filmmaking. She became the first female movie studio owner, one of the most prominent and prolific filmmakers in the industry, and one of the highest paid women in the US. During a filmmaking career spanning more than twenty-five years she was involved in directing, producing, writing, and sometimes overseeing more than 1,000 films. And she achieved all this before women had the right to vote.

Alice Ida Antoinette Guy was born in Saint-Mandé, East of Paris, on July 1st 1873. Her mother, Mariette, had returned to France to give birth on French soil, before returning to join Alice's father, Emile, in Chile where he ran his bookseller chain of stores. Baby Alice was left in the care of her grandmother in Switzerland for three or four years, until her mother returned to Europe to escort her back to the family in Chile. Arriving in Santiago, she met her father for the first time, and growing up in Chile was a happy time.

Alice's father sent her back to France, enrolling her in the boarding school where two of her older sisters were studying, the Sacred Heart Convent in Veyrier, Switzerland. During this time his Chilean business was bankrupted by a series of violent earthquakes, fires, and thefts. He returned to France, but his wife remained in Chile. Alice and her younger sister are transferred to a less expensive boarding school in Ferney, France.

Alice's brother died after a long illness, followed soon after by her father; these two tragedies forced her mother to return to Europe. With her sisters married off, Alice, in her late teens, found herself looking after her ageing mother.

In 1890, Alice was eighteen years old, a close friend of the family advised her to learn shorthand typing, a new technology and a skill that could lead to a good career as a secretary. Alice learned quickly, her teacher was a stenographer in the French Parliament who admired Alice's conscientious attitude. He promised to recommend Alice for the first good position that was offered.

In 1894, Léon Gaumont, a director for Felix Richard's still-photography company, La Comptoir Générale de Photographie, took a chance with such a young candidate and hired her as a secretary. Barely a year into her employ in this company M. Richard was forced out of business, after losing a patent suit. But, Gaumont buys the inventory and starts his own company, taking Alice Guy with him.

By 1895 Léon Gaumont, along with his business partners: architect Gustave Eiffel, astronomer Joseph Vallot and financier Alfred Besnier, built Léon Gaumont et Cie into a business known for motion picture technology. One of their first pieces of equipment they manufactured was an invention of Georges Demeny: his biographe, a 60mm motion picture camera, which Gaumont recognised as innovative and valuable.

On March 22nd 1895, the company received, from the Lumière brothers, an invitation to a demonstration at the Société d'Encouragement pour l'Industrie Nationale. The Lumières put up a giant sheet, and cranking a machine they projected a 'moving picture': employees leaving the Lumière factory. This was a cinématographe (35mm motion picture camera).

After the demonstration that astounded the audience, Alice and Gaumont were excited, maybe a little dismayed that they were still working on Demeny's camera, but they continued on with its development.

At that time the types of films being made were of life on the streets, a train entering a station, or a view of a seaside. Alice, the daughter of a bookseller, who had read many books, had a vivid imagination and had also experienced amateur theatre, thought something more interesting could be filmed. She asked Gaumont to allow her to use his motion picture camera to produce a story film. He agreed, as long as it did not interfere with her job as secretary.

In 1896, Alice Guy directed her first film, *La Fée aux Choux* (*The Cabbage Fairy*), building the set, making cardboard cabbages and wooden babies, as well as using one real baby with the actors. She learned in-camera special effects from still photographer Frédérique Dillaye. This was to be the first narrative film and it sold eighty copies. Gaumont was so pleased with this result, he appointed Alice as the Head of all moving picture production, as well as secretary and girl-friday. She held this post for eleven years, producing and directing about 1,000 films, and setting up the Gaumont film house-style, using real locations. She oversaw script preparation, set design and building, costumes and the work of other directors, as well as being a scriptwriter and director herself. She trained other filmmakers.

Gaumont was an engineering wizard and visionary, he was the first to introduce sound and colour into film and in 1902 he demonstrated his chronophone, a synchronised-sound system. He opened a film studio, Cité Elge at Buttes-Chaumont that became one of the largest studios in Europe and Alice remained head of production and in these studios she directed more than 100 phonoscènes films made for the Chronophone.

In 1906, Alice Guy embarked on her most ambitious Gaumont film: *La Vie du Christ* (*The Life of Christ*). It was thirty-five minutes in length, had twenty-five sets, featured numerous exterior locations and employed 300 'extras'. She used the illustrations from the James Tissot Bible as her guide.

Alice had a few enemies within who tried to sabotage her productions. This was probably because she was a very successful and popular woman at a time that was very much a man's world. One man, René Decaux, tried to make *La Vie du Christ* go over budget so that she would be fired and he would get her job. He slashed all the backdrops and burned them. She picked herself up and her entire staff worked overtime to re-create the backdrops, but there was still a budget overrun. She came close to losing her job, keeping it only due to the full support and intervention of Gustave Eiffel, the company chairman.

In 1906, Alice was asked by Leon Gaumont to take his place on a trip to Berlin to demonstrate to their German clients the process of synchronisation of the chronophone. Protesting that she knew nothing about Germany, nor its language, Englishman Herbert Blaché was appointed as her guide and translator. Alice and Herbert had met earlier that year on the set of her film 'Mireille'; Herbert, who was the manager of Gaumont's German affiliate in Berlin, had been appointed cameraman to relieve Alice's usual cameraman who was unwell. The trip gave way to a whirlwind romance and by the end of the year they were engaged to be married, Alice was thirty-three, Blaché was twenty-four.

Looking to America as being open for business, Léon Gaumont planned to expand the other side of the Atlantic. In 1907, he sent Alice and Herbert to Cleveland in the U.S. to promote a chronophone franchise. Newly married, Alice resigned her position at Gaumont, accompanied her husband and spent several months helping him, unpaid, despite being pregnant with their first child. Their efforts were unsuccessful, business deals did not materialise and Herbert and Alice were living on their savings, which were in danger of running out. Herbert approached Gaumont for work at the newly-built Gaumont studio in Flushing, New York. He was put in charge, to manage the studio dedicated to chronophone film production. Again, Alice helped her husband unpaid, until she gave birth to their daughter, Simone in 1908.

Full-time motherhood did not last long. By September 1910, Simone was only two years old, and Alice had the urge to get back into the cinema. The Gaumont studio was underused, and this kickstarted Alice to create her own film production company, Solax, renting studio space from Gaumont. Her first film, *A Child's Sacrifice*, a true Alice Guy tearjerker, was released in October that same year. She produced and directed one film every week for the next six months.

CELLULOID CEILING

In June 1912, Alice gives birth to her son, Reginald.

Solax was so successful, Alice built her own new and technologically advanced production facility in Fort Lee, New Jersey, which was said to cost more than $100,000, over two million dollars today. Solax produced three one-reeler films a week, collecting a house of well-known star actors. Alice continued to write and direct at least half of all Solax films and oversee all productions.

Fort Lee, was quickly becoming the film capital of America and home to many other major film studios. Her films were social commentaries with role reversals and cross-dressing; comedies full of unruly tension, mayhem and acrobatic stunts; marital problems ultimately patched up with happy endings. She tirelessly experimented with special effects such as split screens, dissolves, camera optics, sound syncronisation and film colorisation. With her directing techniques and her numerous gigantic signs screaming 'Be Natural' all around the studios, Alice transformed the art of acting, from heavily posed pantomime-style and stiff acting to the more 'natural' and unpretentious performance. So much was she praised for her astonishing achievements, it just pushed her to find more spectacular scenes and more daring stunts to satisfy the hungry cinema audiences.

When Herbert Blaché's contract with Gaumont expired in 1913, Alice made him president of Solax so that she could concentrate on writing and directing. But after only three months, weary with working in his wife's shadow, Herbert resigned and started his own film company, 'Blaché Features'. Blaché Features used Solaxs studios, inventory, and actors, making the two companies hardly distinguishable for a few months. Blaché Features' film production eventually superseded Solax production, and in 1914 Solax was virtually defunct. Both Alice and Herbert continued to alternate directing and producing longer films (three and four reels). However, Herbert's business and negotiating skills were not good, he managed to almost give away to a cunning distributor one of Alice's films, *The Lure*. It went on to be one of the biggest box office successes of the day.

The market was now demanding feature-length films (five reels or more). The Blachés joined Popular Plays and Players and US Amusement Corporation, production companies that produced features for distributors such as Metro, Pathé, and World Film Corporation. These films were shot in the former Solax studio in Fort Lee, which still belonged to the Blachés. But these were deals destined to go wrong, resulting in the Blachés distributing the films themselves.

The former Solax studio was rented out to other companies, starting with Apollo Pictures. In 1917, Simone, age nine, and Reginald, age five, became seriously ill with measles. Herbert sent his family to the healthier environment of North Carolina, where Alice Blaché cared for her children and took part in the war effort, volunteering for the Red Cross. Her husband continued to manage business in Fort Lee, and he was also enjoying the attention of young actresses.

In 1918, Herbert Blaché left for Hollywood, California, fast taking over as the film capital of America. He ran off with one of his leading actresses, abandoning his family. Alice gave up her house in Fort Lee and moved into an apartment in New York City. She survived a serious bout of the Spanish flu in 1919, and Herbert, shocked at her condition, asked her to go with him to California to recuperate. Alice moved into a small bungalow in Los Angeles, that he provided, with their children, but Herbert did not live with them. He hired Alice as his directing assistant, and although Alice still loved him, Herbert's affections were elsewhere. Working together became impossible and they split up.

In October 1921, Alice was called back to Fort Lee to oversee the auction of her personal property and the Solax properties and their contents. Everything was sold to pay back taxes owed by the tenants. The Blachés divorced and in 1922, Alice Guy-Blaché returned with her children to France, hopeless and penniless, where she was forgotten by the French film industry. She moved in with her sister in Nice, but was never able to return to work in the cinema.

She resigned herself to looking after her children, as best she could. To make money, Alice wrote children's stories and magazine articles under male pen-names. She only signed her real name to her new screenplays, but none of these screenplays were taken up by film producers. She became financially dependent on her daughter, Simone, who got a job in the Embassy, working in France and Switzerland.

Léon Gaumont published a history of L. Gaumont & Company in 1930 but did not mention any of the film production before 1907. Alice wrote to him pointing out his errors, and Gaumont agreed to add and correct the manuscript, but he never did. Through the 1940s and into 1950s, Alice spoke at high schools and women's clubs in Europe. These appearances lead her to write her memoirs, compile a filmography, and renew the search for her films. In 1953, Alice received the Légion d'Honneur Award, France's highest non-military honor. A decade later, she and Simone moved to New Jersey. On March 24, 1968, Alice Guy-Blaché died in a nursing home in Mahwah, New Jersey at the age of ninety-five.

A 1912 issue of *Moving Picture World* noted,

> 'Madame Blaché is never ruffled, never agitated, never annoyed by the obtrusive effects of minor characters to thrust themselves into prominence. With a few simple directions, uttered without apparent emotion, she handles the interweaving movements like a military leader might the maneuvers of an army.'

As a director for twenty-eight years, Alice Guy-Blaché accomplished things no one was doing at the time and is just one reminder of New Jersey's rich film history, and more specifically, a woman of consequence in her role as one of the founders of the modern-day film industry.

Alice Guy-Blaché was a fearless pioneer in early cinema technology who was betrayed by the history books and forgotten. But new campaigns will see that this is put right.

Author biography

Tania Field is a multi-media producer, with extensive experience in all forms of creative communication from graphics to video production. She is a graduate of the Royal College of Art, a past tutor of degree-level graphic design, typography and advertising, and worked as a marketing consultant for a housing association and local government. She is a member of the Wynkyn de Worde Society.

Tania has directed, filmed and produced short films for non-governmental organisations including Sustrans and the RSPCA.

Tania has researched, written and illustrated historic books, including comprehensive guides for Lee Valley Regional Park Authority, such as: *Three Mills, a heritage walk*. She has also been sub-editor of a number of local history publications.

Contact: taniafield@me.com

18. A Century of Mädchen:

Femmes and Frauen in Facist, New Wave, and Contemporary European Cinema

Heidi Honeycutt

There are literally hundreds of women that deserve to be discussed in a chapter about female European directors and their artistic and technical contributions to world cinema. Many of these women could be (and are) subjects of entire books devoted to their individual accomplishments. Simply put, there is no way to do justice to the subject of European women directors without leaving out much and giving what is essentially a brief overview of the women, both past and present, and the films for which they are honored. The cultural context in which their films, and careers, flourish is significant. Europe in the 20th century was deeply affected by two world wars, fascism, communism and a changing political and economic setting while the 21st century has broken boundaries of sexism and technology in ways that have resulted in there now being, at the time of this writing, more women directors in Europe than in any other period in cinematic history.

Though France's Lumiere simultaneously developed the technology for motion pictures with America's Edison, culturally the two film industries have gone in completely different directions. In the later 20th and early 21st centuries, many European nations' governments have taken steps to subsidise filmmaking on a national level so that their industries can continue to grow despite stiff competition from Hollywood studios internationally. For instance, in France, the Canal+ TV channel must support film production as a condition of its broadcast license. Many nations have created tax breaks for film production, such as Ireland; in 2015 they will have raised their entertainment industry tax incentives to 32%, at least until 2020, to stimulate Irish film production.[1] Still other nations have regulations designating longer intervals between theatrical releases and DVD and digital releases to maximise investor return, encouraging them to continue funding future productions.

International organisations have also grown quite rapidly to facilitate a competitive European film industry. The European Commission's new Creative Europe MEDIA sub-program has a budget of €1.46 billion (from 2013 through 2020) to fund the development, distribution and promotion of European film. European Audiovisual Entrepreneurs (EAVE) provides professional training, project development and networking for filmmakers in the interest of expanding the cultural influence of their films not just in Europe but around the world. Grants awarded by the EURIMAGES *European Cinema Support Fund* and the European Cultural Foundation provide other sources of funding for independent and smaller production companies meaning that, unlike the United States, European cinema is not dominated only by a few major players.

In conjunction with the available funding provided for filmmakers, a new awareness of gender in media and the need for women directors has flourished worldwide largely due to The Bechdel Test,[2] online entertainment news outlets that are critical of the low ratio of women to male directors, and research like that done by Dr Martha Lauzen[3] and The Geena Davis Institute on Gender in Media. As a result, in 2013, major theatre chains in Sweden collectively began to rate films according to their gender representation. Films that are *'A-märkt'* are acknowledged to have passed the Bechdel test and represent gender equally onscreen.[4]

Sweden has also taken steps to ensure that government funding for films is distributed equally among female and male directors.[5] Charlotta Denward, the head of production funding department at the Swedish Film Institute, has said in interviews that 'The fact that there is no international statistical data on gender distribution in the film world speaks for itself.'[6] These exciting cultural and political changes allow for more innovative new women directors to make a distinct and lasting impression on cinema.

Like women filmmakers in the USA, the UK and Australia, mainstream women film directors in Europe enjoyed robust careers prior to the 1920s and 1930s. After that, they largely disappear until the advent of television and the 1960s (except for a few notable exceptions such as Germany's Leni Riefenstahl and Norway's Edith Carlmarl).

With the founding of Hollywood and its studio system in the 1910s, the sentiment towards women directors seems to have immediately shifted; by the time Alice Guy-Blaché (see previous chapter for more on Blaché) moved from France to the United States to found her own movie studio, Solax, in 1912, she found a very different attitude towards women directors awaiting her:

> 'The attitude towards women in America is very different [than in Europe]. It is a constant conflict when a woman in a French studio attempts to handle and superintend men in their work. They don't like it, and they are not averse to showing their feelings.'[7]

Guy eventually stopped making films altogether by 1920; by then only a handful of women directors remained competitive within the studio system.

As the Hollywood studio system continued to be the model for the European industry in the 1920s and 30s, the role of a film 'director' became even more defined, more prestigious, and more commonly male. Women were relegated to screenwriting, costuming, make-up or art department work rather than to positions of authority or creative control. As World War II ended, leaving France, Germany, Austria and Italy war-torn and Eastern Europe shackled with a highly regulated and non-commercial communist film industry, women were practically non-existent as directors until the advent of television opened up new avenues for distribution and caused the studio chokehold on the international industry to topple. Artists, both male and female, began to experiment with independent films and the genre of social realism. Theatres began to open up to alternative forms of cinema and women once again found their footing in a newly blooming industry and in the artistic and independent New Wave cinema of their respective European nations.

Austria

Louise Kolm-Fleck was the first Austrian woman to direct a film. She is rarely mentioned by mainstream media sources except by film historian and Professor Robert von Dassanowsky in his studies of early Austrian filmmaking.[8] As a director, Kolm-Fleck's work spanned the days of the Austrian Empire to the fall of Hitler. Her first husband, Anton Kolm, and their cameraman, Jakob Fleck, formed their partnership in 1906 and their studio, *Österreichisch-Ungarische Kino-Filmsindustrie Ges.m.b.H* (Austrian-Hungarian Cinema Film Company Ltd.), in 1910. The only existing description of Kolm-Fleck's work comes from her son, Austrian film director Walter Kolm-Veltée. He describes her as

> 'energetic and full of humour. She loved fantasy but also desired to comment on the problems of society and the relationships between men and women.'[9]

Kolm-Fleck's fantasy *Hoffmanns Erzählungen* (1911), or *Tales of Hoffman*, is based on the opera by Jacques Offenbach and the stories by Ernst Hoffman. A prolific director in every genre, Kolm-Fleck co-directed romantic thrillers, comedies, and dramas, but sadly, almost no prints of her work survive.

In the 1930s, Leontine Sagan was best known as the Austrian director of a film about a lesbian relationship, titled *Mädchen in Uniform* (1931*)*, based on the then-controversial play *Gestern und heute* (*Yesterday and Today*) by Christa Winsloe. The movie was heavily censored under the Nazi party's influence and remained censored in various forms well into the 1970s. In the 21st century it is an important early piece of queer media valued highly by the contemporary LBGT community.[10]

Valie Export is a surrealist who works in many artistic mediums. In the late 1960s and early 70s, Export became a part of the Austrian Actionist movement: live-action performance artists with a political, social, and artistic agenda. Most of Export's films explore body imagery and sexuality to the extreme, sometimes rolling in broken glass or exposing her clitoris to shocked Austrian theater-goers. Her three-part short film *Mann & Frau & Animal*, made between 1970 and 1973, is a prime example of this kind of body politics. In the first two sequences, the water spout, falling water, and glinting metallic and white surfaces are used to explore the genitalia and sexual experiences of males and females, separately. The third sequence, *Animal*, incorporates bloody hands and vociferous grunting and shrieking in an appropriately animalistic manner.[11] Export's feature films heavily rely on montage and dream sequences, challenging the observer's notions of art and of cinema.

Belgium

Belgium's Chantal Anne Akerman's career spans from the late 1960s into the 21st century. Her short, experimental films evolved over time into feature length dramas such as her 2011 Joseph Conrad adaptation *Almayer's Folly* (*La Folie Almayer*). With the ever-increasing availability of equipment and technology, independent Belgian directors such as Axelle Carolyn (*Soulmate*, 2013) are beginning to enjoy unprecedented success in film festivals worldwide.

Czech Republic/Slovakia/Czechoslovakia

Czech New Wave was the most important film movement to come out of Czechoslovakia (now The Czech Republic and Slovakia) in the 20th century, and Vera Chytilová is one of its most important filmmakers. Rather than make surreal films, Chytilová focused instead on women's interactions and relationships with some experimental storytelling. Her participation in the groundbreaking collaboration *Pearls of the Deep* (1966) and her absurdist art film *Daisies* (1966) have made her an essential player in modern defiance of Soviet Communist censorship. Like Poland's Agnieska Holland, Chytilová was prevented from making films during several years of the Soviet Occupation of her homeland. When the ban was finally lifted, she was able to pursue filmmaking with feminist undertones and female protagonists more extensively.[12]

France

France, like the United States, was a forerunner in the invention of the motion picture camera. Manufacturers like Lumiere and studios like Gaumont ushered in the very first films ever made, and the aforementioned Alice Guy-Blaché is famous for being not only the first French woman director, but the first woman director. Her 1896 short *La Fée aux Choux* (*The Cabbage Fairy*) was perhaps the first narrative film ever made.

After World War I, the French avant-garde film movement grew in France. Germaine Dulac was a leading member and radical feminist and surrealist filmmaker. Her two most-studied films, the *La Souriante Madame Beudet* (*The Smiling Madam Beaudet*, 1922) and *La Coquille et le Clergyman* (*The Seashell and the Clergyman,* 1928), toy with erotic hallucinations, impressionist visions and dream-like explorations of reality. Later surrealist filmmakers like Maya Deren were heavily influenced by the avant-garde films of Dulac. Like Dulac, Marie Epstein also co-directed many early avant-garde impressionist shorts, but her career was unfortunately cut short by the Nazi invasion of Paris and her subsequent incarceration in the 1940s.

Jacqueline Audry's career as a director developed in the 1950s in the Classical French Cinema style. Audrey described her own work as 'a defence of Woman as a human being but also in terms of her femininity.'[13] While showing a preference for period pieces, lavish sets, and conventional narratives, Audrey also tended to direct films with heroines that defied conventions. Her film *Olivia* (*The Pit of Loneliness,* 1951) depicts a lesbian relationship at an all-girls boarding school. *Olivia* has been recognised as important to early queer awareness, and for that reason has screened at several LGBT film festival retrospectives.[14]

In response to the highly decorous, traditional style of Classical French Cinema, the French New Wave was born out of a desire for raw passion and realistic storylines and characters. Agnès Varda, one of the major players in the French New Wave film movement, may be the best-known female director from France. Her best-known film, *Cleo From 5 to 7* (1962), takes place during two hours of a woman's life while she waits for the results of a cancer test. The focus of all of Varda's films was the mundane daily activities that together make up the beauty of life. The small interactions and details, the banal elements, always take the audience and the characters on a greater journey to more substantial themes like love, freedom, death, and happiness. She followed *Cleo From 5 to 7* with *Le bonheur* (1965) and later *Sans toit ni lo* (*Vagabond*, 1985), two pictures that made great use of her talents as a photographer and an explorer of gritty, everyday, non-bourgeois emotions. In the 21st century, Varda has taken primarily to documentary work. Her 2001 documentary *The Gleaners and I* is a subjective, curious look at the lives of everyday peasant women, wine-makers, and other growers in France's countryside. When asked about her distinctive, realistic style, Varda said:

> 'Cinema is not truth. It only tries to get closer to the truth. It's just very difficult to decide what is true… Sometimes even Hollywood movies contain a beautiful truth.'[15]

Nelly Kaplan is a feminist and surrealist, and some of her work has been challenged as nothing more than pornography while others say that her narrative features, such as *La Fiancée du pirate* (1969), are erotic art and undeserving of their soft-core label. Kaplan also resorts to humour and the absurd in many of her social critiques, making her films a strange mix of sexual exploration, direct documentary, and surreal absurdism.[16]

Catherine Breillat began making visually stunning films about women's self-exploration and sexuality in the 1970s, often using sexually explicit close-ups. Constantly challenging sexual taboos and mainstream sex scenes in films, she often incorporates fairy tale imagery and stories into her films, as in *Barbe bleue* (*Bluebeard*, 2009) and *La belle endormie* (*Sleeping Beauty*, 2010) to undercut their innocence and perhaps explore their darker, and more contemporarily relevant, undertones. She is fond of using what is termed 'the female gaze', a cinematic style that focuses on a woman's point of view of sexuality and beauty rather than the more common straight, white, male point of view found in most mainstream films.

Diana Kurys' *Entre Nous* (1983) is a semi-autobiographical

film dealing with anti-Semitism in the 1950s. The film was nominated for numerous Foreign Language Oscars. The film is told from the point of view of the two female protagonists – young married women in a post-WWII Europe racked by war and guilt.

Claire Denis epitomises contemporary French cinema. With her debut magical realist feature *Chocolat* in 1988, she established herself as a keen observer of marginalised protagonists and socio-political issues while maintaining a visual and artistic focus. She followed *Chocolat* closely with several other features, but it was 2001's *Trouble Every Day* that made her a new cause célèbre at that year's Cannes film festival. The story of sexualised cannibalism, vampirism, viral infection, and erotic body horror is an experiment in anxiety and personal sexual turmoil. Several of her films are set in post-colonial communities and the characters deal intimately with the aftermath of Western expansionism. Others, like her film *Bastards* (2013), are about the relationships between parents and siblings. About her female characters Denis has said, 'I don't like films that take for granted that women are victims, so we have to be redeeming them.'[17]

Other 21st century French female directors include Agnès Jaoui, who began directing comedies and dramas in 2000, and Marina de Van, whose disturbing horror and thriller films, such as *Dans ma peau* (*In My Skin*, 2002) have shaken the international independent film festival community with their raw originality and grotesque beauty. Like de Van's *In My Skin*, the 2000 thriller *Baise-Moi* by Coralie Trinh Thi and Virginie Despentes confronts female sexuality head on with violence, bodily harm, and explicit scenes. French directors Julie Delpy, Agnès Merlet, Charlotte Silvera, and Mia Hansen-Love are also actively making films in the 21st century. Hanson-Love is often asked her opinion on how films are discussed in terms of the gender of the director and the genders of the characters in the film. She replied:

> 'I think too many films and film critics are determined by this issue – if it's a film by a man or a woman and if it's a gay film or straight film. I don't like this idea. I think we can have a wider perspective on humanity.'[18]

CELLULOID CEILING

Germany

During the silent film era, Marie Louise Droop was mc
known as a prolific screenwriter in the silent era, penning doz
of romantic thrillers and adventure tales. *Die Teufelsanbeter*
Devil Worshippers) from 1920 was Droop's directorial debut.
Arabian adventure/thriller also featured a then-unknown
Lugosi. That same year Droop co-directed a film version of
Fest der schwarzen Tulpe (*The Festival of the Black Tulip*) by Alexai
Dumas. This shortest Dumas novel is also a brutally violent I
story and detective thriller set in 1672. Because the lead charac
spends much of his time in prison in this faithful adaptat
the film lacked action. The resulting deficient box office d
may have been the cause of Droop's production compa
bankruptcy later that year.[19]

Charlotte Reiniger was a German silhouette artist and anim
in the first half of the 20th Century. Blessed from an early
with a strange affinity for cutting shadow puppet silhou
Reiniger parlayed her imagination and talent into a filmma
career and established the sub-genre of silhouette animated film.
Her *The Adventures of Prince Achmed* (1926) was the first feature-
length animated film ever made (not Disney's *Snow White*, as
many believe). In 1920s Weimar Germany, expressionism was
the artistic choice of the intellectual, and in Paris the avant-garde
movement was in full swing. Reiniger's chosen medium presented
a surrealist quality that appealed to the modern art crowd of
continental Europe: Fritz Lang, Bertolt Brecht and Jean Renoir
were amongst the European avant-garde elite that extolled *The
Adventures of Prince Achmed* as cinematic genius. Reminiscing about
the making of *The Adventures of Prince Achmed* in her much later
years, Reiniger said:

> 'Those were the days, with each new film we could make
> new discoveries…The whole field was virgin soil and we
> had all the joys of explorers in an unknown country.'[20]

Almost everyone in the modern world is at least somewhat
familiar with Leni Riefenstahl, the director of the documentary
Triumph of the Will. Having commissioned the documentary

from Riefenstahl in 1934, the Nazi party acknowledged that film was essential to the Nazi movement. Having pushed out artists like Reiniger, who did not fit in with their fascist policies, they soon replaced independent artists with state-sanctioned ones.[21] *Triumph of the Will* won many awards in European Film Festivals and exhibitions, while Riefenstahl's two-part documentary on the Olympic Games, *Olympia*, was declared the world's best film in 1938.[22] Not too surprisingly, when Germany lost World War II, Riefenstahl's cinematic achievements came to be seen as products of fascist propaganda. Her directing career never quite recovered. She did attempt to direct again with 1954's drama *Tiefland*, and again fifty years later in 2003 with the documentary *Underwater Impressions*, yet she remained infamous for her association with the Nazis through to her death in 2003. Riefenstahl's artistic talents and her ability to succeed in a male-dominated industry made especially difficult for women under the scrutiny of fascism is admirable, and recognised today as so by major film scholars and feminists alike.[23]

Helke Sander began directing during the German New Wave film movement of the 1970s. Sander's film career was tied closely to the German feminist movement, as she founded the political *Aktionsrat zur Befreiung der Frau* (Women's Liberation Action Council) in 1968 as well as *Frauen und Film* (Women and Film), the first European feminist film publication. Many of her films, especially *Redupers* (*Die allseitig reduzierte Persönlichkeit – Redupers*, 1977) and *The Subjective Factor* (1981) deal with the beginning of the New Women's Movement, while *Der Beginn aller Schrecken ist die Liebe* (*Love is the Beginning of all Terrors, 1984*) is considered feminist cinema. Most of her films explore complex female characters, the women's movement, and the political aftermath of the movement particularly from a woman's perspective.[24] Sander was always an ardent defender of artistic freedom and the power that art had over politics. In 1977, she addressed an arts festival in Gratz, Austria with the following statements:

> '…we should consider that until very recently femininity was always defined by others, by men. Only now have women begun to comprehend themselves as social

subjects and to throw off alien interpretations of their nature and being. The organised expression of these efforts is the women's movement. From all sides and with dissimilar results and battles, these organisations are feeling out the question of what women want, more than the question of what women are.'[25]

Sander's directing crosses genres while keeping true to her feminist ideologies and artistic explorations of gender politics and government. *Gluttony Futtern!* (1986) is a cartoonish fable of Adam and Eve in the Garden of Eden as a metaphor for contemporary male/female relationships. *The Germans and Their Men* (1989) is a pseudo-documentary look at masculinity, fascism, sexuality, and femininity in modern German society.

Helma Sanders-Brahms,[26] like Sander, is recognised as an early German New Wave director. Her film *Germany, Pale Mother* (1979) explored her generation's Nazi heritage with valiant and vicious eyes. In fact, it was Sanders-Brahms who famously defended Leni Riefenstahl's *Triumph of the Will*, recognising it as important, if disturbing, as a piece of cinema and German history. 'How is it possible,' she asked, 'that after fifty years the fear of dealing with this film is still so great that just the refusal to view it is considered a correct attitude for German intellectuals?' Sanders-Brahms also argued that Riefenstahl's 1953 drama film *Tiefland* was a rejection of Hitler, Nazism, and the shame of being used as a propaganda machine.[27] Sanders-Brahms continued her unabashed intellectual expression of pain, feminism, and redemption in her narrative dramas and documentaries throughout the 1980s and 90s.

Margarethe von Trotta is another extremely prominent German New Wave filmmaker. Like Sander and Sanders-Brahms, she began making films in the 1970s and tackles political and dramatic stories about women. When the New Wave movement began, Germany was in a time of political upheaval and at the height of the Baader-Meinhof[28] years when government control, fascism, and feminism were hot topics for disgruntled youths and passionate artists dealing with the legacy of the Holocaust.

The Lost Honor of Katharina Blum, which she made with Volker Schlöndorff in 1975, is New Wave social realism at its best. A critique of homegrown terrorism and the backlash against the feminist movement, the film attempts to deconstruct a fragile democracy in the eyes of a new generation of German citizens.[29] Von Trotta, perhaps the most influential female director in Europe in the 1970s and 80s, went on to direct several more decidedly feminist and political movies: *The Second Awakening of Christa Klages* (1977), *Sisters, or the Balance of Happiness* (1979), *The German Sisters* (1981) and *Rosa Luxemburg* (1985).

Von Trotta's more recent films *Vision* (2009), about medieval nun Hildegard von Bingen and her clash with the patriarchal church of her day, and *Hannah Arendt* (2012), the story of the journalist and political theorist who covered the trials of Adolph Eichmann in post WWII Germany, are two of her latest docu-dramas that seek to humanise and deconstruct strong female characters on-screen. Von Trotta is outspoken about the feminist ideals inherent in her filmmaking:

> 'I always fought off that question [do women direct differently from men], as well as the question: Why do you only direct films about women? I simply said: If you ask Wim Wenders why he only directs films about men – he has changed in the meantime however – then you can ask me that.'[30]

Ula Stöckl is yet another New German Cinema director. In 1963, she directed *The Cat has nine Lives*, considered the 'feminist manifesto' of the German New Wave movement by many film scholars.[31] Of the over twenty films that Stöckl has directed, *The Sleep of Reason* (1983) is the most famous, having won the German Critics' Prize in 1984. Ulrike Ottinger has enjoyed a range of directorial styles: documentary, drama and even horror. She is known for eschewing traditional narratives for bizarre and surrealist ones instead, often using an all-female cast. Her Berline Trilogy, *Ticket of No Return* (1979), *Freak Orlando* (1981) and *The Image of Dorian Gray in the Yellow Press* (1984), are her most famous films internationally.

In the late 1980s, Monika Treut ushered in a transgressive, feminist style of filmmaking consistent with the budding Riot

Grrrl[32] feminist and gay rights movements in the United States. Interested in the writings of the Marquis de Sade, she made the 1985 cult classic *Seduction: The Cruel Woman* as a retelling of the 1870 novel *Venus in Furs*. Complicated S&M fantasies, lesbians, and stunning visual displays caused contemporary reviewers to describe it as alternately 'compelling in its insights as well as in its originality' and 'entirely superfluous and annoying.'[33]

Her films *Virgin Machine* (1988), which explores one woman's homosexual isolation and coming of age, and *Father is Coming* (1991), both show a fascination with the outspoken gay rights movement in the United States at the time. With *Female Misbehavior* (1992), she began a series of documentary character explorations. *Female Misbehavior* follows four women who defy contemporary sexuality and femininity. Treut has an ongoing fascination with pornography and deviant sexuality and how they both relate to gender identity.[34] In the 21st Century, Treut has been enamored of Taiwan and continues to use it as a backdrop for her new millennium documentaries and her one 21st century narrative film, *Ghosted* (2009).

In 1997, Katja von Garnier's *Bandits* was a film festival sensation. The movie's protagonists are four women in a German prison who form a band as part of their rehabilitation program. They escape together and go on the run performing shows, but go down in a blaze of glory when the police finally catch up to them. Likened by critics unto a German *Thelma and Louise*, the dark comedy/road movie/rock'n'roll feminist fantasy *Bandits* remains one of the major independent international hits of the 90s.[35] Because it starred women, and was directed by a woman, it was labelled by German and international film press as 'a woman's film' to which the director responded:

> 'If a film is about a bunch of men, no one asks if it's a men's movie. A film is just a film. Men and women differ in that women are allowed to show their emotional wounds but not their anger, whereas men show anger but conceal their emotional pain. All this does is make it difficult for everyone.'[36]

The newest generation of German directors, such as Lexi Alexander (*Green Street Hooligans*, 2005), Katrin Gebbe *Tore Tanzt* (*Nothing Bad Can Happen*, 2013), and Frauke Finsterwalder (*Finsterworld*, 2013) continue to enjoy promising careers both in Germany and in the United States in various genres.

Greece

Like most of Eastern Europe, Greece's filmmakers have been heavily influenced by their nation's politics. Greek director Lila Kourkoulakou's documentary film, *The Island of Silence* (1958), was a dramatisation of the lives of lepers on the island of Spinalogka. Made during a time of conservatism and post-World War II anxiety, it was an attempt to humanise a much-maligned minority in Greece by showing the stark reality of their day-to-day existence.

In 1967, there was a military coup that plunged Greece into a right-wing dictatorship until 1974. The filmmakers that emerged from this repressive political atmosphere turned towards art and created reactionary New Wave Greek Cinema.

Tonia Marketaki's 1973 feature, *Violent John*, is about a serial killer stalking young Greek women. Based on the real-life story of the 1963 murder of Maria Bavea, it is a grim critique of society and politics and the violence they inspire and condone.

Maria Komninos' political documentary *Kavala-November '74* (1974) was made in direct reaction to the fall of Greece's dictatorship. Focusing on the Greek democratic government elections of 1974, Komninos explores worker's rights, candidates' various policies, and labor unions among a newly freed population.

Frieda Liappa was a politically radical film maker of the Greek New Wave. A militant anti-fascist, she spent some time in jail before studying film in London. Her features *Mia zoi se thymamai na feygeis* (*Love Wanders in The Night*, 1981), *Itan enas isyhos thanatos* (*A Quiet Death*, 1986) and *Ta hronia tis megalis zestis* (*The Years of the Big Heat*, 1992) reflect her political and social beliefs.

Antoinetta Angelidi, unlike her contemporaries, concentrated on surreal and experimental films. In *Idées Fixes /Dies Irae* (*Variations on the same subject*, 1977), for example, Angelidi sought to prove that gender is a social construct through the lens of contemporary art by employing time lapse techniques, and plenty of nudity.

Contemporary narrative directors in Greece include Katerina Evangelakou (*False Alarm,* 2006), Kleoni Flessa (*Let's go for an ouzo,* 2002), Stella Theodoraki (*Close…so close,* 2002), Athena Rachel Tsangari (*Ducharon,* 2014) and Marsa Makris (*Dry cleaning,* 2005).

Hungary

Like Chytilová, Hungarian Marta Meszaros (*The Girl,* 1968) began directing in the mid-20th century and challenged traditional and communist ideals of women, gender, relationships, and the notion of feminism. Judith Elit's drama *Mária-nap* (*Maria's Day,* 1984) was a success at the Cannes Film Festival, and more recently, Ágnes Kocsis (*Fresh Air,* 2006) has directed films about female relationships in her native Hungarian.[37]

Italy

Italy's first female director was the prolific Elvira Notari. Forming her own company, Dora Films, allowed her to make over sixty films, both narratives and documentaries. Notari often made films about women and used a female gaze in her work, but her career was put to an end by fascist Italian policies in the 1930s.[38]

In the 1970s, Annabella Miscuglio, a feminist and experimental filmmaker, founded the first Italian Women's Film Festival in 1976: The Kinomata. Misculglio, along with directors Annabella Medley, Rony Daopulos, Martiis De Paola, Anna Carini, and Maria Grazia Belmonti, founded the first Italian women's filmmaker collective, known as 'Collective Romano.' Focusing on TV movies and films with topics as political and social as rape and women's politics, Miscuglio enjoyed a successful career as a director until her death in Rome in 2003.[39]

Lina Wertmüller directed films in the 1960s, after she was assistant to Federico Fellini, but she is perhaps best-known as the first woman to be nominated for a Best Director Oscar (one of only four at the time of this writing) in 1975 with the film *Pasqualino Sette Bellezze* (*Seven Beauties*). Though she didn't win, this was a milestone in cinematic history that coincided with the women's rights movement and the emergence of women as mainstream theatrical directors for the first time since the 1920s. *Seven Beauties* recounts the imprisonment of a decided anti-hero by a fascist government during WWII. Extremely political, but graceful and even funny at times, *Seven Beauties* is Wertmüller's career pinnacle. She has directed numerous films for theatres and television since *Seven Beauties*, but none have captured international attention in quite the same way.

Like Wertmüller, Liliana Cavani was active in the 1970s and became well-known internationally for one: 1974's *Il portiere di notte* (*The Night Porter*). Like Wertmüller's *Seven Beauties*, *The Night Porter* was about imprisonment in a concentration camp and used sensationalism, violence and sexuality to explore the aftermath of the devastating Second World War on the collective Italian psyche. To criticism of the psychological and physical violence in *The Night Porter*, Cavani said:

> 'I am not interested in making people cry, but in making them reflect… Cinema can only be political if it leaves the spectator uneasy.'[40]

Both Wertmüller and Cavani have been active as directors in the 21st Century along with younger independent filmmakers such as Asia Argento (*The Scarlet Diva,* 2000).

Ireland

Tax incentives, film subsidies and grant programs have helped bring films, both shorts and features, to Ireland and the U.K.[41] Pat Murphy is perhaps the first Irish woman director to make full use of this encouragement: her 1981 feature *Maeve* was funded by the British Film Institute. A story of one woman's experience in Ireland's politically volatile climate, *Maeve* was dubbed Ireland's first feminist film by critics.[42] Her 2000 film, *Nora,* was a study of Nora Barnacle, the companion of legendary Irish author James Joyce, and received mixed reviews as a complex piece based on a troubled, but brilliant, female protagonist. Of her female-centric features, Murphy said:

> 'I lived in New York in the late 70s and early 80s, so I was inspired by the women I knew then. Women like Joan

Jonas[43] and JoAnne Akalaitis[44], for example. Also I drew support from all the women I knew who were making independent films at that point.'[45]

Kirsten Sheridan has emerged in the first decade of the 21st century as an important independent Irish film director with varied features such as her debut low-budget *Disco Pigs* (2001), *August Rush* (2007) and *Dollhouse* (2012). When discussing her future film subjects, she says she leans towards the social and political. 'That is where the amazing stories are,' she says, 'in the social sphere.'[46]

Ireland is teeming with new commercial and independent women directors. Maeve Murphy (*Beyond the Fire*, 2009), Juanita Wilson (*As If I Am Not There*, 2011), Farah Abushwesha (*Chicken Soup*, 2006) and Rebecca Daly (*The Other Side of Sleep,* 2011) all have been quite successful in establishing themselves internationally, while directors such as Aisling Walsh (*Wallander*) and Dearbhla Walsh (*The Tudors*) have turned to Irish and UK television series and films.

The Netherlands

Adriënne Solser and Caroline van Dommelen both directed Dutch silent films in the 1920s. Solser, like many early women directors, formed her own production and distribution company, the Hollando-Belgica Film Mij., and created a series of films around a female protagonist named 'Bet', a Dutch folk hero often used in vaudevillian acts or stage shows.[47] Van Dommelen, like Solser, was an actress that also directed several silent films including an adaptation of an Oscar Wilde play (*De bannelingen*, 1911). Neither Solser or van Dommelen directed after the silent era.

In the 21st century, however, there are several renowned women directors from The Netherlands. Marleen Gorris came to international attention when she won an Oscar for Best Foreign Film for *Antonia's Line* in 1995. Later, her adaptation of Virginia Woolf's *Mrs. Dalloway* (1997) also won critical acclaim with major audiences worldwide. At the time of this writing she is developing a film to be titled *Heaven and Earth*, the story of James Miranda Barry, a woman who masqueraded as a man in order to practice medicine in 1814.

Danish/Dutch director Susanne Bier became famous for her 2004 drama *Brothers* (*Brødre*), and her 2006 film *After the Wedding* was nominated for an Academy Award for Best Foreign Language Film. She followed up this international acclaim with 2007's *Things We Lost in the Fire* and 2010's *In a Better World*, making Bier one of the pre-eminent women directors of the early 21st century. Bier commented on the state of women directors in 2011 with the following:

> 'I think it is kind of depressing how few female filmmakers there are. I think it is in general depressing how few women there are in … important positions in society.'[48]

Poland

Ostatni etap (*The Last Stage*, 1947) by Wanda Jakubowska, is set in a concentration camp during the Nazi occupation of Poland. This story of women resisting fascist oppression in Auchwitz-Birkenau during World War II would set the stage for later Polish women directors. By the 1950s, when Maria Kaniewska directed *Niedaleko Warszawy* (*Not Far From Warsaw*, 1954), the influence of the communist regime in place was evident. The film's story of factory workers amounts to little more than communist propaganda, but it is a valuable example of Polish post-war social realism.

Though she had been making films for over 20 years when it was released, Agnieszka Holland's 1991 drama *Europa Europa* made her one of the most prominent European directors of her generation. Having been essentially exiled from Poland from 1981 through 1988 when martial law was enacted in that nation to quell social uprisings, Holland's extremely political and poetic films speak to her native country's troubled past and hopeful future. *Europa Europa*, like her 2011 drama *In Darkness*, is set in Nazi-occupied Poland and tells the stories of the everyday, yet heroic, people that endured and survived. In 1991, *Europa Europa* was nominated for Best Foreign Language Film at the Academy Awards and garnered numerous other awards at international film festivals and events. Holland describes making films about

Poland's troubled past:

> 'In some ways, most of the stories of survivors have this incredible, biblical dimension, and this dramatic and emotional quality and these adventurous qualities. So it didn't surprise me that this is a true story. I kind of expected that true stories are the most incredible. But yes, the fact that it really happened, it gives a special kind of responsibility to the filmmaker, because you have to be faithful to the spirit of those people in the story. You cannot just play with them, so you feel less free in some ways.'[49]

Holland's sister, Magdalena Łazarkiewicz, is also an active film director in Poland. Independent Polish directors such as Dorota Kędzierzawska (*Time to Die* aka *Pora Umierać*, 2007), Urszula Antoniak (*Code Blue*, 2011), Agnieszka Wojtowicz-*Vosloo* (*After. Life*, 2009) and Małgorzata Szumowska (*In the Name Of*, 2013) have more recently found international success at film festivals and theatres, while Mira Hammermesh (*Maids and Madams*, 1986) is a successful documentarian and TV director.

Portugal

In Portugal in the 1970s, there developed a style of filmmaking referred to by critics as 'The School of Reis' that revolved primarily around the films of Portuguese director António Reis. With director Margarida Cordeiro, his wife, they began a new tradition of teaching filmmakers completely through oral training, conveying their concepts at classes at the Portuguese National Filmschool up until the early 1990s. Manuela Viegas is considered a follower of The School of Reis and her feature film *Gloria* (1999) is considered a jewel of modern Portuguese cinema. Set in a small town in rural Portugal, *Gloria* is named for its protagonist; a young girl who comes of age at a time of change and modernisation, where old ways give way to new and new relationships are formed.

Romania

In Romania, Ruxandra Zenide represents the Romanian New

Wave film movement with *Ryna* (2005). This more recent movement developed slowly when the Romanian film industry was allowed to change and blossom after Romanian dictator Nicolae Ceausescu was deposed in the 1980s.[50]

Scandinavia

Sweden's Mai Zetterling's first film as director was 1964's *Älskande par* (*Loving Couples*) which was considered obscene and banned from screening at the Cannes Film Festival. Her second feature narrative film, *Night Games* (1966), was banned from the Venice Festival. To say the least, her films made quite a stir with themes of repressed abuse, straightforward childbirth, nudity and sex. Though she was an actress in the 1940s and 50s before embarking on a career as first a documentary, then narrative director, she was an anomaly as a woman in a predominantly male role. Zetterling recalls being somewhat mystified by the way critics and the film industry reacted to a woman director in her autobiography:

> 'When the reviews of my first full-length feature movie came out, I was horrified to read that "Mai Zetterling directs like a man." What did that mean?'[51]

In 1968, she decided to explore what it meant to be a woman in modern Swedish society with the film *Flickorna (The Girls)*. A clever feminist retelling of Aristophanes' play *Lysistrasta*, *The Girls* focuses on three main female characters involved in a theatre production while dealing with the day-to-day problems presented by their patriarchal social and political system.

Many beneficiaries of modern Swedish programs, such as those run by the Swedish Film Institute and Doris Film network to ensure equal funding goes to male and female directors, include talented women just emerging into a more equitable industry. Still, there are problems that even Sweden's even-handed film industry faces. Director Hanna Andersson (*Erika & Sally*, 2012) explains:

> 'In Sweden, two worlds are completely closed off to women – commercials and crime thrillers. Both are prestigious genres with big budgets. They offer a good wage and give you a chance to try your hand at major

CELLULOID CEILING

projects – you go through a lot of money when you make commercials.'[52]

Director Christina Olofson (*The Steel-Iron-Grey Sky*, 2013) identifies Sweden's remaining issues with women directors as financial:

> 'Financiers are reluctant to entrust a woman with a really big budget regardless of whether it's a woman or a man who makes the decision. Also, men more often than women make their first feature without any financial support whatsoever, on a minimal budget. This is an attitude that few women share.'[53]

Pernilla August (*Svinalängorna*, (*Beyond*, 2010)), Maria Blom (*Masjävlar*, (*Dalecarlians*, 2004)), Helena Bergström (*Se upp för dårarn*, (*Mind the Gap*, 2007)), Ella Elisabet Lemhagen (*Kronjuvelerna*, 2011*)*, and Tova Magnusson (*Fyra år till* (*Four More Years*, 2010)) are just a few examples of directors that have taken advantage of the opportunities presented to them by Sweden's uniquely feminist film industry.

The first film noir directed by a woman was *Døden er et kjærtegn* (*Death is a Caress*), a 1949 Norwegian film that marked the debut feature of Edith Carlmar. It depicted a young newly-wed couple and their disturbing relationship. Film scholars comment on the striking cinematic similarities between *Death is a Caress* and later American noir such as *The Postman Always Rings Twice*. *Death is a Caress* is so widely influential that it is recognised as a precursor to modern Norwegian crime thrillers such as *The Girl with the Dragon Tattoo* trilogy.[54]

Norwegian director Anja Breien, not well-known outside of her native nation, makes political and feminist films such as her 1971 feature *Rape*, a critique of Norway's judicial system and rape politics. In her second film, *Wives* (1975), her characters are allowed to leave behind their traditional housewifely duties and enjoy a day of freedom away from the home and family. Her 1979 film *Next of Kin* inspired legendary director Ingmar Bergman to personally tell Breien that he thought it should have won at that year's Cannes Film Festival.[55]

Like her contemporary Breien, Laila Mikkelsen began her career by directing socially-conscious films in the 1970s. She is most famous for her science-fiction film *Us* (*Oss*, 1976) and her follow up, *Liten Ida* (*Growing Up*, 1981). The new generation of film directors in Norway is not as stringently male-dominated as it had been in Carlmar's generation and many filmmakers that emerged in the 1970s continue to make challenging and provocative feminist films. For instance, Vibeke Løkkeberg, whose controversial short film *Abort* (1971) shocked the then-anti-abortion Norwegian legislature, later made the documentary *Tears of Gaza* (2012). Løkkeberg explained her motivations in a recent interview:

> 'Since I am a woman in film and a writer, I want to use those forms to search for issues that society wants to hide as not important. That is any artist's mission. I only live once and so I want to tell what affects me and what is an injustice. I want to be on the side of the victims, not the powerful.'[56]

Spain

Spain's Anna Mariscal is credited with creating women's cinema in her country. One of only two female directors in Spain during the 1950s, Mariscal was well-respected and her films were known for their recognisable style. Working in both film and television, she managed to direct over fifty films throughout her career. Her first feature film, *Segundo López, Aventurero Urbano* (*Segundo López, Urban Adventurer,* 1952) was a Spanish neo-realist drama. Unfortunately, it was also a box office failure. Nevertheless, Mariscal enjoyed a long career directing despite her early setbacks.[57]

Josefina Molina's first film was *Vera, un cuento cruel* (*Vera, a cruel story,* 1973), a gothic horror tale set in the 19th century. She soon explored other styles and genres of filmmaking including cinema verité, a documentary-like technique, with *Función de Noche* (*Night Function*, 1980), and stories about women with the Spanish TV adaptations of *Hedda Gabler* (1975) and *Anna Christie* (1976). Molina was working in television up until the late 1990s.

CELLULOID CEILING

Pilar Miro Romero, who passed away in 1997, was not only a director but also one of the first government officials in Spain to introduce state funding for film production. She was Culture Ministry director of cinema from 1982 to 1985, and created a government film industry subsidy program for young filmmakers in need.[58] As a director, she had a wide range; her film *Beltenebros* (1992) was about Spanish fascism under Franco, while her last film, *El Perro del Hortelano* (1996), was a 17th century period comedy.

Isabel Coixet is currently the best-known active Spanish female director. Her first film, *Demasiado viejo para morir joven (Too Old to Die Young*, 1989) was not a critical success despite winning numerous awards in film festivals. In fact, between its premiere in 1988 and 1996, she didn't direct at all. Leaning towards intimate dramas and relationships, her films explore the aftermath of wartime rape (*The Secret Life of Words*, 2005) and *Escuchando al juez Garzón* (*Listening to the Judge*, 2011) with a realism that blurs the lines between drama and documentary that is now critically acclaimed as mature and inventive.[59]

Spain's government continues to encourage new women directors; in 2013, Gracia Querejeta's film *15 Años y Un Día (15 Years and One Day)* was nominated for the Best Foreign Language Feature at the Academy Awards. This character-driven film about complex relationships between parents and their children has been compared to Pedro Almodvar's film style, and is described as 'a witty and acidic … film about male role models with a heavily feminine point of view.'[60] Her previous film *Siete mesas de billar francés (Seven Billiard Tables,* 2007), won numerous accolades in Spain at the Goya Awards, launching her into a professional career. Icíar Bollaín's 2011 *Tambien la lluvia (Even the Rain)* was the Spanish entry in the Best Foreign Language Film category at the Academy Awards. María Lidón's independent science fiction film *Náufragos (Stranded*, 2001) continues to be a testament to independent genre films with a decidedly chilling un-Hollywood stance on the fantastic.

The 21st century is an exciting, yet challenging time for women directors in all European nations. Not only are their opportunities as women expanding because of an unprecedented social and gender equality, but the field of filmmaking has evolved with new forms of distribution and production as well as audiences that transcend physical borders. The women directors of early 20th century silent reels would be astounded by the political and artistic progress that not only women, but the art of cinema itself, have made in the last 100 years. However, while Sweden's deliberate efforts to include women directors in funding endeavours and the occasional Oscar nomination for Best Foreign Language Film are nice, it is disturbing that over a century after the invention of the motion picture camera, women still need to fight to be given fair artistic and monetary recognition for their cinematic efforts as directors. At the time of this writing, the media has never covered the lack of women directors in film and television as extensively as it does now. Also at the time of this writing, women directors have never been so outspoken about what they feel is open gender discrimination. In a recent news article, German director Lexi Alexander states,

> 'Only this month, I received two meeting requests from companies whose mandate in 2014 is to hire more women, so the tide may be shifting. And I do appreciate their effort so very much… I loathe the idea of being hired because of my gender and I shudder at the thought that one day I show up on set and half of the crew thinks, "Here comes the quota hire."'[61]

In a film industry devoid of gender discrimination, such efforts as those taken by Sweden, and such statements as those made by women such as Lexi Alexander, will no longer be necessary.

Author biography

Heidi Honeycutt is a film journalist based in Los Angeles. Primarily interested in women directors and genre films, her work has appeared in *Fangoria Magazine, Famous Monsters of Filmland Magazine, The Ms. Magazine Blog, Bitch Magazine, and Bust Magazine*. She programs horror, fantasy, science fiction, and action films directed by women for various venues including the American Cinematheque.

Contact: heidi@planetetheria.com

References

1. Barraclough, L. (October 15th 2013). Ireland ups tax incentive to 32% beginning 2015. (http://variety.com/2013/film/international/ireland-ups-tax-incentive-to-32-from-2015-1200727802/)

2. To pass the Bechdel Test, named after American cartoonist Alison Bechdel, a film has to have at least two women in it who talk to each other about something other than a man.

3. Dr Lauzen is a professor at San Diego State University in California, USA. Her highly relevant research can be read at http://womenintvfilm.sdsu.edu

4. Dewey, C. 'Sweden's plan to bring gender equality to the movies'. (http://www.washingtonpost.com/blogs/worldviews/wp/2013/11/06/swedens-plan-to-bring-gender-equality-to-the-movies/ accessed November 6th 2013).

5. http://www.sfi.se/en-GB/Press/Press-archive/The-Swedish-Film-Institute-celebrates-50-years-with-an-international-equality-initiative/ (accessed May 20th 2013).

6. http://www.swedenabroad.com/en-GB/Embassies/Ottawa/Current-affairs/News/Focus-on-Film---Swedish-women-behind-the-camera-sys/ (accessed April 16th 2013).

7. Blaché, G. (1996). '*The memoirs of Alice Guy-Blaché*' (p. 131), Scarecrow Press.

8. von Dassanowsky, R. (October 2004). Luise Kolm-Fleck. (http://sensesofcinema.com/2004/great-directors/kolm_fleck/)

9. von Dassanowsky, R. (October 2004).

10. Schlüpmann, H., and Gramman, K. (January 12th 1998). Mädchen in uniform (1931). (http://tlweb.latrobe.edu.au/humanities/screeningthepast/reruns/thiele.html)

11. Grossman, A. (2012). 'Finger envy: A glimpse into the short films of valie export.' *Bright Lights Film Journal*, 2012 (76), (http://brightlightsfilm.com/76/76valie_grossman.php)

12. McEaney, K. (2013). 'For country, for women: Women directors in the Czech Republic, Hungary, Poland and Romania. Cinesthesia, 2(1), (http://scholarworks.gvsu.edu/cgi/viewcontent.cgi?article=1012&context=cine)

13. (1994). A. Kuhn and S. Radstone (eds.), *The Women's Companion to International Film* (p. 26).

14. [Web log message] (http://memoriesofthefuture.wordpress.com/2011/06/27/boarding-school-erotics-olivia-and-madchen-in-

uniform/ June 27th 2011)

15. Kramer, R. (August 6th 2009). 'Cinema is not truth'. *Planet Interview*. (http://www.planet-interview.de/interviews/agnes-varda/35020/)

16. Felando, C. (1999). Denis, Claire. *St. James Women Filmmakers Encyclopedia* (p. 114).

17. Adams, S. (October 24th 2013). Claire Denis on bastards and tough women. *The Dissolve*, (http://thedissolve.com/features/interview/235-claire-denis-on-bastards-and-tough-women/)

18. Howell, P. (August 16th 2012). Mia Hansen-Love, a firmly ambiguous filmmaker. *The Star*, (http://www.thestar.com/entertainment/movies/2012/08/16/mia_hansenlove_a_firmly_ambiguous_filmmaker_howell.html)

19. McDonald, J. R. *Das Fest Der Schwarzen Tulpe*, *Carldevogt.com*. (http://carldevogt.org/SchwarzenTulpe.html)

20. Kizirian, S. (2008). *The Adventures of Prince Achmed*, 1926, The San Francisco Silent Film Festival. (https://web.archive.org/web/20130526042308/http://www.silentfilm.org/pages/detail/633)

21. Rentschler, E. (1996). *The ministry of illusion: Nazi cinema and its afterlife*. Harvard University Press.

22. Leni Riefenstahl. (n.d.) (http://www.leni-riefenstahl.de/eng/bio.html)

23. von Dassanowsky, R. (1996). 'Wherever you may run, you cannot escape him': Leni Riefenstahl's self-reflection and romantic transcendence of Nazism in Tiefland. Camera Obscura, 35 (http://web.archive.org/web/20090106231139/http://www.germanhollywood.com/tiefland.html)

24. Helke Sander. (n.d.) http://www.wmm.com/filmcatalog/makers/fm325.shtml

25. Sander, H. (1978). '*Feminism and film. frauen und film*, 15, (http://www.ejumpcut.org/archive/onlinessays/JC27folder/SanderonFemsmFilm.html)

26. Not related to Helke Sander.

27. von Dassanowsky, R. (1996).

28. A left-wing militant German terrorist group in the 1970s led by Andreas Baader and Ulrike Meinhof.

29. Criterion collection: The lost honor of Katharina Blum. (n.d.). Retrieved from http://www.criterion.com/films/726-the-lost-honor-of-katharina-blum & diCaprio, L. (1984) & Marianne and

juliane / the german sisters baader-meinhof fictionalised. *Jumpcut*, 29, 56–59. (http://www.ejumpcut.org/archive/onlinessays/JC29folder/GermanSisters.html)

30. Kramer, R. (September 29th 2009). Margarethe von Trotta. *Planet Interview*. (http://www.planet-interview.de/interviews/margarethe-von-trotta/35032/

31. From Stöckl's personal bio on her website http://www.ula-stoeckl.com/

32. An underground feminist movement of the 1990s that focused on punk rock, art, and multi-media expressions of female power.

33. 'Seduction: The cruel woman.' (n.d.). (http://www.hyenafilms.com/en/films/seduction-the-cruel-woman/)

34. Germunden, G. (1997). 'How American is it? The United States as queer utopia in the cinema of Monika Treut.' In J. Petropoulos, S. Denham and I. Kacandes (eds.), *A User's Guide to German Cultural Studies* (pp. 333–351). University of Michigan Press.

35. Van Gelder, L. (September 24th 1999). 'Bandits': The saga of a criminal band of runaway musicians. *The New York Times*. (http://www.nytimes.com/library/film/092499bandits-film-review.html)

36. Adams, T. (August, 1998). The inside outlaw. US-Interview-Magazine.(http://katja-von-garnier.de/deutsch/interview_interview_199808.htm)

37. McEaney, K. (2013).

38. Bruno, G. (1993). *Streetwalking on a ruined map: Cultural theory and the city films of elvira notari*. Princeton University Press.

39. Annabella Miscuglio. *Cinema Donna*. (http://www.cinemadonna.com/scheda-personaggio.asp?pkey=2688)

40. Marrone, G. (2000). *The gaze and the labyrinth: The cinema of liliana cavani*. (p. 12). Princeton University Press.

41. Irish film board funding programmes. (n.d.). (http://www.irishfilmboard.ie/funding_programmes/)

42. Brady, T. (July 20th 2012). Look back with candour. *Irish Times*. (http://www.irishtimes.com/culture/film/look-back-with-candour-1.540295)

43. Joan Jonas is a video and performance artist.

44. JoAnne Akalaitis is a theatre director and a writer.

45. Murphy, P. (n.d.). Interview by Gabrielle Kelly, email, November 23, 2013.

46. Macnab, G. (November 16th 2007). 'Interview: Kirsten sheridan

follows in her father's footsteps.' *The Independent.* (http://www.independent.co.uk/arts-entertainment/films/features/interview-kirsten-sheridan-follows-in-her-fathers-footsteps-400498.html)

47. Förster, A. (2013). Adriënne Solser In *Women Film Pioneers Project.* (https://wfpp.cdrs.columbia.edu/pioneer/ccp-adrienne-solser/)

48. Curtis, L. (February 27th 2011). 'An interview with Oscar nominee Susanne Bier; she talks Oscar.' *Tonight at the Movies.* (http://tonightatthemovies.com/indexhold/?p=7850)

49. Fish, A. (January 16th 2012). 'Director Agnieszka Holland: Escaping death, Surviving in darkness.' *Iconic Interview.* (http://www.iconicinterview.com/2012/01/16/agnieszka-holland-escaping-death-surviving-in-darkness/)

50. McEaney, K. (2013).

51. Zetterling, M. (1986). *All those tomorrows.* (1st ed., p. 3). Grove Press.

52. http://www.swedenabroad.com/en-GB/Embassies/Ottawa/Current-affairs/News/Focus-on-Film---Swedish-women-behind-the-camera-sys/ accesssed April 16th 2013.

53. http://www.swedenabroad.com/en-GB/Embassies/Ottawa/Current-affairs/News/Focus-on-Film-Swedish-women-behind-the-camera-sys/ accesssed April 16th 2013.

54. Engelstad, A. (n.d.). Doing genre history – the case of the norwegian film noir. (http://english.unak.is/static/files/Nordmedia2011/Engelstad_Audun.pdf)

55. 'Anja breien: Games of love and loneliness'. (November 2013). (http://www.movingimage.us/films/2013/11/01/detail/anja-breien-games-of-love-and-loneliness/)

56. Munoz, L. (September 21st 2012). In 'tears of gaza,' vibeke løkkeberg focuses on children of war. *The Daily Beast.* (http://www.thedailybeast.com/articles/2012/09/21/in-tears-of-gaza-vibeke-lokkeberg-focuses-on-children-of-war.html)

57. Brennan, S. (n.d.). 'Anna Mariscal: Biography'. (http://www.fandango.com/anamariscal/biography/p220289)

58. Goodman, A. (October 1st 1997). 'Pilar miro romero, 57, film and TV director who served in Spain's culture ministry.' *The New York Times.* (http://www.nytimes.com/1997/10/21/arts/pilar-miro-romero-57-film-and-tv-director-who-served-in-spain-s-culture-ministry.html)

59. Minder, R. (September 28th 2011). Isabel Coixet, an

'unclassifiable' director. *The New York Times*. (http://www.nytimes.com/2011/09/29/arts/29iht-coixet29.html)

60. Aguilar, C. (December 5th 2013). Foreign Oscar entry review: 15 years 1 day (*15 años y un día*). *Indiewire*. (http://blogs.indiewire.com/sydneylevine/foreign-oscar-entry-review-15-years-1-day-spain-gracia-querejeta-foreign-language-oscar-submissions-academy-awards-2014-international-film-business)

61. Alexander, L. (January 14th 2014). An Oscar nominated director gets real. *Indiewire*. (http://blogs.indiewire.com/womenandhollywood/an-oscar-nominated-director-gets-real)

19. Hidden Histories on Film:

Female Directors from South Eastern Europe

Dina Iordanova

An aging peasant woman, Ayse, who lives in the mountains above
Turkey's Black Sea coast, begins talking in an incomprehensible
language in Yesim Ustaoglu's *Bulutlari beklerken/Waiting for the
Clouds* (France/Germany/Greece/Turkey, 2004). It is gradually
revealed that she was originally called Eleni and descends from a
family of Pontian Greeks who were displaced during her teenage
years. Most members of her family died during the flight, she
alone was saved by Turkish peasants and raised as a Turk, with
a new name and identity. Now in advanced age, Ayse can no
longer resist the urge to go back in time, haunted by a horrible
guilty memory of having given up on her little baby brother back
then. Her inquiries take her to various places; she learns, to her
astonishment, that the brother has miraculously survived and
now lives in Athens.

Toward the end of the film, Ayse travels to Greece and tries to
reunite with her brother. He is no longer young, in his sixties, and
has built a large family in the city. The brother is not particularly
thrilled by the appearance of this Turkish woman who arrives
out of the blue, claims to be his long lost sister, and starts telling
him stories he cannot recall. Her arrival is disturbing his peace:
he does not remember her and does not need the memories that
she brings along. He treats her with barely suppressed animosity.

In the final scene of the film, brother and sister are seated at
a table; he talks her through a pile of pictures. The viewers are

shown glimpses of the photographs that he displays for her: his leaving orphanage, then a photograph with the girl who would eventually become his wife, then photographs of the family with their first child, him at the door of his shop, then with the second child, then at his son's wedding, then with the grandchildren, and so on. Then the brother puts the pile of photographs down, turns to Ayse and tells her:

> 'Here, all my life is recorded in these pictures, all my family members can also be seen in here. You are not in these pictures; you have not been part of my life. How can you come out of the blue, tell me you are my sister, and expect me to embrace you?'

With trembling hand, Ayse passes on to him a ruffled pale photograph which shows a family: the mother, seated, holds a young baby boy, the father and two older sisters standing beside her. It is this sole photograph that she can present as testimony to her story; not much to offset the overwhelming pile of well documented family history that he has mobilised to counter her story and her claims of a forgotten relationship that disturbs, questions and inconveniences the tidily structured universe of his memories. It is a sole photograph that weighs at least as much as all other photographs and radically undermines the neatly pieced narrative of his life.

Waiting for the Clouds is one of these films that I return to every time I ask myself what is the most prevalent characteristic of female filmmaking from the region of South Eastern Europe. It is a film that clearly demonstrates the desire to expose the 'hushed histories' that circulate in the Balkan realm: these may be stories of displacement and assimilation that are largely absent from official annals but live in oral history, or narratives of suppression that remain hidden, forgotten, relegated to oblivion.

Like many families in the region, my own family has one of these stories: about the migration of my grandmother Kostadina, a Slav woman from Aegean Macedonia, whose family settled in the Kyustendil area of Bulgaria in the mid-1920s. At the age of nineteen, Kostadina gave birth to my father, then to his sister, and then died prematurely at the age of thirty-six, in 1949. We only have one photograph of her – a single ruffled and pale picture. Relatives quietly blamed her husband for bringing about her premature death, but they never wanted to talk openly about what precisely had happened. Like many families in the region, my relatives never spoke about the reasons for her migration nor of the ordeal that she had apparently lived through.

It was only with time, and due to my exposure to the vast panorama of female films from the region, that I gradually came to recognise that many areas in the Balkans are sites of intercultural memory, full of silenced memories that come with a daunting scarcity of record. Different peoples have inhabited the region at different times; earlier settlers have had to leave to open up space for others, who have come to settle in their place, deleting the memory of prior presence. Women have routinely been the quiet sufferers in these processes. Wherever one turns, one encounters the same story: occasional ruffled photograph is the only material that stands against a wealth of later records that obliterate the clandestine realities of singular and apparently insignificant female lives.

Female filmmakers across the Balkans seem particularly attracted to these 'hushed histories'. The stories they tell come from different parts of the region and relate to different memories, yet they are related in that they often refer to a memory of disturbed multicultural co-existence, to people whose presence has been obliterated from memory. In these films, female directors keep asking who is forgotten and why, and explore history from the point of view of those whose trajectories have been silenced.

Recently, female filmmakers from Greece and Turkey have begun to probe the hushed aspects of the 'exchange of populations' between the two countries in the 1920s, a poorly managed process of forced migration that involved 1.5 million Greeks and half a million Turks. In *Between Venizelos and Atatürk Streets* (2004), Turkish director Hande Gumuskemer interviews the remaining survivors, while Peggy Vassiliou's *Hamam Memories* (2000), looked at shared lifestyle features by discovering the use of the Turkish-style bath-houses (*hamams*) across the region.

CELLULOID CEILING

As mentioned above, Yesim Ustaoglu's *Waiting for the Clouds* explores a forgotten ethnic cleansing campaign by dissecting the quiet life of an ethnically homogeneous Turkish village with a hidden multicultural past that still shelters survivors of the massacres of Pontian Greeks. Her *Günese yolculuk (Journey to the Sun,* 1999), spoke of yet another hushed story within Turkey, exposing the racist treatment of the Kurds, which is also the focus of another female film, Handan Ipekci's *Büyük adam küçük ask (Big Man, Little Love,* 2001). This one tells the story of a Kurdish girl, Hejar, who accidentally ends up in the care of a retired Turkish judge, after her parents are arrested and taken away. Ipekçi's new film, *Sakli yüzler (Hidden Faces,* 2007) deals with yet another controversial hidden issue, that of honour killings, where young women become victims of rigid ideas of belonging and family pride.

Another Turkish female filmmaker, Pelin Esmer, follows a group of Anatolian village women as they stage a play based on their own life stories in the documentary *Oyun* (2007), a film that can qualify as a classic feminist text in that it shows little known aspects of female lives.

The female films of the Balkan 'hushed histories' do not seek to revise and establish an ultimate truth about the events behind the story, but focus on presenting the subtle personal dimensions, the way these events have affected the lives of the protagonists and created a personal discourse that may be very different from the stories that are told through officially sanctioned channels. Thus, the films made by women from the region contribute to a daring revisionist project that quietly but persistently undermines the master narratives found in populist nationalist historiography.

Ayse's trembling hand, reaching out with the pale photograph, undermines not only the official discourse that wants the memory of persecuted Pontian Greeks obliterated; it also powerfully protests against the self-sufficient and confident personal story of the brother who is reluctant to accept the quiet suffering of his seemingly irresolute and confused, yet committed, elder sister.

Turning to my native country, Bulgaria, it is easy to discover the same persistent interest in hushed subjects that characterises many instances of female filmmaking here. Since the fall of Zhivkov's government in 1990 Bulgaria has maintained a reasonably good record in suppressing the ethnic tensions of the mid 1980s and has managed to avoid further deepening of the ethnic conflict, but the difficult moments that led to the massive emigration of ethnic Turkish citizens in the summer of 1989 still lingers in people's minds. A succession of governments took various measures to correct the damage of the re-naming process of the Bulgarian ethnic Turks and Pomaks. Remarkably, in cinema, the guilt over the brutal campaign of change of names, has remained a 'hushed history' that has been addressed predominantly by female filmmakers, in a context in which many types of nationalist publications are thriving and one can encounter groups that are more nationalist-minded than ever. These were film productions initiated and staffed almost exclusively by women that set out to promote inter-ethnic peace and to expose the faults of what was called a 'revival process' (a process that was meant to illuminate the Muslim populace as to their inherently Slavic identity, to 'revive' it).

Gori, gori oganche (*Burn, Burn, Little Flame*), was a 1994 television mini-series by screenwriter Malina Tomova and director Roumiana Petkova (and camera-woman Svetla Ganeva). It powerfully told the story of the mistreatment, harassment and humiliation of helpless Pomak villagers in a remote settlement in the Rhodopi region that eventually culminated in a brutal assimilation campaign, as witnessed by a young teacher of Bulgarian ethnicity. She, like the makers of the film, feels guilty over the acts of violence perpetrated by her fellow Bulgarians over this defenseless population. Malina Tomova, the scriptwriter, claimed that her film was a metaphor for the guilt which Bulgarian intellectuals feel due to their silence and failure to condemn the brutality of the 'revival process'. The film's intention was to evoke genuine remorse for the human rights abuses that Bulgarians had committed against their Muslim compatriots. No wonder, the film became one of the most discussed works of the mid-1990s; its hotly contested reception made the gap between intellectuals and nationalist-minded mass audiences visible than ever.

CELLULOID CEILING

The 'revival process' and its difficult aftermath were addressed in other films made by women as well. Adela Peeva's documentary *Izlishnite* (*The Unwanted*, 1999) featured interviews with women inhabiting these same (now depopulated) Bulgarian border regions who bitterly reassess their own role in the re-naming campaign. Today they acknowledge that they suffer from the adverse effects of their own complicit actions. It is an intelligent, subtle film that reveals how, long after those who were abused have found closure, the local perpetrators have fallen victim to themselves, as they are most affected by the repercussions and the guilty consciousness that still haunts them after so many years. Other uneasy aspects of the controversial 'revival process' were also addressed in the made-for-TV work by Tanya Vaksberg, as well as in Roumiana Petkova's documentary *Mezhdinensvyat* (*A World In-Between*, 1995).

The plight of oppressed ethnic minorities has routinely been the theme of other women-filmmakers too. Romanies have been the focus of Eldora Traykova's *Za horata I mechkite* (*Of People and Bears*, 1995) and *Zhivot v geto* (*Life in a Ghetto*, 2000), and the plight of the Jews was explored in Milena Milotinova's *Spasenite* (*The Saved Ones*, 1999).

The commitment to telling hushed or non-conventional histories that women filmmakers have had over the years in Bulgaria led to situations of censorship. I can tell of many incidents that have affected the work of such important women filmmakers from the country like Binka Zhelyazkova, Irina Aktasheva, Nevena Tosheva and Adela Peeva.

The essentially counter-cultural nature of female filmmaking in the region can be discovered in films made by women across all the countries of former Yugoslavia. Women were the first to address awkward or hushed topics and to present them in subtle ways, often as if nothing much happens on the surface while a storm rages inside the protagonist or the small community. In Serbia, Mirjana Vukomanovic's *Tri letnja dana* (*Three Summer Days*, 1997) was one of the first films to look at the ordeal of impoverished refugees from across Yugoslavia who flocked into Belgrade in the mid-1990s, bringing along a few possessions and a lot of memories. In Slovenia, Maja Weiss's *Varuh meje* (*Guardian of the Frontier*, 2002) raised awkward questions of newly erected borders and division lines through the highly personal stories of three women seeking independence. In Macedonia, Teona Mitevska's *Kako ubiv svetec* (*How I Killed a Saint*, 2004) showed the gradual radicalisation and involvement with terrorist activities of her local community as an inevitable side-effect to the presence of the international 'peacekeeping' forces. Before tackling issues of trauma in her acclaimed *Grbavica* (*Esma's Secret*, 2006), Jasmila Zbanic's episode 'Birthday' in the omnibus *Lost and Found* (2005) was probably the best example of subtly addressing the making of new hushed histories, by tackling head on the inept silence in which the members of the split community in Mostar now raise their children. In my view, this is Zbanic's best film today, persuasively critical of the way in which important issues of reconciliation and trauma are still being avoided. It is important to have films that tell the story from the point of view of those who have been overpowered, and pushed aside by the winners, as is the case of the small community of women, victims of trauma and yet finding their own strategies to survive, that we saw in Aida Begic's recent *Sneg* (*Snow*, 2008).

Courage is needed to make films about these contested Balkan themes, and it is women who lead the way. They seek out the hushed memories and commit to bringing them to the fore, thus quietly subverting mainstream narratives with films that have the potential to trigger public controversies. Many of the female films are politically awkward because they bring up suppressed subject matter. Yet, by telling the story of the losing side, they manage to tell the all-important story of women.

Author biography

Dina Iordanova is Professor of Global Cinema and Creative Cultures at the University of St Andrews in Scotland. She has published extensively on matters of East European and Balkan cinema, as well as on global film culture, film festivals and circulation.

DinaView (http://www.dinaview.com) covers world film, culture, festivals, and more. Check it out, subscribe, spread the word.

Contact: dina.iordanova@st-andrews.ac.uk

20. Iron and Reel:

Russian Women Directors Through the Soviet Era and Beyond

Karlanna Lewis

In 2007, director Anna Melikian released her film *Rusalka*, or *The Mermaid*, the story of a woman who occupies a place between worlds, land and water, earth and cosmos. Considering the plight of women in Russia in general, and the blatant inequality of contemporary Muscovite society, the protagonist of Melikian's film represents more than a historic folk legend, and may stand also for the separateness of Russian female film directors. In Russian folklore, Rusalka is the story of a mermaid trickster – a strange creature who plays games and pokes fun at those around her. For many women directing film in Russia, they are treated as 'others', but their earnest work opens doors for other women in the future at the same time as lampooning stagnation in their societies and in the lives of their contemporaries. Today a new generation of women is finding its inner thoughts on the silver screen. For those dreaming of filmmaking careers, this generation may thank Melikian and her progenitors for pushing boundaries to enable these new women to speak for themselves.

Although film is just one of many areas of professional inequality, it is notable because it is offered to an audience of equal gender composition, yet passes through a male lens. Russia will not be the first country to open professional doors to women in film, especially given recent unrest around discrimination against women in a mock astronaut mission (2010), the unjust criminal treatment of the female punk band Pussy Riot (2012) and the widespread homophobic laws (under fire before the Sochi Olympic Games of 2014). However, once the West moves itself toward equal career opportunities, within twenty years, Russian women, no matter what despot may reign, will smash what remains of crumbling Soviet-era ceilings and project their visions worldwide. Hollywood has already recognised its own gaping inequality of the sexes, and since Kathryn Bigelow became the first woman to win a Best Picture Oscar in 2010, excuses about women's lack of interest in film and the time it takes to achieve equality are no longer acceptable. Soon the Russian government, in its aims to show the world its decency and respect, will no longer be able to silence the voices of its Anna Melikians, Dinara Asanovas and Kira Muratovas.

Until women film directors cease to be an anomaly, that unfortunate extra word serves as both sword and shield – sword because these women are fighting for their place, and shield because their work protects all of society. When viewing work by women directors, the audience brings its own biases, reading the films as political whether or not that was the director's intention. In fact, the opposite may be the case, as Russian women film directors today are not radicals as much as voices of 'the woman of the masses, the family woman', speaking 'because woman's equal rights is an economic necessity.'[1] In the examples that follow, some of these voices come to light, and the sensitive reader will recognise them for what they are, not as voices of difference, but of unity: of a people, of daughters and mothers and of the motherland.

The Red List: Notable Russian Women Directors

Olga Preobrazhenskaia by Karlanna Lewis

Although in the West Alice Guy-Blaché was directing movies as early as 1896, the first documented Russian woman director was Olga Preobrazhenskaia, who established herself in 1916, with the film *Baryshnia-Krest'ianka* (*Mistress into the Maid*). Through the Soviet period, when censorship peaked, the West far outpaced its Eastern rival in opportunities for women in film. However, in the past twenty-five years – from 1989 when American men borrowed the centuries-old Russian tale of Rusalka to produce

Disney's *The Little Mermaid* – to the present day, Russian women are carving themselves more than a niche on screen. They are creating a powerful forum for voices too long banned from popular parlance.

Sheryl Sandberg's 2013 book *Lean In* called attention to the disparity women face in many male-dominated professions, and the double standard that forces the work of female directors to be filtered through the additional lens of 'woman'. Preobrazhenskaia will not be recognised for her achievements alone, but because she achieved them as the first woman directing such ground-breaking Russian films as *Baviy Riazanskie* (*The Woman of Riazan*, 1927), *Tihiy Don* (*And Quiet Flows the Don*, 1931) and *Stepan Razin* (1939). Although the extra hurdles Preobrazhenskaia and her sister directors faced in a classist and sexist society make her credits all the more remarkable, her vision deserves recognition for its own sake. One day society may advance far enough toward equality that women film directors, women conductors or even women poets do not need the gendered appellation, but will win respect in their own right regardless of their chromosomes.

Nadezhda Kosheverova by Karlanna Lewis
Another early Russian director, Nadezhda Kosheverova, studied film at FEKS, the Factory of the Eccentric Actor, where she worked with Leonid Trauberg and Grigory Kozintsev and gained her defining theatrical aesthetic. Born in St. Petersburg in 1902, Kosheverova grew up as tsarist Russia fell down. Her first solo feature, *Zolushka* (*Cinderella*, 1947) followed the familiar fairytale without implying any social context, and made it to the screen (succeeding despite the love story's conflict with the obligatory socialist realism in art of the day). Kosheverova's 1963 film, *Cain the XVIIIth*, took the fairytale focus into anti-totalitarian territory, and though the film managed to reach the screen, because of its mere theatricality it failed to reach commercial success. Kosheverova's life gave out in 1989 just before the Soviet state collapsed into itself, but she had lived long enough to witness the emergence of the next generation of women filmmakers.

Larisa Shepitko by Nina Sputnitskaya

Larisa Shepitko was among the next generation of filmmakers. Born in Ukraine in 1938, she studied at the Gerasimov Institute of Cinematography (VGIK). Though she, like Preobrazhenskaia and the early American director Lois Weber (along with many modern women), began her career as an actress, acting was but a way in to her true calling, directing. Shepitko's diploma film, *Heat*, became her first feature in 1963. Though censorship altered her initial vision, turning the film into a history of cinema (with the tagline 'person and war'), *Heat* garnered Shepitko acclaim with debut awards at the 1964 International Cinema Festival in Karlovy Vary. However, it was her second film, *Wings* (1966), which made her career, telling the story of a woman pilot misunderstood by the post-war generation.

Voskhozhdeniye (*The Ascent*, 1977), made at the studio Mosfilm, was Shepitko's final finished film.[2] About World War II, *The Ascent* is also about sacrifice and destiny, featuring torture and attempted suicide, so the censor's near killing of the project is no surprise. She began work on *Matyora*, but a fatal car accident ended her career. Her husband, Elem Klimov (also a director), completed and released the film, renamed *Farewell* (1981), on her behalf.

Dinara Asanova by Vera Zharikova

Hollywood now acknowledges the importance of the emerging markets for film, with the neat acronym BRIC designating the heightened role Brazil, Russia, India and China will play in cinema over the next decades. Given tight content controls at Russia's borders few women directors from Russia have made themselves a global name. Dinara Asanova, a filmmaker from a small Kyrgyz town who directed her first feature *Ne Bolit Golova u Dyatla* (*Woodpeckers Don't Get Headaches*) in 1975, now rests among the other women of Russia film, in the shadows. Her first idealistic feature focuses around universal themes of youth, love and music, but her second film, *Klyuch bez Prava Peredachi* (*The Key That Should Not Be Handed On*, 1967) departs in theme. While still centered around music, *Klyuch bez Prava Peredachi* focuses on the complicated relations between teacher and students, and underneath the surface story, the film explores the dead ends of 1970s society (following 1960s romanticism). Asanova's third feature (of the ten shorts and full-length films of her career) *Beda* (*Calamity*, 1977) details the complexities of alcoholism, an affliction that contemporary society has come to associate with the harsh realities of Russian life and the extreme measures necessary to cope. Twenty years prior to this the optimistic story of war and love, *Letyat Zhuravli* (*The Cranes Are Flying*), had won the Palme d'Or at the 1958 Cannes Film Festival (the only Soviet film to win the festival's highest award). *The Cranes Are Flying* progressed in its depiction of women, featuring a multi-dimensional heroine, but the film's director, of course, was a man.

Though Asanova still awaits the attention she is due, her 1984 feature *Milii, Dorogoi, Lyubimii, Edinstvennii* (*Dear, Dearest, Beloved, Unique...*) was screened in Cannes' *Un Certain Regard* section. Today, though, Asanova's achievements in the year of her death (1985) are overshadowed by the place to which her films have been relegated as 'school cinema' or 'cinema for teenagers.' The fact that she is labelled a 'young adult' filmmaker, operating outside the cinematic mainstream, reflects the discomfort the public continues to feel around the idea of a woman director rather than the content of the films themselves. Asanova's films are not heavy-handed and she uses neither violence nor perversion to compensate for the perception that women are soft – instead she turns the camera toward the bitter reality of the final years of Soviet Russia. Still, like Chekhov's Sonya in his play *Uncle Vanya*, Asanova remains hopeful, believing in the possibilities of the unknown. Though Asanova died decades before women will complete the long journey to equality in film, her work, and its open confrontation of problems in a supposed society of equals, has done its part to build the path.

Kira Muratova by Nina Sputnitskaya

In contrast to Asanova, her contemporary Kira Muratova created individualist stories that, despite the director's distaste for the label 'women's film', focus on women and their varied plights (often with a sharp and critical eye). Born in Soroca, Romania, in

1934, Muratova worked in Odessa, Ukraine for most of her career, employing non-professional actors alongside professionals, and including scenes with animals to contrast the natural innocence of the wild with human depravity. From 1961 on, Muratova directed the Odessa Film Studio. After graduating from Moscow's Gerasimov Institute of Cinematography in 1965, Muratova directed her first feature, *Korotkiye Vstrechi* (*Brief Encounters*) in 1967.

At the time all Russian artists faced the black pen of censorship, and many chose to emigrate to the West, but Muratova spent most of her career near her origins, working with locals in Odessa (aside from a brief stint in Leningrad following a professional conflict). In contrast to the so-called 'women's films' produced by male directors in the Soviet period, Muratova allows her female characters the dignity that they will be criticised when they do not live up to their own personal standards. Without resorting to the kitsch stereotypes her male colleagues employed, Muratova portrayed women in the vein of her admired Leo Tolstoy, with absolute morals and true-to-life psyches.

Many women who have succeeded in directing films, from Alice Guy-Blaché to Kira Muratova, were helped by their relationships with men in the industry. Muratova directed her first two features together with her husband Aleksandr Muratov, but hers is the name history remembers. Muratova's work continues to be compared to that of her teacher, Sergei Gerasimov, and though his stylisation and anti-realism juxtapose with her silver screen humanity, Gerasimov's influence enters into her 'abstraction of speech and gesture through repetition' and her cinematic fascination with heteroglossia in the Russian language.[3] Like other artists of the Soviet era, Muratova also faced the Hobson's choice of either producing work true to her principles that would not see the light of day, or allowing her work to be refashioned into unrecognisable clippings at the hand of the censor.

Like the poet Vladimir Mayakovsky and many other artists, whose early work was taught to Soviet children and whose later work grew more cynical in its view of the State, Muratova's later films, from *Astenicheski Sindrom* (*The Asthenic Syndrome*, 1987) on, grew more vigorous in renouncing the downfall of Soviet social life and morals.[4]

When the state's black scissors butchered her 1983 film *Sredi Serih Kamney* (*Among Grey Stones*, 1983) beyond recognition, she asked for her name to be removed from the credits, and her dissent from the state's artistic systems was born. Constructed during a national 'reorganisation' era, Muratova's *Peremena Uchasti* (*Change of Fate*) and *The Asthenic Syndrome* represent her full creativity and introduced her to the international stage. Critics of her new work, such as *The Asthenic Syndrome*, missed the Tolstoyan moral themes and dismissed the film as '*cherukha*', for what they saw as excessive darkness. Other critics point a finger at what seems to them an over fascination with the 'little man' (in the tradition of Dostoevsky and Chekhov). If Muratova's films bear any excess, though, the excess is not in blackness or the hero's marginality as much as in completeness and the weaving together of many colored threads.[5] Though her work has shifted much in what is now a more than fifty-year career, Muratova's films follow the arc Woody Allen recognised: 'the first three are about love, the second three about death.'[6] However, even her early films met heavy criticism in breaking the only theme the Soviet State endorsed: man and his time.

In any society, the judges of art (the critics) determine much of public opinion, and in Russia part of the lack of respect for women directors stems from a lack of female critics in the field. Muratova's *Brief Encounters*, though not new in its love-triangle theme, was new in placing a woman as a leading government bureaucrat, but the only documented reviews were negative (a film already too radical for the tastes of comfortable Soviet men). As late as 1995, Maya Turovskaya wrote about the difference between Western sexism and Russian sexism – while Western women complained about the attitudes with which men received them and their work, Russian women were still fighting to gain a reception at all. Muratova's films did not win much praise – in part because they broke with linear storytelling and left the viewer to fill in the gaps – and officials ordered her to stop telling contemporary stories because of her potential to disrupt. But fortune turned for her when her *Dolgiye Provody* (*The Long Goodbye*, 1971) was released together with *Brief Encounters* in 1987 and even won a prize at the Locarno festival. The Ukrainian Muratova now occupies the rare place of the artist whose career has spanned two distinct Russian epochs, the USSR and the modern state, in which she has become even more productive and where censorship, if not gone altogether, at least must now tussle with the semblance of democracy.

Valeria Germanika by Nina Sputnitskaya

Her 1984 birthdate places Valeria Germanika among the newest and youngest of Russian film directors, but her own documentarian style and raw authenticity in her portrayal of teenagers place her among the most controversial of Russian cinematic figures. A graduate of the Internews Film and Television School, Germanika studied under documentary filmmaker Marina Razbezhkina. Her initial filmmaking stayed within her mentor's genre, but even so her second documentary *Girls* (2005) won a prize for best short at Russia's largest festival (Kinotavr) and was featured at the Cannes International Film Festival. Still, her debut feature, *Vse Umrut a ya Ostanus (Everybody Dies But Me)* (2008), best showcased her true strength and brought her wider acclaim.

Everybody Dies But Me follows a typical plotline of teenage movies, but the subtext differs in its frank treatment of adult indifference and the fast shift the protagonists must make from child to adult after they experience pivotal, and sometimes bitter, events (attempted suicide, betrayal, loss of virginity). The film nabbed a special mention at the 2008 Cannes Film Festival, and Germanika has continued to focus on the darker side of youth with subsequent works.

Even more than *Everybody Dies But Me*, Germanika's 2010 TV series *Shkola (School)* provoked widespread criticism, with state officials (including the Minister of Education) among those calling for its removal from television. Though individual episodes are lyrical and indirect in their storytelling, the series as a whole is linear, and at times repetitive. Rather than arousing shock, though, *School* seeks to open a conversation about society's youth. The series generated unrest because it destroys the most basic fabric of society – trust. In the finale, graduation and death – two endings, light and dark – are juxtaposed.

CELLULOID CEILING

After *School*, Germanika's work took on an even more sombre tone, as she produced the TV series *A Short Course in how to live a Happy Life*, exploring the love lives of women living in the city. In the series, recognisable heroines reflect the discomfort and alienation which many young people feel in Russia's big cities, presenting the stark reality of modern day life without sensationalism. Much like the heroines of her series, searching to move from a model reality to a place of command over their own destinies, Germanika herself feels trapped in the big cities of modern Russia, in which a woman has apparent freedom, but still seeks true liberty.

Conclusion by Karlanna Lewis

Among the great directors of Russian cinema, many others must not be forgotten. One of the earliest Soviet filmmakers, Esfir Shub, produced documentaries and penetrated Soviet sexism as early as 1927, with her well-known *Fall of the Romanov Dynasty* (part of a trilogy and commemorating the October Revolution). Though all but forgotten today, Margarita Barskaia deserves note for developing children's cinema with her single film, *Rvanye Bashmaki* (*Torn Boots*, 1993) – made 'by children, for children and about children.'[7] Larisa Sadilova debuted with *Happy Birthday* in 1999, telling the story of family and female loneliness through life in a maternity hospital (much in the vein of Shepitko and Muratova). Director Lidia Bobrova won a special jury prize with her film *Babusya* at the Karlovy Vary International Film Festival in 2003. Renata Litvinova is another director (as well as screenwriter and actress) whose work now graces international festivals. In the animated realm, director Irina Evteeva combines animated illustration with documentary. These are but a few of the many Russian women who have left a mark on the cinematic stage through their fearless directing.

Even today, in the Glasnost and Post-Soviet era of Russian film, women are still carving out their cinematic territory. Unlike in the West, where women had to shift cultural perceptions of the motherhood myth, in Russia, where the only myth was that of the motherland, women had to both create their own story and the place for its telling.

Of Muratova's films, she often considered *Poznavaya Beliy Svet* (*Getting to Know the World*, 1978) to be her favorite, a film focused on a building-site, a new world.[8] In this yet-to-be formed world, beauty is undefined, aesthetics await creation and 'chaos may seem terrible, but to me it is wonderful.'[9] This building site also represents the inchoate film world, where directors, regardless of their sex, will be free to express whatever artistic vision strikes them, and where that vision will be received by open minds of all people in Russia and the West, with a single undefined standard. One day, we can hope, women directors in Russia will not face a double sexism, but history will remember Muratova and Valeria as Eisenstein and Vertov's equals.

Only then will every girl, every Rusalka, every mermaid who dreams of becoming a woman with a movie camera, be able to speak with a celluloid voice that resounds across the wide world she builds and calls home.

Author biographies

Karlanna Lewis – her dreams include becoming a bird; she is currently pursuing her J.D.-M.B.A. (2015) at Yale University. She completed her B.A. Honours in Russian and Creative Writing at Florida State University in Spring 2011, with an Honours thesis in Poetry and a Minor in Computer Science. She was a 2011–12 Rhodes Scholar Finalist.

A writer and artist, she published her first book, *Songs of Gypsies with Names of Light* in 2011. Her most recent poetry collection, *Romantic Criminals*, and her first children's book, *Gladyus & the Voodoo Priestess* were published in 2012. She has worked for Raindance Film Festival in London, where she edited and contributed to their weekly filmmakers' newsletter.

Currently she dances for and leads the Yale Ballet Company, Yaledancers and Yale Dance Theater. A native of Tallahassee, Florida, she was a principal dancer for the Pas de Vie Ballet and has led an honours service project teaching dance to local schoolchildren. She volunteers as a DJ at the WYBCX Yale Radio Station. Passionate about the arts and the environment, in 2011 she founded the non-profit Dancearth, an arts for social change initiative celebrating movement and the earth in which we move.

Contact: Karlanna.lewis@gmail.com

Additional Research from:

Tonja Lagutina – Born in 1980, Tonja Lagutina studied social psychology at Lomonosov Moscow State University and is the secretary/coordinator of the Scientific Research Institute of Film Art (NIIK VGIK) organising conferences and projects. Her interests include questions surrounding finding a balance for mothers between maternity and social realisation and it is her hope that politicians may one day dedicate themselves to solving this issue.

Contact: molodyevetra@mail.ru

Nina Sputnitskaya – Born in 1980, she studied cinema research at VGIK and has been published since 2001. Her 2010 master's dissertation focused on the fairytale in children's cinema. Currently Sputnitskaya is a member of the Modern Cinema Department at VGIK, where her research includes the specific sources of a film image, stop-motion animation and modern screen arts. A member of the Union of Cinematographers of the Russian Federation, Sputnitskaya has reviewed and edited several movies and currently teaches at RGGU.

Contact: minadormouse@gmail.com

Vera Zharikova – Born in 1989, she has a PhD in the history of visual arts from VGIK and is a scientific associate at the Scientific Research Institute of Film Art (NIIK VGIK). Her research centres on Soviet films about teenagers and school life.

Contact: verachaude@gmail.com

References

Zharikova, Vera (2014). 'Overview of D. Asanova.' Unpublished paper on file with author.

Makoveeva, Irina (2007). 'The New Century: Has the Russian Pandora's Time Come? *'The Slavic and East European Journal,* Vol. 51, No. 2, Special Forum Issue: 'Resent, Reassess, and Reinvent: The Three R's of Post-Soviet Cinema (Summer)', pp. 247–271. American Association of Teachers of Slavic and Eastern European Languages.

Miller, Jamie (2011). 'Russian Studies: Russian Film Studies The

Year's Work in Modern Language Studies. Vol. 73 (2013 [survey year 2011]), pp. 479–485. Modern Humanities Research Association.

Sputnitskaya, Nina (2014). 'Russian Women Cinema Directors. Unpublished' paper on file with author.

Sputnitskaya, Nina (2012). 'Most Charming and Attractive. "A Short Course of a Happy Life,"' the Director Valeria Gai Germanika. *CINEMA ART*. No. 4, April (http://kinoart.ru/ru/archive/2012/04/samye-obayatelnye-i-privlekatelnye-kratkij-kurs-schastlivoj-zhizni-rezhisser-valeriya-gaj-germanika accessed January 13th 2014).

Taubman, Jane A (1993). 'The Cinema of Kira Muratova'. *Russian Review*, Vol. 52, No. 3 (Jul.), pp. 367–381. Wiley.

Tonic, Lucy (2011). 'Films for the Whimsical, Peculiar & Odd Individual: Anna Melikyan's "Mermaid"' (2007). *Yahoo! Voices*. 7 June 2011 (http://voices.yahoo.com/films-whimsical-peculiar-odd-8600547.html accessed January 13th 2014).

Turovskaya, Maya and Jonathan Flatley (1995). 'Notes on Women and Film.' *Discourse*, Vol. 17, No. 3, 'Views from the Post-Future/Soviet & Eastern European Cinema' (Spring), pp. 7–23. Wayne State University Press.

Endnotes

1. Maya Turovskaya and Jonathan Flatley, quoting Aleksandr Amfiteatrov, in 'Notes on Women and Film,' pusblished in *Discourse*, Vol. 17, No. 3 (Spring 1995), pp. 7–23.

2. *Voskhozhdeniye* (*The Ascent*, 1977) won the Golden Bear at the 27th Berlin International Film Festival. (http://www.berlinale.de/en/archiv/jahresarchive/1977/03_preistr_ger_1977/03_Preistraeger_1977.html)

3. Jane A. Taubman, 'The Cinema of Kira Muratova', *Russian Review*, Vol. 52, No. 3 (Jul. 1993), pp. 367–381 (368).

4. *The Asthenic Syndrome*, in which the title disease serves as metaphor for Soviet society, places responsibility for the moral decay on screen (including abuse of animals and people) with the audience. Beginning with a black-and-white film within the film, *The Asthenic Syndrome* also delves into the self-referential, as a character laments that serious film deserves serious discussion. The film won the Silver Bear - Special Jury Prize at the Fortieth Berlin International Film Festival. (http://www.berlinale.de/en/archiv/jahresarchive/1990/03_preistr_

ger_1990/03_Preistraeger_1990.html)

5. Muratova's 1987 *Peremena Uchasti* (*Change of Fate*), while vibrant, received criticism for dallying too far into the ornamental surreal at the sacrifice of story.

6. Taubman, 'The Cinema of Kira Muratova,' p. 369.

7. Natalia Miloserdova, quoting Margarita Barskaia in 'Margarita Barskaia and the Emergence of Children's Cinema,' *Studies in Russian and Soviet Cinema*, Vol. 3, No. 2 (August 2009), pp. 240–259.

8. Taubman, 'The Cinema of Kira Muratova,' p. 378.

9. Taubman, quoting Kira Muratova, 'The Cinema of Kira Muratova,' p. 378.

21. Where's Britannia?

Melody Bridges

Britannia, the ancient term for Roman Britain is the female personification of the island of Great Britain. With her trident and helmet she graces many public places in England, a symbol of power and female strength. That ancient female power is not much in evidence looking through the encyclopedic tome *501 Movie Directors: A Comprehensive Guide to the Greatest Filmmakers of All Time.*[1] Only Ida Lupino and Sally Potter are mentioned as female directors in the UK.

Potter, prolific director of numerous outstanding films, including *Orlando*, received an OBE from the Queen in 2012 for her services to film. An inspiration to many directors, both male and female, she is outspoken, her work is dangerous and her vision is exciting. But what of the other well-known female directors working in Britain not mentioned in this tome such as Phyllida Lloyd, Lynne Ramsay, Beeban Kidron, Andrea Arnold, Sam Taylor-Wood, Sharon McGuire, and Gurinder Chadra, who have made films recently that have had success in the global marketplace? *Fish Tank* by Andrea Arnold won many international awards, and yet it was shown in less than fifty cinemas in the UK.

Andrea Arnold notes:

> 'I definitely feel sorry more people don't get to see my films. They aren't inaccessible, and if people got the chance to see them, I know they'd like them. I wish cinema [owners] could be braver, or had more money to help them show films like mine.'[2]

There is a sense that 'women's films' are outside of the mainstream and inaccessible to a general audience. But a recent report by David Steele for the BFI called '*Succès de plume?* Female Screenwriters and Directors of UK Films, 2010–2012' contradicts this view and proves statistically that in certain genres women's films are *more* commercial than those by men.

> 'There is a genre difference between male and female written/directed films, with women more likely than men to be associated with biopic, drama, music/dance and romance. Women had greater box office success compared to men with animation, family, horror, music/ dance, romance and thrillers.'[3]

While women film directors in the UK continue to be under-represented generally with only 8% of the total, there has been a slight increase among directors of UK independent films, where the proportion of female directors has risen to 11%. Surprisingly, in the top 20 UK independent films in this study, women directors accounted for 18% of the total and of those films considered profitable, 30% were written by female screenwriters.

What discrimination, love?

Although enjoying hefty subsidies with the same support that is offered in most European countries, the UK lags behind in the proportion of its women film directors. Certainly the legacy of sexism and the historic separation of men to the technical department and women to administration has had a part to play but the on-going recruitment of personnel largely relies on personal contacts rather than openly advertising jobs and this method disadvantages women too.

A report commissioned by the UK Film Council (2007) titled *Barriers to Diversity in Film* by Dr Reena Bhavnani stated:

> 'Most employees are recruited informally, notably by word of mouth, or contacting known individuals to write, produce or direct. In film production 81% of employees were recruited by word of mouth, with half

being approached by a producer or director.' (Skillset and UK Film Council 2005, IES 2006)[4]

The sector is also risk averse, producing films that are similar to the last ones which were successful at the box office, so known people are recruited and newcomers find it hard to break in.

However, in management and production, women such as Elisabeth Murdoch (Shine), Barbara Broccoli (EON), Christine Langan (BBC Films) and Tessa Ross at Film 4 have been heading production, or running film departments, for many decades. Women have been well represented as producers too for over fifty years from Verity Lambert (BBC) to today's Alison Owen (Ruby Films), Elizabeth Karlsen (Palace/Number 9), Debra Hayward (Working Title/Monumental), Emma Thomas (Syncopy Inc), Sue Vertue (Hartswood), Eileen Gallagher (Shed) and Nicola Shindler (Red).

Women writers are under-represented in the film industry too. The BFI report quoted above has acknowledged that commissioners tend to be play it safe and usually commission mid-career writers whom they already know – and these tend to be male. The report recommends:

'To make progress, therefore, an institutional shift is required, in which female writers and directors form better links with producers and funders of films, while producers and funders take a more positive approach to finding and commissioning women to write and direct films.'

Remarkably, in spite of this, there has been some recent progress by women screenwriters in the UK:

'there is evidence of a breakthrough by female screenwriters in the last three years (2010–2012), with female screenwriters being associated with 37% of the top 20 UK independent films and 30% of profitable UK independent films.'

While this recent improvement is very welcome, the lack of successful role models for women directors remains and perpetuates the imbalance. As one director, who requested anonymity, observed,

> 'I wanted to be a director from my late teens… but whenever I used to tell people they would look at me and nod with a forced grin on their face. I knew they were thinking *as if*. It made me feel self-conscious to say what I wanted to do. It felt like I was aiming too high.'

In the report 'Barriers to Diversity in Film', Dr Reena Bhavnani acknowledges the problem:

> 'A lack of female directors, producers and writers leads to different portrayals of women on screen, and provides fewer role models for women to aspire to than men (IES 2006). Films may lack the female perspective, just as fewer minority ethnic or disabled staff may lead to a lack of those particular perspectives, thus not reflecting the heterogeneity of voices for film. If under-represented groups' perspectives are not shown on screen, groups will not feel attracted to working in film (IES 2006).'

Shooting People, the network of Independent Film Creatives (https://shootingpeople.org), runs an online noticeboard for UK filmmakers. They found in their recent membership survey that their subscribers were 33% female and 66% male. A recent posting on their site about the low numbers of female directors drew many complaints about the lack of role models. One correspondent, successful documentary maker Sophie Fiennes, commented:

> 'This is a big theme which probably goes beyond filmmaking. I just hope that my being a female filmmaker is an encouragement. But I have to say I don't think too much about my being a woman. I think it's important to be ambitious in the work itself and take ideas as far as possible, and fight hard for them, (be prepared to be "ugly").'

If being ugly means being tough, uncompromising, demanding, then this goes against cultural perceptions of femininity and the strict confines of women's roles.

Multi-award-winning writer/director Rikki Beadle-Blair added:

> 'Directing is such a parental position that women with
> those strong instincts tend to opt for an actual baby.'

A report done in 1973 by the ACTT (The Association of
Cinematograph Television and Allied Technicians), which later
became part of the Broadcasting, Entertainment, Cinematograph
and Theatre Union (BECTU) called 'Patterns of Discrimination'
listed that in drama and feature films, 8% of directors were
female.[5] The same survey conducted forty years later and in 2013
revealed that figure of 8% of female directors to be unchanged.
It's a shocking result. While the number of female directors
working in documentary/factual film has increased to 27%, we're
still not anywhere near what we can presume is the ideal – a 50%
target – and arguably something like government intervention
will be required before that occurs.

I asked Head of BBC Drama, Kate Harwood, whether quotas
might help ensure parity: 'Quotas? Oh no, I'd hate that! That
would be very anti-creative.'

If not quotas, what's the next step? Directors UK (http://
www.directors.uk.com), a group which was formed in 2008, has
acknowledged the lack of women directors breaking through
today and they have set up their own Women's Working group,
chaired by Beryl Richards. She thinks there were actually more
women directing when she started out in the 1990s but the
numbers have fallen away,

> 'I always took myself seriously and expected other people
> to as well. Feminism was a serious force and it shifted the
> culture but it's been rolled back.'[6]

Show me the Money, Honey

One of the key skills a director needs is fundraising. Current global
instability leads to risk aversion in all fields and when dealing with
a business as risky as the film business, hedging one's bets often
means hiring a male director. Finding a producer and 'the money'

to realise your dream is a difficult undertaking for any director, let alone one who is 'disabled by breasts' as one female director put it. With shrinking pockets of equity finance controlled by a few (usually) male executives, highly talented women often find it hard to raise money for their films or to get hired onto commercial projects. The BFI report quoted above sheds some light on how all-female teams are successfully accessing funding from the public sector:

> '... films with female writers or directors were more likely to have female producers or executive producers, to have been financed and produced by Film4 or BBC Films and to have received Lottery funding.'

The UK Film Council also has a number of funds and statistics show that 26–30% of these funds were allocated to women filmmakers. Where regional funds were made available, women were allocated 47% of these funds (see *Barriers to Diversity in Film* Report, 2007).

Pitching film ideas, packaging projects and especially marketing and publicising one's work and oneself are complex skills that need to be learned if they are not inherent. Mentoring, networking and role models can assist in this process. Women in Film and Television (http://www.wftv.org.uk), an organisation that champions women working in all areas of the media, co-ordinates training and networking events. Recently, The Other Club, an all-female social club was formed in London, to encourage women to network more effectively. Business coach, Clare Bradford stated,

> 'I ban the women I advise from using the term "only", "just" or "little" – they are the most shockingly overused words women use to describe their projects and career to date.'

Recession reduces options

The economic downtown in the UK from 2008 onwards has impacted all industries. While attendance at film schools has boomed, finding an internship or job as a runner, PA or production assistant has become increasingly difficult. In the past, film crews

UK

functioned like old fashioned guilds taking on trainees who learned the skills at the side of an expert. The sheer numbers of those graduates seeking such on-the-job training have made those key starter jobs very hard to get. Consequently, these jobs are often done, as industry publication *Broadcast* magazine notes, 'by young white middle class men who have parental support.' This means that those young people without financial support from parents are less likely to enter the world of film/television. There are schemes to address this such as Creative Skillset's Guiding Lights mentoring programme. See: http://www.lighthouse.org.uk/guiding-lights/about-guiding-lights-scheme and http://www.creativeskillset.org but they are small compared to the crushing economics of a changing world media marketplace.

Where are the role models?

The image of a male director holding a megaphone is a pervasive stereotype. Think of the directors whose names spring readily to mind – Woody Allen, Martin Scorsese, Steven Spielberg, Alfred Hitchcock, Orson Welles. We know what these directors look like and something of their personalities. Our mental image of a film director tends to be white, male and usually American.

On-screen depictions of directors in films include Tim Burton's film *Ed Wood* (1994) with Johnny Depp as the lead; *Argo* (2012) with Ben Affleck; Jack Davenport in the NBC TV Series *Smash* (2012–13) *Mulholland Drive* (2001), Adam Kesher; the documentary character in *Man with a Camera* and the rather fun *Living in Oblivion* (1995) with Steve Buscemi as the director having a meltdown. Even director Sofia Coppola cast a male commercial director in *Lost in Translation* (2003). Women are usually absent in film, in print, in media as that character who defines a movie – the director.

France, in contrast, has recently launched a sex equality charter for the film industry aimed at improving the number and position of women working in the French cinema sector. Our neighbour across the Channel strongly protects its culture, and finances its preservation and promotion. France also showcases the work of its women directors in the long-running Festival des Femmes. Catherine Breillat, in her 2002 film *Sex is Comedy* shows a female director – Jeanne – struggling to direct a sex scene with two actors who hate each other. Jeanne insists on getting the scene right and won't accept any compromises. This fictional scenario was actually inspired by Breillat's own experiences of directing, particularly referencing her film, *Fat Girl* (2001). The movie remains a trenchant examination of the sex and power games that take place on a film set. We know that if it's not in the frame, it doesn't exist and that for women starting out, the reality of seeing directors as women, doing their work without fanfare or excuses is a powerful motivator for their own success.

Who wants to be a director?

Graduate film schools such as the National Film and Television School, and the London Film School, offer key entry level points for those who wish to become directors. These well-regarded institutions train many of the future big film and television makers, and the number of women graduating as directors remain small. Although both institutions declined to comment on the specifics, one professor told me in confidence:

> 'Often, I see these gung-ho women who start off thinking they can do everything. But when it gets to the technical camera classes they slowly get side-lined and by the time they've finished they see it as a boy's job. If they go into production (after film school) they want to produce.'

Radio, which is more modestly budgeted than film, has more women in senior roles. It's inspiring to hear that 'Sound Women' the radio industry group promoting women on the airwaves has gained support from none other than the Director General of the BBC himself for their campaign to bring 50% female voices to the airwaves by 2015. This was as a direct result of their research that found only one in five of the voices that we hear on local radio are female.

But somehow television and film seem to be far behind radio in trying to redress their own imbalances. Andrea Arnold, herself a former on-screen presence as a newscaster, commented: 'You look at men of a certain age on TV and think: "If you were a woman, you wouldn't be there.'"

A successful case of discrimination on the basis of ageism was brought against the BBC by presenter Miriam O'Reilly, after she was ousted as a presenter from *Countryfile* in 2009. Her case and the ensuing publicity may have done much to save the careers of older female presenters, guaranteeing that we continue to see more of older women on our screens. Named by the *Guardian* as one of the UK's 'Top 100 Most Inspirational Women', O'Reilly has now founded a charity called The Women's Equality Network. http://www.womensequalitynetwork.org.uk

Dr Bettany Hughes, the former presenter of ITV's *Britain's Secret Treasures* spoke out at a recent Diversify conference:

> 'I was shocked that there weren't more women with authorial voices on television and I was sickened to the heart by the reaction I got when I tried to break into that field.'

At the same conference, Syeda Irtizaali, Commissioning Editor of Entertainment at Channel 4, where half the staff are female, acknowledged that there were cultural attitudes hindering female progress:

> 'I mentor people who find it difficult to progress because of cultural attitudes but it helps if there are people at the top helping to get them there.'

Elizabeth Karlsen, Producer and co-founder of Number 9 Films and chair of WFTV, commented that childcare, male commissioners, the silencing of women's history, and unconscious bias all impede the progress of women directors in film and television.

Documentary making, which by its very nature has smaller crews and lower budgets, can be seen as more female-friendly. Projects are often shot over long periods and tell stories that would otherwise be invisible to a mainstream audience. With changing models of distribution through digital media, the success of smaller more character-driven stories may start to make an impact. New digital technology is changing the economic model of filmmaking and may actually create more of a level playing field than any government support or affirmative action.

Factual television has a well-established hierarchy – you move up from runner, to researcher to Assistant Producer to Director/Producer. In confidence, a female researcher revealed that male researchers in the production company where she was based were offered camera and lighting training as a matter of course. If you were female you had to write to the (male) Executive Producer to request such training. Equal opportunity in the workplace is supposed to be a woman's right, and yet, because many people are on short-term contracts, they are fearful of complaining in case of being labelled as a trouble-maker.

Children not allowed

As in many other industries, women of child-bearing age may be passed over for jobs due to the risk of a project being interrupted by time off for motherhood. Producers of feature films may find it harder to get insurance cover for women directors as maternity leave can seriously impact budget and scheduling. In spite of these challenges, women directors such as Gurinder Chadhra, Beeban Kidron and Andrea Arnold do combine motherhood and film directing successfully.

Beryl Richards said,

> 'I got my break in drama at the age of thirty-two; women don't usually get that many opportunities and I grabbed onto mine with both hands... Women have reservations that being a director is not compatible with being a mother.'

A recent survey of Directors UK showed that many well-qualified women drop out while younger women coming up struggle to get meetings with senior executives. Certainly any major career is not without its sacrifices: but are motherhood and directing mutually exclusive?

Head of BBC Drama, Kate Harwood (who originally combined motherhood with directing), stated that in all the recent series she has overseen she has actively encouraged shorter working days and time off at weekends so that filming is more compatible with family life.

Theatre director, Sarah Chew, quipped that she needed her own 'wife' to take care of domestic chores whilst she focused on her career. Another feature film director said anonymously that her husband enjoyed her coming home from work (after being in charge of a set with over 100 people working on it), but still expected that she cook the dinner and do the washing up. (They are now divorced.) The traditionally supportive 'stay at home' role of 'wife' is, by its very nature the role the female director is casting aside in order to create her own vision of the world. They have to allow their own uniquely 'female' voice to roar. They listen to others, yes, but ultimately on set somebody has to be in charge, and on a film set it's the director. What happens when this is a woman?

Many working women are simultaneously running a house, marriage, children, homework, housework and job in what I call a 'Jenga lifestyle'. If there is a sick child, a grandparent running late, or a partner who has an impromptu business trip then the whole of this pile of blocks can come tumbling down. The female director needs to manage her 'support crew' at home, just as she must manage the cast and crew on set. To a certain extent she is employing the same skillset and managerial qualities. To be a mother and a director is an incredible feat of co-ordination and many women have decided that it's just not for them.

Crew life can often involve long days, maybe even twenty hours on set. There's travelling, an unstable income, and often a 'boys' club' mentality amongst the crew that is challenging. Young women working on set at the start of their careers see that there are no older women mentors for them. The message is: 'If I become a mum – I'm out.'

Of course, the choice to become a parent can be said to enrich your life, career and creativity. Multi-award winning director Baroness Beeban Kidron, OBE, has created her latest film *InRealLife* inspired by her relationship with her teenagers and the spread of pornographic images. She says,

> 'One of the motivators for me making the film was that
> a friend of my daughter came round to talk to me about

a boy she had her eye on and he said she could be his girlfriend if she gave him a blow job. She's a very bright middle-class girl, now at a great university, and so on. But she was not immune to or even surprised by that sort of transaction culture."[7]

He Shoots, He Scores

There is a complex relationship as to how actors interact with directors and what is expected on and off set. It is perhaps the most intimate artistic relationship in the production. In a *Guardian* article recently (http://www.theguardian.com/commentisfree/2013/sep/16/blue-warmest-colour-terrible-acting), journalist Amy Gray stated:

> 'The dynamic, which most often involves female actors and male directors, often takes the form of svengalis and their ingénues …'

We can see examples of this in David Fincher and Rooney Mara's creepy interview with *Vogue* magazine, Roger Vadim's frequent relationships with his leading ladies, and both Harmony Korine and Vincent Gallo with Chloe Sevigny as their muse. This close relationship can often cross over into abuse but it seems to be accepted by many performers as one of the inescapable difficulties of the filmmaking process. Further examples such at Lily Tomlin being shouted at by David O. Russell on set, or Alfred Hitchcock's alleged 'onscreen torture' of Tippi Hedren on the set of *The Birds* after she refused his advances, highlight the frequent abuse of male power in the role of director. This offers opportunities for women directors to change the process, shift the dynamics, and eliminate bullying and intimidation on set.

Drama on-screen is put together in a different way from documentary and factual television. The size of the team is bigger and the way in which new voices are found is very random. There are specific talent teams in some of the biggest broadcasters and production companies who look out for rising stars in factual. It is down to the individual executive producers to hire a drama director – and they are more likely to choose someone who shares their world view and whose work they know. A very talented drama director with twenty years' experience noted:

> 'The producers hire the same teams they have worked with before. The same people get hired and re-hired and it's very hard to muscle in'.

Yet another documentary director complained:

> 'I know in docs one thing that would be *massively* helpful is if recruitment didn't happen with such short turnaround times i.e. you're approached for a job but they need you to start next week – I know several women who haven't been able to find their way back into telly because of this short-term mindset… they get offered great jobs but simply don't have time to set up the childcare and the companies won't wait for them.'

Treatment on set: 'Well, hello there, little lady'

One of the directors interviewed – who preferred to remain nameless – complained that:

> 'I was treated differently by the Director of Photography, and I can't talk about the way the First Assistant Directors bullied me on set, it's too upsetting'.

The corporate world of broadcasters and production companies is more tightly regulated, and there is a growing demand for diversity schemes and equality of employment opportunities, but the crew environment is totally unregulated. Women who enter this realm must know that they are going into challenging territory.

Successful director, Emma Reynolds explained that when she started she was exploited and paid less than her colleagues:

> 'I was touched up as a runner in a facility house. My VT operator tried to rape me. I was bullied by people both at ITN, Endemol and BBC. The only ways I avoided this was to *not* work for them again.'[8]

CELLULOID CEILING

Current state of play

In 2013, not one female director qualified for the Palme d'Or at Cannes, but there are some signs of change. At the London Film Festival there was much better female representation. Amongst the 234 feature films shown, 45 features were directed by women and of the 134 short films, 36 were made by a female director. *Variety* – the US based industry magazine announced that Gamechanger Films have started a film fund specifically for female directors. (See http://variety.com/2013/film/news/gamechanger-films-creates-film-fund-for-female-directors-1200673875)

Head of BBC Drama, Kate Harwood stated that she would be interested in setting up a directing scheme specifically for young women who are also mothers. Both legally and for many other reasons there is an acknowledgement that including women on teams, such as corporate executive boards, can actually help to generate success for the company. Just as political parties are introducing women-only short lists, there is a sense that women's voices are needed.

Beryl Richards commented,

> 'Over all my years of directing, my best experiences were when there was a balance, when it was gender neutral and I felt I was just as good as anyone else.'[9]

There are currently several film festivals around the world devoted to women's films. However many of the bigger name women directors resist being ghettoized in such formats. They want to be judged as a director first, not a woman.

Award winning director Lauren P. explained what a director needs to do:

> 'She needs to listen. If it is documentary directing she needs to listen and be sensitive. She needs to get on the level of her contributor and understand them. She needs to always, always think about narrative and story. What is this film about? What is the meaning of it? Why am I filming this shot? For me I always like to condense this into a single sentence then if I am filming 200 hours of footage I don't get lost – I always refer it back to my single

sentence – the meaning of the film. In my documentary series it was "expectation vs. reality".

She needs to plan thoroughly and then be able to adapt on the day. If you do not have a plan, shot list, a story board then you have nowhere to go from. If you have all of that and things go wrong you can quickly look at what you were hoping to achieve and then adapt – move to plan B. In the edit, she needs to forget the film she thought she was making, and find the film she has made. It could be more powerful, more dramatic, more beautiful.'

Whether they are working in film or television, directors need to have certain key qualities – 'courage', 'endurance', 'vision', and 'a very thick skin'. These traits were mentioned over and over by the countless different directors I interviewed.

Documentary director, Sophie Fiennes, stated that directors need: 'balls…sorry…boobies – perseverance and a sense of humour'.

Whether the UK film industry will ever address its own diversity issues is a matter for continued debate. We've looked at the struggles at entry level, at mid-point and even for women at the top. Phyllida Lloyd, whose film *Mamma Mia* was one of the highest grossing films in the UK, has serious concerns about the future. She stated that not only do women need to be in the top jobs but the perception of how they are perceived in modern culture needs to change.

> 'Women (in performance) are seldom welding the knife or the axe… They are never the ones crying liberty, freedom and enfranchisement. They are always somewhere back home, putting the kettle on…'[10]

With so few women directing film and television content, the world views of the female half of the British population are not being adequately represented in our media. We started this chapter celebrating the brilliant Sally Potter and we conclude with her words:

> "You can't really divorce women's struggles in the world

from women's in the cinema. As long as there's hierarchy it means that women are somehow secondary or second class or less than. That's going to be reflected in movies because films are the most powerful medium to reflect back society's view of itself".[11]

British directors must continue to champion change. Where public funding is involved there needs to be diversity monitoring to ensure that women filmmakers receive a fair proportion of this available funding. As we go to press the news is released that the BBC, in conjunction with Directors UK, plan two training days to encourage female directors to return to the industry after a break. We can only hope that this heralds a new era and a true commitment to change.

If we want a plural society with a range of perspectives, it is essential that the female voice is heard more forcefully across a range of media. We need to work with the male dominated entertainment industry to ensure that more is done at a high level to protect equality and to deliver fair employment practices and equality of opportunity to women directors at every stage of their careers. Where public funding is involved there needs to be diversity monitoring to ensure that women filmmakers receive a fair proportion of this available funding.

Author biography

After studying English and Drama at Cambridge University, Melody Bridges directed a large ambitious musical at the Edinburgh fringe. She won a place at a London drama school and after assistant directing on a number of fringe shows started working at an award winning documentary company.

She worked her way up from researcher to assistant producer and finally developed, wrote, produced and directed two television series. After winning a place on the prestigious film-directing course at New York University she enjoyed filming in the USA before moving back to England after the birth of her son. Now focusing on writing for stage, radio and tv, her first full length play, PUSH! (a comedy drama about motherhood) was given a rehearsed reading at Theatre Royal Stratford East. In addition to contributing to *Celluloid Ceiling* - through her network of contacts in New York, Los Angeles and the London television world – she writes a weekly page for a newspaper. Melody had six short plays performed in 2013 and was recently awarded the New Buds Award from New Writing South.

Contact: melody@melodybridges.com

Endnotes

1. Schneider, Steven Jay, *501 Movie Directors*, Cassell Illustrated.
2. Andrea Arnold interviewed by David Gritten. (http://www.telegraph.co.uk/culture/film/starsandstories/6093303/Andrea-Arnold-I-wish-cinema-could-be-braver.html)
3. *Succes de plume?* Female Screenwriters and Directors of UK Films, 2010–2012, BFI report.
4. Bhavnani, Dr Reena, 2007. Barriers to Diversity in Film, UK Film Council.
5. Patterns of Discrimination (1973). ACTT.
6. Beryl Richards, interviewed by the author, November 2013.
7. Baroness Beeban Kidron, interviewed in *The Guardian*. (http://www.theguardian.com/film/2013/sep/08/beeban-kidron-inreallife-interview-teenagers)
8. Emma Reynolds, interviewed by the author, November 2013.
9. Beryl Richards, interviewed by the author, November 2013.
10. Phyllida Lloyd, interviewed in *The Telegraph*. (http://www.telegraph.co.uk/culture/theatre/theatre-news/9726761/Royal-Shakespeare-Company-must-be-forced-to-employ-equal-numbers-of-male-and-female-actors.html accessed December 6th 2012)
11. Sally Potter interviewed by Melissa Silverstein, 2012, TIFF: Interview with Sally Potter Women and Hollywood.

References

Steele, D. (2013). *Succès de plume? Female Screenwriters and Directors of UK Films*, 2010–2012. (http://www.bfi.org.uk/sites/bfi.org.uk/files/downloads/bfi-report-on-female-writers-and-directors-of-uk-films-2013-11.pdf)

Bhavnani R. (2007). 'Barriers to Diversity in Film – a research review', City University and UK Film Council. (http://industry.bfi.org.uk/media/pdf/8/n/Barriers_to_Diversity_in_Film_DS_RB_20_Aug_07.pdf cached at Google, March 24th 2014)

Rogers S. (2007). 'Writing British Films – who writes British films and how they are recruited', Royal Holloway and UK Film Council. (http://industry.bfi.org.uk/media/pdf/5/r/RHUL_June_27_2007_-_Final_for_Cheltenham.pdf)

Sinclair A., Pollard E. and Wolfe H. (2006). 'Scoping Study into the Lack of Women Screenwriters in the UK', Institute of Employment Studies (IES) and UK Film Council. (http://industry.bfi.org.uk/media/pdf/4/r/0415womenscreen_-_FINAL_09.06.06.pdf cached at Google, March 24th 2014)

Smith S. L. et al, (2013). 'Gender Inequality in 500 Popular Films: Examining On-Screen Portrayals and Behind-the Scenes Employment Patterns in Motion Pictures Released between 2007–2012', Annenberg School for Communication and Journalism, University of Southern California. (http://annenberg.usc.edu/News%20and%20Events/News/~/media/PDFs/Smith_GenderInequality500Films.ashx)

22. Coming Forth (Day) by Day:

Arab Female Filmmakers Making Strides

Ronan Doyle

The results of November 2013's '100 Greatest Arab Films' poll, mounted by the Dubai Film Festival in celebration of its tenth anniversary and taken from 475 individual critics' ballots, succeeds entirely in its presentation of the scope of Arab film history, if not precisely for the reasons intended. The mere seven women-directed films on the list attest the limited opportunities historically afforded Arab female filmmakers[1], but also – perhaps more importantly – the fact that six of those seven have seen release since 2007 is indicative of changing fortunes for the region's women in cinema. The last decade has seen the international festival success of several such directors, often heralded by a slew of media coverage touting them the 'first' female filmmaker from their respective countries. This international acclaim and newfound awareness, of course growing exponentially in the wake of the Arab Spring, offers the optimum opportunity to examine the reasons for the erstwhile ignorance, and how they've fallen to give way to a bright new future for the region's female filmmakers.

That Moufida Tlatli's *The Silences of the Palaces*, released in 1994, is the only non-recent film of the seven, is as much indicative of the preservation difficulties faced by Arab nations as it is of a modern surge in female filmmakers. Afforded little attention since colonial times, the region's cinema culture has lacked the resources necessary to preserve its own history, relying on outside aid from preservationists the like of Martin Scorsese with his

World Cinema Foundation to commit the earliest works to the collective global canon. Historical strife has hardly helped: the Palestine Liberation Organisation's Film Foundation had its archive infamously lost to the ages when they were driven from Beirut in 1982. Arab film history as a whole has been victim to setbacks innumerable over the years, leaving us scrabbling to establish what few certain forebears we can. Even in Egypt – often referred to as 'Hollywood on the Nile', and so dominant a local cinematic presence that its films comprise almost exactly half the Dubai poll – archival records are exceedingly poor, leaving us only anecdotal evidence of early stars like Aziza Amir, Bahiga Hafez, and Fatma Rushdi helming their own vehicles in the 1930s. Such stories emphasise the Hollywood parallels of the Egyptian industry, which extend to an entrenched sexism that continues almost as a matter of tradition. Indeed, it's arguably the absence of an established industry in the majority of Arab nations that has allowed female directors equal opportunity, at least relatively speaking, historically: their barriers have primarily been cultural and sociological, rather than industrial.

The prevailing Western image of the veiled woman as emblematic of Islam, coupled with media reports focused on certain draconian restrictions such as Saudi Arabia's law against female drivers, has perhaps contributed to a disproportionate amount of blame attributed to religion in keeping Arab women from behind the camera. Certainly it constitutes a major factor: cinema itself, of course, initially saw opposition from Islam, a religion traditionally opposed to the visual portrayal of beings with souls; taken together with its patriarchal structure, it's easy to appreciate how and why Muslim women might thus be viewed as doubly hampered in filmmaking careers. Yet more immediate are those reasons observed the world over: the universal restrictions imposed on women by the demands of the domestic role and the perceived physicality required for work in the film industry. So while Islamic conservatism has inarguably had a significant impact, it's telling that even the comparably liberal Maghreb – where the influence of French culture in Tunisia, for instance, saw women granted full rights shortly after independence in 1956

– saw its first female filmmakers emerge only in the 1970s.

Such figures were documentarians, non-fiction filmmaking being viewed as a form of journalism rather than an artistic endeavour, and thus an acceptable profession for a woman to pursue. The finest used the medium to explore prominent social issues: Heiny Srour of Lebanon became the first Arab woman director to have a film play at the Cannes Film Festival in 1974 with *The Hour of Liberation Has Arrived*, an analysis of the role of women fighters in the Dhofar Rebellion; Algerian author Assia Djebar blended fictional aspects with her two late-70s documentaries – the first of which, *The Nouba of the Women of Mount Chenoua*, won the FIPRESCI prize at the 1979 Venice Film Festival – addressing the role of women in the war of independence; Selma Baccar, meanwhile, made the controversial *Fatma 75* about the historical state of women's rights in Tunisia, which struggled to be shown uncut for decades afterward.

The home media-fuelled decline of cinema audiences throughout the 80s and 90s across the Arab world saw the industries essentially decimated, Algeria in particular falling from a peak of four hundred theatres to just ten by the start of the new millennium, forcing the privitisation of the industry in 1993 and the shutting down of the Algerian Institute of Art and Film. With few such training and educational opportunities available at all outside of Lebanon and Egypt, let alone to women, these decades saw little growth in the numbers of female filmmakers. What few features came from women through the 80s and 90s tended to be from those who managed to work their way up through the business, such as successful editor Tlatli, assistant director (to directors as noted as Roman Polanski and Franco Zeffirelli) Nadia El-Fani, or the Moroccan screenwriter Farida Benlyazid.

That these figures should stand out as so exceptional is indicative of the anomalies they were, unlikely achievers in a system that seemed intent on denying them the opportunities they nonetheless forged for themselves. So why, given the historic rarity of women directors in Arab cinema, are we seeing such significant change now? The reasons are many, aided additionally by the fortuitous coincidence of their simultaneous arrival.

CELLULOID CEILING

Chief among these is, simply, the growth of cinema itself: digital technology's democratisation of movie-making has seen the sudden arrival of a new wave of filmmakers both male and female, allowing near-universal access to the means of production previously withheld from the great majority. This is particularly true in the Gulf states, the majority of which – courtesy of the massive influence of the Egyptian industry, which remains the dominant force over indigenous productions – have only in recent years seen their first features.

Recent progress in the field of gender equality, of course, has provided perhaps the most significant factor in expanding the opportunities afforded these new talents. Most visibly in Morocco, which revised its Mudawana 'family code' in 2004 to improve women's rights, even the most conservative of Arab states have made moves toward legal equality. The efforts of women in high places have helped enormously: the Doha Film Institute, which splits its funding evenly between men and women, was founded by Sheikha Al-Mayassa bint Hamad bin Khalifa Al-Thani; Kuwait's Sheikha Al-Zain Sabah Al-Naser Al-Sabah, meanwhile, has founded the Eagle Vision Media Group with intentions of offering funding to women who wish to get their start in filmmaking after her family were reluctant to support her own efforts. And in Saudi Arabia in 2013, courtesy of the support of women's rights advocate Prince Alwaleed bin Talai, the kingdom's first ever feature – let alone first directed by a woman – was *Wadjda*.

That film, directed by Haifaa Al-Mansour, is as much indicative of Western media's monumental new interest in the Arab World in the wake of the ongoing uprisings as anything else. Fittingly, given its eponymous heroine whose desire is only to ride her bicycle in public – a banned activity in the country – the film has become an extraordinary emblem in the recognition of and revolution against the second-class standing of women in this society. Indeed, it's as much because of those conditions and the significant achievement the film marks in spite of them as its affecting content that *Wadjda* came to be the enormous success was; in a country where a woman cannot cross the border without having a male guardian alerted, Al-Mansour's is a film of enormous importance in how it's managed to make women's voices heard.

But this, of course, is far from the only example of how Arab women are taking matters into their own hands and using cinema to ensure they are listened to. Khadija Al-Salami's aptly-titled *The Scream* (2012), set in the midst of the 2011 protests and following the women whose presence on the streets evidences their role in the revolution,[2] is only the latest of a series of documentaries from the Yemeni director to interrogate the country's treatment of women including the acclaimed short *A Stranger in Her Own City* (2005), which bears witness to a barrage of threats and insults thrown at a teenage girl whose refusal to don a veil jars with particularly conservative local sentiment. In Syria, meanwhile, Diana El Jeiroudi – whose debut documentary short *The Pot* (2005) saw women discussing pregnancy and the female body – has similarly taken on the idea of the veil with her feature documentary *Dolls* (2007), inspired by the marketing of veiled Barbies.

The difficulty of life as a woman in a faltering society of men is a concern of Egyptian Hala Lotfy's *Coming Forth By Day* (2012), in which the bed-ridden patriarch for whom the mother and daughter protagonists care might easily be seen as a symbol for the collapsing order. Hers is a country cautious of such allegory: Inas El-Degheidy, a rare success who has worked since the 80s, had her script for *The Silence* scrutinised by censors who insisted its incestuous father figure be portrayed as mentally ill and by no means representative. But such sensitive censorship has showed signs of waning in Mubarak's wake: Nadine Khan, a well-known assistant director on films the like of *Transformers: Revenge of the Fallen* (2009), had her oft-rejected script *Chaos, Disorder* (2012) at last accepted after his removal.

Much as they may be working to right the balance of female representation in Arab cinema, the women directors of the region have tackled a striking array of ideas from all social spheres, expanding far beyond what might dismissively be termed 'women's issues'. Take for instance the Emirati Shaikha Awad Al

Ayali, who progressed from a PSA on domestic violence to a pair of documentaries on her country's hip-hop scene entitled *Heat the Beat* (2008/2010). And she's not alone either in intermingling such ideas: in Palestine, Jacqueline Reem Salloum followed up her documentary *Slingshot Hip Hop* (2008) with a music video decrying violence against women. Arab women have proved themselves to be every bit as diverse in their subject matter as their male counterparts: indeed Sandra Nashaat's comedy capers *Thieves in KG2* (2002) and *Thieves in Thailand* (2003) have become some of the most successful Egyptian blockbusters of recent years. Nadine Labaki, meanwhile, while of course working on a considerably more independent scale than Nashaat, has melded a populist narrative style with subtle social critique, a blend that gives her the unique honour of being the only female director with more than a single feature on the Dubai poll. *Caramel* (2007) and *Where Do We Go Now?* (2011) address issues of gender and religion within Lebanese society. While not without transgressive elements, (*Caramel* is notable for its inclusion of lesbian characters) the film has earned commercial as well as critical acclaim, breaking native box office records.

A fascinating phenomenon that should not go ignored in any overview of Arab women directors is the proliferation of first and second generation émigrés returning to explore the issues of their homeland. Be they from women who fled in times of uncertainty or foreign-born filmmakers keen to discover themselves in their ancestral home, films like Iraqi Maysoon Pachachi's ironically yet appropriately-titled *Return to the Land of Wonders* (2004) bring a literal aspect to the idea of rediscovering these nations via their new cinema. Perhaps the most well-known of these filmmakers is Cannes- and Sundance-fêted Cherien Dabis, whose twin tales of Palestinian women coming to the US and Americans moving to the Arab World in *Amreeka* (2008) and *May in the Summer* (2013) have explored the very cross-cultural phenomenon she herself embodies. It's a concern similarly tackled in *Salt of This Sea* (2008), the feature debut of acclaimed director Annemarie Jacir, whose self-reflexive *Like Twenty Impossibles* (2003) was the first Palestinian rt screened at Cannes, and whose subsequent features – *Salt of*

This Sea and *When I Saw You* (2012) – have both been Palestine's submission to the respective years' Academy Awards.

As greater numbers of Arab female filmmakers attain international success amidst a culture that – despite the many moves still yet to be made – grows more supportive of these women and the issues they eye, the audience for these voices can only grow. And with them the opportunities too: where the aforementioned names were trained in Europe or America, if at all, the comparably considerable in-region educational opportunities afforded young filmmakers now ensures – or at least makes more likely – that talent remains within the area. While organisations like the Palestinian Women's Affairs Centre have offered training since as far back as 1994, the new proliferation of university courses in such institutions as Dubai Women's College and the University of Qatar is producing an unprecedented amount of eager talent with the kind of formal know-how their forebears where lucky to be able to learn on the fly. And it's a talent that's being increasingly embraced: in June 2013 Oman hosted its first Extraordinary Women Meet, touting a number of prominent female citizens, among them filmmaker Laila Habib Abdullah al Hamdoon.

So the future seems bright, for all its challenges: in a region where female filmmakers were once almost singular exceptions, women in cinema are thriving and forging the way for the generations to come in a manner that's fast becoming an international example. At the 2010 Gulf Film Festival over half of the student shorts screened were directed by women. Some 80% of the University of Qatar's media students are female. The ongoing efforts, only increasing in the wake of the Arab Spring, to ensure equality for women across all spheres of society has seen the rise to prominence of the same figures who once lamented the lack thereof. Nearly four decades after chronicling the story of women's rights in her country, Baccar was appointed to Tunisia's new constitutional assembly. And then there is Tlatli, whose appointment in 2011 as Tunisia's Minister of Culture, provides evidence of exactly how valuable the contribution she and her contemporaries have made to their society, is. And international recognition for these filmmakers only continues to grow: the 86th Academy Awards in 2014 will include not just the first Oscar-nominated Arab woman director, but the second too, with Yemeni Sara Ishaq's documentary short *Karama Has No Walls* (2012) competing alongside Egyptian Jehane Noujaim's feature documentary *The Square* (2013). It's not solely for their Arab Spring subject matter that these films will be recalled as revolutionary.

Author biography

Ronan Doyle is an Irish freelance film critic and programmer who has contributed to Indiewire, Film Ireland, and FRED Film Radio, as well as Next Projection, where he is senior editor. He is fuelled by tea and has heard of sleep, but finds the idea frightfully silly. He can be found on Twitter at @baronronan.

Contact: ronan@nextprojection.com

Endnotes

1. No more so, it should be noted, than their American counterparts; the AFI's own equivalent list features not a single female helmer.
2. In Algeria, Yamina Bachir-Chouikh's *Yesterday, Today and Tomorrow* told much the same story.

23. In Their Own Words:

Interviews with Contemporary Women Directors from the Middle East

Annemarie Jacir in her own words

Annemarie Jacir is a Palestinian filmmaker and poet. She was named one of *Filmmaker* magazine's 'Twenty-five New Faces of Independent Cinema in 2004' after her short film, *Like Twenty Impossibles* (*2003*), went on to be a Student Academy Awards Finalist. In 2007, Jacir shot the first feature film by a Palestinian woman director, *Salt of This Sea*, which premiered in Cannes. Her most recent film *When I Saw You* opened at Toronto International Film Festival (2012). She is chief curator and founder of the ground-breaking 'Dreams of a Nation' Palestinian cinema project, dedicated to the promotion of Palestinian cinema. In 2003, she organised and curated the largest travelling film festival in Palestine, which included the screening of archival Palestinian films from Revolution Cinema, screening for the first time on Palestinian soil.

Filmography

2012 *When I Saw You*
2008 *Salt of This Sea*
2006 *Palestine, Summer* (Short)
2006 *An Explanation: And Then Burn the Ashes* (Short)
2005 *Quelques miettes pour les oiseaux* (Short)
2004 *Until When* (Feature Documentary)
2003 *Like Twenty Impossibles* (Short)
2001 *The Satellite Shooters* (Short)

CELLULOID CEILING

Annemarie Jacir: My influences have mostly been in literature and poetry. I was a Literature major. My grandfather was a writer. It's where I started and where I always return. I am particularly influenced by our poets, from Hafez to Darwish, to Adonis and and also Neruda, Belli, and so many others. I loved how it all came together – how poetry, theatre, photography, storytelling and music… all the things I love could come together in one form. That was the original draw to cinema and still is.

I believe independent cinema should be independent, on all levels. So I am a filmmaker who is very careful about who I take money from, and what conditions may be tied to it, and what is the agenda behind any organisation I work with. It's why I choose to make a film for only one quarter of the necessary budget rather than the full budget. It's not ideal for the production, but I prefer to work that way rather than be involved or used for people's political agendas. With Palestinian art, unfortunately it's often the case, so artists need to always be aware. I do that not because I believe filmmaking is a political statement but because filmmakers and artists are used politically.

I am very proud that the production of *When I Saw You* was entirely funded by Palestinians and every single one of the producers involved is Palestinian. It's what I have been working towards for years and am so delighted that it actually worked. I believe we have to look to our own community for support and not rely on European sources of funding only. If these films are made by us, and made for us, then why shouldn't we be the ones who also support them? The funding landscape has changed drastically in the last few years. When I made *Salt of This Sea*, it was a very different situation, and in fact, not one Arab organisation supported the film. It took me six years to find the funds. For *When I Saw You*, the situation was different and many Arab organisations were involved, including the Arab film festivals, which now support Arab cinema. And thanks to crowd-funding being made more 'official' such as with Aflamnah, it also helps get the word out. That being said, I have been 'crowd funding' all my films for the past fifteen years. I have never felt my gender was an issue on the ground, or rather on set.

The places where I do feel gender affects my work is when it comes to financing as well as in festivals. But specifically from organisations and institutions which seem to play a big role in questioning and taking female directors as equals. It's a fact that women all over the world have a harder time financing their films. And are also underrepresented in film festivals around the world, excluding the Arab world and Iran where we see quite a large representation from women directors. As far as my own choices go as a writer and director, I have tried never to let any issues around gender affect my work.

Hala Lotfy in her own words:

Hala Lotfy is an Egyptian filmmaker and producer. Born in Cairo in 1973, Lotfy studied economics and political science at Cairo University, then filmmaking at the Cairo Film Institute. Her first feature film, *Coming Forth By Day* has been recognised through awards including the Fipresci Award for best film at the Abu Dhabi Film Festival and the prestigious Katrin Cartlidge Foundation Award, given to a new cinematic voice reflecting integrity of spirit in independent film. She is committed to nurturing a new independent film industry in Egypt.

> 'Cinema is more than ready for an exciting new female auteur from the Arab world, and, on the basis of her long-gestating debut *Coming Forth By Day* (Al-Khoroug Lel-Nahar), Egyptian thirty-nine-year-old writer-director Hala Lotfy might well be it.' *The Hollywood Reporter*

Filmography

2012 *Coming forth by day* (feature film)
2005 *Feeling Cold* (Short documentary)
2001 *Images of water and earth* (Short documentary)
2000 *Greeting Pattern* (Short documentary)
1999 *Four Scenes* (Short documentary)
1999 *No waiting please* (Short fiction)
1998 *A Rehearsal* (Short documentary)
1998 *That beautiful voice* (Short fiction)

CELLULOID CEILING

Hala Lotfy: I love films and wrote film reviews for one year in a weekly newspaper in Egypt, but I was so hard to please and hated most of the Egyptian films I wrote about. Then I thought that it's not positive enough to write that the films we produce are not to my taste, so I studied filmmaking in the Cairo Film Institute. My filmic influence is not only one director... Tarkovsky, Bela Tarr and Shady Abdel Salam are my favorites though.

I used to make documentaries, and I loved making documentaries because you don't do tricks, you don't use music, you don't cut too much. I can't work with professional actors because they are full of tricks, and they don't get involved in a real way in what they do in front of the camera. *Coming Forth By Day* started as a documentary – it was my father who was ill, and I was so helpless... I wanted to express my feeling of despair, but I didn't dare to shoot my father, and I had to turn it into a fiction film because it was easier.

We started shooting in 2010, stopped after two weeks because we didn't have enough money, then resumed in May 2011, with big hopes just after the revolution.

We are trying our best to change the miserable situation of independent filmmaking in Egypt. Only last week, we finally managed to register the new syndicate, we will knock on every and each door trying to do some further movement towards giving more space for new voices in the Egyptian independent scene. We are engaging in many projects aiming to change our situation, for instance, we are establishing a residency program for filmmakers in four different places outside Cairo, as we don't have any in Egypt, and we find it essential to secure such a platform to free the newcomers of their financial needs in the most crucial time/stage in the filmmaking process.

We are building a network of Egyptian producers to manage distributing our films, and we are initiating small film labs/schools in the remote villages in Egypt to build audience and give a voice to deprived artists around the country... we've fundraised and we now can buy the equipment for these facilities and start with three film schools in Asyout (Upper Egypt), El Wadi El-Gedid (Western desert) and Luxor.

Haifaa al-Mansour in her own words:

Born in 1974, Saudi filmmaker Haifaa al-Mansour studied comparative literature at the American University in Cairo, and later went to film school in Australia. Her first feature-length film, *Wadjda*, has received worldwide acclaim, endless awards and theatrical releases around the world. It was selected as the Saudi Arabian entry for the Best Foreign Language Film at the 86th Academy Awards.

Filmography

    2012 *Wadjda* (Feature)
    2005 *Women Without Shadows* (Documentary)

Haifaa al-Mansour: Film is a great medium to present new ideas and perspectives, as it is a universally accessible medium. I think it is a very useful tool in shifting the tone of a political conversation. In Saudi Arabia, the act of filmmaking in and of itself is a political act, as film is essentially illegal in the Kingdom. For sure the lack of a film industry was the greatest barrier to getting *Wadjda* made. Without the basic infrastructure of a film industry, every aspect of the film's development presented challenges. There had been previous attempts at films from Saudi Arabia, but they were filmed outside of the Kingdom and all of the principle cast and crew were non-Saudis. I knew I would have to look for international partners who could assist with both the physical infrastructure of the filmmaking process and the know-how to help me develop my film. I started with international writing and script labs to develop the script (Script Station, Berlin International Film Festival, Berlinale / RAWI Sundance Writer's Lab, Jordan / Dubai Film Connection, Dubai International Film Festival / Atlanta Screenwriters Lab, Atlanta International Film Festival / Torino Film Lab, Italy). I then partnered with Razor Film in Germany because they had been involved in two very successful films from the region (*Paradise Now* and *Waltz with Bashir*). By building up a German-Saudi co-production we were able to tap into so much expertise and equipment from Europe, while maintaining the authenticity of the film as a Saudi product.

I think the European partners were more supportive of my insistence on shooting inside of Saudi Arabia than most of our local partners – probably because the local partners were more aware of the risks involved!

A big problem came in casting the female characters, since we can't have open casting calls in Saudi because of the sensitivities relating to women acting. In Saudi Arabia, we don't have casting agencies and we always have to depend on word of mouth, so finding them was not easy. We had to rely on the small production companies that recruited kids for cultural fairs. We had found a lot of great potential actresses, but their families would ultimately get cold feet and decide that they couldn't let their daughters act in a film. It was really sad to see so many beautiful, talented young girls with so much potential being denied the opportunity to act. But luckily Waad [Mohammed, Wadjda's eponymous lead actress] came in at the last possible moment, about one week before principal shooting, wearing jeans and an 80s style jacket. She was listening to Justin Bieber and she did not speak English, but she understood Justin Bieber and his songs, so she was a great example of modern youth culture.

My gender wasn't really an issue until we actually started filming. Filming in Riyadh was quite a challenge, and would be for a director of either gender. People aren't used to having cameras around so we were especially cautious, even though we had permission to shoot publicly. For the outdoor scenes we knew we were going to face a lot of difficulties, from conservative bystanders to sandstorms to nervous partners, so we had to be ready to work with what we had on any given day. We used a handheld camera sometimes to save time and give the actors freedom with their movements. I occasionally had to direct from a protected spot, like a van, so people wouldn't see me (a woman) interacting publicly with the crew (men).

I think it is always difficult for women in positions of power to direct men and have to deal with the negative reactions that they get from it. I think it was certainly a shock for a lot of the Saudi men on our crew to take directions from me! I try not to focus on the challenges and look for ways where I can instead build up my own place within the system. In a lot of ways being a woman helped me get this film made, as Western audiences are very eager to hear from female voices from this region. The fact that I was a woman, in fact the first female director from Saudi Arabia, and that I was making a film that focuses on women's issues helped me gain a lot of traction with the project at its early stages.

Censorship is the biggest obstacle for artists in the Gulf region. Because of censorship, and just social pressure in general, creative people of both genders in the Kingdom face all kinds of pressure. Aside from the very real threat of criminal consequences to self-expression, a lot of artists practice self-censorship, and try to play it safe. But making any type of art requires putting out an opinion and a perspective on how you see the world. Even the most basic art forms somehow talk about the world and a person's search for a place within it. I hope that my film makes the medium itself less threatening to people who think it is intrinsically evil or misleading, and I hope it gives Saudis pride to see themselves and their world represented on the big screen.

I think Western audiences have ideas and concepts about women in Saudi but don't know much about Saudi women and the actual ways they live and things they care about. It is hard to be a woman in Saudi Arabia, of course, but through my films I want to show the world how strong the women are in my country. I'm not sure if there are misconceptions, but I don't think people realise how tough Saudi women are. They are brash and sassy and fiery, and the new generation has a whole new outlook and window to the world. They are empowered and motivated to improve their status within the society in ways my generation could never have imagined. They are survivors and they will change the world.

Nujoom Alghanem in her own words:

Nujoom Alghanem is a poet and a multi-award-winning film director from the United Arab Emirates (UAE), who is widely acknowledged as one of the most significant Emirati filmmakers. Born 1962 in Dubai and educated in Australia and the USA, Nujoom came to filmmaking after working as a journalist for a decade.

CELLULOID CEILING

Filmography

2013 *Red Blue Yellow* (Feature documentary)
2011 *Amal* (Feature documentary)
2011 *Salma's Dinner* (Short fiction)
2010 *Hamama* (Feature documentary)
2008 *Al Mureed* (Documentary)
1999 *Between Two Banks* (Short documentary)
1997 *Ice-cream* (Short fiction)
1997 *The Park* (Short fiction)

Nujoom Alghanem: From a very young age, art and literature were essential to me. The house in which I was raised, my grandfather's, was rich with respect for culture, including literature, photography, and art. We had a tradition: every Eid holiday we would go to the cinema. At the time, they were primarily Egyptian or Indian films. I discovered the emotional impact that films could have on me. It was like magic. Cinema introduced me to how one can tell a story with a visual impact that is full of feelings.

Although I have made four films about women, I do not consider it to be my niche. That said, I do believe that presenting women, particularly Emirati and Khaleeji women, is extremely important. It may indeed be our role as Khaleeji women to work on these types of films because, as we share similar stories and culture, our representations will be more authentic. What is important to me, outside of gender or nationality, is the human story of the individual.

Through my experiences, I have discovered an important reality: that women here are oftentimes more daring, open, and accepting in front of the camera than men are. The women in my films have been willing to share their lives and open their homes to my camera. The men whom I have filmed, on the other hand, have shown greater reluctance to allow me into their lives. I am often restricted to filming in their living rooms, unable to film their wives or children. Unfortunately, when these films travel outside of the Arab world, it is difficult for international audiences to recognise the amount of audacity and courage coming from these women when they allow me into their homes and share with me their stories, the line that it crosses within our social landscape. And this is true particularly for documentary film, which requires real people.

We have colleges and universities in this region that do teach media and you'll find that, within these programs, a greater number of the students are women. But we need to see how many professional feature length films, not student films, have been produced by female filmmakers.

Personally, I have never made my gender an issue or a barrier to my career or work. I don't see it in this way at all. I follow the same paths for opportunities that are available to both men and women. I think that the opportunities themselves, for both genders, are what are still limited. To accommodate three festivals in this country, I think that we require more grants and fund providers not only locally but also regionally and internationally through co-production agreements.

Sara Ishaq in her own words:

Sara Ishaq is a Yemeni-Scottish filmmaker. She was born in Edinburgh in 1982 and grew up in Sana'a until the age of eighteen when she moved back to pursue her education in Humanities and Social Sciences, followed by an MFA in film directing. Her debut award-winning documentary film *Karama has no Walls* (2012) was later nominated for the BAFTA Scotland New Talents, One World Media awards and recently for an Oscar. In 2013, she completed her first feature film *The Mulberry House* which deals with her relationship with her Yemeni family against the backdrop of the country's 2011 revolution.

Filmography

2013 *The Mulberry House* (Feature Documentary)
2012 *Karama Has No Walls* (Short Documentary)
2012 *Marie My Girl* (Short Drama)
Television credits:
2011 *Yemen Uprising* for Newsnight & Our World Episodes. Role: Assistant Director / Camera Operator
2013 *Yemeni Child Prisoners On Death Row* for Channel 4 – Unreported World. Role: local producer

CELLULOID CEILING

Sara Ishaq: I got into filmmaking after working on a BBC documentary in Yemen and Egypt straight out of University. Documentary filmmaking appealed to my journalistic and curious (yet fleeting) nature – by making films, I could explore one subject closely for a period of time, and then move on to a completely different subject, work with a new group of people and in most cases, move to a different country too. For a while, I pondered studying Investigative Journalism but felt I would miss out on the creative/artistic process of making a film and did not feel as passionate about writing as I did with filming. It also felt like the most powerful medium through which to tell stories, real and fictional, to a wider audience, and so I took a diploma course, then bought a camera, travelled and filmed in Palestine in 2009, then returned to Scotland in 2010 to do my an MFA in film directing."

To be a female filmmaker in Yemen means putting up with feeling like an outcast a lot of the time, particularly while in the thick of working, and quite often, feeling under threat by skeptics and constantly surveyed and monitored by the authorities. Along with trying to break ground in the field, it's a question of also trying to break ground with social and cultural norms and contend with restrictions imposed by family. Considering that there are few established independent filmmakers in Yemen, let alone female filmmakers, it can sometimes be a solitary profession, particularly if you do not have credibility. It took me a few years to gain this credibility (socially and privately) and once that was accomplished, I was astounded by how much support, respect and space I was given by all.

I think the Arab revolutions made way for the emergence of all sorts of talent. Artists could create and be heard, through social media and on the ground. During my time in Yemen throughout 2011–2012, I came across more emerging talent than I had my entire life spent in Yemen. Hopefully, the Academy Award nomination will encourage many more aspiring filmmakers to follow through with their ideas and realise that Yemen is a treasure trove containing endless incredible stories waiting to be told.

Interviewer/Author biography

Elhum Shakerifar is an independent film producer and Program Manager of UK based Birds Eye View Film Festival, which showcases and explores the outstanding contribution of international women film practitioners to cinema. Elhum is a research fellow at Goldsmiths, University of London, and lectures at Freie Universitaet Berlin.

Contact: elhum@birds-eye-view.co.uk

24. Voices of Israeli Women Filmmakers

Amy Kronish

Based on a previous article which appeared on the Jewish Women's Archive website.

An analysis of the history and contemporary trends of Israeli cinema undeniably shows that quality filmmaking has developed along unique thematic and stylistic lines. These characteristics represent the beginnings of a national filmmaking expression, one which has developed in the wake of the new Israeli Jewish identity. As seen through the cinema, this identity is the sum of many parts – the history, the complexity of the political and social issues, the years of tension, and the character of the people of Israel. It is a mixture of the ideal and the real, the political and the personal, war and the search for peace, the universal and the particular. It is also about the preservation of Jewish tradition and culture, and conversely a longing to be ordinary, to be like everyone else. Israeli filmmaking has become a national cultural expression and Israeli film directors, both male and female, are major contributors to that expression.

Women filmmakers who have made a significant contribution to Israeli film, in both the narrative and documentary film genres, have added a particularly feminist perspective to Israeli filmmaking. The films which may be included under the rubric of 'feminist perspective' comprise films directed by women and/or films scripted by women, as well as adaptations based on works by female authors. In contrast to Israeli films made by men which deal with political and military issues, issues of national identity, ethnic situations and stereotypes, the complex narrative films made by women deal with relationships and family issues and include sensitive portrayals of human beings grappling with personal issues. The first feature film directed by a woman in Israel, albeit not an Israeli woman, Ellidah Geyrah's *Before Tomorrow* (1969), was also the first to deal with male-female relationships in a universal context. Since that time, many women have joined the ranks of filmmakers in Israel.

Autobiographical filmmaking

Actress, director and scriptwriter Michal Bat-Adam, the most prolific woman filmmaker in Israel, made nine full-length narrative films between 1979 and 2003. They are intimate portrayals of women which deal with complex relationships, unique friendships, passionate loves, conflicts and tensions, marriage and coming-of-age. All are heavily laden with autobiographical elements, and all are strong and sensitive.

Bat Adam's first film, *Moments* (1979), which received much critical acclaim, expresses emotions and feelings cinematically rather than through the use of dialogue. Seen in flashback, the story is about a pensive young writer (played by Bat-Adam), who meets a French tourist on the train from Tel Aviv to Jerusalem. This chance meeting between two women develops into a complex, intense relationship expressed without physical contact but certainly with lesbian overtones.

Her second feature, *A Thin Line* (1980), is a psychological study of a woman with emotional problems. Bat-Adam's mother was emotionally ill and, as a young child, Bat-Adam often found herself caring for her mother. This is reflected in the film, which focuses on a mother's dependency on her young daughter, who struggles to sustain her in times of need. The film is similar to *Moments* in its emphasis on mood, feelings and facial expressions. As a child, Bat-Adam was sent to a kibbutz boarding school because her mother was unable to care for her. This experience is reflected in her next film, *Boy Meets Girl* (1983), in which Bat-Adam tells the story of a fourth-grade city girl who goes to study at a kibbutz where she finds herself the outsider in a closed society. The film is about conflicts and friendships between girls and boys at this age.

Bat-Adam directed two literary adaptations – *The Lover* (1986), based on the book by A. B. Yehoshua, and *A Thousand and One Wives* (1989), based on the novel by Dan Benaya Serri. The first is a film about unfulfilled love, family tensions and relations between Jews and Arabs within Israeli society, all against the background of the period of the 1973 Yom Kippur War. Bat-Adam stars as Asia, a middle-aged schoolteacher, married to Adam, a garage mechanic. Yehoshua's story is a literary commentary and middle-aged Asia symbolises a slumbering Israeli society, searching for fulfilment, caught unawares by the perils of the Yom Kippur War. In a completely different style, *A Thousand and One Wives* is a period piece, a delicate tale of superstition, naiveté and jealousy, set in the Bukharan quarter of Jerusalem at the end of the 19th century.

In addition to *The Lover*, Bat-Adam directed another political commentary, *The Deserter's Wife* (1992). This is the story of a French concert pianist who moves to Israel with her new husband during the period of the first intifada (Palestinian uprising). Her husband returns from his military reserve service unable to speak or respond to his environment. His incapacity to communicate must be interpreted as a direct result of his frustrations and powerlessness at not being able to oppose the Occupation of the West Bank. While providing a unique perspective on how the wife copes with her husband's incapacity to function, the film also conveys how Israeli society copes with issues of war.

In her later films – *Aya, An Imagined Autobiography* (1994), *Love at Second Sight* (1998) and *Life is Life* (2003) – Bat Adam mixes the contemporary period with memories of the past. *Aya, An Imagined Autobiography* is a touching personal document about relationships between mother and daughter and the hardships of young girls growing up. Bat-Adam herself has stated that one must look at this autobiographical film as a reflection of the emotional memory of the filmmaker, the accumulation of little fantasies and important things that occur in one's mind, which are the elements that make up the 'real' or 'imagined' autobiography. *Love at Second Sight* is a film which portrays a woman who has the courage to act upon her gut emotions. Nina is a photo-journalist who discovers, in one of her photos, the image of a man who stirs her curiosity. As she sets out to find this man, about whom she knows nothing, she becomes obsessed with him and imagines him as her destiny. Also in her film *Life is Life,* Bat-Adam blurs the lines between reality and fantasy. This is a film about love and the meaning of life. The film includes a wonderful cameo appearance by filmmaker Moshe Mizrachi (Bat-Adam's life partner) and a pointed look at two aging ladies – one is losing her hold on her son, the other is losing her grasp on reality.

Women's issues in contemporary society

As further narrative films about women in Israel are being produced, the images are changing. Women on the screen are no longer appearing against the backdrop of stories about men, as they once were; they are no longer seen as war widows, prostitutes or ethnic stereotypes. The Israeli women portrayed are becoming 'normal' and are appearing in roles with depth and sensitivity which reflect the new individualism of the 1990s.

The best example of this new individualism and professionalism can be seen in the adaptation of Irit Linur's bestselling novel, *The Song of the Siren* (directed by Eytan Fox, 1994). Extraordinarily popular with Israeli audiences, the film, a romantic and quirky comedy, rich in texture, colour and humour, is set against the stress and absurdity of the Gulf War of 1991. The film, whose title refers to the air-raid sirens which sounded almost every night during the six weeks of the war, is the story of an assertive professional woman who experiences emotional growth and genuine romance. At the same time, the film is critical of the superficial lifestyle of trendy Tel Aviv urban society.

The new professional woman is also seen in another literary adaptation, *Blind Man's Bluff* (directed by Aner Preminger, 1993). Based on a book by Lily Perry Amitai, the film portrays the story of a young concert pianist, a single woman and second-generation Holocaust survivor. The narrative follows her as she acquires independence and learns to live according to her own dreams for herself rather than according to the expectations and manipulative demands of her mother. Another film which deals with a mother-daughter relationship is Mira Recanati's *A Thousand*

Little Kisses (1981), which portrays the complexities and jealousies in mother-daughter relationships and focuses specifically on a stormy period following surprising discoveries after the death of the father.

Upon his death, Alma is inexplicably drawn into his past and discovers that her father had not only had a long term secret affair, but also had a child by the other woman. Torn between her father's two lives, Alma becomes passionately involved with the other woman's son. Her newly widowed mother, who already feels betrayed by her husband's infidelity and robbed of her own memories, now feels even more betrayed by the daughter who has seemingly abandoned her for the father's other family. After a claustrophobic sequence in which the mother suffers a month-long siege of hiding from reality and coming to terms with her own subjugated needs and desires, she overcomes her feelings of betrayal, despite the pain and suffering that she has endured.

Three other films which deal with the single woman trying to assert herself in the milieu of urban life are *Circles* (1980), *Tel Aviv Stories* (1992) and *Noodle* (2007). Idit Shechori's study, *Circles*, is about life in the modern Israeli urban centre of Tel Aviv. Four women spend a Friday evening together – one is a swinger who knows everyone and seems to sleep with just about everyone she knows; one is a depressed divorcée; one is a young and innocent girl who grew up in a small town and has just completed her military service; and the fourth is a lesbian. The drama follows their developing relationships, their worries and pains, all set against a bustling Tel Aviv nightlife.

Tel Aviv Stories, made by two young filmmakers, Ayelet Menachemi and Nirit Yaron, comprises three short dramatic episodes about Tel Aviv women. The first two episodes are about working women who suffer alienation in the jungle atmosphere of big city life. The third episode, entitled, *Divorce (Get)*, is about a woman willing to resort to desperate means in response to discriminatory rabbinic laws governing divorce. Ayelet Menachemi went on to make a full-length film, *Noodle*, which takes place on the background of the large number of illegal foreign workers who began to appear in Israel with the beginning of the Second

Palestinian uprising (intifada) in 2000. The storyline deals with two inter-connected subjects – about a bereaved woman learning to love again and about how she can make a difference by doing *tikun olam* (repairing the world). Winner of the Jury Grand Prize at the Montreal World Film Festival, the film is a dramatic and sensitive story about an El Al flight attendant named Miri, whose Chinese housekeeper is suddenly deported, leaving her with the woman's six-year-old little boy. It is also about Miri's relationship with her sister, and with her sister's estranged husband. This is a charming story about the issues of foreign workers, about bereavement, about the bond between sisters, and about learning to love again. Miri learns to love this little Chinese boy, and she decides to move heaven and earth to return him to his mother, especially because she loves him – even if she has to take risks to do it.

The contemporary period has brought about a new consciousness concerning the issue of abuse in the family and female filmmakers are bravely beginning to portray these 'women's' issues on the screen. Filmmaker Tsipi Trope has made two intense studies of the relationships between husband and wife, both of which deal with contemporary domestic issues. *Tell Me That You Love Me* (1983) portrays two intertwined tales of married women – one about the pressures of a two-career family and the other about physical abuse. Trope's *Chronicle of Love* (1998) deals with similar issues.

Director Julie Shles began her filmmaking career as a documentary filmmaker. Her first attempt in the area of feature filmmaking, *Afula Express* (1997), is an award-winning comedy about love, fantasy and dreams, portraying quirky characters with much depth and charm. The film's success lies in its small magical moments of humour, intimacy and serendipity.

Dina Zvi Riklis is well-known to Israeli filmgoers – her first feature film, *Dreams of Innocence* (1993), portrays two adolescents who comprehend life and its illusions better than their own father, an immigrant, uprooted from the world of his youth, forever searching for his childhood dreams. Her television drama, *Purple Lawns* (1998), dealt with issues of religious versus secular. Her complex narrative film, *Three Mothers* (2006), is about love and devotion between sisters, love that becomes bitter over the years due to betrayal, jealousy and pain. Based on the personal story of the director, it portrays the story of three strong-willed women, a film mixed with historical sweep – from life in Alexandria, to the Six Day War, to the visit of Sadat to Jerusalem. This is a film of stunningly rich detail, and complicated, in-depth characters.

Based on a novel by Rachel Eytan, Dina Zvi Riklis made an additional historical film, *The Fifth Heaven* (2011). It is a touching and authentic period piece, set in 1944 Palestine at an orphanage for girls. The story takes place on the background of the greater political issues of the period – the war in Europe, fighting the British in Palestine, building a state, and the tensions between the idealistic socialists and the capitalists. Not surprisingly, these issues intrude upon the lives of the girls and the workers, all living together in the orphanage outside of Tel Aviv.

Hannah Azoulai-Hasfari is known to Israeli audiences as an actress of stage and screen. Searching for her own cultural roots, she wrote the screenplay for *Sh'chur* (directed by her husband, Shmuel Hasfari, 1994), which is based partially on her own family's story. A film about cultural conflicts, it deals with superstition, family hardship and sacrifice. The conflict lies imbedded in the childhood memories of the Israeli-born daughter of a traditional and old-fashioned Moroccan family – a family which solves domestic problems through the use of white magic (*sh'chur*) and the casting of spells. Looking back years later, the daughter, who as a youngster had been sent to Jerusalem to attend high school (as was Azoulai-Hasfari), finds it hard to repress her ambivalent feelings, which hover between nostalgic love and angry contempt.

Jellyfish (2008), directed by Shira Gefen and based on stories by Etgar Keret (a husband and wife team), is a quirky and complex film, which provides a comment on marriage, memory, unfulfilled promises and alienation in the post-modern urban setting. The story is about Batya, a grown woman living in Tel Aviv, who is remembering a trauma of her childhood – her parents' divorce and their unfulfilled promises to her (as represented by an ice-cream man on the beach). A strange, little girl with a life-preserver represents Batya herself, holding onto her childhood memories like a life-preserver. In fact, her friend the photographer says that her parents are survivors; we are all second generation. In fact, we are all living with memory of one kind or another, in this case, with trauma about relationships between parents and children. Indeed, most of the film is about relationships between parents and children. Eventually, Batya succeeds in letting go of her traumatic memories. As she is reborn in the water and saved by her friend, she smiles up at the heavens, and we realise that she will now be able to move on.

Israeli society seems to find images of the ultra-orthodox world strangely compelling and many films of the last twenty years have portrayed this community. Only one of these films, however, was made by a female filmmaker, *Fill the Void* (2012) by Rama Burshtein. Perhaps more important, she is also the only filmmaker who is portraying her own community from within. Although not born into the world of ultra-orthodox Judaism, Burshtein has chosen it and in this, her first feature film, she portrays it in an intimate and loving manner. This is a unique and tight-knit community in which people go to ask their rabbi for advice and girls dream only of marrying their *bashert* (promised match). The film is a romantic drama – charming and somewhat artistic (including traditional music and frequent use of close-ups). The film was screened in the competition at the Venice Film Festival (2012), where the lead actress, Hadas Yaron, won an award for best actress. In addition, the film received the highly acclaimed Israeli Ophir Award for Best Feature Film.

After-images of the Holocaust

It is never easy to raise children, and it is even more difficult if one is raising them in the shadow of another, nightmarish, time and place. Relationships between parents and children become increasingly complicated against the background of such memories. There are often feelings of guilt – the parents feel guilt at having survived, at not having enough emotional strength to pass along the memories of each and every one of the relatives who were lost, at not telling their stories or perhaps the opposite, telling their stories too much – while the children feel guilt at being incapable of replacing loved ones lost in the ashes of the past. This complex relationship between parents and children, mothers and daughters, especially those which involve survivors of the Holocaust into the second and third generation, is the subject of a number of Israeli films produced during the 1980s and 1990s.

In an attempt to come to terms with her own experiences as the daughter of a Holocaust survivor, actress Gila Almagor wrote a book and produced a one-woman play which told her story. This autobiographical story provided the material for two full-length dramatic films, both directed by Eli Cohen – *The Summer of Aviya* (1988) and its sequel, *Under the Domim Tree* (1995). Both films deal with Almagor's own difficulties growing up as the child of a mentally unbalanced survivor, living in the shadow of her mother's memories. Almagor does not attempt or intend to portray her own version of history. Rather, she portrays the daughter's understanding of what happened to her mother – not so much the story of the mother-survivor as the tale of the daughter's living with that story.

Another Israeli dramatic film about a Holocaust survivor living in the past is Tsipi Trope's *Tel Aviv–Berlin* (1987), which confronts the survivors's difficulties in adapting to his surroundings and portrays him as a man obsessed with memories of a world which was destroyed. Benjamin, a survivor of Auschwitz, lives with the memories of his lost family and surrounds himself with the music and art of pre-war Berlin. Although he is a married man, he finds himself attracted to a beautiful and elegant woman from Berlin, who represents for him the world of culture that he misses. At the same time, he becomes obsessed with a local blacksmith, who had been the Kapo in charge of his father's barracks at Auschwitz. This is a film about revenge, moral choices and a person's difficulties in adapting to a new life and culture.

It is significant that foreign portrayals of the Holocaust concern themselves overwhelmingly with images from the Nazi period, whereas Israeli cinema deals primarily with the after-images. In fact, Israeli cinema has placed an unspoken, self-imposed censorship upon itself – no one has yet attempted to dramatically portray the events of that terrible time. As a result, there is no body of narrative films produced by Israeli filmmakers which deal with the brutality of the Holocaust period and the machinery of death.

Documentary filmmaking

What is history and how does it enter our consciousness and become historical fact? Even documentary films are somewhat 'staged', but to what extent does this enter our consciousness when we are viewing them? Our memory of the Holocaust is certainly through films, both drama and documentary, which have engraved on our minds a sort of cinematic memory of that time. But how can we know what is propaganda and what is reality?

Filmmaker Yael Hersonski has taken an otherwise unknown and unfinished Nazi propaganda film about the Warsaw Ghetto, and has created new layers of reality in order to help us remember. Her film, *A Film Unfinished*, which won a prize for best documentary at the Jerusalem Film Festival (2010), utilises the partially edited, never completed film that she found in the archives of Germany, a propaganda film created by the Third Reich, shot in the Warsaw Ghetto during May 1942. In voiceover, she tells the viewer that,

> 'the cinematic deception was forgotten and the black-and-white images were engraved on memory as historical truth.'

This is the story of a propaganda film.

Hersonski combines the footage of the archival film with the story of the Warsaw Ghetto. We see so many faces, so many children, so much suffering. The soundtrack includes readings from the daily diary entries of the head of the Judenrat and readings from the diaries of Ringelblum. In addition, she has interviewed survivors watching the footage, looking for people they knew, while their comments and impressions are used to help us identify what we are watching. There is also an interrogation protocol with the man behind the camera, who talks about what he saw and what he filmed, the contrasts and extremes of life in the ghetto – staged luxury versus actual poverty, hunger, dead bodies and mass graves. We also see footage shot in colour by another cameraman for his own personal collection. This was May 1942, thirty days of shooting, only two months before the beginning of the deportations to Treblinka.

Two additional female documentary filmmakers, Orna Ben-Dor and Tsipi Reibenbach, have also grappled with the subject of the Holocaust and Holocaust survivors. Orna Ben-Dor's highly acclaimed film, *Due to That War* (1988), documents the impact of the Holocaust on the lives of two second generation survivors – singer Yehuda Poliker and lyricist Ya'akov Gilad, popular rock figures (of rock band 'Benzine' fame). The film tells the story of a Sephardi and an Ashkenazi, one working-class, the other an intellectual. Poliker's father, Jacko, was born in Saloniki and was deported by the Nazis to an extermination camp. Gilad's mother, Halina Birnbaum, is an expressive writer and poet from Warsaw, whose memories haunt her work.

In a more personal and painstaking style, Tsipi Reibenbach, in *Choice and Destiny* (1993), provides insight into the details of her parents' lives – their routines, obsessions and memories. The lingering camera emphasises small gestures and habits in its intimate portrayal of the everyday lives of these two survivors. During most of the film, her father relates stories from his past, while her mother lurks in the shadows, a silent image, a woman who never spoke about her Holocaust experiences throughout all the years of her daughter's growing up. Suddenly and spontaneously, the mother opens up emotionally.

On a completely different subject, but also in a highly personal style, documentary filmmaker Anat Zuria grapples with issues of the intersection between Orthodox Judaism and contemporary feminism. Zuria is an Orthodox woman, a graduate of the Ma'aleh Film School, who has chosen to use filmmaking as a form of religious criticism, feminist activity and, if she is successful, a way to influence the Orthodox Jewish discourse. Her films do not grapple with the hard-to-grasp larger issues, but rather with individual stories of specific women.

In her first prize-winning film, *Purity* (2002), Zuria exposes subjects generally not discussed in religious circles – married life, sexuality, family purity, laws of female impurity and *mikveh* (ritual immersion). Zuria looks sensitively at the stories of three women. One of the stories is about Katie, the mother of many children, who has a uterine problem and experiences staining almost all the time, making her impure and, as a consequence, unable to have any physical contact with her husband. They have decided to make an accommodation by differentiating between intimate relations and normal, everyday contact, such as holding hands, a hug at the end of the day, emotional contact – which they have decided to permit even when she is 'impure'.

In her second film, *Sentenced to Marriage* (2004), Zuria has chosen to handle the stories of women who are trapped in marriage by religious law. Tamar, Sari and Smadar are young, married women who, even though separated from their husbands, are unable to obtain a divorce without their husbands' consent. While waiting for their husbands to agree, they are not permitted relations with another man, are not permitted to bear children and, as the years tick by, are ensnared in a Kafkaesque trap.

Her latest documentary, *The Lesson* (2012), is also about a religious woman – in this case, a Muslim woman named Layla who grew up in Egypt and came as a young bride to live in Jerusalem with her new husband. Layla is not her given name – it is the name that was assigned to her when she came to live in Israel at the age of fifteen. This is the first hint of strange circumstances, which even she appears not to fully understand. Today, Layla is an elegant, mature woman who is learning to drive. Through the discussions that she has with her driving teacher, we get to know her, to see her as a remarkable and expressive woman, and an intimate portrait is drawn. All of Layla's children were brought up in Jewish schools. Her daughter, Hagar, writes compelling and beautiful songs – but her mother, in a moving moment, expresses her disappointment that her daughter addresses God in Hebrew and not in Arabic.

As the circumstances of Layla's life are slowly unfolding before the viewer, one realises that this is a complex story. It is about the hardships of being a Palestinian in Jerusalem, the difficulties imposed by the security wall/separation barrier, about loneliness and being a woman on her own, struggling to hold on to her own identity and her ties to her past. It is also about her troubled relations with her children and about their issues of national and religious identity. A haunting and sensitive film, *The Lesson* won an award for best documentary at the Haifa Film Festival (2012).

Conclusion

Israeli society is a developing and maturing society, no longer obsessed solely with cosmic and political issues of existence, but interested also in the needs of the individual. This is reflected on the Israeli screen and in the significant contribution made by female filmmakers. Israeli cinema has moved from an emphasis on communal issues to an in-depth understanding of the individual, from the sacrifices of the pioneering period to the materialism and personal egotism of the contemporary period, from stereotypical heroic male images to more complex and problematic images of the Israeli (both male and female) in contemporary society. Moreover, the screen images produced by female filmmakers, scriptwriters and authors, raise new issues and present new perspectives on how Israeli society regards war and morality, family relationships and women's issues. The woman's vision in Israeli filmmaking also reflects a deep awareness and sensitivity in dealing with issues of memory.

Author biography

Amy Kronish lectures and writes widely on film and is the author of two books on Israeli film – *World Cinema: Israel* (Flicks Books, Trowbridge, England and Associated University Presses, NJ, 1996) and *Israeli Film – A Reference Guide* (co-author, Greenwood Publishing, Westport, CN, 2003). She worked for three years as the Director of Coexistence Activities of the Jerusalem International YMCA and prior to that, she worked for fifteen years as the Curator of Jewish and Israeli Film at the Jerusalem Cinematheque – Israel Film Archive. Born and bred in the United States, she has an M.A. in Communications from N.Y.U. (1973), and has lived in Jerusalem since 1979. She blogs at http://www.israelfilm.blogspot.co.uk.

References

Kronish, Amy W, 1996. *World Cinema: Israel*. Trowbridge, Wiltshire: Flicks Books and Cranbury, Associated University Presses, New Jersey.

Shnitzer, Meir, 1994. *Israeli Cinema: Facts, Plots, Directors, Opinions* (Hebrew) Jerusalem.

SUMMARY

Gabrielle Kelly

Certain themes emerge from the diverse voices speaking out in the previous chapters that may be summarized as follows:

Waves of Feminism

Many chapters reflect three waves of feminist politics; the pre-1950: 'Androgyny' of women filmmakers such as Arzner and Lupino when Hollywood was gender blind. The push for women's issues can be seen in the radicalism of the 60s and 70s as women emerged from theatre and politics to use film as a medium for advocacy and the most recent 80s and 90s new wave of women filmmakers who have greater training and explore more unique female subjectivities/heroines within their home/geographical boundaries. From 2000 onwards we see post-feminism and neo-feminism, cinema without geographical boundaries, more trans-nationalisation, a deeper exploration of issues that cross gender, including homosexuality, transgender, less self-declared feminists, and a focusing on larger political, social and religious issues. The extreme of this was the turn to magic realism in Latin America, which was an escape from the realities of civil war.

Today there is a rejection of the label of 'women's films' in countries such as Africa and the US.

Actresses Turned Directors

This is a key theme in films emerging from Canada, Mexico, China, South and SE Asia and in the early days of Hollywood when actresses had so much more power. Women exploited their on screen personaes to fund/enable their power behind the camera as they continue to do more recently with Barbra Streisand, Helen Hunt, Julie Delpy and others. Many directors such as Lynn Shelton were actresses but found the roles less than challenging and looked to directing as a role with more agency, less subject to physical appearance and age. Indeed, as actresses age and find fewer roles, especially in the US, their knowledge of filmmaking can be a powerful push toward directing.

Documentaries as a Way In

In the late 1900s many women directors in Australia, South America, Africa, India, Korea and Singapore worked on documentaries before embarking on feature films. Access to these smaller budgets, and in many cases, a less complex medium allowed women to prove themselves professionally but also allowed them closer access to the social and political issues impacting on women. Barbra Kopple's Oscar win for *Harlan County,* a raw insider view of a coal miners strike and more recent docs on charged political subjects often put women in the centre of provocative subject matter.

Independent Film as a Gateway

Women filmmakers tend to start in independent film, which usually has lower budgets, less risk and a greater chance of telling stories that may be deemed less commercial. Women also tend to work in specific genres such as romantic comedy, television, especially in Australia, NZ, Africa and USA.

Elitism, Social Class and Education – The Connection

In South-East Asia, India, Philippines, South America and Iran, women directors are often daughters or wives of powerful filmmaking families, as is Sofia Coppola in the USA. Nepotism has always been a large part of such a desired occupation as film directing but weighing against it is the increasing growth of film school education, labs and mentoring which seek to diversify and also acknowledge the disparate level of opportunity between men and women.

CELLULOID CEILING

Film Education Training

The explosion in film education training both in national and for profit film programs has given women, especially from the 1980s onward, the chance to study in national or overseas film schools. Scholarships can even up the income disparity and the related fields of critical studies have allowed for greater research and training for film critics and scholars to bring the achievements of women directors to light. Especially in Australia, Asia, Africa, South America, and Korea, many key directors have come out of film school programs.

Women as Primary Audience for Film

Increasingly in countries such as US, India, Japan, Korea and China, women are becoming the majority of ticket buyers and therefore the demand for stories featuring women has increased. Profound changes in access to the means of production have meant distribution is the greatest issue filmmakers now face. Finding their audience however may allow women directors to succeed without gatekeepers who decide what audiences want.

Lack of Institutional Acceptance

The difficulty for women to be nominated or win Sundance and Oscars may have led to a subversion of feminist politics. Women Academy Award finalists such as Bigelow, Coppola, Campion and Wertmuller do not engage in dialogue about feminism preferring to let their work stand for itself. Individual directors have struck out alone forcing dialogue away from questions that start with "As a woman…" in order to mediate the gender difference and keep the focus on their work.

Global Changes Force Power Shift

Older models of production have been supplanted by the financial, technical and other changes rocking the status quo. Women, who may be more used to working nimbly and with a strategy that must constantly change and reinvent may be better able to take advantages of opportunities where they arise. The dominant story trope in the biggest market in the world – China, is that of the romantic comedies beloved by young women who have left their villages for work in the big city. That they number fewer than their male counterparts who now must woo them as the gender imbalance is not in favour of males wanting to marry, is a direct result not only of China's one child policy but of the forced extinction of girl babies considered less valuable than boys. Dennie Gordon, US director of such a rom com, was able to find more freedom directing in China than in the US. She is an example of the complex forces of global change stimulating both chaos and opportunity.

Work-Life Balance

Despite any gains women may have made in equal pay, housework and childcare are still the second job of most mothers and wives/partners. Especially in Western countries such as the US and Australia, women find it difficult to balance motherhood and their professional careers in countries which lack established childcare systems. As society changes and more people live away from family and clan systems we can expect to see this in other societies. Much lauded women directors have often refused work that could have been ground-breaking due to making motherhood their priority.

In many fields other than feature filmmaking the question of 'having it all' does not seem to be answered in a way that is beneficial to women. Like many high-pressure jobs and demanding career paths, women in directing often have to eschew family life for the ever changing demands of this high profile business and art.

It remains to be seen in the very different countries and societies all over the world, how this unfolds but we can be sure the silence of past decades will not prevail. Women film directors are breaking through and will push hard to do so.

There will continue to be many firsts by women directors until there is no more need for it. Finally, they will become just directors, without the additional qualifier "woman" and can stand as artists and filmmakers to be judged solely on the merits of their work.

For more titles on Women and the Arts see

www.supernovabooks.co.uk